BORNEO and the MALAY ARCHIPELAGO

PACIFIC OCEAN

NEW GUINEA

OR

AUSTRALIA

BORNEO
PEOPLE

Borneo People

BY THE RIGHT HONOURABLE

Malcolm MacDonald

NEW YORK: ALFRED A. KNOPF
1958

L. C. Catalog card number: 58-10962

THIS IS A BORZOI BOOK,
PUBLISHED BY ALFRED A. KNOPF, INC.

FIRST AMERICAN EDITION

CONTENTS

v

CONTENTS

ILLUSTRATIONS

Follow pages 122 and 282

PART ONE

THE COUNTRY

CHAPTER ONE

THE LAND AND ITS PEOPLES

I

BORNEO LIES across the equator. It is a land where men are simple men, women are unsophisticated women, monkeys are uninhibited monkeys, orchids are blooming orchids and all manner of other living creatures are their own natural, unspoiled selves.

Sarawak is a small state in Borneo, a country enjoying a certain romantic fame as the sometime realm of the White Rajahs. Its shores are washed by the South China Sea, which in olden times was notorious for the traffic which it bore. Innocent ships voyaging over it were liable to sudden assault by pirates, whose craft were light, swift prahus operating in fleets like swarms of darting, deadly mosquitoes. Manned by crews of human fiends, they made Sarawak's coast a place of wicked reputation.

That was a century ago; but for those with eyes to see beyond mere physical forms the ghosts of those days still haunt the sunshine and shadows when a breeze whispers and the tide murmurs on tropical evenings along the shore. I have often felt their presence as I lay becalmed in the estuaries of their ancient hiding-places up sultry rivers.

Now Sarawak is a peaceful place. Its coastline is bordered by long white beaches. When the monsoon blows, giant breakers thunder along those pleasant strands, strewing them with flotsam and jetsam; but in clement weather the sands lie clean and smooth like endless race-tracks for motor cars. Inland the country is covered with jungle, save in small patches where man has cleared and tamed the ground for agriculture. It is like the luxurious growth of a vast hothouse, for the equatorial climate bathes Sarawak in perpetual summer. Nowhere on earth is natural vegetation more lavish.

The prospect is always green. A visitor gazing on it from an

3

aeroplane sees, wherever he looks, billions and billions of leaves. The country is a paradise of foliage, not flowers; but in shadowy recesses the forest hoards its floral treasures. Exquisite and languid, they dangle in mid-air, suspended from the tree trunks. In places these orchids flourish abundantly. Hundreds of different species are native to Borneo, among them some of the most fancifully shaped and exuberantly tinted of all their strange, magnificent tribe. In the deep woodland, too, grow many varieties of pitcher-plants, fantastic beauties with a sinister reputation for devouring insects.

Heavy rainfall and hot sunshine conspire to produce this extravagant growth. High above the jungle spreads the sky, a blue canopy often ornamented with floating clouds. The Sarawak scene is usually a pleasing combination of green earth and blue-and-white heaven; but periodically black storms pass over the land, lashing it with hurricanes of wind, illuminating it with fitful streaks of lightning, blasting it with shattering roars of thunder, and drenching it with sharp, tumultuous rain. The torrents which descend unevenly throughout the year sustain many rivers. Except for paths worn by the feet of native hunters, these rivers alone penetrate the jungle. They are the great highways and the small byways of travel in roadless Sarawak.

Animal life is plentiful. Parts of the jungle are as empty as a desert, but others are alive with innumerable residents of a fascinating wild zoological garden. Among its myriad forms are many species of strange stick and leaf insects. Nature never had a more ingenious inspiration than when, to protect them, it made these creatures in the image of the twigs on which they feed. Other Bornean insects are less passive. Unwary travellers are stung by mosquitoes, bitten by ants and sucked by leeches wherever they struggle through the jungle. By day in the more open spaces their eyes are often delighted by spectacles of gorgeous butterflies, and at night everywhere their ears are entertained— if that be the right expression—by massed orchestras of cicadas and other tedious musicians.

The varieties of small, furry animals include several which took to aviation long before Man did. There are flying squirrels, flying foxes, flying lizards and even flying frogs. In the tree-tops other aero-acrobats disport themselves. Monkeys galore swing and leap from branch to branch like troupes of trapezists. Among the apes is a renowned monster found only in Borneo and Sumatra —the orang-utan or "man of the trees". Short-legged and long-armed, with massive torsos covered with brick-red hair, these members of the *Order Primates* contemplate you, when you meet them, with melancholy eyes, as if they had just read Darwin's *Origin of Species* and were painfully aware of being your poor relations who have not done so well in life.

Wild pigs, mouse deer, leopard cats, bears, pythons, rhinoceros and many other interesting beasts live in the jungle. Elephants roam in a small area of neighbouring North Borneo. They were not original inhabitants, but arrived generations ago as an impressively large gift from the Sultan of Sulu to his fellow ruffian, the Sultan of Brunei. In their new home they thrived, but soon grew weary of the artificial pomp of court life and escaped to the freedom of the jungle, where they have lived in happy natural state ever since.

Up the rivers lurk crocodiles, and among their companions in the muddy waters are some strange fish. They include poisonous fish, stinging fish and even singing fish. I am told that if you sit silent in a boat above the aquatic bower of one of these sirens, you can hear the faint mumble of its modest dirge. On islands off the coast turtles produce their young, each mother laying several scores of eggs like a collection of battered ping-pong balls.

Bird life is also plentiful. Among the large specimens are grotesquely majestic hornbills, and among the lesser is the spider-hunter, a charming creature with a small green body and long, down-curving bill, who plays, unwittingly, a significant part in the lives of the native peoples, for its movements determine the omens by which conduct in pagan society is ruled. Sun-birds, flower-peckers, bulbuls, fly-catchers, trogons, drongos, parrots, bee-eaters, kingfishers, goatsuckers, kites, parakeets and hundreds of other species inhabit the swamps and forest.

So Sarawak is the home of a splendid menagerie of birds and beasts; and among the other animals in the jungle lives that astonishing species, Homo Sapiens — Man.

II

Peoples of several different races inhabit Sarawak. Their creeds are as varied as their origins. They include primitive tribes who are mostly pagans, Malays who are exclusively Moslems, Chinese who are predominantly Buddhists, Europeans who are usually Christians, Indians who are generally Hindus, and Melanaus who are an impartial mixture of pagans, Christians and Mohammedans. The total population of the country is less than 600,000 men, women and children. Rather more than half belong to the pagan tribes, fewer than twenty per cent are Malays, about twenty-five per cent are Chinese, and the Melanaus and other races compose the rest.

No one knows when man first lived in Borneo, nor precisely what type of human beings the aboriginals were. The ancestors of the present inhabitants arrived in a series of migrations spread over several centuries. Each invasion of newcomers came from the sea; they established themselves first along the coast and then penetrated inland. Usually the earlier, more savage settlers retreated before the later comers, withdrawing ever farther up the rivers. So the most primitive types of residents are now found in the remote interior.

These natives in the deep jungle are "uncivilized" pagans. They associate together in primitive tribal organizations and are divided among distinct ethnological groups called Punans, Penans, Kayans, Kenyahs, Ibans, Land Dayaks, Muruts and various others. They are the real "wild men of Borneo". Except to a trained eye, they appear physically much alike. Judged by European standards they are of less than medium height; their hair is black, long and lank; and the pigment of their skin ranges from dark brown to pale *café-au-lait*. Their faces show, in almost all cases, though in divers degrees, the customary Mongoloid characteristics: "wide cheek-bones, the small oblique eyes, the peculiar fold of the upper eye-lid at its nasal end, and the scanty beard", while "the nose varies greatly in shape, but is usually rather wide at the nostrils."*

None of the tribes has any written history. Vague traditions

* From *The Pagan Tribes of Borneo* by Charles Hose and William McDougall, Macmillan, London, 1929.

concerning their earlier adventures are handed down by word of mouth from generation to generation, and the rest is lost in the thick mists enshrouding the past. As I have said, they came to Borneo in successive waves of immigration, and each brought its own characteristic social organization, customs and dialects. To some extent they have influenced one another since, but many differences still distinguish their various groups. In particular, they have not evolved a common language, though they have lived for ages as neighbours on the same rivers. They speak a multiplicity of unconnected tongues, each incomprehensible to the next-door communities up- or down-stream.

The most interesting fact about human society in Sarawak is that much of it has scarcely changed for centuries. The earlier immigrant peoples still live in similar conditions to those which existed when they arrived several hundred years ago. Indeed, the simplest among them are not merely like men near the dawn of history: they *are* men near the dawn of history, authentic examples of primitive man. Sarawak is an anthropologist's dream.

The lowliest peoples are the Penans and Punans and a few similar tribes. Perhaps they are indigenous to the country, true aboriginals; but the generally accepted opinion seems to be that ages ago even they were immigrants. It would be difficult to imagine a human society simpler than that, for example, of the Punans. Its members lead no settled existence, and are nomads forever wandering in small family groups through the half-lit world of the tropical forest. They build no permanent dwellings, keep no domestic animals and engage in no agriculture. Hunters pure and simple, they erect temporary shelters of leafy roofs supported on sticks wherever they happen to stay for a few weeks or months, then drift onwards, living on jungle fruits, wild sago and such game as they can kill. They use primitive tools and weapons. Their home-made spears are fashioned from sharpened wood. Occasionally they now acquire steel spearheads and parangs (short swords) from more sophisticated tribes, bartering them for jungle produce such as gutta-percha, dammar and rattans; but their favourite weapon is still the blow-pipe, a rod of hardwood some eight feet long bored through its centre with a barrel like a gun. Into one end of the weapon the

hunter fits a bamboo dart tipped with poison brewed from the
sap of the ipoh tree. Holding the blow-pipe to his lips and aiming
at the object of his chase, he fills his cheeks with air and puffs
the poisoned arrow through the bore. The dart flies straight
and true for a short distance. At twenty yards a Punan's aim is
unerring. The missile buries its sharp barb in the victim's flesh,
and the poison quickly does its work. Wild pigs, deer and monkeys fall prey to the nomads' spears and arrows.

The extraordinary skill with which, by means of simple
mechanical devices, the Punans bore barrels in their blow-pipes
marks a certain degree of attainment which elevates them a little
above utter savagery. They also make fine rattan mats and baskets, and are clever at singing rude, melancholy songs. These
are their chief claims to craftsmanship and art. Their clothes are
as unsubstantial as could be, the men wearing skimpy loin-cloths
and the women brief skirts made from tree bark. With no other
adornment these light-brown Adams and Eves drift through the
shadowy places of Sarawak's jungle and the even darker recesses
of human history.

III

The other pagan peoples in Borneo are also lightly clad.
The men wear only loin-cloths and the women short skirts.
When they work in their padi-fields or travel along the rivers
in the heat of the day they augment these brief costumes with
straw hats almost the size of parasols, to protect them from the
scorching sun. They have reached that stage of development,
however, when their garments are made of woven cotton or
cloth, and the men and women alike often don small trinkets such
as ear-rings, necklaces and bangles. They have an eye for pretty
things, and enjoy dressing up. On gala occasions their costume
assumes barbaric splendour.

Unlike the Punans, the Kayans, Kenyahs, Ibans, Land Dayaks
and others live a settled life. Except in the case of some Land
Dayaks, their dwellings are the famous long-houses. These interesting and in many ways charming wild men, and for that matter

wild women also, of Borneo will fill a large part of this book, so I shall not start now on a fuller description of them. But I must mention in passing the accomplishments for which they are most renowned. The outside world knows little about them beyond their passion for taking human heads.

In bygone days head-hunting was their favourite sport. They collected heads with as much zeal as acquisitive people in more advanced countries devote to collecting furniture, pictures, porcelain and other *objets d'art*, though perhaps with a less discriminating eye for period pieces. Frequently the men of a long-house felt an urge to raid another house, slay its inmates and bring back their severed heads as trophies to hang in their own home. In this hobby they received hearty encouragement from their wives and sweethearts. It is said that in some groups the taking of a head was regarded by the women as an essential test of masculine virtue, and that no maiden would accept the advances of a youth who had not so proved himself.

I shall not attempt to probe deeply into the dark mystery of how Bornean natives originally acquired this habit. One opinion is that it had something to do with ending the period of mourning after a chief's death. The restless spirit of the departed leader could find no peace in the next world until a retainer was killed to attend him; so the head of a sacrificial victim was placed beside his grave as proof that this last earthly service had been performed. Speculation upon the accuracy of the theory is a subject for anthropologists and psychologists, and interested readers may pursue it in their learned works.

At first the gruesome pastime of head-hunting was probably kept within some sort of decent bounds by religious taboos as well as by prudent social restraints. In time, however, the original checks were relaxed. No one can tell how the change took place. Possibly it happened much as a similar development might occur if a people's religion decreed that on certain sacred occasions their priests should smoke opium. The priests would become increasingly zealous devotees of this holy duty, and then helpless slaves to it. They would find good reasons why the special days when they performed it should dawn with ever

greater frequency. In due course the ecstasy of their spiritual
elation at the moment of celebrating the rite would communicate
itself to their followers. So impressed would the ordinary members of the sect be by the remarkable piety of their priests that
they would seek to emulate it; and they too would take to the
pipe. As time passed their devotion would become as conspicuous as that of their clerics, until it was a matter of honour with
them to spend as little time as possible on mundane pursuits and
as much as possible expressing their religious fervour by puffing
the witching poppy. In fact a whole people, influenced originally
by a lofty spiritual impulse, would become drug addicts. What
had started as a sacred ritual, the performance of which was
strictly confined to a few, would end by degenerating into a
national vice indulged in by the entire population.

Whether or not the custom of head-hunting spread in Sarawak in some such manner, it is certain that man's most savage
inclinations became a predominant characteristic of many Bornean tribes. They were intoxicated by blood-thirstiness, and engaged with little or no restraint in orgies of murder. It was a
sadly depraved chapter in the human story.

The originators of head-hunting in Borneo enjoy the anonym-
ity of most other characters of antiquity. Some authorities believe
that the Kayans introduced the practice. These pundits suggest
that the Ibans did not engage in it until they learned it (as they
have learned many more attractive habits) from the Kayans. If
that be so, the Ibans proved sedulous pupils. I feel warm admiration and affection for the Ibans; but no one can deny that until
recent times they were the wickedest head-hunters in Borneo, and
perhaps in the whole world.

Head-hunting thus became a national sport pursued passionately by most pagan tribes in Sarawak. The resultant battles were
not conspicuously heroic or honourable affairs. A victory gained
by low cunning was as praiseworthy as one secured by noble
prowess. An attack from behind an opponent was generally regarded as better, because more likely to succeed, than a frontal
assault; and the head of a defenceless old woman was as triumphant a capture as that of a vigorous young brave. Few hand-to-

hand encounters occurred, for the natives did not relish that kind of combat. A party on the warpath preferred to surprise a rival long-house in the darkness, to get below its floor and set the building alight while its inmates were still unaware of their presence. If discovered before the ruse succeeded, they retreated behind jungle trees and, from safe cover, hurled a few missiles and many insults at their enemies. Only when resistance was feeble would they storm the house. If, by some aggravating mischance of war, an engagement developed in a way which involved the two parties in hand-to-hand fighting, the conflict did not last long. One side or the other, or both, soon turned tail and ran. In any case the thick forest did not lend itself to such actions; you could not see the foe for the trees. I do not suggest that the pagans of Borneo lack physical courage. They possess it, but it rarely expressed itself in that particular type of battle.

When British administrators assumed responsibility for the government of Sarawak, they had great difficulty in eradicating the practice of head-hunting. For decades they were only partially successful; but by perseverance, precept and punishment they eventually succeeded. Comparatively few serious outbreaks of murder are recorded after the early years of the present century, and the last serious relapse in peace time occurred in the early 1930's. Then the second World War gave the deplorable old pastime a brief fresh impetus. I shall describe in due course that final hilarious spasm of head-hunting.

IV

The pagans who wander through the pages of this book, sometimes searching for heads and sometimes seeking more civilized expressions of their egos, live far up the rivers. Other peoples reside near the coast. They belong largely to two races, Malays and Chinese.

A comparatively small community of different antecedents, character and customs inhabits a stretch of the coastal plains. They are called Melanaus, and in some ways they constitute a physical and cultural link between the "uncivilized" natives of

the highlands and the "civilized" peoples of the lowlands.
Though fairer of skin, they betray many of the Mongoloid features of the up-river tribes. Originally they too were pagans
and long-house dwellers, though they were never enthusiastic
head-hunters. Being of gentle and peaceable disposition, they
came off worst in warlike encounters, and so acquired a distaste
for getting involved in them. Yet they could never establish an
effective exemption, because their women happened to be strikingly good-looking. A reputation for beauty was unenviable in
those days, since it attracted the slave-hunting pirates who roamed
the coasts. Melanau girls were the favourite booty of these buc-
caneers, and Melanau men had to fight desperately to defend their
wives and daughters.

After the coming of orderly government they shook off
their last traces of bellicosity and settled to honest work. They
are daring sailors, and as fishermen have no superiors on the
South China Sea. Throughout the season of the northeast monsoon, when high ocean breakers and flying surf keep most
mariners ashore, Melanaus launch their boats, scud before the
breeze, cast their nets and make good catches. Along the coast
they have come in close contact with Malays, and been so deeply
influenced by them that recently large numbers were converted
to Islam. Others fell under the influence of European missionaries and became Christians, while a third section still retained
their pagan beliefs.

All alike have adopted Malay dress, except to the extent that
more "modern" Malay and Melanau men have taken to Western
shirts, jackets and trousers. Almost all the Melanaus now live in
the Malay domestic style, congregating in villages where each hut
stands in its own plot of ground. This is a development of comparatively recent years. Within living memory the Melanaus
were long-house dwellers; but gradually individual families broke
away from their communal residences to build their own separate
homes. Today only three or four inhabited Melanau long-houses
remain, and already the drift of population from these has begun.
In a few years they too will be empty, and the traditional
Melanau house will become extinct.

V

The precise order and dates of arrival of the immigrant races who successively composed Sarawak's mixed populations are unknown. Even the most learned historians of Borneo can form on the subject only infirm speculations based on scrappy foundations of folk tradition and other vague evidence. At some time or other, long ago, the first Malays landed. They were very different types from the pagan tribesmen. To explain their presence in Sarawak we must peer for a moment into ancient, dimly perceived events.

Centuries before the Malays reached Borneo, peoples of their race had roamed and settled, then roamed and settled again, only to roam and settle once more in various parts of southern Asia. When they first appeared in the pages of manuscripts, they inhabited the island of Sumatra and the peninsula of Malaya. Whence they had come no one knows; the birth-place of their forbears is forgotten. What is certain is that they were folk with an inveterate urge to travel, who in the course of many journeys mingled and married with sundry other peoples. Thus the modern Malays, spread widely over several countries, are of mixed breeding and present no one representative type.

Ages ago, responding to their wanderlust, Malay voyagers ventured outwards from Sumatra and Malaya through the innumerable islands of the eastern archipelago. On many shores they landed, settled and established new societies. This process can be simply described. A few families would arrive in a small fleet of boats on an unoccupied beach. Building huts near a river mouth, they prospered and multiplied. As time passed the colony spread and joined other communities of immigrant Malays who had likewise populated neighbouring areas. By their superior weapons they held the local natives in check, making them subject peoples. Gradually considerable settlements grew and, by a process of amalgamation of one with another, they eventually formed sizable new states. The ruling families produced sultans. In this way Malay sultanates thrived along the shores of many islands scattered through the ocean, dozens of them existing in Java, Sumatra, Malaya, the Philippines and elsewhere.

That happened in Borneo, and eventually several independent principalities existed at various points round the huge island's coast. The largest and most powerful was a state called Brunei. For centuries its sultans governed virtually the whole of north Borneo, and Sarawak was a mere province in their realm.

VI

Among many amazing qualities which make the Chinese perhaps the pre-eminent people in history is their genius for colonization. They are indefatigable voyagers, invincible traders and imperturbable settlers, able to adapt themselves to any climate in any country at any time.

Their connection with Borneo stretches back to the dawn of the island's story. The earliest known written description of Borneo was scribbled by a Chinese traveller in the sixth century A.D. Apparently at that time the Sultans of Brunei, like many other minor Eastern potentates, acknowledged a remote suzerainty of the Emperors of China. Occasionally they sent envoys bearing tribute to the Imperial court. Spices, camphor and other crude but desirable jungle products were laid at the feet of the T'ang and Sung rulers when Chinese civilization was achieving its finest flowering. For centuries this rough Bornean homage continued. A letter sent nearly a thousand years ago by a Sultan of Brunei on the occasion of the presentation of a gift to the Son of Heaven is still preserved. Scratched on what appears to be thin tree bark, it begins with the required obsequiousness, "The King of Puni, called Hianzta, prostrates himself before the most august Emperor and hopes that the Emperor may live ten thousand years."

From very early times Chinese traders seeking spices, edible birds' nests and other tropical produce sailed across the China Sea in small but wonderfully ocean-worthy junks. The winds of the northeast monsoon blew them to Borneo, and the breezes of the southwest monsoon blew them back again. To establish their commerce, some settled on the island and married native women. One or two of the recognized Bornean tribes are reputed to be descendants of those unions. No one can tell when anything like an organized group of Chinese immigrants arrived to live permanently in Borneo, nor which part of the country attracted them. The earliest colonizers in the Sarawak region were probably lured by the alluvial gold in some of its rivers. They conducted such successful operations that fresh recruits from the motherland came constantly to join them, and at that stage the men started to bring their Chinese wives. A Chinese population maintaining unimpaired its national character and customs began to grow. It established vegetable gardens and trading kongsis, secular schools and Buddhist temples, opium dens and secret societies exactly as at home. By the middle of the nineteenth century the gold-miners were a flourishing community settled in a little El Dorado up the Sarawak River, Chinese antimony miners and proprietors of pepper gardens thrived elsewhere in the province, and Chinese merchants lived in the local capital, Kuching.

As the area where business could be pursued with a fair prospect of gain grew larger, fresh immigrants poured in from China. They came mostly from southern ports like Canton, Swatow and Amoy. Speaking many different dialects, they formed among themselves distinct groups with clannish rather than national loyalties; yet they were all indelibly, unmistakably Chinese. They promoted the economic progress of Sarawak, just as other multitudes of Chinese settlers have helped to develop neighbouring countries in South-East Asia.

Until a person has seen Borneo, Malaya and adjacent lands, it is difficult for him to comprehend how much these tropical territories owe to the enterprise of tens of thousands, hundreds of thousands and, in some cases, millions of Chinese. The indigenous peoples usually had neither the inclination, the experience nor the means to promote mining, planting and commerce. European brains and capital assisted the work, but swarms of Chinese have provided not only vital additional capital and ability but much of the essential labour. These hardy, adaptable people engage in any activity that may give them a modest livelihood. As coolies, market-gardeners, planters, miners, laundrymen, artisans, shopkeepers, traders, bankers, doctors, lawyers, teachers, journalists and workers in scores of other occupations they have overrun much of South-East Asia. Their hard-headed shrewd-ness turned for many of them the original modest livelihood into the spacious affluence of millionaires.

In Sarawak they have been as successful as anywhere else. Many businesses in the towns are in their hands; along the rivers their sampans and launches speed perpetually in search of trade; on the river banks their small-holdings occupy countless acres of good land; and in the jungle they build bazaars and engage in barter with the pagan gatherers of forest produce. No recesses of the wilds are too remote or solitary for their habitation, pro-vided that their enterprise can yield a profit. They thrive almost everywhere.

VII

Settlers of other racial origins have also made contributions to Sarawak's growth. Scions of Arab trading families have long lived there, intermarrying with the local peoples. During the last fifty years Indians and Pakistanis have arrived, though not in large numbers; and throughout the last century Europeans, espe-cially British nationals, have come as administrators, business men and missionaries. Their numerical importance has always been comparatively small, but their work has left the most decisive mark on the country's progress.

Thus Sarawak's population of little more than half a million is remarkably diversified. About half of it belongs to pagan tribes, and the rest is a mixed company. The people's skins run the whole gamut of flesh-tints from white, ivory and café-au-lait through many gradations of brown to a very dark shade. Their ways of life vary from the simplicity of primitive savagery to the complexities of twentieth century civilization. They worship their gods, each man according to his conscience, in pagan long-houses, Moslem mosques, Hindu temples, Buddhist pagodas and Christian churches. The blending of this mixture of communities into a coherent, harmonious nation is Sarawak's principal political problem.

CHAPTER TWO

THE WHITE RAJAHS

UNTIL A CENTURY AGO the state of Sarawak had no separate existence of its own. The name "Sarawak" belonged to a river, and was later used to describe the province through which that river flowed in the ancient and once honourable state called Brunei.

Brunei was a sultanate on Borneo's coast. Occupying about a third of the island, it was a place of impressive size. Its ruling family and governing class were Malays, its trade was largely in the hands of Chinese, and its inhabitants were mostly simple, savage tribesmen.

Its sovereign lords, the Sultans of Brunei, sprang from long-established, though not always impeccably correct, lineage. They were assisted—or perhaps it would be more accurate to say impeded—in their royal duties by a host of Malay feudal barons. For more than a thousand years Brunei had played a respectable part in the affairs of South-East Asia, but by the beginning of the nineteenth century it had grown decadent. Its reigning prince was degenerate almost to the point of imbecility, its aristocracy were corrupt and cruel tyrants, and its population was sunk in poverty, misery and fear.

Its coast was a trysting place for the worst pirates who roamed the southern seas. These wild characters manned fleets of sea-going canoes, swift in attack and elusive in defence, which were a threat to all lawful shipping. They were not wholly to blame for the vigour with which they developed their desperate profession. The Malays of some localities had shown in earlier centuries a natural inclination to piracy, but many others were honest traders doing regular business throughout the archipelago. Then the Dutch, who became the paramount European power in the region, tried to insist that Netherlands ships should have a monopoly of commerce passing from the islands over the oceans. This prohibition on the activities of native people who had long been skilled mariners and free traders drove them into illicit operations; and as Dutch efforts to enforce their policy grew more severe, the response of the Asian seafarers became more vicious. For them there seemed to be no alternatives but piracy or poverty.

Whatever the cause, some Malays became as unruly a tribe of plundering cut-throats as ever sailed salt water. Most notorious among them were the Illanun and Balanini pirates from the Sulu Islands east of Borneo; and of all the inlets in the region, Brunei Bay afforded the best anchorage from which they could pursue their sport. Its spacious waters, shallow channels and protective headlands provided ideal conditions in which their light craft could muster unseen before an attack, and withdraw to safety afterwards.

To keep their hand in, and to maintain a livelihood between assaults against wealthy ocean-going vessels, they made a practice of raiding Brunei villages along the coast. On these expeditions they captured everyone who had the misfortune to escape death, selling the prisoners into slavery. This nefarious business received tacit support from no less a person than His Highness the Sultan of Brunei himself. He and his courtiers acquiesced in these high-handed actions against his faithful subjects because they often received a share of the loot, including the slaves.

In the 1830's Sarawak was a province of this disreputable realm. Its Governor was a Brunei noble called Pengiran Makota, who resided in the provincial capital, Kuching. He proved himself the cruellest of all the Brunei chiefs, and after a while his oppressions provoked trouble. Accustomed though the local people were to plunder, kidnapping and murder as the normal methods by which administrators increased their wealth, filled their harems and expressed their power, his excesses became altogether more than they could tolerate.

Sarawak's population was then a mixture of Malays and Land Dayaks. The former were of a different breed from the Brunei Malays and resented their overlordship, while the Dayaks hankered after their own tribal freedom. Makota's misrule whipped both communities into open revolt. They built stockades in the upper reaches of the Sarawak River, withdrew behind them, and defied the government to come and defeat them.

The situation became so grave that a viceroy named Rajah Muda Hassim was sent to Kuching to supervise Makota's civil administration and organize military action against the rebels. He was no less a person than the sultan's uncle and the heir to the Brunei throne. But that availed him little. What he needed to subdue the enemy was determination, energy and a reliable force of fighting men; and all these he lacked. In particular his bands of warriors were unworthy to be called soldiers. The lethargic spirit in which they attacked the insurgents was no match for the fiery resolve with which those stubborn men resisted. The rebellion continued, and the Sarawak government exerted no authority over large parts of its domain.

Into this scene sailed casually in the summer of 1839 a high-minded young Englishman called James Brooke. As it happened, he was a man of destiny casting around to discover what his destiny might be. A curious stroke of fate had unsettled him at the age of twenty-seven. His father was a civil servant in the East India Company, and as a lad James acquired a commission in the Company's army. A few years later he was severely wounded in a battle in the Burmese War, and returned to England with a mention in despatches and a bullet in his person as honourable souvenirs of his military career. When the musket ball was extracted from his body, his mother mounted it under a glass case and displayed it among the other Victorian bric-à-brac on her drawing-room mantelpiece. If another tale be true, the little scrap of metal was not unworthy of this singular honour, for it played a decisive part in a fragment of modern history. It was said that young Brooke's wound deprived him of the capacity to beget children. If that were so, then paradoxically the bullet which prevented him from rearing a family caused him to found a dynasty.

He could not resume soldiering. Abhorring the idea of becoming a mere gentleman of leisure, his thoughts turned to exploration in the China Seas. He felt especially attracted by the spice islands of the Malayan Archipelago, where the Dutch were attempting to monopolize commerce and, in his opinion, the British had hitherto shown insufficient enterprise. He bought a yacht, the *Royalist*, selected and trained a crew, and sailed for the

islands of his dreams, flying at his masthead the flag of the Royal
Yacht Squadron and nursing in his bosom a vague ambition to
perform some useful service to mankind.

Several months later he landed in Singapore, then a new
British settlement of twenty years' establishment. His intention
had been to proceed to the coast of what is now North Borneo,
but on receiving a commission from the Board of Commerce to
convey a letter of thanks to Rajah Muda Hassim in Kuching for
some unaccustomed kindnesses to a crew of shipwrecked English
sailors, he changed his plan. The course of the *Royalist* was
diverted from more northerly waters to the mouth of the Sarawak
River, apparently at the behest of the merchants of Singapore
but in reality, no doubt, at the decree of Providence.

On August 15th, 1839, the ship dropped anchor twenty miles
up-river opposite the group of attap huts called Kuching. James
Brooke went ashore and called on the Rajah Muda, whom he
found an amiable and well-meaning but irresolute man. The
pro-consul discoursed to his visitor on his troubles with the
Sarawak rebels. Brooke gained permission to travel in areas unaffected by the revolt, and made some expeditions to Land Dayak
villages which whetted his appetite for further knowledge of the
country and its people. On returning to Kuching he cultivated
a friendship with Hassim and, before sailing away, promised to
visit him again.

In the following year he went back. This time he landed fair
and square in the middle of Sarawak's disordered politics. The
rebellion was still maintained, and its leaders now received encouragement from the Sultan of Sambas, in neighbouring Dutch
Borneo. That potentate was incited by the Dutch, who hoped to
extend their influence into independent Brunei. The Rajah Muda
was deeply despondent. He seemed doomed to remain in Sarawak as long as the revolt continued, and his chances of ending
it were remote. Meanwhile his reputation as an administrator
was steadily deteriorating, and at the sultanic court two hundred
miles away his enemies were undermining his position as heir
apparent. In desperation he appealed to James Brooke to help
him to defeat the rebels.

Partly because he thought that he could perform a useful

service, partly from curiosity to see what might happen next, and
partly no doubt at the prompting of personal ambition, Brooke
accepted. With a small party of sailors he went up-river to join
the expedition against the insurgents.

On arrival at the battle-front he was appalled by the state of
affairs existing there. Led by the despicable Pengiran Makota,
the commanders of the government forces sat in craven passivity
in their jungle huts, resolved not to run the risk of action against
the foe. Neither by argument nor threats could the Englishman
induce them to attack. Returning in disgust to Kuching, he
reported this impossible situation to Hassim and declared that
his further stay in Sarawak was useless. He proposed to embark
on the *Royalist* the next morning and sail away.

The Rajah Muda replied with an astonishing proposal. He
offered Brooke the governorship of Sarawak, with full powers to
rule the province, if he would return up-river, assume command
of the local forces and end the rebellion.

Brooke was no adventurer, but a scrupulous and honourable
man. He refused the offer, at any rate for the time being, recognizing that it had been made under duress. Yet his interest was
now strongly engaged in the Sarawak problem. He liked the
people, thought that an unhappy situation had arisen from bad
rule, and reckoned that he could set it right. He felt sympathy
with the insurgents, who had revolted against vile tyranny by
Makota, and believed that, if he could induce them to submit, he
could give the population just government afterwards and open
a new era in their country's affairs. So he agreed to lead a re-
invigorated expedition against the rebels, and left the Rajah Muda
free to renew his unique offer after victory was won.

I do not suggest that Brooke's decision was unaffected by selfish
motives. He was an ambitious man, and probably expected that
Hassim would confirm his proposal when peace was restored.
The idea of becoming the Rajah of Sarawak doubtless appealed
to him, as it would to anyone with a romantic imagination. But
to him thoughts of his personal position were secondary. His
primary impulse was a conscientious urge to perform high public
service, to help to improve the lot of his fellow-men. There was
a streak of the crusader in him. His sentiment had been touched

by the simple character and horrid plight of the natives of Sarawak. He was also aware of the Dutchmen's attempts to extend their rule over all Borneo, to the prejudice of British interests, and he felt that he could perform a patriotic duty to his own country by responding to Hassim's invitation.

So the crusader, having now stumbled on the purpose to which he would dedicate himself, began his mission by leading a motley array of Malays, Chinese, Dayaks and English sailors up a tropical river into deep jungle to meet a native rebel host.

This book is neither a biography of James Brooke nor a history of Sarawak, and I shall sketch only briefly the subsequent achievements of the first White Rajah and his successors. Partly by a show of force and partly by an exercise of diplomacy he secured the surrender of the insurgents. Afterwards his main difficulty was to induce the Rajah Muda to pardon their leaders, since the customary punishment in such cases in Borneo was death for the chiefs and slavery for their wives and children. Brooke's opposition to this made him appear a strange eccentric to his Malay friends, but when he threatened to leave Kuching unless he were satisfied, he won his point. So he began the work of reconciling the population with their rulers.

Hassim then hesitated about appointing Brooke as the governor of the territory. The Rajah Muda was the best of a bad bunch of Brunei lords, but he was weak. He wished sincerely to elevate his English benefactor, yet was fearful of criticism from his enemies in Brunei. By this time, however, Brooke's prestige in Sarawak was high, his appointment was desired by large sections of Malay and Dayak opinion, and only Pengiran Makota and his supporters opposed it. Those ruffians realized that his assumption of supreme authority would end their despoiling of the country.

In the end, after intrigue and counter-intrigue, the remarkable change was achieved. Hassim signed a document declaring James Brooke Rajah, and on September 24th, 1841, at a colourful ceremony in the astana, he was formally proclaimed.

For the time being he was only a feudatory Rajah, owing allegiance to the half-witted Sultan of Brunei. His territory was of limited extent. It included but a fraction of modern Sarawak,

being confined to the immediate neighbourhood of the Sarawak
River and a few smaller waterways. Embracing about 3,000 square
miles of swamp and jungle, it was inhabited by a scattering of
Land Dayaks, a small community of Malays and some hundreds
of Chinese. All told, the population did not number more than
8,000.

The new Rajah was content to start from those small beginnings. His purpose was to give the people of his province just
government, the best in Borneo. In spite of obstruction by
Makota's clique within his territory, and of interference by head-
hunting, slave-gathering pirates from without, he succeeded. He
put a check to tyranny and exploitation, ended robbery, kidnapping and murder as instruments of government policy, and established benevolent rule throughout the small area where his writ
ran. The local inhabitants enjoyed a measure of security and
well-being which they had never known before.

Nevertheless the situation was precarious, and would not have
lasted long if Brooke had confined his activities inside his own
territorial boundaries. Across the borders, in the next-door provinces of Brunei, some highly unsavoury characters lived. They
were the infamous Ibans of the Saribas and Sekrang Rivers, among
the blood-thirstiest pirates in even that hot corner of Asia. Incited by local Brunei governors—Malay or half-breed Arab
chieftains who after each expedition took the largest share of the
loot—they had long been accustomed to sally forth on head-
hunting jaunts into Sarawak. The pirate-masters now recognized
that the introduction of orderly government was a challenge
to their licentious way of life. They vowed to upset it. Deliberately they organized fresh raids to despoil the new Rajah's
people and to bring his authority into contempt.

With the permission of his ally, Hassim, Brooke struck back.
Certain Dayak groups who had long suffered as victims of the
Ibans welcomed the prospect of protection, and joined his forces.
In his initial campaign he also received aid from the Royal Navy.
H.M.S. *Dido* came from China waters, and an expeditionary
force of its sailors, with the Rajah himself on board the leading
pinnace, penetrated far up the Saribas and Sekrang Rivers and
captured the Iban strongholds. The story of their fights makes

reading appropriate to the most thrilling pages of *The Boys' Own Paper*.

For many years, however, the story seemed to be unending. The first defeats of the pirates crippled but did not destroy them. Some of their leaders always managed to escape from their stockades and withdraw into jungle fastnesses, to lick their wounds, rally support and prepare to fight another day. And beyond each discomfited community of Ibans were other settlements of like-minded savages encouraged by Brunei overlords. Under the corrupting rule of a decadent sultanate such lawless characters flourished in every province. They resented the introduction of good government in Sarawak, knowing that if its insidious influence spread, they would be put out of business. Their means of earning a livelihood, their thieving and murderous profession, the whole rapacious, free-booting system of society on which they depended for their power and riches would collapse. They adopted every possible resource in court circles in Brunei to upset Rajah Brooke's growing influence, and resorted to every intrigue that cunning minds could devise to accomplish his overthrow in his own capital at Kuching.

He had to contend with other difficulties elsewhere. As I have said, in his earliest battles he received aid from one of Her Majesty's ships; but later his activities became a subject of unfriendly questions in the House of Commons. Zealous, reforming Parliamentarians heard rumours misrepresenting what the English Rajah was doing in far-away Borneo. These tales described his attacks on cut-throat gangs of pirates as unprovoked assaults on innocent, peace-loving natives; and some legislators repeated them at Westminster as gospel truth. Among the critics were a few distinguished men like Richard Cobden, and even Gladstone once hurled the thunder of his eloquence against James Brooke, whose courageous efforts to bring enlightened rule to primitive peoples should have earned the great Liberal's staunch support.

Both before and since those days well-meaning but ill-informed agitation of that kind has sometimes been a feature of Parliamentary discussion. It seems an unavoidable part of the system of free, democratic public criticism, which must be forever alert against any possibility of tyranny. Occasionally some of the watch-dogs of liberty are not sufficiently well trained to distinguish the champions of freedom from its enemies, and they bark as viciously at the former as at the latter. In Brooke's case the Parliamentary pressure of the critics had unfortunate results. Though most Ministers recognized the worth of his efforts, they thought it inexpedient to maintain a firm line against the opposition, and withdrew from him their active help. For many years he continued his hard tasks of stamping out piracy and head-hunting, extending good government, promoting trade, and increasing British influence in Borneo without aid from the British Navy, support from the British Government or thanks from the British public. The expense cost him his fortune and the strain cost him his health; but gallantly he persevered.

The progress of his administration, if slow and painful, was inexorable, because the natives who lived under it recognized its worth. His province was a haven of security and well-being compared with the misgovernment and anarchy of neighbouring districts in Brunei. Peaceable people in those places soon asked that their areas should be transferred from their existing governors to the authority of the good White Rajah. So began the decline and fall of the Brunei empire and the steady rise of Sarawak state.

The process continued for about fifty years and was accomplished in stages. At first, for more than a decade, it involved no question of adding new territory to Sarawak. Brooke was busy improving his government, introducing reforms and ensuring security against internal and external perils. During that period he also sought to establish beyond challenge his position and rights as Rajah. For some years he remained a feudatory of the Sultan, owing allegiance to him as supreme ruler of all Brunei and paying him a sum of $2,500 a year for his governorship. In 1846 he negotiated an agreement with His Highness which ceded outright to him and his successors full sovereignty over Sarawak.

Brooke was now the absolute master of his realm. So successful was his rule that large communities of natives from neighbouring, less well-governed territories, in both Brunei and Dutch

Borneo, left their homes and settled in Sarawak. Whereas its population in 1840 was reckoned at about 8,000, ten years later it was estimated to be 50,000.

After that the demands of the peoples of near by provinces for incorporation in Sarawak grew insistent. Brooke did not resist this development; on the contrary, he welcomed it. Law and order could not reign in the areas beyond his borders so long as they remained under the authority of unscrupulous Brunei chiefs, and in their disturbed state they were a constant threat to the tranquillity of his own small kingdom. Frequently he had to seek the Sultan's permission to lead expeditions against disturbers of the peace next door. In addition to such practical considerations in favour of absorbing new areas, he felt a mission to bring benevolent government to the largest possible number of the wild men of Borneo.

In 1852 the old Sultan died. Unfortunately Rajah Muda Hassim, his former heir, was no longer in the land of the living. Some years earlier a faction at court, disliking the prospect of such a reasonable man ascending the throne, plotted his overthrow; and in a characteristic orgy of assassination he, his entire family and many of his supporters were, to use a modern expression, liquidated.

The new Sultan, Mumin, was another uncle of the deceased ruler and a worthy successor to him, though his outstanding characteristic was not half-wittedness but avarice. This weakness served many of his unhappy subjects well, for it provided a means by which they ceased to be his subjects. Pestered by their requests to become citizens of Sarawak, embarrassed by the unruly conduct of his local governors, and passionately desirous of money, he was ready—for a consideration, of course—to part with his country bit by bit to Rajah Brooke.

He sold the Rajah one huge region in 1853 and another in 1861. He similarly disposed of large areas to James Brooke's successor in 1883 and 1885. In the meantime, in 1878, he received a good price from the promoters of the future British North Borneo Company for the cession of another slice of his dominions farther east.

James Brooke did not live to see all these developments. In

1868 he died. Not the least of the achievements of this remarkable man was that he passed away peacefully in bed. Many times
he risked death from a pirate's sword or a head-hunter's poisoned
arrow, and once he came within an ace of assassination by Chinese rebels. But he died in his country house in Somerset in
England, far from the excited jabber of pagans in long-houses,
the obsequious obeisances of Chinese towkays, the mumble of
prayers in Malay mosques, and all the other familiar sights and
sounds of his well-loved Sarawak. He was worn out by toil.
In a hard, heroic and creative life he had suffered many disap-
pointments, but in spite of them all he achieved astonishing
successes.

Among the Englishmen who have played notable parts in the
affairs of South-East Asia two are outstanding: Stamford Raffles,
the founder of Singapore, and James Brooke, the creator of Sarawak. Their characters, experiences and achievements were in
many ways similar. Both were inspired by a mixture of philanthropy and patriotism; both sought to bring sympathetic government to hitherto misruled native populations; both endeavoured
to expand British interests in the Malayan Archipelago; and both
were remarkably successful in the achievement of their purposes. In each case their efforts were more appreciated in the
wild jungles of Malaysia than in the tame offices of Whitehall.
Both the men had a genius for benevolent autocracy over Asian
peoples, and natives felt deep trust and affection for them. Both
also saved Britain's position in an important area, the one in
Malaya and the other in Borneo. But in both cases the British
authorities kept blowing hot and cold. Sometimes they encouraged and praised the distant empire builders' work, but as often
as not they turned lukewarm and withdrew their support.

The splendid quality of the two men is only now beginning
to be widely recognized. Hitherto the thoughts on Imperial
affairs of politicians, publicists and voters in Britain have been
mainly concerned with the "white" Dominions and with India
and Africa. Until recently the significance of Britain's position
in South-East Asia was not appreciated, and neither Raffles nor
Brooke received adequate recognition. The latter in particular,
as the White Rajah of a land populated mostly by head-hunters,

tended to be regarded as a strange figure of romance rather than
a solid hero of history. Also one or two light, gay incidents in the
later story of his family filled too large a space in the public
mind, and for a while gave the royal house of Sarawak an unde-
served reputation for frivolity. The Brookes must be taken very
much more seriously.

The first Rajah was a noble figure. It is true that the range
of Stamford Raffles' abilities and achievements was greater than
his. The Governor was a more considerable man than the Rajah.
Nevertheless James Brooke stands in the same rare class of makers
of eastern states and rulers of dependent peoples. In Brooke's
own mind, Raffles was his model. When he first sailed from
England to the region of his future activities he wrote in a letter
to a friend, "I go to awake the spirit of slumbering philanthropy
with regard to these islands, to carry Sir Stamford Raffles' views in
Java over the whole Archipelago." In the many-statued halls of
fame his effigy is worthy to stand in a niche beside that of his
great master.

Before he died James Brooke had the satisfaction of recaptur-
ing a measure of support from the British Government. Parliamentary agitation against him diminished; his constructive work
began to be understood; the honour of knighthood had some time
earlier been conferred upon him; and in 1863 the Government
recognized Sarawak as an independent sovereign state under his
rule. The old Rajah felt deep satisfaction at another circumstance.
He knew that after his death the succession would pass to a young
man whose ability to rule in his own spirit had been amply
proved. Himself a bachelor, Sir James had for many years been
helped in the government of Sarawak by two nephews. The
second of these in particular, Charles Johnson, devoted his whole
life to the service of the people of the country.

His first visit to Sarawak was in 1844, as a midshipman in
H.M.S. *Dido* on its expedition to suppress piracy up the Saribas
and Sekrang Rivers. He took part then in a brisk hand-to-hand
fight to recapture an Iban stronghold, and found this sample of
Sarawak life so much to his taste that a few years later he obtained
leave of absence from the Navy to try his fortunes in Borneo.

In 1852 he resigned his naval commission and joined his uncle's service as a District Officer.

When he ceased to be a sailor and became a land-lubber he did not cease to be a man of action. In a period when recalcitrant sections of the population in and around Sarawak had to be subdued by force of arms and governed by force of character, he displayed admirable qualities for both tasks. He was that unusual combination, a fighting man and an administrator. From 1852 onwards he took part in almost every military excursion against head-hunters. His bravery, resource and leadership on jungle campaigns won him unbounded respect from Malays and Dayaks alike, while his sympathetic government of the latter simple but far from docile tribesmen in peaceful periods between jaunts along the warpath gained him their devoted loyalty. The Rajah's confidence in him grew steadily, and Charles was given ever heavier responsibilities. As the older man's health failed, the younger assumed many burdens of rule, and when finally the Rajah left Sarawak for the last time, Charles Johnson was appointed head of the administration. In the meantime he had changed his name by deed-poll to Brooke.

As soon as news of James Brooke's death reached Kuching, Charles was proclaimed the second Rajah. He continued to rule in a spirit of benevolent autocracy. His government remained as popular with his subjects, and his subjects were as envied by other peoples in Borneo, as had been the case during his uncle's reign. The natives of next-door provinces in Brunei continued to covet their neighbour's sovereign and to demand that their own regions should be transferred to him. In 1883 and 1885 the Sultan gratified their wish by selling fresh tracts of territory to the Rajah.

In the latter year Sultan Mumin departed this life. It was high time, since he was already past a hundred years old, perhaps the most aged miser in history. Sultans might come and go, however, but the diminution of their kingdom went on almost forever. The process by which Sarawak gradually swallowed Brunei continued under Mumin's successor, Sultan Salleh, yet another specimen of depraved Oriental royalty. In 1890 and once more in 1905 additional provinces and populations broke away from his dominions and were joined to the Rajah's.

The process might have continued until it reached its logical conclusion in the complete disappearance of the ancient, historic state of Brunei. What with cessions of vast areas to Sarawak on one side and to North Borneo on the other, very little of Brunei remained by the beginning of the twentieth century. The fragment which survived was poor, miserable and misgoverned. Its population numbered less than 40,000, and the place brought little except discredit to the Sultan. On the verge of bankruptcy, he was prepared to sell it lock, stock and barrel to Charles Brooke.

The Rajah was not averse to this, but the British Government intervened with another solution. Having first, through many years, consented to Brunei's steady disintegration, and then in 1888 reversed their policy and declared the country a British Protected State, the Cabinet in London now suddenly decided to make the King's protection effective. In 1906 they appointed a British Resident in Brunei, with nominal powers of advising His Highness but actual powers of dictating to him. A period of reform in the financial and administrative affairs of the country commenced, and Brunei began to pull itself once more onto its feet. Thus at the last moment the tiny state was saved from utter destruction, and under British guidance it survives to this day. In recent years the development of an oil-field has brought it wealth and the accession of its present wise young Sultan, His Highness Sir Omar Ali Saifuddin, has restored its hope and pride.

Only a few minor boundary adjustments between Sarawak, North Borneo and Brunei have altered their geographical relationship since 1906. By that time Sarawak had grown to its present size, a land covering nearly 50,000 square miles with a population now reckoned at more than 550,000 people. Through most of this long period the second Rajah stayed at the head of affairs. His fearless character, iron will and just mind were appropriate qualities for an Eastern potentate in those times. They led Sarawak and its peoples through all the difficulties of an age when the rival imperialisms of European powers caused upheavals in Asia. For close on seventy years he strove for the good of his state, and the gallant young midshipman of the 1840's became a sagacious old statesman of the 1900's. The celebrated cartoonist "Spy" included him in his gallery of notable Englishmen. In that picture the second Rajah's erect, spare figure clad in a neat frock coat, and his eagle-like head rising above a high "choker" collar are impressive. His handsome face hewn ruggedly as if from granite, with white locks of hair, curling moustachios and fierce, authoritarian eyes, is that of a grand Victorian worthy. If the first Rajah was the founder, the second was the builder of Sarawak; and he deserves greater fame as a maker of history than he enjoys.

He lived and ruled, active and imperious, until 1917, when he was succeeded by his eldest son, Charles Vyner Brooke. The new Rajah governed according to the well established traditions of his forbears, remaining universally popular throughout yet another long reign. When the centenary of Brooke rule approached in 1941 the third Rajah still sat on the throne, and it seemed that the dynasty was as firmly rooted as any reigning house in the world. Indeed, the White Rajahs of Sarawak appeared more secure than most royalty in these revolutionary times, when not only crowns but even several kingly heads have rolled in the dust.

CHAPTER THREE

CESSION

I

ON SEPTEMBER 3RD, 1939, Hitler's panzer divisions marched into Poland, and Europe and the British Commonwealth were hurled into war. On December 7th, 1941, the Japanese assaulted the United States fleet in Pearl Harbour, and the conflict spread across the whole earth. Sarawak was sentimentally engaged in the first phase of the struggle; in the second it was physically overwhelmed.

The Japanese took swift advantage of the crippling blow which they inflicted on the United States of America and its friends at Pearl Harbour. Having at one stroke broken the shield on which the democratic nations depended for protection in the Pacific, they let loose their navy, army and air force. These fierce hordes poured like lava thrown from a volcano over the islands and coasts of the Western Pacific. In December they marched into Siam, laid siege to Hong Kong and attacked Malaya, the Philippines and Borneo. By Christmas Day they had captured Hong Kong and made formidable progress elsewhere. In January they subdued North Borneo, Brunei, Sarawak and Dutch Borneo, and pounced upon the Solomon Islands, Celebes, New Guinea and New Ireland. In February they completed the conquest of Malaya by occupying Singapore, and overran Sumatra and Bali. In March they drove the Allies from Java and helped themselves to the Andaman Islands. In April they finally defeated the stout-hearted defenders of Bataan, and by early May had destroyed all organized resistance throughout the Philippines. After five months of lightning and savage warfare they had made the Western Pacific a Japanese lake.

It was almost exactly a hundred years since James Brooke was proclaimed the first Rajah of Sarawak. In September 1941 centenary celebrations were held in Kuching, where the third Rajah ruled with the hearty acclaim of his subjects. He marked the occasion by enacting a new constitution for his state qualifying the absolute, if benevolent, monarchy which he and his predecessors had maintained so long. To quote his own words written in the Constitution Order, "It is Our will and intention to commemorate this Centenary year . . . by terminating forever the era of auto-cratic rule which has so far characterized Our government."

Thus even in backward Borneo the breeze of democratic po-litical reform blowing across the world was faintly felt. How-ever, the new constitution was of little practical value to the citi-zens of Sarawak, for a few months later the Japanese overran their country. The Rajah and some of his principal advisers withdrew to Australia, all his British officers who stayed behind were thrown into a prison camp, and for the next four years Sarawak remained under the heel of the conqueror.

Japanese administration was almost unbelievably bad—inef-ficient, neglectful and often cruel. In fairness it must be said that the Japanese concerned were the brutal military class, the worst representatives of their talented nation. With few exceptions the people of Sarawak detested them. The pagan tribes in particular were wretched under their rule. Since the principal anxiety of the Japanese was to secure for themselves all the good things of the country, they commandeered the natives' crops of rice, made the chiefs hunt jungle game for them, and confiscated their shot-guns for fear of insurrection. They showed no respect for pagan custom, and in every way broke the friendly connection which had long existed between the Rajah's government and the up-river peoples. The natives loathed them. They nursed their hate, hoping for a day when they might give practical expression to it. In due course their patience was rewarded.

At about the time of the padi harvest in 1945 rumours spread through the long-houses that white men had landed again in Sarawak. The tales were true. The war in Europe was about to end in Germany's overthrow, and the war in Asia was moving towards a similar conclusion for Japan. At that moment sixteen Allied soldiers parachuted into the interior of Borneo. Their exploits became a small epic of daring which will have its place in military history. Some members of the expedition are still in Sarawak. Its leaders were Major Toby Carter, now an officer of the Shell Company in the Miri oil-field, Major Tom Harrisson, the brilliantly gifted curator of Kuching museum, and Major Bill Sochon, the Commissioner of Prisons in Singapore. As these brave men and their comrades floated earthwards they were uncertain which of two fates would greet them on landing. Either they would have their heads chopped off by Dayaks and hung as trophies in the long-houses, or they would lead a triumphant revolt of the head-hunters against the Japanese.

Discussing the episode one day with Sochon, I asked him whether he thought that his worst troubles were over, or that they had only just begun, when he alighted safely on the Kelabit plateau, where they came to earth. He replied that his most anxious moments were spent in the air coming down. He was a practised parachutist, having made twenty previous jumps, and his parachute, too, was experienced at the game, for this was to be its eighty-first drop. Together they were therefore a professional combination who might be trusted to perform the descent with credit.

Weather conditions over the appointed landing ground were difficult, so the invaders made their leaps from only 3,000 feet. The first nine-tenths of their drop was through cloud, and not till they came within 300 feet of the earth could they study the prospect below. Sochon jumped last, and then beat all his companions on the way down, landing in record time for a live descent from 3,000 feet. I write "live" advisedly, for men whose parachutes failed to open have been known to travel faster.

Soon after leaving the aeroplane, when his parachute had spread to take the breeze and check his fall, he realized that he was tumbling more swiftly than usual. Looking up, he observed something which made his heart miss a beat. In the umbrella above him were seven gaping slits. While he counted them they grew gradually larger, and two or three additional rips appeared in the parachute. His speed accelerated. The holes kept increasing in size and number until they totalled fourteen, and by then his pace was spanking.

When he cleared the cloud and saw that he was indeed ap-

proaching the earth with undue haste, he searched for a handy
piece of ground which might be softer than the rest. Noticing
a small marsh on one side of his line of descent, he pulled the appropriate strings on his parachute, changed course and splashed
into a foot of water. He suffered no harm.

At that moment he felt a strong conviction that the worst was
over, and that thereafter his fortunes would be good.

He was right. He and his colleagues experienced many hard-
ships and perils, but they found friendly pagans who hid and fed
them while a campaign was organized. The leaders of this native
conspiracy were the great chief of the Kenyah tribe, Tama Weng
Ajang, the wise Scapan, Penghulu Puso, and afterwards the remarkable Iban, Temonggong Koh. The reader will meet all these
men in this book.

Quickly the news of the return of white men spread through
the jungle, and by secret messengers Kenyah, Kayan and Iban
chieftains summoned their followers to take revenge on the Japanese. Soon British officers were leading bands of natives down
the rivers of Sarawak, driving the enemy before them towards
the sea. Bill Sochon captained an expedition among the Ibans on
the Rejang River, and Toby Carter led one among the Kenyahs
and Kayans on the Baram. In many places the Sarawak natives
did not wait for the arrival of organized military units, but
attacked the foe by their own means. For many years under the
strict rule of the Rajahs they had been reformed characters,
restraining reluctantly their desire to set forth on head-hunting
sprees. Now, however, the Rajah's enemies were occupying
Sarawak. His devoted subjects felt that it would perhaps not be
wholly inconsistent with their duty to His Highness if they fell
to the temptation of cutting off Japanese heads. Fetching out
their blow-pipes and parangs, they enjoyed a short Indian summer
of unrestricted head-hunting.

Many a Japanese soldier who strayed incautiously along a
forest path never returned to camp to regale his comrades with
tales of the odd tropical creatures or beautiful wild orchids which
he had seen. At some lonely spot he would suddenly, unaccount-
ably stumble and fall. A small, wispish object flying through the
sunlight and shadow had struck him. Whence had it come?

What could it be? Ah, how it hurt! Examining his person he discovered a dart embedded in his flesh, like a porcupine's quill. It was a poisoned arrow from a blow-pipe. How sleepy it made him feel as he lay helpless on the ground! The fatal juice of the ipoh tree was doing its work.

Something stirred in the near by bushes, a head-hunter stepping from his hiding place. Stealthily he moved to the prostrate body, laid his blow-pipe on the grass and drew his parang from its sheath. With a single stroke of its blade he claimed his prize— and the number of Japanese heads taken by the pagans was increased by one.

When a marksman thus bagged his quarry he took it home and hung it in his house, just as other big-game hunters do. All head-hunters—both those who claim to be civilized and those who make no such pretensions—delight in displaying the trophies of the chase in funereal rows upon their walls. In some cases they may be the heads of elephants and tigers, and in others the heads of men. Many Japanese heads now hang, unrecognizable among older skulls, in long-houses up the Sarawak rivers. I am told that the most valued possession in one Iban mansion is the head of a Director of Artistic Endeavour in the Imperial army of occupation in Borneo. He was a man of earnest, student-like appearance who wore a pair of gold-rimmed spectacles. It is said that the glasses still perch on what is left of his nose, and that each day the chief of the house removes them, gives them a polish, and solemnly puts them back.

Probably the tale is not correct. The Ibans are great romancers. Boastful lying about their exploits does not strike them as being bad form. But in this case any inaccuracy in the fanciful embellishments of the story is of little importance; its substance was overwhelmingly true. The pagans of Sarawak, accustomed for several generations to rule by benevolent English autocrats, resented the reversion to government by harsh Oriental despots, and they expressed their resentment by helping themselves one by one to a few hundred Japanese heads.

Now British government has returned, and they are once more reformed characters.

II

The Japanese in Sarawak surrendered in September 1945. The people rejoiced. Their country was free, and they assumed that their Rajah would return to his throne.

During the war, however, discussions had taken place in London about Sarawak's future. Representatives of the British Government and of the Rajah reviewed the treaty relations between their two countries, and at the war's end the Colonial Office proposed that when His Highness resumed the administration of his state, he should receive advice from a British Resident. The purpose was to ensure that economic, social and political development in Sarawak kept pace with that in other dependent communities in the British Empire.

The plan was sent to the Rajah, who studied it and returned it with the comment that it did not go far enough. To the astonishment of Ministers in Downing Street he said that he wished to cede Sarawak to the King. In later public messages he gave his reasons for the proposal, explaining that he feared that if Brooke rule continued, the future of Sarawak would be uncertain; that if the territory depended entirely on its own resources, it could not meet the costs of rehabilitation after years of Japanese occupation; that he trusted the British Government more than any other authority to give native peoples a fair deal; and that only with British assistance could an expansion of Sarawak's health, education and other social services, the exploitation of its natural resources and an improvement in its people's conditions of living be achieved.

The Government in London agreed to cession on condition that it was approved by the Legislative and Executive Councils in Kuching and effected by the proper constitutional processes. In April 1946 a majority of members in each Council accepted the plan, and on July 1st an assembly was held in Kuching to witness the transfer of sovereignty.

I was then Governor-General of Malaya and British Borneo, and flew to Sarawak to represent His Majesty at this historic ceremony. As my flying-boat crossed Borneo's coast I sat in the pilot's cockpit gazing upon the verdant land below. I caught my first glimpse of Kuching when it was twenty miles away.

The smoke from its kitchens hung like a grey mist against the tropical green surrounding it, and as we approached the little capital gradually revealed itself below. I was charmed by its neat streets and buildings on either side of the Sarawak River.

The seaplane splashed to a landing on the channel several miles beyond the town, and I proceeded to Kuching by launch. The calm of evening lay upon the water, which flowed as smooth and polished as a mirror. As we went up-stream it reflected in pools of liquid crimson and molten gold the colours of a gorgeous sunset. A moment in history was passing, and Nature was bidding a regal farewell to the White Rajahs.

Dusk fell quickly, the lights in the sky and on the water faded, and when I reached Kuching the place was hidden in darkness. I did not go ashore, since it would have been tactless for the King's representative to set foot on land before the hour for the transfer of sovereignty next day. So I slept aboard H.M.S. *Alacrity*, which had come to Kuching to take part in the ceremonies. Beyond the porthole of my cabin glided the placid river, and on the opposite bank stood the palace of the Brookes. I could not see it in the darkness, but I felt the presence of distinguished ghosts.

At first light next morning I went on deck and set eyes for the first time on the royal mansion standing amidst green lawns and shady trees. Its fabulous architecture accentuated its romantic character, for in the heyday of the Victorian Gothic revival its author, the second Rajah, built it partly like a mediæval castle and partly as a modern tropical bungalow. I pinched myself to make sure that I was awake, and not just dreaming this strange mission to receive on behalf of His Majesty the King the realm of the famous Rajahs.

As I stood in reverie on deck a thunderous roar suddenly shattered the silence. With ponderous deliberation the ship's armament had begun to fire a salute of seventeen guns. It was a signal that Mr. Archer, the Rajah's envoy at that day's event, had arrived at the courthouse for the ceremony. Ten minutes later, when I descended the ship's side and embarked in the captain's pinnace, the battery roared a salute of nineteen guns.

At the jetty Mr. Archer and Mr. Dawson of the Malayan Civil Service (who was to act as Governor) greeted me. We were dressed in white and gold uniforms, flags decorated the streets, and a huge crowd watched me inspect a guard of honour formed by sailors from the warship and constables from the Sarawak Police. The day was marked with suitable pomp.

Shortly afterwards, in the crowded courthouse, Mr. Archer handed me the Deed of Cession of Sarawak. At that moment the little territory became a colony in the King's dominions. The rule of the White Rajahs had ended and that of His Britannic Majesty had begun.

III

The act of cession caused much controversy, some of it bitter. That was inevitable, for the situation was one where certain personal and political feelings were grievously hurt. A section of Malay opinion in Sarawak opposed the change, and the Rajah's young nephew, Anthony Brooke, who was previously second in the line of succession, sought to visit Sarawak to assess the measure of this discontent. The British authorities banned his entry to the country, and for a few years hot arguments continued.

I shall not enter into the details of the charges and counter-charges which the two sides hurled at one another. Those who criticized Mr. Anthony Brooke showed an extraordinary lack of sympathy for one who had suffered a terrible reversal of fate. He would have been more than human if he had not resented deeply a sudden and, in his opinion, unnecessary change which robbed him of the proud destiny to which he had been born. The bearer in his generation of a famous name, he was an heir to unique responsibilities. Everyone had expected that he would ascend the throne of the Rajahs of Sarawak and uphold in his astana at Kuching the traditions of his ancestors.

Suddenly that prospect faded. The glory of a life of kingly rule dissolved before his gaze. In the face of such a blow to an ambitious and honourable young man's expectations, I for one never felt disposed to rouse anger against him, but only to express heartfelt understanding and sympathy. But the issue was not one in which considerations of the personal prospects of an individual could unduly influence judgement. As Mr. Brooke himself was the first to agree, the decisive questions were: what was in the best interests of the people of Sarawak, and what did they themselves wish? Judged by those tests I think that at that time cession was right.

The people's feelings were apparent to everyone who travelled widely in the country. At the liberation of Sarawak in 1945 no difference of opinion existed among them. For a hundred years they had been ruled by the Brookes. They were loyal to their Rajah and they rejoiced at his impending return. Everyone was happy, too, at the prospect of renewed British guidance and protection for their small state; but few contemplated the possibility of the cession of the country to the King.

If anyone but the Rajah himself had suggested it, the idea would have been summarily dismissed; but when he proposed the change, that was a different matter. His subjects at once considered the idea with respect, and when he published the practical reasons for his decision large numbers of them agreed. Though a section of Malay opinion opposed the plan, an equally strong section favoured it; the Chinese community almost unanimously approved cession; and the pagan chiefs were attracted by the assurance that British rule would lead to the introduction of education for their hitherto unschooled children. Naturally the great majority of the primitive natives were not affected by any such enlightened thought; they were merely devoted to the Rajah, and trusted his judgement. His word had long been law for them, and if he advocated cession, then they were prepared to accept his counsel.

They had only one doubt, one fear. Accustomed to a certain way of life founded on ancient native customs—an unwritten code of laws known as the "adat lama"—they were afraid lest a new ruler would sweep aside these traditions and govern according to new-fangled notions incomprehensible to them. It was strange how little things had changed in Sarawak in a hundred years. A century earlier, when James Brooke sought to become the first Rajah, the Dayak chiefs' sole apprehension was lest he should interfere with their adat lama, and the one condition which Rajah Muda Hassim urged him to accept was that these ancient customs of the people should be guaranteed. Only when he promised to respect them did the chieftains acclaim him.

Now again, in 1946, the same point troubled their descendants. The Secretary of State for the Colonies, however, gave a public assurance that the British Government would maintain the adat lama. That settled the matter. The natives' doubts were allayed, and they were ready to acquiesce in the change of rule.

Nevertheless, on the day of cession a profound sadness affected the people. Brooke rule, they thought, had been wonderful. When the last Rajah withdrew, the simple men of the jungle felt that someone closer to them than a mere friend or leader had departed. For generations three just and sympathetic Englishmen had governed them with the compassionate understanding of a father watching over his children; and as children love a good father, so they loved the White Rajahs.

However, they heard that King George was an even greater, wiser and more generous father. Well, if that proved true, they would be happy. They looked forward uncertainly but hopefully to the future.

So much for the people's own wishes. Was cession in their interests? Again I think the answer is yes. The Rajah was undoubtedly sound in his main arguments.

In many ways Brooke rule had been conspicuously good. It established order where there had been chaos, brought security and justice to the tribesmen, was sympathetic to their simple way of life, and preserved them against harmful influences from outside. It was a model of the benevolent autocracy of the old days. But it had grown out-of-date. Its attitude to the natives was negative, not positive. Apart from introducing a few Christian missions among them, it sought to leave them as they were, completely unchanged in their "savage" habits except for the suppression of head-hunting. It was right to shield them from the unfortunate, corrupting influences which have sometimes destroyed native races after the arrival of white men in their lands, but it was wrong, in my view, not to introduce gradually more of the good, beneficial developments which can result from that crisis in primitive societies. After a century of Brooke rule many capable administrative officers served the Rajah's subjects, but there were deplorably few trained agriculturists, doctors, teachers and other specialists. There was no adequate health, agricultural or education service. Such institutions as dispensaries, hospitals, schools and experimental farms were lamentably insufficient. Moreover, plans for training the natives in the management of their own affairs did not exist. Sarawak was stuck in the jungle mud.

Its population enjoyed excellent nineteenth century government; but they now needed twentieth century government. The Rajah's resources in men, experience and money could not provide that. Peering into the future, he felt that the Brooke dynasty could never do what was required. He believed that Britain, with its unrivalled experience in modern colonial government, was better able to do it than any other existing authority; and so he proposed cession.

Some critics urged that the advantages which cession would bring to the local peoples were all material—healthier bodies, a higher economic standard of living and an education which would give various individuals a chance of promotion to better-paid jobs. In return, these observers said, they lost something spiritual, because they lost their liberty. They were no longer citizens of an independent state, but dependent peoples in a colony.

That was a specious argument. No population in history was ever more dependent on its rulers than the people of Sarawak. They are at least as free today under the Queen's Governor as they were yesterday under their own Rajah; and as time passes they will become freer than they would otherwise have been. If the people of Great Britain fulfil their trust to them as faithfully as they have fulfilled it to the once "dependent colonial subjects" in Canada, Australia, New Zealand, South Africa, Eire, Newfoundland, India, Pakistan, Burma, Ceylon, Central Africa, the Gold Coast, Nigeria, and other countries, the natives of Sarawak will be encouraged to practise ever fuller self-expression and to assume ever greater responsibilities, until they become the masters of their own destiny.

PART TWO

THE LAND DAYAKS

CHAPTER FOUR

A VISIT TO SINGGI

I

THE RAJAH'S GOVERNMENT in Sarawak was personal. His word was law. Problems in his small kingdom were so few and simple that he could virtually cope with them all himself. He had officers, of course, who advised him on the affairs of their various departments, but he was not obliged to take their advice. All the Rajah Brookes were men of independent character, firm opinions and strong will, and their officials existed less to influence their decisions before they were made than to carry them out afterwards.

Most of the time the Rajah (or, when His Highness was in England, his sagacious brother and heir) resided in his astana in Kuching, and issued his edicts there; but every now and then he proceeded on tour, visiting different parts of his domain. Wherever he went he held court, conferred with local government officers, hob-nobbed with native chiefs and met crowds of his subjects. On these journeys he was accessible to everyone. Penghulus* consulted him about tribal affairs, Chinese leaders told him of their community problems, petitioners sought his aid in the settlement of grievances, and all and sundry paid him homage. Mixed with a certain amount of ceremonial, a pleasant, friendly informality graced these occasions. If the relationship between the Rajah and his people was authoritarian, it was also intimate.

The high functionaries of the administration established similar personal contacts with the population. Especially in the outstations they lived close to the people under their charge. No barriers of official etiquette or entanglements of red tape separated them from the natives. At their headquarters the Residents

* Native chiefs

and District Officers were accessible to all callers, and they often journeyed through their territories. On these travels business and pleasure were judiciously combined. First the visiting official would sit in court, trying criminal and civil cases, then he conferred with chiefs about local public affairs, and after that he was entertained with refreshments, music, dancing, gossip and merriment through the rest of the waking hours. Periodical visits of this nature to all the people of his area were among an administrative officer's duties. The authorities in Kuching insisted that a District Officer in a Dayak area must stay at least one night each year in every long-house in his region; and his contacts with the Chinese in the bazaars and the Malays in their kampongs* had to be equally regular.

This close personal association of the Government with the public was the secret of peaceful, harmonious rule throughout the land. It was the means by which benevolent autocracy did its work. The Rajah was an absolute monarch and his representatives were, each in his own sphere, all-powerful; but instead of being a remote tyrant he was a presiding father to his people, and instead of being a body of bureaucrats his officials were a company of popular leaders for them. The ruler, his advisers and his subjects were like a large patriarchal family in which authority filtered down from above and obedience rose up from below with mutual goodwill.

My first resolve as Governor-General was that this tradition of personal rule must be preserved. I wished the people to be as happy under the King's jurisdiction as they had been under the Rajah's. Familiar personal relations between the governors and the governed become to some extent impossible in large, populous countries, but in small states the relationship can still exist in its purest form. It is especially important where autocratic power lies in the hands of administrators, as it must do in colonies at an early stage of political development. The new régime in Sarawak is working gradually towards self-government; but that will grow slowly. At present the natives are accustomed to authoritarian rule. They like it and would feel lost without it. But they wish to see their autocrats from time to time, to discuss

* Villages

problems with them, and to feel that the powers-that-be have a close, sympathetic interest in their affairs. If the authorities reciprocate this wish, meet the people frequently and pay due heed to their opinions, some of the best features of both autocracy and democracy in government can be combined.

Therefore I started early to travel widely in Sarawak, meeting the pagans, Chinese, Malays and others in their own homes, discussing with them every public matter which concerned them, explaining to them the Government's policies, and listening carefully to their comments and criticisms.

II

One of my early expeditions was to the Land Dayak villages on Singgi Mountain, about forty miles from Kuching. Land Dayaks were the principal inhabitants of the original territory acquired by James Brooke. That great man himself visited the Dayaks on Singgi Mountain shortly after ascending his throne. One or two of their leaders were then threatening trouble, and he went to bring them to heel. The natives whom I visited in 1946 were direct descendants of his hosts of almost exactly a hundred years before.

The Land Dayaks used to be long-house dwellers, but many have abandoned that form of residence. They did this from necessity, not choice. Land Dayaks are not vigorous types like most other pagan peoples; they are easy-going, pacific and even timid. Their very name bears a hint of this. Early European visitors to Borneo called them Land Dayaks to distinguish them from the Ibans, whom they nicknamed Sea Dayaks, because the former were not sea-farers. They had not the daring which made the Ibans take to the ocean and, incidentally, to piracy.

So the Land Dayaks became convenient prey for their aggressive neighbours. In the centuries of slave-trading and head-hunting their long-houses were favourite objects of attack by combined forces of Brunei Malays and Ibans, as well as by Illanun and Balanini pirates from farther afield. The peace-loving Land Dayaks put up little resistance. This naturally encouraged their persecutors to return whenever they desired loot. Harassed, bullied and despairing, the Dayaks abandoned their homes, retreated up the rivers, and in some cases left low-lying country altogether and fled to higher, more defensible ground. Ultimately many built their homes near mountain tops.

The change of site had a profound influence on their architecture. Flat ground is required for building a long-house. If one were erected on the irregular and often rocky slope of a steep height, it would collapse, its length and weight making it slip down the hillside. So the mountain Land Dayaks adopted a smaller type of home. Where the nature of the ground allowed it they built miniature long-houses, dwellings accommodating perhaps four or five families; but in their kampongs many households had separate shacks of their own. The collection of buildings looked like a Western village, with individual huts and short rows of huts scattered in groups.

When the White Rajahs enforced law in their kingdom, the Land Dayaks were left in peace. They prospered and multiplied, and some descended from the hilltops to live again in the valleys. Among these the long-house became fashionable once more, but the most characteristic Land Dayak dwellings remained fortress villages in the highlands. Singgi Mountain was one of the heights chosen by a group of Dayaks in an earlier age for a last stand against their enemies, and its steep, stony slopes achieved what their meek character could not. It successfully defied attack and gave them security until the blessings of Brooke rule restored their hope. Even then they chose to stay in their mountain resort.

A jeep took me from Kuching on the first stage of my journey. Datu Bandar, the senior Malay chief in Sarawak, accompanied me. A man in his early forties, he was a prudent leader in the public affairs of the colony, and a charming, cheerful friend. Our way lay for several miles along a road through rubber plantations and jungle, and then it came to a crossing of the Sarawak River. Embarking on a primitive ferry, we were poled by a Malay crew across an angry current which strove to wash us down-stream. After a grim struggle we landed safely on the farther bank, climbed into our jeep again and continued on our way. Soon the road began to deteriorate, and we bumped along its corrugated surface until we reached a small gold-mining town called Bau.

The little settlement lay amidst beautiful highland scenery. Its main street was flanked on either side by shop-houses filled with all the strange foods and simple household goods which beguile Chinese. Not far beyond the end of the street a solitary crag rose abruptly from the plain to a height of almost two thousand feet. This was Bau Mountain. A few miles farther away other rugged limestone hills half encircled the landscape—an assembly of steep, jagged heights clothed in thick green jungle so tattered that here and there large spaces of bare grey rock appeared. Their loftiest peaks rose four thousand feet, and they had the grotesque, dramatic shapes of an artificially constructed scenic railway in an amusement park.

The local District Officer, Mr. Lloyd-Thomas, joined Datu Bandar and me. We continued our journey for several miles by jeep, advancing erratically along a rough, twisting track so narrow that stems of forest undergrowth reached out from either side and scratched our faces as we passed. At length we came to a rivulet opposite a village named Tondong. We jumped out, waved good-bye to such lordly means of locomotion as jeeps, rowed across the stream in a sampan and thereafter depended on our legs for further progress.

Tondong is a small huddle of Chinese dwellings situated on the river's bank. Beside its bazaar stands a temple where Buddha is worshipped, a school where the local youngsters are taught Confucian ethics, and a police station where laws made by a Christian Queen are enforced by Moslem and pagan constables. That mixture is typical of Sarawak. The village exists to provide a market for Land Dayak and Chinese husbandmen scattered over a wide area. We drank coffee with its principal towkay in his shop, then sallied forth to walk four miles to the Dayak kampongs near the top of Singgi Mountain, accompanied by a group of native porters carrying our baggage. We were to spend the night with the highland villagers and return next day.

At first our path led through untidy Chinese rubber plantations. Shafts of sunshine penetrated irregular rows of trees, dappling the ground with light and shadow. Not even the ceiling of foliage, however, could make the place cool. The time of day was early afternoon, and the equatorial sun had hardly

declined below its zenith. Lloyd-Thomas set a sharp pace for
walking, and within a few minutes I was soaked with perspiration
from head to foot. During the next twenty-four hours my clothes
were to be almost continuously sopping wet from tramping, climbing and dancing. I kept changing them until I had no more
dry shirts or trousers left. After that I changed every now and
then into whichever garments in my wardrobe happened at the
moment to be the least damp.

Though walking strenuously in these conditions was uncom-
fortable, it was splendid exercise. It stretched limbs and tested
muscles which had long been lazy in the relaxed life of Singapore. Our pace was swifter, however, than Datu Bandar considered agreeable. In his athletic youth his figure was no doubt
spare, but now it was gradually assuming a portliness in keeping
with his position as a promising statesman. It checked his speed
on jungle excursions, and he fell far behind us, where the more
elderly Dayak porters kept him company. The younger natives
leaped forward quickly, carrying their loads easily over rocks,
through gullies and up steep inclines. They were not cumbered
by garments other than loin-cloths, and their brown skins glistened
moistly in the sunshine.

After half an hour's trudging we came to the first Land Dayak
village, lying at Singgi Mountain's foot. It was a Christian
settlement. Once upon a time its inhabitants were pagans living
with their fellows on the mountain. Then their headman fell
under the influence of missionaries, turned Catholic and converted some of his family and friends. This little congregation
of Dayak churchmen grew intolerant of its neighbours who
maintained a stout animistic faith in good and evil spirits. Their
pagan neighbours were willing for them to stay on the mountain
top, enjoying freedom to build their own kampong and practise
their strange new religion; but the Catholics felt upset by the
propinquity of savage worship, and resolved to build a new
kampong elsewhere. They could not travel far, for the traditional lands on which they grew their padi were in Singgi's
neighbourhood; so they merely descended the height and settled
at its foot.

We tarried for a while among the Christians, sipping refreshing orangeade, and then continued our journey. The steep, upward slope of the mountain started immediately beyond their village boundary. Singgi's summit rises to a height of 2,000 feet, and its Dayak residents have built their huts at about 1,700 feet above sea level. There seven hamlets cluster together in a group reached by a precipitous, rocky path twisting among jungle trees. The time was now four o'clock in the afternoon, and climbing in the tropical heat was punishing work. As we ascended perspiration ran down me as if I stood under a bathroom shower, but the uphill track was a nice challenge to our stamina. We went forward like goats from foothold to foothold, and after an hour's exertion came to the entrance to the Dayak homesteads.

Over the pathway rose an arch of welcome, a high bamboo structure decorated with palm leaves and tropical flowers. Beyond it waited a reception party led by the orang kaya or chief of the group of villages. Behind him stood the tua tua kampong, or headmen of each separate village, with a throng of local inhabitants.

"Apa khaba, orang kaya?" I called to the chieftain, using the traditional words of greeting. They mean, "What is the news, rich man?"

"Khaba baik, Rajah," replied the orang kaya. ("The news is good, Rajah.")

He and his companions stepped forward to welcome us.

"Tabeh, Rajah; tabeh, tuans," they murmured, meaning, "Hail, Rajah; hail, masters."

Their brown faces betrayed great shyness, many looking at the ground instead of into our eyes as we greeted them; yet they grinned with pleasure and their voices were glad. They wore an extraordinary variety of clothes. An assortment of inappropriate Western garments had recently arrived for them from America, provided by the United Nations Reconstruction and Rehabilitation Agency. One old man stood sweltering in a thick fur coat, while another wore upon his savage head a lady's cocktail-party hat of chic New York design. Several natives were dressed in Malay costume, sporting bodices or tunics above their ankle-length sarongs, but most favoured their own customary garb, the upper parts of their bodies naked and the lower skimpily clad in brief loin-cloths or skirts.

The orang kaya conducted us to his house. It was a building of bamboo and attap raised a few feet above the ground on wooden stilts. We climbed a notched tree-trunk staircase to its platform and were introduced to the chief's relatives. Then I went to visit the neighbouring kampongs before darkness should fall. They were grouped close together, connected by well-worn paths meandering through the undergrowth. The buildings looked wild, rising here and there among the lanky forest trees, with floors made of split bamboo and walls and roofs constructed of overlapping layers of attap which made them look like hay-stacks. Some were erected on such steep slopes that, although the inner end of the house stood on piles jutting only two or three feet from the ground, the outer end was skied thirty or forty feet in the air and supported on tall stilts like high scaffold-ing. They seemed flimsy, yet were strong enough to survive the fearful storms which sometimes lashed the mountain. How they managed to stand firm and give safe shelter to large households through many years, I do not know. The Land Dayaks have an uncanny genius for crazy building.

The orang kaya led me from kampong to kampong, intro-ducing me to many people. He was an elderly man with a gentle disposition and sensitive face. The other village chiefs were also veterans. That was one of the weaknesses of Land Dayak society; the elders had too much say in public affairs and the younger men too little. The headmen exerted great authority, the ordi-nary folk were accustomed to obey, and so there was a tyranny of aged conservatism.

After touring the villages I returned to the orang kaya's kam-pong for a much needed bath. By special leave of my host a tub was placed for me in a small round house which is the nearest thing in a Land Dayak village to a temple. One such building stands in each community, a sacred place especially constructed to lodge heads taken in battle. Unlike the other pagan tribes of Borneo, Land Dayaks may not keep these honourable trophies in their homes; so in the centre of every village is this circular building raised on piles, with a steep, cone-shaped grass roof crowned by a carved finial. It looks like a fancy hayrick propped on stilts, and is so holy that no human being may stay or sleep in it.

The local authorities did me the singular honour of letting me have a wash in it—as if the Archbishop of Canterbury had given me permission to take a bath on the chancel steps of Canterbury Cathedral. With soap, towel and dry clothes I climbed a tree-trunk staircase to its door. The shadowy interior was cool, and I felt more comfortable as I slipped off my clammy garments and stood naked on the split-bamboo floor. But as I poured canfuls of refreshing water over myself I felt that I was not alone. I sensed that strange eyes were watching me. This seemed odd, for the place was empty. Then, looking up at the rafters, I saw that I was indeed being observed. On a pole hung a couple of aged, fleshless skulls, inclining their bone faces towards me with grinning teeth and round, vacant eye-holes, scrutinizing my every splash. I realized that they disapproved of my sacrilegious conduct; but there was nothing that they could do about it. I finished my bath, dressed leisurely, waved good-bye to the heads, and left.

III

The Dayaks planned to make merry that evening, for the occasion was unique. Lately they had begun their annual planting of padi, and they had a notion that if I blessed their work a good harvest would result. I was the first Governor-General whom they had ever met, and they had touching faith in my influence over the good and evil spirits. So they organized a ceremony with appropriate solemnities and gaieties. The programme commenced at seven o'clock that evening and continued without cease until three o'clock the next morning.

It began as soon as I returned from my toilet. I was ushered into the orang kaya's living-room and seated on a rustic throne, with Lloyd-Thomas and Datu Bandar placed courtier-like on either side of me. Dusk was falling, and the dark chamber was faintly lit by two flickering flames from oil lamps. Men, women and children crowded every inch of space, some standing, some crouching and others squatting cross-legged on the floor. A hush of expectation filled the room.

At a given signal the orang kaya advanced towards me, bowed reverently, stretched out his hands and tied round my right wrist a rattan string on which hung a small, tinkling bell. As he did so he spoke earnest words in his mother tongue which Lloyd-Thomas translated for me.

"The chief says," he observed, " 'May your padi-fields produce much padi! May your fruit trees bear rich fruits! When you go hunting may you kill many pigs! May you have numerous children, and when they are married may their first-born be sons! May you have a long life and prosperity!' "

I reciprocated these friendly wishes, Lloyd-Thomas interpreting my remarks to the chief. He smiled contentedly, expressed thanks, retired and resumed a seat on the floor.

Then another elder came to me and tied a second bell on my wrist, wishing me similar good fortune in planting, hunting, procreation and all other manly pursuits. Again I expressed my sincere hope that he would share in these fine things. Afterwards many more natives did the same, advancing to me one by one. Some of them tied little bells also on Lloyd-Thomas's and Datu Bandar's arms. At first only men approached us, but later several women joined shyly in the ceremony; and then a few girls and boys plucked up courage to do likewise. Some people brought eggs as presents for me, and even live hens tied in baskets. These offerings were placed on the ground at my feet.

The ritual continued for nearly two hours, one person following closely upon another. As it proceeded we sipped rice-wine and gossiped pleasantly together. When this introductory episode ended, I had sixty-five small bells jingling on my arm, their thin rattan bangles stretching from my wrist almost to my elbow. Nearly one hundred and fifty eggs were heaped in baskets beside me, and I was the owner also of more than twenty domestic fowls.

The eggs and hens were distributed later among the porters who carried our baggage, but the bells were not so quickly disposed of. Lloyd-Thomas advised me that the padi crop would be a failure if I took them off too soon. So I wore them all that evening, all night and most of the next day. Only when we had descended the mountain, trudged and jeeped back to Bau and reached Lloyd-Thomas's house did I cut them off.

The bells were symbolic; they had deep significance in connection with the next harvest. My arm, I was told, represented the branch of a tree, and the bells were fruits growing on it. They were supposed to communicate their abundant fecundity to the padi-fields and wild orchards of all my companions who during the evening's rites brought bangles as offerings for me.

When my belling was over, I presented the assembly with many bottles of rice-wine (called tuak) and packets of cigarettes which I had brought as gifts. The Dayaks were delighted. Their natural reticence began to dissolve. Usually unable to express themselves readily, or to reveal openly their feelings, on this occasion they soon commenced to talk freely and to declare unreserved friendship. As the party progressed they became ever more at ease.

After the long-drawn introductory incident we should have passed immediately to the solemn, supreme ceremonial in which I would bless the padi-planting; but some of the elders were still sitting in a huddle on the floor in the next room, debating certain points of procedure. No similar occasion had been known in the lifetime of these Land Dayaks. The Rajah had never paid them so seasonable a visit—and a Governor-General, they reckoned, was a creature of the same rare, exalted breed. So no precedents existed to guide them in the mysteries of proper practice. This gave the learned men a fine chance to argue delicate questions of etiquette. They had already spent several hours discussing the subject, and still had not settled matters to everyone's satisfaction.

As we waited for them to reach conclusions, a native approached Lloyd-Thomas. He seemed nervous and diffident, and was obviously the bearer of a message. Eventually he explained that "the children" were indulging in a little amusement two rooms away, but that they were not sure whether I would approve of their behaviour. They asked Lloyd-Thomas to inspect their frolics and offer them advice on my opinions. I told him to go and condone whatever the youngsters were up to, however deplorable it might be, and to say that, if they felt no embarrassment, I would come and witness the fun.

When he returned he reported that the merry-makers were not children but young women. They were dancing. According to Land Dayak custom, such behaviour on the part of females was of doubtful propriety on an official occasion in the presence of strangers; but, the revellers urged disarmingly, they felt so joyful at my arrival that it was difficult for them to restrain their gaiety.

I drew the orang kaya aside and said that I hoped that he would give men, women and children alike that evening permission to enjoy themselves as thoroughly as they wished. This was a noble day. My heart was filled with gladness at being with him and his people. If they shared my delight, let us all express unreservedly our happiness.

He was pleased with these sentiments and conveyed them through the house. I heard a mighty shout of glee from the dancers.

Soon afterwards I went to watch their revels. The room was lit by an oil lamp hung from the ceiling, and its yellow rays fell on a crowd of eager brown faces of women and children filling the place almost to suffocation. A few men were also present. In the company's midst a small space of floor was cleared for dancing, and somewhere in the background a musician methodically struck a gong while another thumped a drum. Two or three voices accompanied this monotonous, throbbing, strangely stirring music with chanting, and several people clapped their hands to the rhythm of the tune.

Two girls were performing a *pas de deux*. After a while they tired and withdrew, but immediately another pair of damsels succeeded them on the stage. The music continued without interruption. The audience watched every movement of the dancers and maintained a running fire of comment. Everyone was in gay humour. The local wits occasionally offered observations which convulsed the crowd with laughter.

I studied the steps of the dance. They were simple, like the restrained, to-and-fro motions of Malay rongging, though more lively and spirited than that mild jigging. When the two girls retired after their effort, I said that I would perform. The announcement caused a sensation and the assembly buzzed with excitement.

Elderly matrons looked round the company to select a worthy partner for me. They chose a maid of about eighteen summers, who came forward with diffidence and even embarrassment, her walk hesitant and her gaze cast demurely towards the floor.

I enquired her name, and someone translated the question to her.

She raised her eyes, smiled at me and answered, "Gawang".

When the Creator made Gawang, He made a very lovely thing. Her figure was neat and comely, clad in a Malay blouse and sarong falling to just below her knees. She had long black hair and honey-coloured skin. Her eyes were dark and slanting, and she had a sweetly modelled nose and a delicious mouth. She bore herself modestly, without a trace of affectation. I was told that she loved dancing, and that she was the best dancer in all the seven villages on Singgi Mountain.

Gawang and I performed for a long time, she leading and I following. Her footsteps were deft and light, and when she turned to pirouette she swayed her hips with a gentle, graceful movement. As she overcame her shyness, she looked at me unabashed, smiling encouragement to my efforts. But I could not equal such skill and beauty. The audience, however, was not in a critical mood. They watched with rapt attention, and when at length the music stopped and we ceased to dance, they gave us an ovation.

Shortly afterwards the learned elders in the next room reached decisions on the procedure which I should follow for blessing the padi; so we all adjourned to a long, covered gallery in front of the house where this rite was to be performed. The throng of people was so dense that it overflowed into apartments behind the gallery and on to an open platform in front of the dwelling. The hour was past ten o'clock. A heavy shower of rain had fallen earlier, and the sky was still cloudy and the night pitch black. Our lamps threw beams of dim illumination into the outer darkness, and beyond that lay the sleeping forest. The world of modern cities and societies which I knew seemed infinitely distant. Only this gathering of Dayaks seemed to be reality. There was a feeling of all-pervading peace and goodwill on the solitary mountain-top in the silent night.

The orang kaya led me to a seat facing a large wooden bowl filled with many kinds of food, and the assembly drew close round me. An old man, aided by Lloyd-Thomas as interpreter, gave me whispered instructions as to what I should do at every stage of the impending proceedings.

First the orang kaya advanced with majestic steps towards me, holding a live hen upside-down by its feet. I rose, took the bird and passed it slowly backwards and forwards over the bowl of food. As I did so I murmured heartfelt wishes for a good padi harvest, rich fruit crops, successful hunting, multitudinous progeny, incredible longevity and other desirable gifts for my Dayak friends. Then I returned the hen to the orang kaya, stooped and picked up the bowl. Holding it aloft before me, I marched the length of the gallery four times, every now and then waving the viands over the heads of the onlookers on either hand, like His Holiness the Pope pronouncing benedictions on a congregation. The natives shouted gratefully. Datu Bandar and a couple of village headmen preceded me, one of them performing a few clownish capers, while the orang kaya followed with simple dignity in my wake.

That was all. The mountain of talk by the wiseacres had produced this mouse of ceremonial.

Afterwards the orang kaya invited me into his room for political discussion. Datu Bandar, Lloyd-Thomas and the headmen joined us, and a large company of interested listeners also gathered near a lamp-lit table where we sat. Bottles of tuak passed round the principals, and all our glasses were filled. As the earlier gathering for dancing had consisted almost wholly of women, so this company to talk politics was mostly composed of men.

One or two youths began to ask me questions about public affairs, but the orang kaya angrily reproved them. He declared that he was the authorized spokesman for the community, and that he would lay before me the matters on which they wished to receive enlightenment. At that the audience was hushed. He rose and began a formal speech.

After some delicately phrased compliments to myself, he expressed the Land Dayaks' delight at the return of the British to Sarawak following the Japanese occupation. He referred to the harshness which they had experienced at the hands of the Japanese, and described the natives' sense of renewed freedom to be themselves, to live their own lives in their own way, when white men returned to rule in Kuching. They were glad to be subjects of His Majesty the King. Provided that the new Government did not interfere with their adat lama, cession did not worry them. His only reference to the Brookes was a complaint that whereas the Rajahs had educated the Malays, they had provided no schools for the Dayaks. He and his people hoped that the British administration would remedy this. Then he mentioned local problems: the destruction wrought by wild pigs in their padi, the shortage of guns and cartridges with which to kill these marauders, the lack of cloth for making new sarongs, and sundry other village topics. He asked me for information on the Government's policy in these matters.

I dealt with his points one by one, answering all his questions. When my words were translated, murmurs of agreement with some of my comments passed round the company, and expressions of doubt at others. Where scepticism existed, either the orang kaya or one of the headmen plied me with further queries, or began to develop an argument. The discussion between us was frank and free. I told the orang kaya that if he would give permission, anyone in the room could state his views or ask me questions on any subject, and many took advantage of this invitation. Each spoke in his turn, and none was afraid to express an opinion. By the time we finished, everyone who wished had had his say and received his answer.

As this primitive council proceeded, I reflected that it must be similar to the popular assemblies held by early Anglo-Saxon tribes in England—those embryonic beginnings from which modern parliamentary government has sprung.

When at last our talk ended, the orang kaya remarked that I

must be tired after so strenuous a day, and that they would now release me to go to bed. But I could hear the music of gongs and laughter from the gallery. Asking what was passing there, I learned that the people were still celebrating the day's events with dancing. They expressed a hope that I would not mind them keeping it up a little longer. I answered that, far from displeasing me, the plan suited me well and that I would join them.

They made room for me on the floor of the covered gallery, at the edge of a mat spread for performers. There I squatted cross-legged. Gawang came immediately to sit beside me, bringing a bevy of other young females to be introduced. Datu Bandar sat with us to act as my interpreter in this pleasant circle, while Lloyd-Thomas was the centre of another group of girls close by. Children crawled and settled near us to get a good view of the entertainment.

A kerosene lamp hung from the ceiling above the dancing mat. It threw gleams on the lively faces of a large audience sitting, crouching and standing all around. Rowlandson would have drawn a brilliant sketch of that crowd. They were merry but sober, for the tuak bottles had circulated freely yet judiciously. One of the many good features of this party was that few people got inebriated. Three or four old men became mildly drunk, but they soon disappeared to sleep off their stupor. There was joviality on every face, but it was the product of high, not strong, spirits.

Two men danced first. Buckling on swords and grasping wooden shields, they presented a dramatic version of a fight. It was not a convincing action, lacking the emotional tenseness and artistic execution which I witnessed later in dances by the Ibans, the Kayans and the Kenyahs. This was a mechanical jog-trot affair, full of clumsy steps and awkward postures; but the inhabitants of Singgi Mountain knew no better, and they gave friendly applause to the worthy warriors.

When they retired and the stage was empty, the audience called for Gawang and me to dance. Gawang plucked at my sleeve, and we rose and started to repeat our earlier performance. News that we were dancing spread swiftly through the kampong

and into the neighbouring villages. Many more people flocked
to the house, standing on tiptoe at the back of the crowd and
craning their necks to catch a glimpse of us. The gallery was
too small to hold them, and we decided to adjourn to the open-
air platform outside.

The clouds had now dispersed, and we sat beneath a vast, black
firmament jewelled with stars. The grass huts of the orang
kaya's kampong and the leafy trees of the forest loomed from the
shadows around. The platform, made of long split bamboos
raised on stilts, was built spaciously for spreading padi to dry in
the sunshine. It made a splendid stage, lit by lamps hung along
the eaves of the roof. But the area for performance on it was
restricted, since part of the audience sat crowded over its floor.
Other spectators adopted various stations, peering from the gallery
of the orang kaya's house, from the high windows of near by
buildings, and from rocks, grassy banks and even the branches
of trees overlooking the scene. The dancing mat was the only
uncovered space in the middle of this multitude. At its edge
sat the orchestra—a girl banging a gong, another pounding a
drum and three more chanting.

Gawang and I opened the programme in this wild jungle
theatre. We stepped a gay, bucolic jig, and again our patrons in
the stalls and dress (or rather undress) circle, the pit and the
boxes received our act with kindly favour.

Then four men danced a mock battle. It was greeted with
acclaim. After that Datu Bandar selected a partner, and together
they executed a vigorous sort of shimmy-shake. Next Lloyd-
Thomas and a pretty child in her 'teens showed their paces. These
were all popular performances. Everyone was happy. Lloyd-
Thomas murmured to me that he had never known Land Dayaks
express themselves with such unrestrained delight and friendship. I suggested that the orang kaya should dance, and he did
so with right goodwill; but after that there were cries again for
"Gawang" and "the Rajah".

So we took the floor once more. The gong and drum began to
beat their well-known rhythm, and the voices of the singers gave
these bare bones of sound the flesh of a tune. Gawang and I were
soon well set in the quick, half-jigging, half-shuffling steps of

the dance, swinging forwards and backwards, shifting to this side and that, occasionally exchanging places, giving a high kick, making a circle of pirouettes, she leading and I following wherever she moved. As the act progressed, the approval of the audience became more boisterous, and soon everyone was clapping their hands in time with our steps. Beneath us the bamboo floor swayed gently. Gradually the gong and drum increased their tempo, and we did likewise. Encouraged by the spectators, the musicians were testing our skill. Gawang added new, complicated figures to our dance, and I did my best to imitate them. Her eyes shone brightly and a smile played upon her lips. Men and women shouted words of admiration.

The bamboo stage was being tried even more severely than we. It began to rock beneath our feet, and once or twice the stakes supporting it creaked in protest at their burden. Suddenly a loud report like a pistol-shot sounded above the rest of the din— the crack of breaking timber. The floor collapsed and Gawang and I descended with it to the ground.

For a few minutes there was pandemonium. Many members of the audience had fallen with us, and were slithering and rolling on the sloping floor. Others near the edge of the platform, where it still held in position, were raised above us; but most people had lost their balance and were tumbling over one another. There were shrieks and yells—near panic. I heard the word "Rajah" oft repeated. Anxious natives were enquiring whether I was hurt. When they saw that Gawang and I were still dancing unconcernedly in the middle of the wrecked stage, they burst into roars of laughter and applause.

The accident demonstrated the cunning with which Land Dayaks make their bamboo floors. The central stake supporting the platform had fallen over, shaken from its upright position by our dancing feet and the weight of the crowd. When it fell, other foundation props tipped sideways and ceased to maintain the structure, yet the flooring held together and descended in an unbroken piece. It continued to give Gawang and me firm enough foothold as we sank downwards with it. I merely felt as if we were dropping one story in a flimsy elevator.

When the Dayaks had recovered from their shock and rearranged the auditorium, the dancing continued on ground level.

Performer succeeded performer. We all took turns. Gawang and I tripped a measure half a dozen times. The orang kaya, solicitous and kindly as ever, began to grow worried about my health. He feared lest, as I sat in damp clothes, the chills of night would attack me with fever. The prudent man did not wish me to die on his hands. Several times he suggested that I should go to bed; but the women declared that they would dance till daylight, and they dropped hints that they hoped that I would stay. I replied that I would outstay them all. So the orang kaya's warnings were uttered in vain, and I changed my clothes for the umpteenth time. We danced until the very ground seemed on the verge of collapse.

At last the ladies weakened. They grew sleepy. They heard, moreover, that I proposed to take photographs of them when day dawned, and they wished to look their best for the pictures. Fearful of appearing with dark circles under their eyes, they asked at what time I would rise to make the portraits. When I answered "Six-thirty", they were visibly shaken. Their eye-lids blinked and they permitted themselves a few yawns.

At three o'clock Gawang said, "Salamat teedor!" which means "Sleep well", and went to snatch forty winks in her hut in the next kampong. The others dispersed soon afterwards.

I retired to bed in the orang kaya's room. Already a dozen exhausted natives of various ages and both sexes were stretched on the floor, deep in slumber. Others squatted on their haunches, gossiping. I crept under my mosquito-net. For some time chatter continued round me, but it quickly grew fainter in my consciousness, until profound sleep banished it altogether.

In spite of the fact that I lay in damp clothes, I slept well. Two or three times the cry of a child or the growl of a dog somewhere in the house half woke me, and whenever I shifted my right arm the sixty-five bells dangling on it tinkled in my ear. I dreamed that I was about to:

> Ride a cock-horse to Banbury Cross
> To see a fine lady on a fine horse.
> With rings on her fingers and bells on her toes,
> She shall have music wherever she goes.

At six o'clock the sounds of people stirring in the room woke me. I felt muzzy with sleep, and at first wondered where I was. Then gradually the events of the previous night reconstructed themselves in my mind, and I remembered that I lay in a Land Dayak home near the top of Singgi Mountain. Realizing that I was soon to depart, I felt a momentary sadness. I wished that I were a Dayak and that I need never leave this simple existence with my warm-hearted friends. My drowsy imagination started on pleasant trains of thought. I could learn to plant padi and hunt wild pigs. I was then still a bachelor, and the thought of wooing and winning lovely Gawang had attractions. In time, I reflected ambitiously, I might rise to be an orang kaya. . . . Then these unsubstantial day-dreams were interrupted by the grunting of substantial pigs rootling among the garbage below the house and the sight of some all too realistic dirt in the room dissolved my idealized conception of life in primitive society.

The inmates of the house were rising to commence their early morning duties. Men fetched wood for the cooking fires, women set dishes on the floor for breakfast, through the door I could see girls lifting baskets filled with bamboo "bottles" to fetch water from a near by spring. The routine, humdrum activities of a new day had started.

I rose and shaved. A group of children watched me with amusement. They giggled every time that I scraped my cheeks with the razor, for the bells on my wrist shook and jingled. Then I went for a wash in the round house, once more under the hostile scrutiny of the skulls. Returning, I consumed some excellent coffee and eggs, and finally sallied forth to take the promised photographs.

Soon afterwards Lloyd-Thomas, Datu Bandar and I were ready to depart. I need not describe our leave-taking from the great company of Dayaks who lined the mountain path to wave us good-bye. It was the heartfelt farewell of friends.

Oh, Land Dayaks of Singgi Mountain, you were generous and good to us! With all my heart I hope that your guardian spirits will ensure that your padi harvests are bountiful, that your fruit trees bear rich crops, that when you go hunting you will catch many wild pigs, that your children will be legion and that you will all live long and happily. And I pray that my God also, who is the Giver of Life, will watch over you and bless you always.

PART THREE

THE IBANS

CHAPTER FIVE

UP-RIVER

I

MY FIRST CONTACT with the Ibans was at Simanggang on the Batang Lupar River. They possess very different characters and capacities from the Land Dayaks, being energetic where the latter are easy-going, clever where the others are slow-witted, aggressive where Dayaks are retiring, and ambitious where Dayaks do not care a straw what happens to them so long as they have enough food to eat and a roof over their heads. I doubt whether the Ibans are the ablest natives in Sarawak. The Kayans and Kenyahs are doughtier warriors, wiser councillors and finer artists. But the Ibans are the most dynamic, and since they are more numerous than any other community, with the possible exception of the Chinese, their qualities will probably make them, as they become educated, the pre-eminent people in the country.

As I say, I caught my first glimpse of them during a visit to Simanggang. Denis White, the Secretary for Native Affairs, a knowledgeable and congenial officer of the Rajah's government, was taking me on an introductory tour of the colony. Sarawak is divided into five provinces called Divisions, and Simanggang is the capital of the Second Division. This pleasant little town is therefore the headquarters of a Resident. It is a considerable trading centre inhabited by large Chinese and Malay communities, while the country round is Iban territory with a scattering of long-houses. It stands on a high bank overlooking the Batang Lupar River. When we arrived, a vast crowd waited to greet me. Courtesy to the King's Representative and curiosity to see what this unprecedented functionary looked like combined to bring Simanggang's entire population, and many visitors from neighbouring districts, to the jetty.

It was a gay throng, for the Malays, Chinese and Ibans were

attired in their best clothing. Malays have splendid taste in
costume, liking brightness and contrast in colours. Frequently
no two parts of their dress are similarly hued, and some of the
combinations are startling, yet invariably the harmony is as successful as it is bold. That morning at Simanggang the reds
and browns, blues and greens, mauves and purples of turbans,
veils, bajus and sarongs were a brilliant spectacle.

The Chinese men were soberly clad in black and white, but
their women were dressed as for a festival. Some wore gay bajus
and sarongs like their Malay sisters, but others favoured the neat
tunics and long wide trousers of their motherland, with picturesque patterns and colours like frivolous beach pyjamas.

Most striking of all, however, were the Ibans. Many men
from the long-houses had come to town for the occasion. Few
women accompanied them, for the month was August, when
padi-seed is planted. As the females do most of the labour of
sowing, we had asked that they should stay in their fields, otherwise the next harvest might have been seriously prejudiced.

The Ibans at Simanggang that morning were husky specimens,
superbly clad in bronzed flesh decorated with blue-black tattooing
on their throats, shoulders, backs, arms and thighs. Most of them
were naked except for a slim loin-cloth, called a sirat, a silver bracelet above each elbow and a black rattan garter below each knee.

A particular group of Ibans was more sumptuously clad.
Drawn up in formal file, like a platoon of soldiers, they were
to be my bodyguard. One bachelor had been selected from
each long-house for miles around, so that every native village in the
district should be represented. The fourteen youths had been
picked for their good looks, and they knew it! Their faces were
not only handsome but arrogant, and their bearing betrayed
swagger as well as grace. They were all in the prime of masculine youth and beauty, with strong torsos, slim hips, firm thighs
and muscular limbs.

They were dressed to kill, in both senses of the term. Indeed,
they were over-dressed, for they had donned every article of
finery that they possessed. On their heads were silver crowns sur-
mounted by tall black-and-white hornbills' feathers. Iban males

do not cut their hair, and the long, jet-black locks of these splendid bucks fell in loose, thick tresses far down their backs. From their pierced ear-lobes dangled heavy brass ear-rings, round their necks were silver chains, across their chests stretched tinselled sashes, and their arms bore many bracelets of beaten silver. Brilliantly coloured loin-cloths circled their waists, with one tasselled end suspended like a sporran in front and the other hanging like a tail behind. Some warriors wore silver belts supporting short skirts so thickly encrusted with Chinese dollars that they seemed solid metal kilts. Below their knees were red and black garters strung with small tinkling bells. Not content with all these sartorial falderals, most of them sported in addition wrought silver anklets above bare feet. The men wore at their waists head-hunter's swords, weapons with richly carved staghorn hilts tufted with locks of the hair of slain enemies.

Mr. John Barcroft, the Resident, greeted me and introduced me to the local Malay and Chinese notables. Then he presented me to the members of the guard. When we turned to stroll to the Residency, the Ibans broke their rank and collected in formation round me. To my astonishment, their leader shouted a word of command, and as I began to walk the troop moved forward too. All the way to the house three guardsmen marched ahead of me while the others followed in a triple column behind. The tall plumes of their head-dresses nodded, and the coins and bells on their persons jingled at every step. Their bodies glistened like burnished metal and their ear-rings and necklaces, sashes and kilts, bracelets and anklets glittered in the sunlight. Her Majesty the Queen driving to Parliament with an escort of the Household Cavalry and Yeomen of the Guard is not more regally conducted.

Barcroft told me that traditionally an Iban cannot wear a hornbill's feather on his cap unless he has taken a head. The number of plumes which a man wears should therefore indicate the number of fellow-beings whom he has decapitated. I saw that some members of my guard wore nearly a score of feathers, but Barcroft assured me that they had not earned them in the customary way. That morning's display was a revelation of the decay of ancient tribal codes, and also of the streak of vanity in Iban character. The young men's selection as members of my body-guard had gone to their heads, and they were swanking.

During the next two days I was almost perpetually busy, for I inspected the government offices, a hospital, two or three schools, the bazaar, the prison and various other institutions, as well as attending numerous functions. Wherever I went, the Ibans felt it their duty to accompany me. When occasionally I snatched half an hour's leisure in the Residency, they crouched on the grass beneath its elevated verandah, awaiting my next engagement. At the first sound of my footfall descending the stairs they rose, set the various articles of their costumes in order, took their stations in the escort and, at the captain's word of command, conducted me on my way.

One item in the programme was a ceremony in the court-house, where the leaders of the several racial communities presented me with addresses of welcome. The hall was crowded with Chinese, Malays, Ibans and Europeans. It was a friendly occasion, but a stranger seeing the members of my bodyguard in attendance might have thought it a meeting being harangued by the dictator in a police state, with the local Gestapo in charge. Dressed in their full panoply, they lounged round the door and peered through the windows, their fists gripping the hilts of their parangs, apparently ready to lop off the head of anyone who cried "Boo!" during my speech.

Once I escaped from their surveillance. If their regimental march round me was stately and Viceregal, it was also slow. At that pace I should never have reached the Anglican mission school a mile outside the town. Moreover, since there were no motor cars in Simanggang, the best means of locomotion was a bicycle. But the dignity, not to mention the limbs, of the Iban braves would be grievously hurt if they attempted to ride in precise military formation over the bumpy path on push-bikes —machines of which they had no previous experience. So when they were not looking, Barcroft and I slipped through the back door of the Residency and cycled unescorted to the school.

This truant act displeased them. They were mightily upset. As temperamental as a group of prima donnas, they felt hurt that I should think them dispensable. In their own eyes they were an essential condition of my well-being. Like vain actors in a male chorus, they wanted to be perpetually in the limelight, to remain on the stage from the first raising of the curtain until its final fall on our little Simanggang drama.

So they murmured discontent and showed signs of sulking when they heard that I had appeared before the public without sending a call-boy to summon them for their act. Children who had dressed up and were then prevented from showing off would behave so. But if they had the touchiness of spoiled youngsters, they had the simplicity, too, of all young things. If they were quickly offended, they could be equally swiftly appeased. When I heard a rumour of their displeasure, I sent a message asking them to come for refreshments with me on the Residency verandah. I added that I wished to take photographs of them in full dress. The gesture immediately healed their wounded feelings.

At the appointed hour they arrived in all their glory, but for comfort when squatting on the floor discarded most of their clothes. The feathered head-dresses, glittering sashes, coin-draped kilts, sheathed parangs and other unnecessary articles were carefully laid aside, and the youths retained only the bangles on their arms, the sirats round their loins and the garters below their knees as they settled cross-legged with Barcroft and me. They grinned with satisfaction when tumblers of tuak were served, and helped themselves generously to heaps of tobacco set before them.

Without hesitation they made themselves at home. Nor were they shy about talking. At once they started chattering volubly, completely at their ease. Before long they betrayed one of their native weaknesses. Ibans are inclined to be scroungers, and these young men begged me to present each of them with a shot-gun, arguing that it would be an appropriate reward for their devoted services to me. I parried successfully with a promise to send them enlarged copies of the group picture which would be taken of us all. The prospect of this unique possession enchanted them and satisfied their acquisitive passion. After that we gossiped about Iban life and customs, sipping our tuak and puffing contentedly at hand-rolled cigarettes.

At length the moment for photography arrived. As I have

said, the Ibans had stripped off most of their costumes, and were sitting in a minimum of clothing. At my invitation to appear before a camera they rose eagerly and hastened to their clothes, afraid lest the pictures would be taken before they were properly adorned.

They dressed deliberately, taking all the precise, extravagant care of dandies. It was a fascinating spectacle. Some used window-panes as mirrors, studying their reflections appreciatively as they fitted on their fabulous hats. Tilting their heads this way and that, they glanced at the effect to make sure that the feathers slanted at proper angles. Others twisted their bodies in graceful, statuesque poses as they fastened kilts or buckled swords above their hips, and they stretched their legs elegantly to fasten tas-selled garters below their knees. Several lingered lovingly over the correct arrangement of many necklaces or the exact order of innumerable bangles. All fourteen performed these exercises at the same time, with noddings of plumes, tinkling of bells and jingle-jangling of silver ornaments. I never saw a more magnificently exotic sight. The verandah appeared like the dressing-room of a corps of ballerinas robing for some fantastic, barbaric ballet.

That was my introduction to the bumptious, aggressive and lovable Ibans.

II

From Simanggang White and I returned down the Batang Lupar, heading for a greater river farther east called the Rejang. On a mud bank as we voyaged down-stream I saw my first croco-dile. It basked close to the water's edge, so deeply engaged in the main business of the afternoon, a post-prandial nap, that it did not notice our approach and remained motionless only thirty yards away. I have seen many crocodiles since, but they were usually so thickly coated with dirt that they were mud-coloured. This brute was spotlessly clean, exhibiting to perfection its bright green hide mottled with dark stripes and splashes. It had fallen asleep with its mouth open, and the long, gruesome upper man-dible pointed skywards at an angle of nearly ninety degrees while the lower jaw rested on the ground, as if the beast had been petrified in the middle of a gigantic yawn. It offered a perfect target for a sportsman, but we had no gun on board. So we left it undisturbed, like a statue of Evil brooding over the river.

From the mouth of the Batang Lupar we turned along the coast. It was August and the southeast monsoon had broken. As we put to sea a vicious tropical storm arose. Black clouds rolled swiftly across the evening sky, forked lightning ripped the murky heavens, and thunder mumbled and crashed on every side. Suddenly torrential rain pelted down, millions of drops descending with such force that they lashed our faces like whips. The sea heaved tumultuously. We were tossing wildly when I retreated to my bunk and fell asleep.

I woke at dawn, went on deck, and found that we were approaching the mouth of the Rejang. The storm had passed, the sky was clear and the ocean lay as calm as a mill-pond. A flock of terns fished in the shallows, and a pair of sea-eagles stood like sentinels on protruding stakes flanking the entrance to the river. Occasionally, as the prow of our boat nosed its way towards the estuary, a flying-fish leaped from the sea and fled in a series of panicky hop-skip-and-jumps in and out of the water, until it felt safe from our monstrous craft and plunged back into the deep.

Ahead the coastland appeared flat, a monotonous line of dark-green mangroves, though in two or three places a strip of beach obtruded, with a group of coconut palms rising gracefully above its strand and the huts of Malay fishermen huddled in their shade. Entering the Rejang, we journeyed hour after hour along its broad channel. At first the landscape was unchanging and dull. On each side a dense, tangled mangrove swamp stretched away from the water's edge as far as the eye could see. A mangrove tree is an uninteresting object, and its virtues do not become any more apparent when tens of thousands of its kind are gathered together to fill a whole scene. They form the sort of monotonous prospect which occasionally turns a tropical explorer into a raving lunatic.

Later the view began to improve. Muddy swamps gave way to solid earth and the mangroves were replaced by a variety of jungle trees. Here and there on the river bank huts indicated the presence of human settlers, and in their neighbourhood the ground was cleared for crops. Soon we came to a small town called Sarikei, the trading centre of a wide district.

We went ashore. The town's five thousand inhabitants were all in the streets to greet us. Arches of welcome spanned the roadways, flags hung from every window, and the populace were dressed in their most colourful garments.

The local police force mounted a guard of honour. Behind them waited rows of notables; beyond them again were ranks of Chinese and Malay school children; and at their backs crowded the rest of the population, a motley, silent, inquisitive assembly.

The corporal in charge of the guard shouted a word of command and his men presented arms. I inspected the troop. Then I moved to the ranks of local leaders, who each in turn bowed and shook my hand.

"Tabeh, tuan," said some.

"Good afternoon, Your Excellency," others observed with precise, oft-rehearsed enunciation.

I could see the Chinese school children glancing from the corners of their eyes at their teachers, waiting for a signal. As I approached them the word was given, and the youngsters instantly burst into a high-pitched song of greeting. The Malay children remained dumb, but saluted smartly. Their faces betrayed the solemn view which they took of the occasion, and I had difficulty in coaxing grins from them.

The men and women in the crowd stared in awe, but when I waved to them their faces were quickly wreathed in smiles and they gleefully waved back. They were charming, friendly people.

Afterwards we strolled through the town, visited the bazaar and viewed the government offices, then embarked again on our launch and continued up-stream. The country became more populous, though villages were still few. Mostly the land was overgrown with jungle. Where the huts of a Malay kampong huddled at the water's edge we saw men and women peering shyly through their doorways. They sat motionless in the shadowy interiors, observing us but hoping not to be observed. They wore Malay dress, the men displaying their Moslem faith in the caps on their heads and the women by the way that they drew veils across their faces if they thought we detected them.

Occasionally we saw the lengthy, barn-like structure of an Iban long-house stretching along the river bank. Its inmates were less retiring than the Malays. They flocked inquisitively to the outside platforms of their homes, or ran down the tree-trunk stairways to catch a closer glimpse of us as we passed. The men and women wore only loin-cloths or brief skirts, while the children spurned clothes altogether.

Forty miles beyond Sarikei we reached Binatang, another trading settlement. Going ashore, we were accorded the same friendly reception as at Sarikei. I was to grow accustomed to those whole-hearted welcomes from the entire population wherever I landed in Sarawak.

From Binatang we headed for Sibu, twenty-five miles farther up-river. Once more the character of the scenery changed. Now both banks carried rubber trees. Many years earlier several hundred Chinese families from Foochow were settled on this stretch of the Rejang under contract to grow rice. The land appeared ideal for cultivating padi. At that moment, however, a rubber boom began in the world, and before the authorities knew what had happened, the Foochows had all planted rubber. Whatever the conditions attaching to their title deeds, these shrewd businessmen could not resist the temptation to make the largest available profit, and when the Government protested, it was too late. The rubber trees were already firmly rooted in the ground, and there they have stayed ever since. Hardly an acre of padi is grown in the whole district.

The Rejang wound onward, one long reach succeeding another, until we saw at a bend ahead a considerable concourse of buildings with ocean-going vessels lying alongside wharves. It was Sibu, the capital of the Third Division and the largest town in Sarawak after Kuching.

The place looked attractive with greensward stretching like lawns beside the river, fine trees such as might grace the precincts of an English cathedral, and neatly trimmed hedges surrounding the gardens of pleasant houses. As we approached, however, we saw that the town wore scars of battle. We had reached the region where fighting took place in the previous year, when British officers and Iban braves drove the Japanese helter-skelter down the Rejang. Sibu was a Japanese military headquarters, and Allied aircraft bombed it. When I arrived the Residency was still only a broken shell, a victim of a direct hit, and some other buildings, too, were in ruins.

A portly, dignified figure standing on the quay was the Resident, Mr. Gordon Aikman. With him were his principal officials. Near by stood the customary guard of honour, along either side of a path were ranks of Sibu notables, beyond them waited row upon row of school children, and at their backs was a tremendous throng of citizens.

I went through the customary ceremonial of greetings, and in due course came to a score of Iban chieftains grouped among the local personalities. They were dressed in their finest feathers, loin-cloths, bangles and garters. Beside them, drawn up like an immaculate line of chorus girls in some fabulous revue, stood a dozen maidens from the long-houses.

This was my first glimpse of Iban women in gala dress, and I confess that their startling loveliness made me catch my breath. Could these wondrous creatures be real, or was I dreaming? They stayed as motionless as statues, with eyes cast towards the ground. Their dusky Mongolian faces had the mysterious serenity of idols in Eastern temples, with arched eyebrows, slanting eyes and full-lipped mouths. Their costumes were in keeping with this exotic style. Finely wrought silver tiaras with countless tiny bells crowned their heads, and in their ears hung long gilt ear-rings. Small shawls of many-coloured beads fell from their shoulders to just above their bare breasts. Corsets of brass hoops encased their bodies from the midriff to the hips, and beneath these the girls wore short skirts of red silk and gold thread. On their arms were silver bangles and round their legs thick silver anklets.

So motionless did they stand that they might have been waxworks models, and only the gentle, scarcely perceptible rise and fall of their bosoms betrayed that they were living figures of flesh and blood. I shook hands with each maiden in turn, and felt that I had crossed the threshold into a strange, new world.

That night I stayed in Aikman's house. After dinner we went to see the town illuminated in honour of the occasion. Many

streets were lit from end to end with torches, their flames flickering and glimmering on the faces of a multitude of Chinese,
Malays, Ibans, Melanaus, Indians and Europeans. Those who
knew Sibu before the war remarked on a significant change which
distinguished this crowd from festive pre-war gatherings. In
those days women were conspicuous by their absence. They did
not join in fun out-of-doors, for age-old custom decreed that
Chinese ladies should stay at home, while Mohammedan tradition kept Malay women out of sight. That night in the
crowded streets women were as much in evidence as men. Ancient
taboos were decaying; restrictions on the freedom of wives and
daughters were disappearing; even in remote, backward Borneo
the emancipation of women from conservative prohibitions was
dawning.

Parties of Malay girls tripped gaily along the roads. For
them it was a bold and novel venture. They enjoyed the expedition, whispering and laughing softly to each other as they shuffled along the streets. Their bodices were close-fitting, and their
long sarongs so nearly touched the ground that they had to lift
the hem when negotiating puddles, revealing little brown feet
in pretty slippers. Though their outing that evening was evidence
of modernity, they were not yet so radical that they left their
heads uncovered. In many parts of Malaya that innovation had
come, but these young women in Sarawak wore silk scarves over
their hair and drew them across their faces when they passed close
to men.

The various racial communities had organized different public
entertainments in the town. In one place a group of Melanau
ladies demonstrated their skill as makers of fine straw mats, hats
and baskets. In another an amateur theatrical company of
Malays staged a comic opera, while elsewhere some Iban braves
delighted an eager crowd with head-hunters' dances. The deep,
rhythmic booming of their gongs and drums throbbed like the
heartbeat of the jungle.

Beneath the glare of hurricane-lamps lighting their stage
sat the dozen Iban girls, still clad in costumes of fairy-like prettiness. But they were no longer stiff, impassive figures like temple
images. They had come to life. As they watched the dancers

their faces wore lively expressions, and often they broke into merry peals of laughter as they chattered together. It was as if a group of goddesses were visiting the earth and condescending for a while to assume human form.

III

Next day we travelled farther up-river. Aikman led us on a tour of his far-reaching dominions, and no traveller in Sarawak could have a better guide. His knowledge of the country and its peoples was deep, sympathetic and wise.

The Rejang remained a broad highway for two hundred miles beyond its mouth. During the early part of our journey Chinese rubber plantations were the principal feature of the landscape, interspersed with patches of wild jungle; but long-houses began to appear more frequently. The Rejang is the most populous area of Iban occupation in the colony, and we were penetrating far into native territory.

First we landed at Kanowit, three hours' journey above Sibu. No bigger than a large village, its site was selected by the second Rajah for strategic reasons in the period when he was suppressing head-hunting throughout his kingdom. It occupied a point of land where the Kanowit River flows into the Rejang. On a hill commanding both waterways stood the Rajah's fort, an imposing, two-story white-washed wooden building with walls pierced by rows of trap-doors through which, in the wicked old days, pro-truded a battery of cannon. The stronghold was called Fort Emma. Many such places in Sarawak were christened after female relatives or friends of the Rajahs, and the names of these ladies spatter the map of Sarawak as plentifully as the names of explorers mark charts of the polar regions.

After a conference in the fort to discuss local problems, I strolled through the bazaar. While we inspected the wares in a shop, I heard a gay tinkling of tiny bells behind me, as if a cavalcade of Lilliputian sleighs were approaching. Every now and then the music ceased for a few moments, then commenced again. Looking round, I saw a party of Iban girls tripping along the street, the same idol-like beauties who had greeted us in Sibu, now returning to their up-river homes. They still wore their fine party dresses.

Curiously I watched their progress. First they passed a few shops filled with unexciting stuffs like pickled vegetables and dried fish; then they spied a counter laden with pretty necklaces, ear-rings, lockets and other tempting trinkets, and stopped to consider purchases. After a few minutes of eager, talkative deliberation they decided to view other stores before reaching final judgements. Hastening on, they came to another emporium where glass cases were crammed with rings, hair combs, belts, bracelets, anklets and coronets; and again they halted for consultation. The Chinese shopkeepers hopefully watched their advance, while a trail of inquisitive Chinese children followed in their wake. Eventually the damsels reached decisions and acquired a little hoard of jewellery.

From Kanowit we continued far up-river. Few Chinese rubber holdings now appeared, but here and there an industrious pioneer family from Foochow, Canton or Amoy cultivated a patch of ground-nuts, vegetables, wet-padi or tropical fruits. Frequently we passed long-houses, some standing immediately above the river bank and others withdrawn a short distance behind a screen of trees. Always the people ran from their rooms to stare and wave at us as we passed. My memory is filled with attractive pictures seen that day of Ibans in their home environment. I remember, for instance, a child of about ten years rushing excitedly down a muddy path among close-growing trees to jump into a prahu, paddle towards mid-stream and rock on the waves made by our launch. The youngster was naked except for a loin-cloth, and his long black hair flew out behind him like a galloping horse's tail. The track down which he ran was steep, slippery and twisting, yet he skipped from foothold to foothold with the speed and agility of a gazelle. As he boarded the canoe, he might have tipped it over, for it floated unmoored in the water some way from shore, but he took a flying leap and landed in it as surely as a wild cat springs on a branch of a tree. His nakedness, his flowing hair, his fitness of body, and the lithe cunning of all his movements made him seem as natural an inhabitant of the forest as any creature of the wild.

Aikman told me that as we advanced into the interior, travelling farther from the influence of towns, we should find progressively finer representatives of true Iban physique and character. He said that the natives near Sibu and similar places had become sophisticated. The best, the most unspoiled Ibans lived far up the rivers.

IV

As we went up-stream we frequently passed native boats gliding as silent as shadows along the river. They were slight craft, each hollowed from a single tree trunk and usually so loaded with people or goods that only an inch of freeboard appeared above water. At every paddle stroke it seemed that they must ship a wave, be swamped and sink from view. The danger was all the grimmer because a hungry crocodile might be swimming below. Yet the catastrophe never occurred. The oarsmen's strokes were deft, the passengers sat with calm nonchalance on their frail seats, and the canoe skimmed smoothly and safely forward.

Our next stop was at a small station with the engaging name of Song, perched on a hill with slopes falling steeply into the river. One of the Rajahs decided to build a fort there, for its guns could cover the entrance to a tributary flowing into the Rejang where some particularly vicious Iban bands lived. They were tamed long ago, but the magnificent landscape of highlands and jungle surrounding the hilltop remained untamed.

The village was almost completely destroyed towards the end of the war, for the Japanese tried to revive its military strength, and stationed a garrison there. As Bill Sochon and his warriors advanced down the Rejang, the Japanese made a stand and had to be forcibly ejected. In the battle, various types of weapons, from the most primitive to the most modern, were used. First an aeroplane made a reconnaissance flight over Song, with Temonggong Koh, the paramount chief of the Ibans, sitting in its cockpit. He pointed out to Air Force officers the enemy's positions, as these had been secretly reported to him by his followers still living in Song's neighbourhood. Next morning the aircraft returned and emptied a load of bombs on the place. Their explosions were the signal for Ibans on the ground to attack with blow-pipes and parangs as well as shot-guns. After a stubborn resistance, the Japanese withdrew, leaving several of their soldiers' bloody, decapitated corpses in battered fox-holes.

During the operation the fort and almost every other building were burned to the ground, and at the end of the day the site was a wilderness amidst a jungle. However, the civil affairs authorities advancing behind the troops soon built a temporary government office on the hilltop, and local Chinese traders lost no time in constructing attap shops in which to recommence business as usual.

When we visited Song, these provisional buildings were still doing duty. A handful of Malay officials, a dozen Chinese towkays and a group of Iban headmen met us at the foot of a path leading uphill. As I approached them, a native chief waved a crowing cock over my head, a traditional Iban gesture believed to ward off evil spirits. That desirable object achieved, we climbed to the crest of the hill.

There stood the temporary government building; there too was a guard of honour of six policemen; and there, also, waited a reception committee of Iban women. Once more I was momentarily startled by the gracious appearance of these ladies; yet I was now growing more accustomed to them, and began to regard them with a more objective eye. I noticed certain features which, to my taste, slightly marred the perfection of their forms. For example, when their sweet lips parted they revealed teeth and gums spattered with red stains acquired from chewing betel-nut; and, not content with this disfigurement, some girls had filed their teeth into stunted shapes. In offering criticisms of these fashions I betray an Occidental prejudice for teeth gleaming like rows of white pearls—a preference which many Asian peoples scorn. And if I remark that I thought the legs of some Iban beauties a trifle short, or their feet a little flat, I expose myself to the charge of harbouring a crude partiality for the long, athletic limbs favoured by tribes like the Greeks two thousand years ago. So these are expressions of personal opinion, and it would be unchivalrous to dwell on them unduly. The Iban girls at

Song were a group of exquisite tropical blooms, and if they showed an occasional blemish, it appeared significant only in contrast to the charm of the rest of the flowers.

On the hilltop the Ibans had built a bamboo pavilion for our reception. They conducted us to it, and a throng of people crowded round. Then an old chief with a face like a he-witch raised a hand to command silence, and called for drink. Assistants brought many bottles of tuak. The venerable man poured a goodly portion into several glasses, and summoned the troupe of Iban damsels to his side. One of the duties of women in long-houses is to ply distinguished visitors with liquid refreshment, and this was to be my initiation into the hallowed technique which they employ.

A girl lifted a glass and held it towards me. When I grasped it, she maintained her hold on it and helped to raise it to my lips. After a few hearty gulps I wished to stop drinking; but she pressed the tumbler resolutely to my mouth, tilting it so that the fluid flowed ceaselessly down my throat. Feeling that it might be impolite to reject such hospitality, I continued swallowing until the wine was all inside me.

Other maidens then refreshed Aikman and White in the same generous way. When my companions were duly regaled, the first girl approached me again, holding another tumbler towards me. This time, however, before treating me to a drink she favoured me with a song. In a thin, tremulous, piping voice she began a monotonous chant like a dirge, which Aikman assured me was an expression of joyous welcome. He explained that young women in long-houses are trained to compose these musical greetings, called pantuns, to special guests. Each soloist improvises the verses as she proceeds, like stanzas in ancient folk poetry, and the theme is the personality of the visitor being honoured. No bounds are set to the flattery which a singer may employ.

The crowd in the pavilion listened intently to the girl's words. She continued her performance for two or three minutes, then suddenly seemed at a loss for a phrase, sniggered and held the glass up for me. When I grasped it, she once more helped to guide it to my lips and held it there until every drop of the wine had flowed down my throat. The concoction had a sharp, acid taste which displeased me, but the friendliness of our hosts was captivating, and I resolved to consume without demur as many glassfuls as they, in their wisdom, judged that I should imbibe. The path of duty is not always a hard uphill climb; sometimes it is a slippery downhill slide.

I had scarcely swallowed the last dregs of my wine before the young lady attending Aikman broke into song. When he had manfully responded by quaffing another half-pint, Denis White's handmaiden took up the tune. So the ritual continued, with alternate singing by the girls and drinking by the guests. The audience was delighted at our receptivity, and encouraged us to ever nobler efforts. We accepted every challenge until the bottles could yield no more.

The intoxicating power of tuak varies according to the brew, and fortunately that morning's sample was reasonably mild. It produced a pleasing but sober sense of good-fellowship. I personally could not dismiss my initial dislike of the sickly, bitter-sweet drink, but my affection for the gay-hearted, open-handed natives who dispensed it warmed with every mouthful.

That was my first experience of wine and women at Song, and I resolved that it would not be my last.

CHAPTER SIX

TEMONGGONG KOH

I

WE BADE GOOD-BYE to our friends and descended the hill to the launch. Later that afternoon we were due at Kapit, an up-river centre where a vast, important assembly of Iban chiefs and their followers was gathered to meet us.

Kapit is a small town 180 miles from the Rejang's mouth, but the river still flowed broad and deep past the high bank on which it stood. Before the war the place had a reputation as a beauty spot. A succession of District Officers with a flair for landscape gardening made it a charming station. Green lawns, bright flower beds, an artificial lake, and bridle-paths winding among the surrounding jungle-covered hills distinguished it. The District Officer's bungalow had simple architectural merit, and Fort Sylvia, the local stronghold, stood with dignity on a knoll overlooking the river. A street of Chinese shop-houses neatly associated Commerce with Art.

Most of these amenities were lost during the Japanese occupation. The lake was drained of water, the flower beds became breeding grounds for weeds, and the bridle-paths returned to jungle. At the end of the war the post was the scene of vicious fighting. Ibans assaulted it with murderous gusto, the Japanese garrison resisted with obstinate courage, and in the skirmish many buildings were destroyed. The entire bazaar was burned to the ground, though Fort Sylvia survived amidst the ruins.

We arrived at tea-time, stepped ashore and climbed the path to the fort. On the upward slope we met grim evidence of the recent battle. The Ibans had raised a flamboyant arch of welcome, decorated as always with palm fronds, orchids and other bright tropical blooms. Its principal adornments, however, were more unusual. They were two Japanese heads. Already one was almost a bare skull, but on the other scraps of flesh still clung to the bone. The cropped black hair of a soldier sprouted from its pate, and eye-lashes grew in withered eye-lids half closed over lack-lustre eyes. For the rest, little of the countenance remained. The nose had mostly disappeared and the face looked like the mask of a dead leper. These horrifying relics of the head-hunters' victory hung among flowers. Beyond the arch stood rows of Iban chiefs, Malay officials and Chinese towkays, while at their backs swarmed a huge crowd of natives. The first man to receive us was the redoubtable Temonggong Koh, paramount chief of the local Ibans and the most important pagan in Sarawak. Now over seventy years old, the grey hair and wrinkled skin of his handsome face were marks of a life as strenuous as it had been long. Though age had sunk the flesh on its bone structure, his features still expressed lively qualities. His eyes were crafty yet kindly, his nose showed pugnacity, his mouth was sensuous and generous, and his jaw indicated great firmness of will.

Apart from his distinguished countenance, his most notable physical attributes were the backs of his hands. From the wrists to the finger-nails they were completely blue, as if they had been washed in ink. The decoration had honourable significance, being a sign of a mighty head-hunter. In olden days when a man took a head he earned the right to have one joint of one finger tattooed. With each additional head to his credit another joint was pricked and dyed with blue-black juice. When the number of slain enemies could no longer be counted on all the joints of all the fingers and two thumbs of both hands, the pattern was continued down the back of the hand. Temonggong Koh's fingers, thumbs and hands were completely covered with these proud symbols.

Chieftainships among the Ibans are acquired by personal merit, not by family inheritance. The title "Temonggong" attached to Koh's name signified a leader of supreme stature, and he owed this pre-eminent position to the outstanding strength of his character. It had enabled him to survive unscathed the whole series of changes in Sarawak, from the age of unbridled head-hunting, through years of gradual pacification by the White Rajahs into the period of misgovernment by the Japanese and finally the beginning of British Colonial rule. During the Japanese occupation he remained secretly loyal to the Rajah in exile, and when British liberators parachuted into Sarawak he assured them of his support. His immense influence with his people greatly aided them. He rallied his followers to the Allied cause, and in the attack on Song made Iban history by taking wing in an aeroplane and showing the Air Force where to drop its bombs.

At our first meeting I did not foresee the warm friendship that would grow between him and me. Since then I have come to know him well. Though he is intelligent, his intellect is not outstanding. Other, younger Iban chiefs have better brains or sharper wits; but none possesses in the same degree his shrewd common sense, personal magnetism and rare powers of leadership.

That afternoon at Kapit he introduced me to his subordinate colleagues, men assembled from long-houses for scores of miles around. They belonged to two classes: "penghulus", who are the chosen chiefs of wide districts including many houses, and "tuai tuai rumah", who are the heads of individual dwellings. Among them were Jugah and Sibat, Grinang and Jinggut, Sandai and Rabong, Koh's most trusted lieutenants in his captaincy of his people. I was to meet them many times on later visits, and to know and love them as brothers.

Koh led us to a lawn where a banqueting table stood in the open air. On it were tea-pots, milk-jugs, sugar basins and other properties for an English garden party, with dishes of sandwiches and cakes. All of us—Europeans, Ibans, Malays and Chinese—settled down to eat and drink. But the men of the jungle were not comfortable propped on chairs at a table; nor did they like the insipid tea and sweet pastries. This alien form of entertainment was a concession to us British visitors, and having initiated the gesture they were not sure how to carry it through. The atmosphere was restrained and polite. Local policemen and government clerks acted as waiters. They lacked professional dash and skilled hands, and in their nervousness poured tea into saucers and dropped cakes on the grass. The head-hunters fingered the food uncertainly, picking at a few crumbs and leaving the rest uneaten on their plates. In any case the heat ruined the sandwiches.

The scorching sunshine dried and curled them like dead autumn leaves.

Throughout the meal a crowd of Iban men and women of the lower orders stood round the table, staring at us, as a party of civilized human beings might gape at the strange feeding habits of animals in a zoo. Our pagan hosts at the table looked increasingly awkward and bored; so as soon as possible I made a speech of thanks, which brought this frigid entertainment to an end. With sighs of relief everyone rose, and we passed to the next item on the programme.

II

After that the real fun began. My travelling companions and I were conducted to a long row of native mats laid on the ground. On these were spread many scores of small plates piled with native foods, and dozens of bottles of home-made tuak. We were invited to squat cross-legged on the grass facing this formidable repast.

I sat in the centre, with Temonggong Koh beside me and Denis White close by to act as interpreter. The other dignitaries of all races crouched likewise at the edge of the mats. Then a group of Iban maidens stepped forward, one female kneeling opposite each guest to attend upon him during the ensuing ceremony, much as a geisha girl would do in a Japanese tea-house. They were young relatives of the penghulus—wives, daughters and nieces—a choice assortment of distinguished native ladies.

None wore the fanciful, tiara-like head-dresses which the women at Sibu had favoured. I began to realize the truth of Aikman's remark that the farther we went up-river, the simpler would Iban manners become. Those down-river headgears were not, I learned, original parts of an Iban female's gala dress, but foreign importations into Sarawak, introduced recently by enterprising Chinese merchants who foresaw that such cheap magnificence would appeal to the vanity of local beauties. Their style was copied from Chinese bridal coronets, or from the crowns worn by girls on ceremonial occasions in certain other islands of the Malayan Archipelago. They had proved popular and become "the rage" in Iban communities on the lower reaches of Sarawak's rivers; but they had not yet penetrated the remote interior.

So the women at Kapit wore in their hair only silver combs and small posies of flowers. In other ways, too, they were more scantily attired than the damsels at Sibu. A few favoured brass-ring corsets, but most were completely naked above their waists. Slender gold necklaces, ear-rings of delicate workmanship, numerous bracelets, short skirts of gay local weave, and anklets of beaten silver were all the adornment that they added to God's gifts of enchanting figures and honey-coloured skins.

I was honoured by having more than my fair share of hand-maidens, for two waited upon me. Both were daughters of Temonggong Koh. During his eventful life he had acquired four successive wives, four daughters and two sons. The pair at Kapit that day were his two youngest girls, Mindun and Segura.

Mindun was a smiling, vivacious female, over twenty years old and already married. Segura was a child of about thirteen. Both had charming looks and figures, but Segura was especially engaging. With an angelic face, golden-brown skin, small virginal breasts and elegant young limbs, she was an exquisite creature. When she overcame her first awe of me she grew extraordinarily friendly, sitting at my side and chattering gaily to me in her mother tongue, regardless of the fact that I did not understand a single word of what she said. Frequently she nudged me, or pulled at my arm and pointed a finger to draw my attention to something of interest which she feared that I would miss. At any humorous event her eyes twinkled and she broke into happy laughter.

Let the reader take note of this pleasing youngster, for she will play an important part in this book.

The mat on which we sat was littered with plates of food and bottles of drink. I felt apprehensive lest I should be forced to over-eat, for I had partaken heartily of the sandwiches and cakes at tea, and was already satisfied. Now, I feared, politeness would make me sample all these exotic dishes, with evil consequences to my digestion.

I need not have worried. None of the delicacies spread before us were for human consumption. They were dedicated to a higher purpose. We would offer them to the good and evil spirits, to appease the local hobgoblins who might otherwise resort to malicious interference with our evening's entertainment.

To explain this, let me describe the religious beliefs of the pagans of Sarawak. Most wild men of Borneo still retained animist notions inherited from countless generations of their forbears. They acknowledged the existence of certain superior gods, and especially of three who were respectively the creator of man, the benefactor of agriculture and the arbiter in war. Lower in the hierarchy of supernatural beings was a host of spirits. The forest and rivers, mountains and padi-fields, earth and sky were inhabited by countless sprites, some good, who were minor deities, and others evil, who were absolute devils. They manifested their will through the behaviour of animals, and particularly in the conduct of certain birds like the little green-bodied spider-hunters, the trogons brilliantly clad in scarlet, black and yellow, and the great hovering hawks. Before engaging on any important undertakings such as building a house, preparing ground for planting, contracting a marriage or setting forth on an expedition, the Ibans studied the movements of these creatures. If the birds behaved in one way, the omens were good; if in another, the omens were bad; and the natives shaped their own conduct accordingly.

Another creature through whom the spirits spoke was the barking deer, which often indicated the intentions of the unseen powers who determine the fates of men. Sometimes they also conveyed strong hints of their wishes in dreams to medicine men, who claimed to be in communication with the other world, and of whom there was usually one in every long-house. The spirits made their thoughts known with equal force through natural occurrences, like the growth of crops, the flooding of rivers and the rumble of thunder. All these phenomena conveyed their meaning to superstitious native minds.

The pagans' whole life was governed by their desire to be on correct terms with the spirits, to appease the bad ones and gain the friendship of the good. In order to achieve this they conformed to a well-established code of social conduct, observing

religiously various taboos and performing certain propitiatory
acts. One of these deeds was the periodic refreshment of the
deities and demons with food and drink. It was prudent, for
example, when a distinguished visitor arrived in a house, to ask
him to prepare a meal for the sprites. The invisible multitude of
good and evil ones was flattered by this attention. The meal
provided on such an occasion was elaborate, and its preparation
was accompanied by a solemn ceremonial called the bedara.

That afternoon at Kapit I was to play the leading part in
performing a bedara.

As a preliminary, Temonggong Koh asked me to stretch out
one arm. I did so, and round my wrist he fitted a rough copper
bracelet. This was an introductory gesture of friendship, an
initiation into the good-fellowship of the Ibans of the Rejang
River. The old chief then placed a large plate before me and he,
Mindun and Segura instructed me in rites which would gain
the benevolence of the hobgoblins.

On the mat in front of me twenty-seven saucers were arranged
in four rows, each piled with some native delicacy. I was to take
samples from every one in turn and place them on the large
plate which Koh set before me. First I took a wad of tobacco
from one saucer and a sirih leaf from another, then a few grains
of rice from a third, a pinch of salt from a fourth, some betel-nut
from the fifth, and so on. All these I mixed together on the plate.
It was commodious, and yet soon began to appear too small to
hold its accumulation of offerings. Adding a few crystals of lime
to the tobacco and other ingredients, I afterwards picked several
slices of glutinous rice, a generous scattering of puffed rice and
contributions from all the other dishes. Koh and his daughters
watched my progress with keen interest, occasionally lending a
hand in arranging a new item on the pile in such a way that the
whole edifice would not totter and spill on the ground.

When bits of the contents of every saucer were thus collected,
Mindun produced a dish of hens' eggs. She asked me to balance
four of them perpendicularly on top of the mound of viands.
So poised, they made the concoction look like a fantastic creation
by a lunatic conjurer. Finally Mindun handed me a tiny cup of

tuak, which I placed on the summit of the refreshments between the quartette of eggs.

Then a chief appeared carrying a live cock upside-down. On Koh's instructions I took the fowl and waved it, still in reverse, above the plate of food. As I did so I muttered Bornean blessings on my friends. The rooster took the incident with commendable calm, but its subsequent fate was unenviable, for it was a sacrificial bird. When I restored it to the chief, he took it away, slew it, and returned a few moments later with some feathers plucked from its tail. They had been dipped in its blood and thereby acquired special virtue. Koh, Mindun and Segura stretched out their hands to stroke the quills where they were bloody, to be imbued themselves with a share of that virtue. Then I stuck the plumes like triumphant flags on the peak of the mountain of food before me. The dish was ready for the sprites.

Koh asked me to rise and offer it to those unseen guests at our party. Behind us several bamboo poles had been planted in the ground. The topmost section of each was cut into half a dozen splinters, splayed outwards like the fingers of a wooden hand. At Koh's prompting I fixed the dish in one of these bamboo clasps. There, I was advised, the spirits would enjoy it.

Meanwhile Aikman, White and two or three others had prepared similar dishes for the edification of the demons, and these they perched on the tops of other poles. Collectively the portions composed a splendid banquet. We left them there, and returned to squat once more in our places on the mats. Female attendants carried away the saucers with the remnants of food. None of us had taken so much as a bite of it. Having thus dealt with the edibles, we now turned to the drinks.

They were disposed of in a different fashion. First Mindun poured a mouthful of tuak into the bottom of a tumbler and handed it to me. Koh signalled that I should sprinkle it on the ground behind my back, and White whispered in explanation that the goblins would notice it there and gratefully slake their thirst. I did as I was told—and that was all that the spirits ever got of the bountiful supplies of drink. The rest we dealt with ourselves.

I handed the empty tumbler back to Mindun, and now she filled it to the brim. This time there was nothing half-hearted about her pouring, none of the restraint which had somehow held her hand when she measured the meagre ration for the sprites. The drink was for me, and evidently she considered me ten times as thirsty as all of them put together. Holding the glass before me, she started to sing a pantun. I sat patiently as the song continued for many verses, admiring the sparkle of Mindun's personality revealed in her performance. At last it ended amid a burst of applause from the spectators, and she held the tumbler to my lips, pressed it against my teeth and coaxed back my reluctant head. Not until every drop of tuak had slipped down my throat did she relax her pressure.

Then Segura filled a glass for me, and we went through the same exercise. She sang a pantun sweetly, and her childish grin as she invited me to drink was such that I needed no compulsion. Simultaneously every other guest at the party and some of our chieftain hosts were regaled. The men sat in a long row and their attendant women knelt in a rank facing them. Chanting and drinking proceeded merrily all down the lines.

III

I gossiped with Temonggong Koh, with Denis White as our interpreter. The old man reminisced about his wild youth, and time passed pleasantly. When at last all the bottles were empty, our entertainment changed once more. Preparations were made for dancing. The performers would appear on a stretch of grass in front of our mats, and a large audience lolled comfortably beside it. Mindun sat on one side of me and Segura on the other, with Koh near by.

Dusk was falling. Night comes suddenly on the equator. Almost before the dancers took their first steps, stars were twinkling in the sky, and rays of light from "fairy lamps" round the greensward illumined the scene.

When the show had proceeded for a while I was distressed to discover Mindun and Segura weeping silently beside me. Their tears flowed without restraint, and I wondered what could have upset them. I hoped that this was not an expression of distaste for my company. Unable to talk their language, I could make no amends for any fault that I had unwittingly committed, by speaking gentle words of comfort. I appealed to White to unravel the mystery. He enquired of Koh, who then told him that Aikman had just brought bad news to Kapit. The Resident had reported the death of one of the old man's nephews, a favourite with him and his family. They had lost touch with him during the Japanese occupation, and now heard for the first time that he had been taken prisoner in a jungle skirmish and afterwards executed by his Japanese captors.

The girls cried quietly for some time, tears rolling freely down their cheeks. In a daze they watched the dancing, for in imagination they were looking upon the corpse of their murdered cousin. At first I thought that they would be inconsolable, but then their father muttered sharp, reproving words to them, and they made an effort to be calm. Drying their eyes, they soon became so engrossed in the entertainment that for a while they forgot their sorrow. Before long Segura was chattering gaily again, tugging my elbow to draw my attention to incidents which amused her, and laughing cheerfully.

Two or three Iban warriors opened the programme with solo jigs. Then we were privileged to witness an event rare in these days, the initiation dance which used to be performed when a newly captured head was brought to a long-house. The head in this case was one of the mellow skulls which had decorated our archway of welcome, but the actors pretended that it was a fresh trophy not yet prepared for hanging in a house. Three women began the dance by strolling in single file to the centre of the stage, their steps slow and their faces wearing funereal expressions. They formed a small circle and started shuffling round like witches clustered about a cauldron. No steaming and bubbling pot, however, stood in their midst; instead one of them held at arm's length the head, tied in dried banana leaves. Soon four men with long staves appeared. They were medicine men, and they paraded solemnly round and round outside the circle of women, beating the ground with their staves and repeating an incantation. The women continued their slow "ring-a-ring-a-roses" movement silently and mournfully. This dull action continued monotonously for some time. After that I suppose the head was qualified for hanging, for the performance gradually faded out and the dancers disappeared.

Then more Iban men danced. Afterwards a Kayan visitor from the farther interior performed. Dancing is the finest of the up-river peoples' arts, and the Kayans and Kenyahs are its noblest exponents. Among them it is an accomplishment of unforgettable grace and beauty, beside which the efforts of the Ibans are amateurish. So I shall reserve a description of it until the reader travels with me into Kayan country up the higher reaches of the Rejang and the Baram Rivers.

It is sufficient now to say that the Kayan dancer at Kapit gave a superb performance. He did the customary, dramatic *pas seul* of the men of the jungle, stepping and leaping with savage stylishness. The hour was late when his act ended; but no one was ready for bed. The final item of our entertainment had still to be witnessed. The pagans having completed their parts, it was the local Malays' turn to put on a show. They were few in numbers, but a small caste of officials and policemen had rehearsed a play for the occasion.

The rest of us crowded round an open-air theatre, where hurricane lanterns strung on poles provided footlights and arc-lamps for the stage. The drama turned out to be an extremely funny skit on Iban life. Its script was written by a government clerk named Inche Sulaihi, and he and his friends presented the piece with zeal. Malays are endowed with a strong sense of the comic, and many of them have a sparkling gift for clowning. The actors that evening were amateurs, but they achieved something of the wit and satire of the Little Revues which used to receive vociferous acclaim on Shaftesbury Avenue and Broadway. Incidentally, their dialogue had occasional flashes of the same robust naughtiness. Iban social life lends itself to that.

The Malay author showed an intimate, almost scholarly knowledge of pagan character and customs, and no aspect of the subject open to burlesque was spared. He poked fun at the Ibans' sartorial vanity, their outrageous boasting, their inordinate passion for taking heads, some odd habits connected with their courtship, their superstitious belief in good and evil omens, and many other features of long-house life. In one scene he presented a hilarious take-off of the solemn initiation dance for a new head which we had witnessed earlier that evening.

The Ibans themselves were a sympathetic audience for this buffoonery. Their sense of humour appreciates jests against themselves as much as jokes at other people's expense. This trait is part of their conceit, for they are pleased when people take notice of them even for the purpose of poking fun. They sat crowded on the grass, peering eagerly at the players and roaring with laughter at every fresh sally. Like children watching a Christmas pantomime, their mouths kept opening wide to emit loud guffaws, and their eyes glistened with delight.

A full moon had risen in a cloudless sky, and it shone eerily on the assembly. At last the final curtain fell on the play, and the glaring arc-lamps were extinguished. Then only the moon illumined the scene with silvery, ghostly light. The hour was midnight. Many in the audience yawned, stretched their limbs, and rose to disperse. Silently they walked across the lawn, like shadows of human beings in a dim, unreal, dissolving world.

I bade good-night to Temonggong Koh and his daughters, and to all the lesser chiefs and my other new friends. Before going to the river, where I was to sleep on our launch, I visited the row of bamboo poles holding refreshments for the evil spirits. I was curious to see what had happened there. Several times during the earlier evening I had slipped across to observe how the hob-goblins were progressing with their meal; but on those inspections I could never detect that they had made any impression on the food. I presumed that this was due to the fact that my eyes were not trained to perceive the effects of spiritual consumption on physical matter.

Now I was much relieved at what I saw—or rather, at what I did not see. The miracle had happened; the splayed tops of the poles were empty. The rice, betel-nut, boiled eggs and other fare had disappeared, and, what was more, the half-dozen plates had gone with them. I felt that our hospitality had been thoroughly appreciated, and that the sour disposition of the evil ones must be distinctly sweetened in our favour. Henceforth, until their hunger needed further appeasement, all would be well.

With a comforting sense of security at this prospect I descended the path to the river and climbed aboard our boat. The air was warm and humid. To cool myself before sleep, I stripped and plunged into the Rejang. In spite of the benevolent protection which we could now expect from the guardian sprites, I did not venture far from shore nor stay long submerged in the cold, refreshing water, lest a crocodile should be swimming near by seeking its supper.

My caution was perhaps wise. Next morning my confidence in the goodwill of the spirits was shaken. On making discreet enquiries, I learned that shortly before midnight the Ibans themselves had removed from the bamboo poles all the dishes prepared for the holy ones, with full complements of untouched food. It was their habit, I was told, to keep some of them religiously for three days, after which they would eat such of the viands as remained fit for human consumption.

Could the jungle demons, after all, still be dissatisfied?

CHAPTER SEVEN

LIFE IN A LONG-HOUSE

I

ON THE FOLLOWING DAY we returned down-stream to Sibu, and eighteen months passed before I travelled again along the Rejang. This time I was to penetrate much higher up-river. My travelling companions included the Governor, Sir Charles Arden-Clarke, and his private secretary, Bob Snellus, as well as Gordon Aikman.

Arden-Clarke had arrived in Sarawak a year before, and was an ideal first Governor for the young colony. An inveterate traveller, he believed whole-heartedly in the principle that good government depends on close contact between the rulers and the ruled. All through his earlier life in other territories he had acted on it. First as a District Officer in Nigeria, and later as Resident Commissioner in Bechuanaland, Swaziland and Basutoland, he journeyed far and wide, meeting the Africans on their own ground, seeing their problems through their own eyes, and then applying to them his ripe wisdom. As a youth in the Northern Provinces of Nigeria he had even emulated on occasions the exploits of the first two Rajahs Brooke, for he was the solitary British representative in areas where wild pagan tribesmen still conducted murderous expeditions. By his strength of personality, supported by two or three police rifles which would have proved pitifully inadequate if they had been challenged, he brought the outlaws under civilized rule.

On our way up the Rejang we visited Sibu, Kanowit, Song and Kapit, meeting the local peoples and informing ourselves on conditions in every place. At Kapit Temonggong Koh and other Iban chiefs gave us again a superlatively friendly welcome. It was late in March, and everywhere the padi grain was ripening. Many men and most women had therefore stayed on their farms to gather the harvest. Among others, Mindun and Segura were at home. Koh's long-house was twenty miles away, up a beautiful tributary of the Rejang called the Balleh, and his wife and daughters were busy bringing in the crop. So the two girls were not at Kapit to pour drink and sing pantuns for me.

Instead another maid called Siah performed these services, with a grace and skill second to none. I remembered her from the previous visit, for she too was conspicuous then among our hostesses. About a year older than Segura, with something of the same fresh beauty of person and gaiety of character, she was a daughter of Penghulu Jugah, after Koh the most influential native on the Rejang. The padi on his remote river, the Merirai, had ripened early, so Siah had finished her harvesting and was free to come with him to greet us.

We stayed three days in Kapit. During the visit Arden-Clarke and I held a conference with the local penghulus and tuai tuai rumah, more than a score in number. They were angry about a recent incident. Two Malay supporters of the anti-cession organization in Sibu had come up-river, visited a few long-houses and tried to induce the Ibans to demand the restoration of Brooke rule in Sarawak. At our conference the Iban chiefs reported the affair, speaking with contempt of these strangers of another race who sought to tamper with the Ibans' loyalty to their King. With a hot flash of passion Temonggong Koh asked whether, if the visitors came again, the Ibans could take their heads. His request was supported with fiery words by Jugah and enthusiastic grunts of approval from every native leader squatting on the floor.

Arden-Clarke replied firmly that no heads must be taken, whatever the provocation. He said that the Government would not tolerate such action, and would punish it as murder. If strangers tried to stir up trouble among the Ibans, let the chiefs report the offenders to the District Officer. He would deal with the situation. It was not for the head-hunters to take the law into their hands and decide what was appropriate treatment for uninvited political agitators.

The chiefs accepted the prohibition philosophically, but with evident regret. If Arden-Clarke had not spoken decisively—if he had given them any excuse to feel that we even partially shared their zeal for capital punishment—blood would have flowed on the Rejang at that time.

Early next morning we left Kapit to continue our journey much farther up-river. We were to voyage beyond the remotest Iban territories into the country of the Kayans and kindred tribes, our goal being a small trading centre called Belaga over a hundred miles away. Two days' hard travelling was needed to reach it.

Since shallow waters and turbulent rapids lay ahead of us, we abandoned our launch and proceeded in native long-boats, called temois. Arden-Clarke and the District Officer at Kapit, a capable young man called Francis Drake, were passengers in one craft, Bob Snellus lolled in lordly state in a second, and Aikman and I travelled in a third. Each vessel measured some eighty feet in length and was wide enough at its centre to accommodate two people reclining on the cushioned floor. Its keel and main hulk were made from a single tree trunk, its sides were raised by the addition of planks, and awnings with kajang roofs amidships sheltered voyagers from the scorching sun. Each boat was driven by an outboard motor.

The prow of Aikman's and my vessel was rudely carved into the shape of a dog with ferocious mien and wicked face. The native builders had posted it there to frighten away evil spirits. Immediately behind its tail crouched the leading member of our crew, the bow-man. An unbelievably ugly Iban, he was, in my humble opinion, more likely than the hound to terrify anything in heaven or earth which sought to harm us. The flesh of his face hung loose and pouchy, his eyes were small and pig-like, he had ears elongated to take heavy ear-rings, and an appallingly swollen nose drooped over his large, lascivious mouth. Locks of untidy hair hung far down his back, and on his head was a basket-shaped hat with a few hornbill's feathers sprouting from its crown. As we sped up-stream they fluttered briskly in the breeze and completed the grotesque fellow's resemblance to a scarecrow.

The rest of the crew consisted of a Malay outboard motor driver and his assistant, both sitting in the stern. The first of these was Inche Sulaihi, the author of the bright burlesque played by the Kapit Malays on my earlier visit.

For several miles above Kapit the Rejang flowed placidly, its water slipping smoothly past our craft. Later the channel grew rough. We were approaching hilly, even mountainous country. The river bed became rocky and treacherous. Eddies, swirls and occasional whirlpools disturbed the stream's calm flow. Our boat began to toss and twist with sudden impetuosity. In places it tipped from side to side in a frolicsome way not lacking a hint of mischief, and sometimes a shudder passed along its spine. In the ruffled, patchy, baffling river it was perplexed to find the right, safe course. By itself it could not have done so, but would have foundered and sunk. That was why our ugly bow-man sat in the prow.

He crouched cross-legged, his eyes keenly searching the water ahead. He was our guide, our pathfinder, who knew every yard of the river as well as he knew the track to his own home. His swift glances detected the easiest channel, and what they saw he communicated with eloquent gestures of his arms to the motor driver in the stern. Sulaihi squatted there, firmly gripping the tiller, ready to change direction instantly at the slightest signal from his colleague eighty feet ahead of him. The partnership between them was perfect; they co-operated like two sections of one efficient machine. It was well that they did so, for in the dangerous rapids higher up the Rejang they were to hold our lives in their hands.

For most of the journey the scenery was beautiful, presenting various aspects of a river twisting through equatorial jungle. The thick vegetation was uniformly green, but the limbs of some of the lankiest trees were grey, and the shadowy woodland depths beyond were black. Almost everywhere the forest came to the water's edge, a confusing mass of close-growing timbers and tangled undergrowth; but occasionally a space of pebbly shore or a mudbank intervened between it and the river, and here or there a small clearing in the jungle contained a long-house.

In some places islands stood in the river, rocky and wooded. They were as wild and shaggy as hairy apes. No taming hand of men had touched them; only the beasts of the jungle and the

fowls of the air knew them as habitations. The same was true
of almost all the land which passed before our gaze in a splendid
succession of savage, unkempt landscapes.

Sometimes we caught glimpses of its inmates. At one spot
a party of monkeys gambolled on a sandbank beside the water.
As we approached them a large male chased a female, caught her,
clasped her to him and started making love with impatient passion. At another place a giant lizard, three feet long, basked
lazily on a grassy path. I saw no crocodiles that day, for Arden-
Clarke's boat travelled ahead of mine and frightened them away.
At the first sound of an approaching outboard motor they would
hurriedly end their sun-baths and slip into the river.

Brilliant kingfishers were plentiful. Hornbills flapped their
ponderous way above our heads. Eagles, kites, crows, doves,
swifts, swallows, sandpipers and bitterns were common. They
eyed suspiciously our invasion of their territory.

Now and then we saw the lord of this animal kingdom, the
great hunter, Man. Along the river small groups of Ibans waited,
half-hidden in forest. Some squatted in prahus moored at the
water's edge and others crouched on the boughs of trees, peering
like wild cats through the foliage. They stared inquisitively at
us as we passed. In their hands were spears. Motionless, silent,
alert, watchful, they seemed like scouts on the warpath. They
were indeed expecting battle, but their ambush was set to catch
pigs, not men. Annually large herds of wild boar migrated across
country, fording the Rejang at certain established places; and
each year bands of Iban hunters lay in wait for them, to attack
them as they swam the river.

After a three hours' journey from Kapit we reached the
lower edge of the notorious Pelagus Rapids. For the next four
miles up-stream a series of swift, rocky shallows agitated the river.
They were so vicious and dangerous that many extra oarsmen
were needed to pilot a boat through. Passengers were a risky
liability, so we landed on a sandspit below the cataract.

Soon two score Ibans arrived in a fleet of small prahus as reinforcements to aid our crews. Each craft carried three or four
men, and was so light that the playful waters at the foot of the
rapids tossed it furiously, striving to upset it. The natives handled

their boats with bold skill, guiding them safely to land and leaping overboard with shouts of greeting to us. They were fierce, husky savages dressed in primitive loin-cloths made of tree-bark. A generation ago they would have taken our heads with pleasure, and I doubt whether any of them would have felt objection to doing the same that day. Instead they shook us warmly by the hand, grinning and declaring themselves to be our obedient, humble servants.

While their team gathered they squatted on the beach, puffing at cigarettes and gossiping in their native gibberish. They were in merry mood, emitting much boisterous laughter. Afterwards they divided among our long-boats and started the voyage up-stream.

We foot passengers walked along a path winding beside the rapids, often high and precipitous above their seething waters. The track was narrow, passing sometimes between thick clusters of tropical vegetation and at other times across bare, rocky promontories overhanging the river. In one place it completely disappeared on a cliff-face, where only stone protuberances for handholds and crevices for footholds provided a precarious way. At another place the route lay along a solitary tree trunk felled to act as a bridge over a ravine. The tree was continuously splashed by flying spray from a near by waterfall, and the trunk was as slippery as a greasy pole. No handrail was provided to steady our balance, and we had to progress across the bridge much as a tight-rope walker advances along his wire. Giddiness would be rewarded with a fall and probably broken limbs on the rocks in the gully below.

In all this region hills impinged upon the river, and our views of jungle-covered peaks, beetling crags, rushing waters and wooded isles were magnificent. Almost always the pictures were framed in leaves, for although the ground beneath our feet descended steeply to the rapids, trees sprang from every pocket of earth lodged among the rocks. At points we caught glimpses of our boats below, struggling up-stream. They were a brave sight, bobbing like corks in turbulent stretches of water, hesitating momentarily in the face of particularly strong currents, and then suddenly shooting forward again, like arrows released from bows, when they overcame the obstruction and entered a patch of quieter river. In the wildest spots we could see the crews plying their oars like fiends. They took almost four hours to complete a journey of as many miles. By then we were waiting for them at the farther end of our walk. We had survived our jaunt with no injuries more serious than innumerable bites from leeches. These repulsive, avid creatures lurk at every turn in the jungle, intent on sucking the blood of innocent wayfarers. Their sense of smell is keen, and they detect the presence of blood through thick layers of woollen garments or tough casings of leather boots. Ravenously they hasten towards their meal, dropping from trees or climbing from the ground towards their prey. With unerring aim they find any chink in your protective armour of clothing, insinuate themselves through it, puncture your skin and fasten their lips to the wound. So light is their touch that for a while you remain unaware that they are helping themselves to copious draughts of your life's blood. Their hold is horribly strong. When you discover a leech, swollen and red with blood, clinging to any part of your person, beware of taking it between finger and thumb and trying to pull it off. So treated, its body comes away easily enough, but its hungry jaws are fixed so firmly in your flesh that the head remains behind. It is difficult then to extract it, and a festering sore may result. The proper, and infallible, method of detaching a leech from one's body is to touch its tail with a lighted cigarette. That so startles and pains the little creature that at once it unlooses its grip and drops harmless to the ground.

I chain-smoked cigarettes all the way along the path above the Pelagus Rapids, and several times they came in handy for dealing with these jungle pests. Yet one or two extra-clever leeches managed to evade my gaze and find my flesh. I discovered them, bloated and clinging, when I was free to search the more remote parts of my anatomy as we waited for the long-boats to arrive. Then they, too, succumbed to ordeal by fire.

As soon as the Ibans brought our boats to shore, they stepped out, smiling and sweating, and we stepped in, to recline once more at ease while the bow-men and motor drivers resumed charge of our fates.

II

The rest of that day's trip was tranquil. The most exciting
voyages through rapids were to take place on the morrow. Then
our calm and poise would be severely tested, but in the meantime
our temois glided on smooth waters, mile after mile and hour
after hour, until we came to Penghulu Sandai's house. There we
disembarked, for we were to spend the night under his roof.

Sandai was one of the chiefs who had greeted me with Temonggong Koh on both my visits to Kapit. In the latter stages of the
war he showed conspicuous character, initiative and courage. His
long-house stood at the farthest limits of Iban territory, close
to the land of the Kayans, where Bill Sochon and another member of the parachute party, Sergeant Barrie, lay in hiding. The
Kayans were preparing to fight in support of the British officers,
but the attitude of the Ibans, who controlled vast regions lower
down the river, was still uncertain. Much depended on their
decision.

Sochon made contact with Sandai, the nearest Iban leader of
consequence. They met privily, and the chief listened to the
Englishman's tale. He gave cautious thought to the proposal
that the Ibans should join an expedition to expel the Japanese,
then said that he must consult his people, and left the meeting.
He promised to give an answer later.

At that time a party of fourteen Japanese soldiers was camped
close to Sandai's house. He could easily betray Sochon and Barrie,
and thereby gain a handsome reward. Many an Iban would
have fallen to the temptation, and some of Sandai's followers
with whom he discussed the situation were not averse to that
course. But Sandai argued earnestly against them.

For two days Sochon and Barrie waited anxiously for his
return. They did not know what his answer would be. On the
next night they were wakened in their hiding place beside the
river by the plash of oars. Peering through the bushes, they
saw the silhouettes of men alighting stealthily from boats. The
first to leap ashore was Sandai, betraying no sign whether he
came as friend or foe. Over one shoulder he carried a heavily
loaded sack.

Flinging a word of greeting to Sochon, he untied the sack

and spilled its contents on the ground. In the darkness they looked like a heap of coconuts. Inspecting them, Sochon discovered that they were the heads of fourteen Japanese soldiers. That was Sandai's answer. On their way up-river to join the white men he and his braves had attacked the enemy garrison and killed every member of it.

We arrived at Sandai's house above the Pelagus Rapids in the late afternoon. He was waiting on the river bank to greet us. His pleasant face expressed a modest character, though he wore the full, proud panoply of an up-river Iban chieftain—on his head a tall plumed cap, in his ears heavy brass ear-rings, round his neck a huge oyster shell suspended on a necklace, over his shoulders a feathered war-cloak, round his loins a finely patterned sirat, and on his arms and legs bangles and garters.

A reception party of the principal men and women of his house stood at his side. As we landed an elder waved a cock over our heads and spoke friendly words of welcome. The bird expressed in unmistakable language its wish that we would go to an even hotter place than the Rejang on that sweltering afternoon. Then we climbed a muddy path to the long-house.

As we ascend the bank, let me introduce the reader more adequately to the Ibans' homes, the famous long-houses of Borneo. No more authentic example of savage architecture exists in the world. At one time most pagan peoples of Sarawak lived in them. Nomadic tribes like the Punans never acquired such settled or splendid habitations and, as I have already explained, many Land Dayaks abandoned long-houses when they fled for safety to mountain retreats. Recently the Melanaus, too, have deserted communal dwellings and adopted a style of individual family huts; but the Ibans, the Kayans, the Kenyahs and kindred peoples still live invariably in their traditional massive abodes. In some respects their building materials and architectural features differ from one another, but the general plan of their houses is similar. I shall describe a long-house belonging to Ibans as an example of the characteristics common to the homes of all long-house dwellers.

Usually a house is built beside a river. Since rivers are the only highways in Sarawak and the natives must travel and conduct trade by boat, it is convenient for them to live close to water. Their dwellings stand on cleared ground along the tops of the banks. A long-house is built of wood, is raised on piles and stretches continuously for a remarkable distance over the ground. I can perhaps convey to the uninitiated reader an impression of its appearance by saying that it looks like an enormously elongated English barn on stilts. To enter it one must climb a tree trunk propped steeply from the ground to its doorway, with notches cut in the trunk to make rough steps. Sometimes a hand rail is provided, but often this aid is lacking and a visitor must trust to his powers of balance. The footholds are sometimes quite large, but even so on a wet day the ascent is more like climbing a greasy pole than strolling up a staircase. I know to my cost, for once I slipped and fell in the mud.

This hazard illustrates the effectiveness of the elevation of the house as a means to achieve its original purpose, for long-houses were raised on stilts primarily for defence. In the bad old days in Sarawak it was wise to dwell a dozen feet above the earth. Then if enemies rushed the outer stockade round a house, they still could not easily enter the residence. Several yards of empty space yawned between the intruders and their intended victims. Prudent men constructed their home at a height which made it impossible for a foe to stand below the building and jab his spear through the floor.

The building's great length also is partly explained by requirements of security. A century ago Sarawak was a land where peace and order scarcely existed. Might was right, and the good things of the earth belonged to the strong. Every family's and every community's prime anxiety was for its safety, and each must be in a constant state of military preparedness. For this reason the Iban's home was literally his castle. The stronghold would be more formidable if it were not a small building containing one family, but a large place containing many families. The bigger the house, the stouter its walls. The more numerous its inmates, the more plentiful its guards. That was the simple explanation of the remarkable size of Bornean residences. They sheltered many households. Other reasons besides security may have played a part in producing this arrangement. Sociability, the instinct of primitive men to live in herds, the economic advantages of communal life, and other considerations perhaps influenced the decision; but the primary, compelling need was to create an effective fortress.

Insecurity of life and limb throughout Sarawak did not disappear automatically with the arrival of James Brooke. For the next two generations he and his successor gradually extended the area of peaceful government, but even during the reign of the third Rajah occasional head-hunting expeditions were conducted by bloodthirsty chiefs reluctant to abandon their ancestors' favourite sport. Almost until the present day, therefore, the original reason for building long-houses remained to some extent valid. Over the country as a whole, however, security has steadily increased during the last few decades, and mainly for this reason there has been a tendency for long-houses to be shorter. They now vary considerably in size. Small dwellings shelter about ten families, or approximately sixty persons. At the other extreme a few houses still accommodate almost a hundred families, or some six hundred inmates. Many are the homes of fifty or more families, but an average long-house probably accommodates between twenty and thirty.

In fact, a long-house is not so much a house in our sense of the term, as a village. Every inhabitant of the community lives under one common, continuous roof. Except occasionally in the case of Kayans, long-houses are not grouped together. Each stands by itself, isolated. The nearest neighbouring residence is probably a few miles away, and may be many miles distant. In its own locality a long-house is the home of every living human being throughout the surrounding countryside.

So one building may house anything up to six hundred people. It is in that sense like a large block of flats in a modern city. In such buildings, however, the apartments of the individual families are raised in stories, one on top of the other. The structure is lifted upwards towards the sky, not stretched outwards along the ground. A long-house, on the other hand, extends horizontally over the earth. It is a one-story building, a bungalow. Moreover, instead of the separate family apartments forming a compact group covering, say, a square area, they are set end to end in a

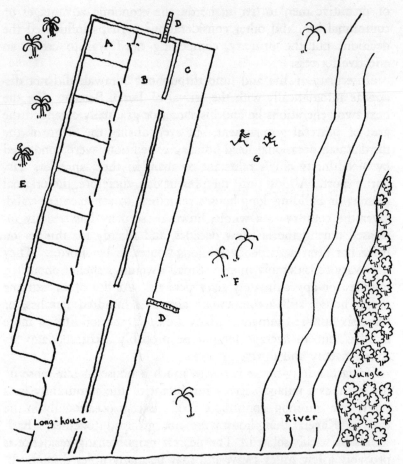

PLAN OF AN IBAN LONG-HOUSE

A. Private Rooms
B. Public Gallery
C. Open platform

D. Tree-trunk staircases
E. Banana orchard
F. Coconut palms
G. Head hunters

M.M.

continuous row. A large long-house may stretch for more than a quarter of a mile.

The dwelling's interior design is simple. The sketch plan on the opposite page indicates its domestic arrangements. Let the reader imagine that he has successfully climbed one of the tree-trunk stairways and reached the entrance to the house. In an Iban home on the Rejang he arrives first on an open platform running the whole length of the building. Crossing that, he steps into the dwelling proper. He will notice four elementary facts about the interior. First, the outer wall through which he has entered rises only two or three feet above floor level, the space between it and the roof being open except for posts supporting the rafters. Thus light and air enter the place. Second, a continuous wall stretches the length of the house and divides it longitudinally into two more or less equal halves. Third, the half of the building in which he now stands is open from end to end, forming a long, uninterrupted gallery. Fourth, in the central wall dividing the house a succession of doors leads into the other half of the dwelling.

If he walks through one of these doors, he will discover on its other side a very different plan. He enters a room lit by a small window. The place contains an open fireplace and is usually sparsely furnished with a few belongings of an Iban family. Every door in the central wall of the house leads into such a chamber. The rooms are set side by side along the building, and each room is owned by one family. The number of these apartments in a long-house depends on the number of families living in it. If twenty families inhabit a house, there are twenty rooms; if forty-three families inhabit it, there are forty-three rooms, and so on.

The room is the private quarters of a family, and is used for sleeping, eating and gossiping *en famille*. Its inmates spend much of the rest of their time in the gallery outside. This gallery is, so to speak, a common-room for the whole populace. Everyone uses it. Indeed, it is much more than a common-room, for it fulfils many purposes. It is like a village street on which all the separate family apartments open, and along which the villagers walk when paying calls on friends. It is the village club where the lads and worthies of the place gather to exchange news, tell stories, talk scandal and imbibe drink. It is the village hall where concerts and dances are held, where public meetings of the community take place, and where distinguished visitors are ceremoniously received. It is, in fact, the hub and centre of social life in this communal society. At nights it also becomes a dormitory. While parents, grandparents, newly-wed couples and children in an Iban family sleep in their private apartments, the young bachelors are relegated to the public gallery outside, and the unmarried girls occupy a loft above.

To complete this account of an Iban house I need add only one further explanation. Along the front of the roof-covered gallery extends, as I have said, an open platform or verandah. Its main function is achieved at harvest time, when the crop of padi is spread there in the sunlight to dry.

Kayan and Kenyah houses are similar in principle to those of Ibans, but differ in important architectural details. The principal difference between the two types lies in their comparative sizes. Iban dwellings are usually shorter and lower than the others. The roof is less spacious, the gallery narrower and the rooms more cramped. Kayan and Kenyah architecture is conceived on a grander scale. It is a noble example of these tribes' mastery of arts and crafts. Their houses are in many ways rough and primitive, for they are built by jungle people with a few simple implements; but their construction is a triumph of the builder's craft. They are splendid in their vastness, and have a strength which in a temperate climate would endure for a thousand years. In the equatorial forest, however, perpetual damp and voracious insects slowly but steadily devour their substance, and even the mightiest among them last effectively little more than a human generation.

III

Penghulu Sandai's house was comparatively small, being only half finished. The chief and his followers had moved into it a few months earlier. Previously they lived on the other side of the river; but an epidemic of sickness afflicted them there and persuaded them that evil spirits had placed a curse on their home. They resolved to flit, and the elders studied the omens to decide where their new dwelling should be. Observing the flights of spider-hunters and listening for the cries of trogons, they permitted these significant ornithological phenomena to point the general direction and then the exact site was settled when the medicine man saw clearly in a dream the location of the present house.

Sandai and his friends at once began to build, and had completed seven family quarters with the gallery attached before work was suspended while they gathered their padi harvest. When that task was done the house would be extended to include several more apartments.

Although the place was comparatively small, the common-room running its length was already very spacious. When I entered it, I was reminded of a long gallery in a stately Elizabethan home in England, though its almost naked inmates contrasted sharply with the original extravagantly over-dressed, hooped, breeched and ruffed first inhabitants of those lordly mansions. We had arrived at an hour when the natives were returning from their daily toil, when they like to gather sociably in the gallery for gossip. The great chamber was gradually filling with people. Men strolled to and fro or squatted in talkative groups on the floor. A few women stood inquisitively by, with babes-in-arms cradled in scarves round the mothers' necks. Other ladies of the household were for the moment too busy to join the evening assembly, for they were preparing their families' and our suppers, cooking rice, roasting chickens and boiling eggs over fires in their private apartments. But they kept making shy appearances in the darkening gallery, flitting from one room quietly into another where they wished to fetch things—or pretended to fetch things, so that they might have another excuse for a surreptitious glance at us white strangers. Mostly they wore only necklaces, belts and brief skirts; but the younger girls had donned all their finery.

The concourse of human beings did not complete the company. Countless dogs scampered through the gallery, sniffing unceremoniously at the walls and at each other, a pack of flea-

infested mongrels kept by the Ibans for hunting deer and wild
boar. Chickens strolled through the house, stepping delicately
between the feet of their owners, and cackling with fright when
they misjudged a situation and received a kick in the tail. On
either side of the door of Penghulu Sandai's room a pair of
splendid cocks were tethered by their legs. Cock-fighting is a
popular sport unlawfully enjoyed by the up-river people. Sandai's
birds were handsome, colourful creatures, and they stood with a
proud air, as if conscious of their aristocratic status among the
domestic animals. Every now and then they drew attention to
themselves by lusty, long-drawn "cock-a-doodle-doos".

This mixed assembly made a considerable noise, and to the
conversations of men, yapping of dogs, crowing of cocks and
clucking of hens was added also the grunting of pigs. The pigs
did not actually live in the gallery, but stayed below its split-
bamboo floor, sniffing ceaselessly at the dirt which accumulates
beneath an Iban house. Most of the household slops and refuse
were disposed of by being pushed through the floor to make a
meal for the pigs.

Night fell quickly and lights were soon lit in the gallery.
Half a dozen brass lamps like tall candlesticks stood on the floor,
spaced at equal distances along its length. Beside each collected
a circle of squatting men, and some women also began to settle
in the shadows behind their husbands and sons. It was attractive,
looking down the gallery and seeing the successive small points
of light illuminating the vivid faces or accentuating the black
silhouettes of people gathered round them. The men smoked
and talked. The women stayed silent, puffing cheroots or chewing betel-nut as they listened to their lords' words of wisdom or
mirth. Aikman and I joined one group and engaged in conversation on local politics.

In the gloom of the gallery I perceived bamboo fish-traps and
wooden mortars for pounding padi. A painted war-shield leaned
against one pillar, and two or three parangs hung on the walls.
A gong and a drum stood in one corner beside rolls of cane
matting. For half its length the great apartment rose clear to
the rafters, but the other half had a lower ceiling which formed the

floor of an upper chamber. There the padi was stored, and there the unmarried girls slept at nights.

In an Iban house the bachelors sleep in the public gallery and, in some districts, the unwed damsels sleep in this upper chamber or loft. A wooden staircase leads to their dormitory, and up it after dark climb youths who are courting.

A young buck so inclined will approach the couch of the girl who attracts him. She sits within her mosquito-net, perhaps expecting him. He crouches beside her and speaks of his love or discusses the weather, according to which tactic he thinks more prudent. If, after a while, she asks him to roll a cigarette or to wrap a betel-nut for her, he knows that he has her permission to stay the night. If, on the other hand, she asks him to go and poke the fire, or to perform some other task outside the bed, he knows that she does not desire him. Alternatively, she may light her small bed-lamp as a sign that he should go. He never questions her decision, nor seeks to overcome her reluctance. That would be bad manners. He leaves her, returns to the bachelors' quarters, and hopes for better luck next time.

A system of trial marriage is a recognized part of the Rejang Ibans' social code. A youth may sleep with a girl a few times without particular importance being attached to their liaison. It is publicly regarded as an experiment between the pair, to see whether they would suit each other as husband and wife. But if a boy visits a girl several times and does not then propose marriage, her parents question him about his intentions. If he plans to wed her, they are satisfied. If he does not, he is forbidden to enter her mosquito-net again.

After a brief trial period the young man or woman is still free to refuse marriage. This practice is a deliberate test of the compatibility of their physical temperaments, the couple having presumably already decided that in other ways they would suit each other. A youth or girl may try several sleeping partners before he or she makes a final choice. When the resolve is made, the wedding is celebrated with traditional pagan ritual. At the climax of the ceremony a betel-nut is split in two, and one half is given to the bride and the other to the bridegroom. It is a symbol of a partnership in which they share all things together.

Ibans marry early, the girls often at fifteen or sixteen, and the youths when they are a year or two older. They are invariably monogamous, and after marriage are usually faithful to their mates. Divorce is not difficult, but is at least no more frequent than in "civilized" societies. Generally the Bornean tribesmen are good husbands and devoted fathers.

When our dinner was cooked that evening, the Governor and our party ate from a table specially made for us in the gallery. Afterwards we squatted on the floor while the women of the house laid before us those rows of little dishes which serve to curry favour with the demons who haunt the Iban world. Dutifully we performed the whole ceremony of bedara, from throwing splashes of tuak over our shoulders for the spirits, to planting a cock's feathers on the pyramid of food arranged for their refreshment. The evil ones thus appeased, we turned to appeasing ourselves with rice-wine. As usual, girls came forward to fill and refill our glasses, and to sing a ditty before each drink.

Penghulu Sandai being a widower, his daughter Sri acted as our hostess. She attended upon me. In age she counted some twenty years and in looks she surpassed almost any native woman whom I had seen. She was tall and long-legged for an Iban, standing almost five and a half feet high. Her oval face was handsome and her figure had the grace of a Greek statue. She moved with dignity, having a stately walk. Quiet and shy in manner, she nevertheless laughed quickly at a jest. At the moment she was unmarried, having lately divorced her husband. He must have been an idiot to allow himself to be separated from such a partner.

She knelt like a suppliant before me, poured a bumper of tuak, and held it towards me while she sang a saga of countless verses. I thought that it would never end. Bob Snellus sat beside me and translated her words. She began, it seemed, by saying that she felt diffident in the presence of so renowned a visitor, but that she was overjoyed to welcome me to her home. My fame had spread up the Rejang after my first visit to Kapit, and the people of her long-house had been eager to see me. They were glad that this time I had come so far up-river. Then she resorted to outrageous flights of fancy, declaring that I possessed in high degree all the virtues of a great Iban. These she recounted in detail and at length, but at last she exhausted her list and handed me the drink. I quaffed it to the applause of the grinning head-hunters crouching around.

Meanwhile a buxom young lady called Luli performed a similar service for Arden-Clarke. A cousin of Sri, she was fashioned in coarser, plumper mould. Yet if her face was plain, it was also jolly, and with unaffected smiles she praised in song Arden-Clarke's manly virtues and gubernatorial gifts. Other girls regaled Aikman and the rest of our party with carols and tuak. Each solo was an essay in shameless flattery.

Sri and I conversed for a while, with Snellus as our interpreter. We discussed the prospects for the padi harvest, the nature of Sri's household duties, her taste in jewellery and trinkets, and other pleasant topics. Suddenly she filled my glass again and burst into fresh song. This time she told of the Iban gods, each one in turn, describing what they meant to her people. Snellus said that she would end by comparing me to the whole lot. Whether she did so or not I never learned, for his attention was distracted by a wild-eyed maiden who wandered up to him and began singing his praises in high falsetto.

Then a couple of minstrels started to strike their gongs, and another native gave a few hearty thumps on a drum. Everyone settled to enjoy some dancing. Sri shifted from her suppliant posture before me and reclined at my side, propping herself comfortably against a large, unused gong.

A man hung a hurricane lamp to the ceiling, where it cast a circle of light on the floor in front of us. A youth stepped from the outer darkness into this arena of illumination. He donned a war-cloak of hornbill's feathers and a cap crowned with Argus pheasant's plumes, strapped a parang round his waist and laid a shield upon the floor. Then he struck a statuesque pose, hesitating for a few moments before breaking into the first strutting steps of an Iban dance. With a sudden fierce yell and leap he began his performance.

The crowd of savages watched with the expert scrutiny of professional critics, such as sit in the stalls in London, Paris and New York on the first night of a new ballet. For the next two hours dancer followed dancer. Among them Sandai himself performed with gay, jaunty steps. He was happy that evening, smiling often at us and sometimes to himself. Whenever he glanced towards Sri his pride glowed in his face. He felt that she was doing the honours well.

Sri did not dance. She laughed at my urging that she should do so, declaring that she could not. But she told Luli and another girl to perform, and fetched some colourful sarongs for them to wear. They giggled, and the three retired to a room to dress up. When they emerged they were so splendidly attired that they looked like mannequins exhibiting a set of palace fashions. The orchestra started another throbbing tune, and Luli and her partner did a slow, restrained, arm-waving, foot-tapping women's dance.

When at length everyone who wished to jig had done so, the entertainment ended. Then the whole company gathered round the Governor and me, so that we could address them. In simple, friendly terms Arden-Clarke spoke of Sarawak affairs and outlined the Government's policies. He described plans to instruct the natives in improved methods of agriculture, to bring health services to them by sending mobile dispensaries up-river, to build Iban schools and train Iban teachers, and to promote local self-government by the appointment of district councils. His audience listened carefully, made comments and asked questions. He answered them. The proceedings promised to be a good session of a long-house parliament.

Suddenly, however, a distant roll of thunder sounded, and a moment later rain began to patter on the roof. Before long a terrific storm was raging. Crash after crash of thunder broke above the house, a mighty wind howled round it and torrents of rain fell on it like a tidal wave. Perhaps the evil spirits had taken umbrage at some defect in our offerings earlier in the evening, for they seemed determined to destroy us. The enraged elements made a tumultuous noise. Simultaneously the animals in the house took fright; dogs barked fearfully, cocks crowed vociferously and pigs squealed in terror. Unless we shouted at the tops of our voices, none of us mere human beings could make ourselves heard above the din. We roared with helpless laughter, and adjourned the meeting.

It was past midnight. Arden-Clarke and I went to bed in the penghulu's room, but not to sleep. The storm was one of those brief, impetuous, tropical affairs which soon subsides; but the excitement in the house was not so short-lived. The pack of mongrels whined periodically, the fighting-cocks raised their voices in lusty competition, and from beneath the floor came now and then the whimper of a pig suffering, it seemed, a nightmare. In the next room someone snored, from other apartments came the coughing of old men, and sometimes a baby cried in misery until comforted by its mother. Meanwhile outside our door Penghulu Sandai and his followers had resumed their political discussion. They argued keenly and loud, maintaining an incessant, noisy babble of talk. For an unconscionable time sleep was impossible, and after that it was fitful. Thus we passed a short night in a long-house.

It seemed only a few moments between the last throaty spasm of coughing which I heard before I fell asleep, and the first cock-crow that woke me in the morning. The dawn chorus of bird song in Sandai's home was a raucous outburst of crowing by chanticleers.

Arden-Clarke and I rose, put on bathing-trunks and walked down the path for a plunge in the river. When we arrived we found Sri and Luli in occupation of the jetty, having their morning baths. They were clad in work-a-day sarongs which clung, sopping wet, to their legs, for the girls had been immersed up to their necks in water. Now they sat on a raft of logs, douching their faces and soaping their bodies.

They smiled cheerily, waved hands to us and called, "Tabeh, Tuans!"

"Tabeh, Sri! Tabeh, Luli!" we answered.

They continued their toilet and we joined them. In the presence of so much splashing humanity the place seemed safe enough from crocodiles, so we dived into the river for a swim. The girls continued to lather and rinse themselves. They joked together, and laughed heartily when I slipped by mistake beneath the logs and nearly got drowned. When they had finished their ablutions, they filled gourds with water and carried them to the house, the first domestic duty of native women every day.

Arden-Clarke and I followed them shortly. Soon afterwards we travellers were ready to depart, and descended the path to go aboard our temois. The entire population of the house came to wave us good-bye.

IV

The prows of our long-boats turned up-river. For the next nine hours, with a short break for lunch in the shady jungle, we voyaged ever deeper into Borneo's interior. The scenery was splendid most of the way, the country growing steadily more mountainous.

During the journey our boats had to fight their way through three separate stretches of rapids. The first and second were comparatively simple, but the third was not. This passage was the infamous Tekok Rapids, which have drowned many men. In the middle of their wicked course they form an "S" bend. Their twisting, erratic channel is rock-strewn, and when the river is swollen with rain they grow particularly angry. That day they were in a towering rage.

Aikman's and my craft led the attack. As it approached the rapids we saw their white outer frill of ruffled water spanning the river. When we crossed it our boat began first to toss and then to jig. Farther on lay the more formidable defence lines of the cataract. Chopping waves and swirling pools were locked together in a wild dance of frantic waters—but that was mild compared to the chaos beyond.

There jagged boulders split the river into a number of seething alleys. Sharp twists in the channel added to the confusion of torrents rushing together from different directions. Every few yards contained a fresh whirlpool, not usually spinning on the same axis as the one which we had navigated immediately before. More rocks than appeared above the surface were hidden beneath it, with rills pouring over them in mighty leaps and bounds. The river's downward course was apparent. Besides contesting against a host of obstacles in the water, the boats had to fight every inch of the way uphill.

After several preliminary skirmishes, our temoi passed boldly into the area of greatest danger. Sulaihi released the full power of his motor, and the craft leapt forward with a defiant roar. For a few moments it raced onwards unchecked, then met head-on the full force of the enemy. It hesitated, shook itself, steadied its balance, gathered its strength and began to push obstinately forward again. But its progress was now slow and uncertain. The galloping rapids dashed at it without mercy and for a while they appeared to make it their plaything. The prahu was pushed this way and that, sometimes keeling over so sharply that it seemed about to capsize, and at other times sinking so low in the water that we seemed on the point of being sucked to the bottom of the river. It rocked, turned, jumped, twisted, hesitated and advanced, not so much at its own sweet will as at the sour, embittered will of the tumultuous torrent. My most vivid impression was of the craft's frailty, of the narrow margin of strength which at almost every moment lay between its triumphant survival and its helpless destruction.

Yet it always just managed to keep an adequate control of the situation. Its old tree-trunk keel and stout plank bulwarks knew a thing or two about the elements. They were not amateurs but professionals, not novices but veterans at this game. When they stood upright as giant trees in the forest they weathered many storms, and now that they had been laid horizontal and made by cunning builders into a boat with trim form and firm lines, they preserved their tough resilience to overcome all the tempestuous wiles of the Tekok Rapids.

Nevertheless, by itself that quality would not have sufficed. Inanimate wood, however well carpentered, would have lost the battle against madly animated waters. The boat prevailed because at its prow was an expert pilot and in its stern an expert helmsman, who worked together with transcendent skill.

The ugly old Iban in the bow sat keenly alert as we entered the rapids. His back appeared stolid. Possibly his face registered some mildly emotional response to the perilous confusion ahead; but he gave no hint of concern.

Fascinated, I watched him perform his duty. As we approached the outer edge of the turmoil his arms and hands began to issue orders to his comrade at the tiller, talking volubly in silent sign language. Their movements were quick and precise. With each yard that we advanced the conditions of the next stretch of water altered and some change in the boat's course was necessary. This he must convey instantaneously by an appropriate signal to Sulaihi. A single error might lead to disaster. There was no time for hesitation, indecision or second thoughts. So his gestures were emphatic and decisive, like the commands of an officer leading troops into battle.

I was astonished at the ease with which he maintained his balance on the sharp, high prow of the violently swaying temoi. He seemed as much a part of the vessel as a steeplechase rider is part of his horse. But this amazing riverman could achieve even more startling things. Twice in the middle of the rapids he leaped to his feet and stood erect as he shook a warning fist at some particularly treacherous piece of water in the neighbourhood. These extreme antics seemed to be only partially for Sulaihi's benefit, and partly for the assistance of the two younger, less experienced bow-men in charge of the other temois. I learned that one of these youths was his son; so our pilot was moved by paternal solicitude. On each occasion he turned round and peered in the youth's direction, waving an arm vigorously, clenching his fist and contorting his face into minatory expressions. Why he did not lose his balance and fall headlong into the river, I do not know.

At last we reached the upper limits of the rapids. The wild waters subsided and our boats ceased to sway and jig. I learned later that in the middle of the falls Arden-Clarke's temoi shipped a wave, which soaked him and gave him a nasty fright. For a moment he thought that the craft would sink with all hands.

Not far above the rapids the river paid him compensation for this piece of impertinence. On a mudbank he spied a crocodile, fast asleep. Firing three shots at the beast before it struggled into the water, he claimed that he had mortally wounded it. He felt that on the day's reckoning he was quits with the Rejang River. His surmise proved correct. On our return journey two days later we heard that a dead crocodile with three bullet holes in its carcase had been found on a sandbank near the spot where the Governor fired his gun.

In the late afternoon after our adventure in the rapids we reached Belaga. That small, remote administrative post lay 270 miles by water from the sea, yet the Rejang still flowed nearly a hundred yards wide past its white-washed fort. The river continued far beyond Belaga, up winding reaches, through narrow gorges and over leaping rapids into the wildest heart of Sarawak. A journey of another two or three weeks, accomplished partly by motor-driven prahu and partly by hand-poled canoe, would be required to reach its source. We did not make that voyage, but stopped two days in Belaga. Our companions there were Kayan chiefs and tribesmen, so I shall postpone an account of the sojourn with them till the next section of this book.

CHAPTER EIGHT

THE BALLEH

I

Two YEARS PASSED before I returned to the Rejang. My principal purpose this time was to keep a promise to visit Temonggong Koh in his long-house up the Balleh River. He had planned for the occasion a ceremony of extraordinary pagan significance and solemnity, and a small party of official notables accompanied me to witness the event. Arden-Clarke was away on leave, so Christopher Dawson was Acting-Governor and came in his place. Dawson's wife Jill joined us, with John Barcroft, now the Resident at Sibu, Willie Geikie, a capable Eurasian officer who was the "mayor" of that town, Terry Dilks, the Governor's private secretary, and Major Martin Gilliat who, as Comptroller of my Household in Johore, thought that he might pick up some useful tips about house management from the vast communal dwellings in Borneo. Failing the acquisition of anything to his advantage in that line, he came simply, like the rest of us, to enjoy a remarkable experience.

It was April, 1949. When we reached the Iban country we saw that the padi was ripe and that harvesting was in full swing. Long-houses beside the river were almost empty, only small children and decrepit elders standing on the platforms to stare at us as we passed. All the able-bodied natives were in their "fields" gathering the crop. Many husky young men and women appeared near small, flimsy farm huts, where they often stay for the harvesting, and countless others were hidden from view beyond contours of undulating country. Large areas of hillside were denuded of trees and undergrowth, having been cleared a few months earlier to receive the rice-seed. Now the slopes were covered with acres of tall, waving padi.

Native economy in Sarawak is simple. All the pagan tribes

"Rivers are the highways and byways in roadless Sarawak" (p. 4)

"The country is covered with jungle" (p. 3)

"Their famous saws are in all the villages." (p. 131)

"On gala occasions their costume assumes barbaric splendour" (p. 8)

"Melanaus launch their boats" (p. 12)

The mosque at Kuching

"Huts near a river mouth" (p. 13)

"Rocky path twisting among jungle trees" (p. 51)

"Their own customary garb" (p. 52)

"The buildings looked wild" (p. 52)

"A small round house" (p. 52): *on the left is the platform which collapsed as Gawang and the author were dancing* (p. 62)

Kanowit (p. 78)

"Frequently we passed long-houses" (p. 79)

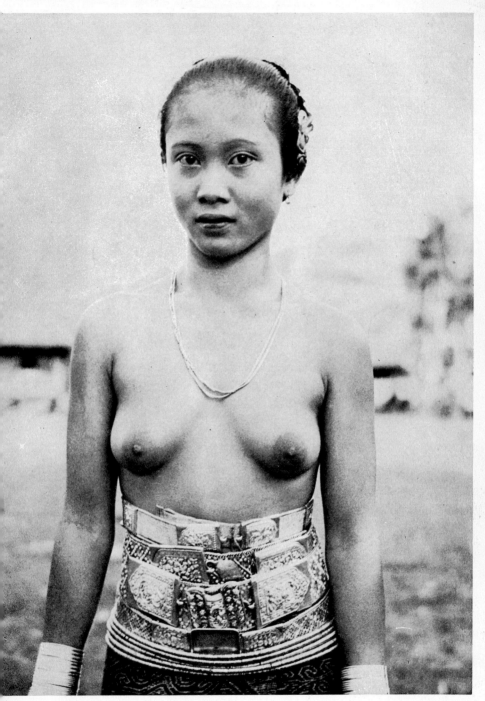

Siah (p. 98)

Koh's hands (p. 85)

"Fierce, husky savages" (p. 102)

"Glimpses of our boats struggling up-stream" (p. 102)

"Reinforcements to aid our crews" (p. 101)

"Women with babes-in-arms"
(p. 111)

Kanyan (p. 137)

"Filled gourds with water" (p. 117)

Penghulu Jugah (p. 142)

"Adorning themselves like brides": Anchang and Sani (p. 153)

"A young pig lying helpless on the ground" (p. 152)

except the Punans and other nomad groups live mainly by agriculture, with a certain amount of fishing, hunting and trading in addition. Their principal food is rice and their most important activity is growing padi. Some cultivate small quantities of wet-padi on flat, irrigated ground, but mostly the natives grow dry-padi on hillsides prepared in a crude fashion for this elementary agricultural effort.

At the appropriate season, and when the omens are good, the wise men in a long-house select an area suitable for sowing the year's crop. The males sally forth to clear the land of jungle. Having felled the trees and undergrowth, they burn them to provide wood-ash as fertilizer. Each family acquires in the cleared area its own patch of ground. Then men and women together plant the seed. Usually they cultivate tapioca, maize and other foodstuffs as well, but the greater part of the land is sown with rice. The men walk ahead boring holes in the ground, and the women follow, dropping seeds into the holes. Afterwards they build a fence round the area to keep out wild pigs, deer and other marauders.

Tending the padi as it grows is a duty left to women. They weed the plots and watch over the young shoots. When they report that the harvest is ripe, the whole population of the long-house turns out to gather it. Its conveyance to the house for drying and storage is attended by dancing, drinking and other jovial celebrations. Harvest festivals among the pagans last for several days and are sometimes marked by debaucheries which would be severely prohibited at other times.

A piece of land cannot generally produce good crops in two consecutive seasons. In the following year, therefore, the wise men choose another hillside of virgin soil not too far from the long-house. A particularly fruitful bit of ground may be worked again in a later spring, but in time all the suitable country in the neighbourhood is exhausted. Then the people of the house migrate.

In dreams the medicine man sees visions of a likely new site. He and other village worthies go exploring to discover it. The flight of spider-hunters and the calls of trogons are studied, until by these omens the location for a fresh home is finally determined. Then the people throw their possessions into their boats, step aboard, and travel up- or down-river to the chosen spot.

There they build another house. Settled in it, they start afresh to transform acres of the surrounding forest into temporary padi-fields. When these in turn are exhausted for agricultural purposes, the community flits again, and the deserted land once more produces the inexorable, prolific vegetation of jungle.

This system of shifting cultivation accompanied by widespread destruction of forest along the river banks has some grave consequences. It causes soil erosion on a significant scale, and leads to wasteful despoiling of valuable timber resources. How to check these, while maintaining native agriculture, is one of the Government's major problems.

Besides growing rice, every village breeds pigs and keeps hens, and some of them own goats as well. The Kelabits on their distant plateau tend herds of cattle. Variety is added to the natives' diet by the profits of their chase after wild pigs, deer, monkeys and other woodland creatures, as well as by fish from the rivers and fruit from the jungle. From the forest also the men gather various kinds of produce with commercial value in the outer world. Gutta-percha, camphor, rattans, beeswax, honey, vegetable tallow, dammar, wild rubber, sago, illipi nuts and edible bird's nests are all collected. These goods are loaded in the community's boats and paddled up- or down-stream to the nearest trading centre.

Many such centres exist along the Sarawak rivers, like Kanowit, Song and Kapit, which the reader knows. Each small township is the administrative headquarters of a District Officer or a Native Officer. In the former case its principal building is generally one of the old wooden forts of earlier, troublesome days. There, too, stand the local police barracks, a lock-up for criminals and a court-room where the majesty of the law asserts its just, impartial sway. In such stations enterprising Chinese merchants settle to pursue their eternal aim of making money. Their row of shop-houses is a magnet for the men and women of the jungle, for in them the traders display popular articles of food, brass lamps, betel boxes, rolls of pretty cloth, cheap jewellery and other wares to tempt the natives.

Periodically the long-house chiefs bring their wives and daughters to spend a day or two in these bazaars. Wild produce of the forest is exchanged for slick objects from workshops in Singapore, Hong Kong and beyond. Business is conducted by barter. It is amusing to watch the tattooed up-river men bargaining with inscrutable, smiling Chinese towkays shrewd in the ways of commerce. And there is strange romance in the spectacle of Iban girls in native finery strolling along the street on shopping expeditions, seeking yet more pretty necklaces, bangles and earrings to adorn their persons.

A faint atmosphere of the larger, cosmopolitan, civilized East hangs about these ever so small, ever so remote, ever so lonely places. Wherever the Chinese go they erect other buildings besides shop-houses. Each township has its Confucian school and its Buddhist temple. There is also for Malay government officers and their wives a mosque, and sometimes a Christian mission is present with a Catholic, Anglican or Methodist church and classroom. Around this little oasis of Man's faiths and strivings crowd the jungle trees.

II

On our way up-river we stopped a night at Kapit. It bore numerous signs of development since my last visit. The temporary bazaar of flimsy timber and kajang stores which I remembered was half demolished, and the ground was levelled to form the foundation of a more modern shopping centre. Already several new cement buildings were rising from the dust. The greensward around Fort Sylvia had been cut and neatly trimmed, the paths and lawns of the District Officer's garden began to look tidy, fresh flowering shrubs had been planted everywhere, and clumps of water lilies were budding in the lake. The place was gradually assuming once more its pre-war graces.

A Methodist mission school on a hilltop at the edge of the village, which flourished before the war but had suffered the indignity of bombing during the Japanese occupation, had been reopened. We visited it. Its master was the Reverend Burr H. Baughman, an austere but friendly American with a gentle

Chinese wife whom he had married during an earlier period of schoolmastering in Penang. This zealous couple conducted us through their establishment, introducing us to their staff and pupils. The buildings were simple, clean and prim. The assistant teachers were a Batak youth and his wife from Sumatra, themselves excellent products of Methodist education. The students numbered almost a score of Iban boys and girls of various ages from eight to eighteen, collected from several long-houses up the Rejang and the Balleh rivers. They included children of chiefs, among them two charming daughters of Temonggong Koh's nephew, Penghulu Sibat, one of the best Iban leaders on the Rejang.

I personally was sorry, though not surprised, to find that the missionaries discouraged the children from wearing native dress. Indeed, a foreign style of costume seemed compulsory. The boys' long hair had been shorn as completely as Sampson's locks were cut by Delilah. Their loin-cloths, too, were discarded, and the young Ibans strolled round with their hands thrust into the pockets of short trousers, like small Western schoolboys. Some of them were so modern as to wear shirts. The girls likewise were not immediately recognizable as Ibans. In place of their natural three-quarters nudity they were covered from necks to ankles in Malay bajus and sarongs. Two or three even wore European blouses and skirts. Except for their Bornean features, they might have been sophisticated children from Singapore.

Thus Western civilization was creeping into the interior of Sarawak, not, as sometimes happened in native states in earlier times, by means of guns and commerce, but with the Cross and the Christian ethic. These apparently gentler instruments are equally destructive of indigenous, traditional ways of life, and whether they create more than they destroy depends on the tact and understanding with which they are employed.

It was a sultry, tropical afternoon. The river seemed sluggish, and an oppressive heat fell from a cloudless sky on the huts of the little jungle settlement. We abandoned our launch and embarked in temois. The air was cooler under their kajang awnings, and their outboard motors drove the small, slim craft at a pace which created for us a refreshing breeze.

A few miles above Kapit we turned from the broad highway of the Rejang into the by-way of its tributary, the Balleh. The water at once became ruffled, betraying rocks below. The river narrowed, and its banks grew steeper and higher. A thick tangle of tall trees and dense bushes covered them, shaggy and impenetrable. So we passed into the intimate embrace of the jungle. After long months of staid, formal, official life in Singapore, my heart leaped for joy.

Sulaihi's steady hand once more held the tiller of my craft, while in the prow sat a jaunty Iban bow-man. He led with dash our advance up the Balleh. The river was in flood, and its waters raced swiftly down-stream. Half-drowned tree trunks, torn by the force of the torrent from their footholds in the upper reaches, kept sweeping towards us as wild as rogue elephants. We swerved this way and that to avoid them, and sometimes the bow-man thrust a paddle overboard to beat off their attacks. Progress was hard for the prahus and the men who worked them, but pleasant for us passengers lolling on cushions under shady roofs, idly watching a succession of savage landscapes slip by.

In the late afternoon we reached Penghulu Jinggut's house, where we were to lodge the night. Jinggut was the youngest of Sarawak's chieftains, a lad still in his earliest twenties. He looked even younger than his age, but had the ripe dignity of captaincy as well as the fresh vigour of youth. That afternoon he stood at the water's edge to greet us. Beside him stood a girl who turned out to be his sister. His wife was pregnant and would shortly bear their first child. In those circumstances ancient tribal custom imposed on her a strict taboo. She could not appear before strangers, and throughout our visit remained as effectively concealed as if she had been a lady in a Moslem potentate's harem.

When I landed, Jinggut received me warmly, and his sister handed me a tumbler of tuak.

"Buai," she said.

This meant "Give it to your attendant spirit." According to Iban belief, an invisible companion, a sort of guardian angel— or it may be devil—accompanies everyone wherever he goes. The first act of hospitality when a visitor arrives at a house must be extended to this ghostly being, so that it feels welcome and shall be benevolently inclined towards the inmates of the home.

When I had done my best to encourage a genial mood in my unseen partner by spilling wine for it on the grass beside me, our hostess offered me a second tumbler, this time for myself. I dutifully drank it. Then similar rites were performed first to the spirits and afterwards to the human forms of Christopher and Jill Dawson, Barcroft and all the others in our party.

This act of propitiation of the spiritual guardians of visitors appears to be peculiar to the Ibans in the Balleh region. It is part of a comprehensive code of entertainment of the deities and demons who inhabit their animist world which I shall describe later in greater detail.

Its first manifestation over, we ascended the hill to Jinggut's house. The building stood high on a rocky bluff overlooking the river, the approach lying first up a sharply climbing path through a banana orchard and then up two successive tree-trunk stairways giving access to the verandah. With ape-like tread I climbed the arboreal staircase. At the top was a startling company. On the verandah rows of the house's most presentable ladies were assembled. Some appeared in customary seductive South Sea adornment, with flowered heads, bare breasts and skimpy skirts. I was accustomed to them, and they did not unduly disturb my equanimity. But other damsels were dressed in a style which made me blink and marvel. They were covered from head to foot in hats and robes of coloured beads so thickly meshed that their bodies were as completely hidden as the forms of mediæval knights encased in armour.

These extravagant costumes were the most fabulous that I had seen in Borneo. Each girl wore a hat like a vast pincushion, in which hundreds of long spikes bristled like the quills of a porcupine alerted for battle. On every spike were threaded small, many-hued beads, and from the pinheads hung ribbons, artificial flowers, ornamental marbles, silver coins and other bits of feminine nonsense.

This amazing superstructure was matched by the garments covering the girl's body. Her principal robe was a one-piece, long-sleeved suit falling from her neck to her ankles, made wholly of glass beads so closely woven that it had the texture of a coat-of-mail. An apron of smaller beads was attached at her back, with two or three bells the size of cow-bells suspended from its lower extremity. Girdling each damsel's waist was a silver belt supporting numerous smaller bells, and all the girls wore beaded cravats, silver necklaces and silver-thread sashes criss-crossed over their bosoms. Whenever the ladies stirred, the beads rustled like trees of crystal leaves, the coins jingled, the small bells tinkled and the large bells jangled all at once.

These strange apparitions did not move more than they could help. Their costumes were hardly the ideal dress for life on the equator. The close-fitting glazed robes stored heat from the sun's rays as efficiently as a hermetically sealed glass-house. The poor females dripped with perspiration, and appeared to be visibly melting before our gaze. Each held a towel, which she applied frequently to her brow, cheeks, chin and neck to wipe away trickles of sweat.

As soon as the young women had done their duty by offering me further draughts of tuak, they strolled in single, jingle-jangle file to the shade of the house's covered gallery. There we all settled on the floor to celebrate a bedara. The girls in the fabulous dresses performed the rites as serving maids while I acted as head-waiter for the good and evil spirits.

Let me now explain the order and significance of the various obsequies to the spirits which are performed when an important visitor arrives at an Iban house on the Balleh. Three separate, formal acts of propitiation occur.

The initial act is that which I have already mentioned. As soon as I set foot on the river bank below Jinggut's house his sister handed me a half-filled glass of tuak, the contents of which I flung to the ground as an offering to my private, personal spirit.

There are many other spirits also to be appeased. The Iban world is filled with a vast host of unattached sprites who rove at random through the jungle, entering the long-houses at will. These characters exert a great influence over the fates of men, and are therefore to be treated with the utmost care. Many of them, by nature, have rather evil dispositions and require particular attention. A suitable occasion for gaining their favour is a visit by a distinguished stranger, for many of them may have accompanied him to the house. The spirits appear to be snobs, who are flattered if a personage like a touring Resident or Governor makes an offering to them. So a household eagerly exploits a call from any such officer to achieve a grand propitiation of all the goblins who at that moment haunt their home. The means of doing this is the public bedara performed in the house's gallery.

In dwellings up the Balleh it is customary for another act of entertainment of yet another group of spirits to be performed. During the evening the guest is invited to visit each room in turn, to celebrate a private bedara with the occupying family. This little act of thoughtfulness is, the pagans reckon, deeply appreciated by the group of personal spirits of the individuals composing the domestic circle. It is, so to speak, an intimate party given partly in honour of the visitor's spirit, and partly in their honour.

Thus, by a series of conciliatory acts, the individual spirits attendant upon the guests in the house, the mob of unattached spirits who hang around the dwelling, and the personal spirits of every inmate of the place are all regaled. None can complain that it has been forgotten. The process is costly, since it consumes large quantities of tuak and heavy rations of eggs, rice, popcorn, betel-nut and other ingredients. But it sets the minds of the pagans at rest. They are convinced that such lavish hospitality disposes the hobgoblins to shower blessings on their homes. Nor do they think that this desirable result is prejudiced by the fact that much of the food prepared for the demons is, after a decent interval, eaten by the supplicants themselves. Their reasoning and faith in such matters are touchingly illogical and childlike.

III

That evening in Jinggut's house we relaxed for a while after the bedara. I descended to the river for a swim, then dressed and joined Barcroft and a group of Iban braves on the outer platform of the dwelling. Darkness had descended upon the Balleh, the night air was cool, and we lolled with a delicious sense of ease under a million stars.

Talk turned on pleasant rustic topics. The padi harvest, we heard, was neither particularly good nor especially bad. Too much rain had fallen recently, and there would be no surplus rice for export. On the other hand, the crop was ample to supply all the needs of the household itself.

Hunting of late had been profitable sport. Deer were plentiful in the surrounding jungle, and so were monkeys. The latter lively beasts were difficult to chase. They were better killed by blow-pipes than by shot-guns, for pellets wrought too much havoc on their small bodies. It was easy to slay a monkey with a poisoned arrow blown from twenty yards. No hunter worthy of the name could miss at that range; the difficulty was to get so close without the target taking fright. Monkeys were alert, nervous creatures who leaped away at the slightest disturbance, chattering alarm to all the other inmates of the forest.

There was a pleasant village atmosphere about that long-house talk. The platform might have been the parlour of a pub anywhere in rural England, with monkeys taking the place of foxes in the conversation.

We dined in Jinggut's room and then my travelling companions and I divided forces to perform the series of individual family bedaras expected of us. Like a troupe of philanthropists dispensing charity, we went from door to door. The conscientious performance of a bedara is a lengthy process. I celebrated ten that evening with as many separate families, and they occupied me till midnight.

It was tiring work, this constant squatting on the floor and repeating monotonously the same solemn, tedious set of rites. The girls who sang the pantuns laboured as long and hard as I did, for only a few young women in a house are sufficiently skilled to perform on special occasions. They were in constant demand. One in particular was easy on the eye. She joined me in the celebration of several bedaras, and chanted a pantun each time. The flowers in her hair, the jewellery about her person and the skirt round her waist were enchanting in quality and brief in quantity. She had the beautiful face and body of a dancing apsara in the sculptured frieze on the great temple at Angkor. Lit by a candle-flame flickering amidst the long-house shadows, her dark eyes sparkled brightly, and she favoured me with Mona Lisa smiles as she sang paeans in my praise. In the middle of one softly tuneful song I was about to fall head-over-heels in love with her, when she stopped singing for a moment, lifted a corner of the mat on which we sat, and spat a juicy, blood-red gob of betel-nut through the floor. That brought me to my senses.

I escaped to bed in the small hours of the morning, but the pagan celebrations continued all night. Eventually I was lulled to sleep by the dirge of a pantun sung in a neighbouring room; and the first sound of which I became conscious when I woke next morning was another pantun gently carolled in the outside gallery.

We rose and departed early, for we had far to go before we reached Temonggong Koh's home.

CHAPTER NINE

PAGAN CEREMONIAL

I

A NIGHT OF RAIN had further filled the river, and our long-boats fought the flooded waters for ten hours before we reached our destination. Eventually, towards five o'clock in the afternoon, we saw an unusually large fleet of boats moored at a spot ahead of us, and learned that they were craft assembled at the landing stages before Temonggong Koh's house.

The party there started with a bang, or, to be precise, with several bangs. The old chief stood on the house verandah, peering eagerly along the river for the first glimpse of our temois as they rounded a distant bend. As soon as we appeared he gave a signal to natives crouching by his side, where a battery of two ancient Brunei cannon was mounted on the rickety platform. They promptly announced our arrival to the penghulus and people in the dwelling, the sprites and hobgoblins in the atmosphere and the monkeys and hornbills in the forest by a salute of nineteen guns.

So long as they maintained their erratic explosions we approached with more discretion than speed. On the previous afternoon, during a similar reception at Jinggut's house, a cannon had blown a piece of flesh from the leg of a girl standing close by. We prized our lives and limbs too highly to throw them away unnecessarily, at any rate at this early stage of the proceedings.

As we cautiously advanced I looked with interest and pleasure on Koh's house. It stood on a hillside overlooking the Balleh, perched about fifty feet above the river. Before it several tree-trunk stairways sloped to the water's edge, and behind it the hill climbed higher to a jungle-clad ridge. The building was extensive, for it was the home of thirty-eight families, and work was in hand to add rooms for another ten. We saw many scores of inmates crowding the platform, while numerous pagan dignitaries descended the stairs to greet us when we landed.

After their royal salute of savage barks, the Brunei cannon relapsed into silence. The hush of the river and forest once more prevailed, and our boats plucked up courage to go ashore. At the foot of the central staircase waited Temonggong Koh, wearing a gay turban of wild-animal fur on his head and a broad grin of welcome on his face. With him were his two elder daughters, Iba and Mindun, clad in habitual finery. A local chief called Tedong, a brother of Penghulu Jugah, was mantled in a war-cloak of monkey's fur and crowned with a plumed helmet. Behind this picturesque group stood a row of long-house worthies like a crew of pirates on parade, old men with fearsome faces and costumes of garish, barbaric style.

Koh laughed joyously and clasped my outstretched hand in both of his as I stepped ashore. Tedong muttered words of blessing while he waved a protesting cockerel over my head. Mindun held out to me a glass of tuak, repeating insistently as she did so the word "Buai".

Her beseeching tone meant, "For the love of Mike don't drink the stuff yourself, or our party will be a failure. Throw it over your shoulder into the river, where your attendant spirit can taste it. Then he will be pleased and the success of our gathering is assured."

I threw the wine into the water, and Iba immediately handed me another glassful. I quaffed it without drawing breath, then held the empty tumbler upside-down to show that not a drop of the repulsive liquid had been wasted.

After that Koh led me to a party of penghulus, visitors from other houses up and down the Balleh who were his guests at this special ceremonial in his home. They were the principal chiefs on the river, officers of the Temonggong's general staff in the management of Iban affairs. Jugah, Sibat, Grinang, Kulleh, Rabong and Jinggut were in the group, the last named having come with us in our boat. One and all were now old friends of mine, and we hailed each other with pleasure.

As the Dawsons and my other fellow-travellers landed they were each received with the same cordiality, and they too did their bit to ensure that the spirits were thoroughly appeased. There was a buzz of friendly greetings.

I started up the tree-trunk staircase to the house. On a landing half-way some Iban women lay in wait with fresh glasses of tuak. The contents of the first I hurled into space, but the ladies insisted that I partake of all the rest. Thus fortified I went upward to the verandah. At the top a green archway of sprouting foliage spanned the entrance. As I reached it two damsels stepped forward with further profferings of food and drink. One held a plate heaped with rice, eggs, popcorn, pancakes and other viands, while the other carried the inevitable glass brimfull of wine. Fortunately, as the first thrust her dish into my hands she murmured "Buai", and made signs that I should cast its contents over the edge of the verandah for the local goblins. I did so gladly, and saw some pigs scamper to the food and gobble it up. Then the second girl gave me the drink to dispense in the same reckless fashion. This, too, I did with gusto. I had now tumbled to the excellent idea that we should make the evil spirits so hopelessly intoxicated that they would be incapable of interfering with our revels. Behind me the Dawsons, Barcroft, Geikie and Gilliat joined in turn in forwarding this admirable conspiracy.

Entering the house, I was led to the centre of its gallery. There I would perform at once a bedara, to start with a seemly mixture of solemnity and hilarity a pagan programme of festive yet religious ceremonial which, we were warned, would continue throughout the next two days and nights.

There was a short interval while people found their places in the gallery. I squatted on my haunches and surveyed my surroundings. The scene was such as one would expect to see in a theatre at the rise of the curtain on some strange Oriental drama. A street scene in *Chu Chin Chow*, a market scene in *Ali Baba* or a court scene in *The Arabian Nights* would not appear more fabulous. A shifting crowd of people moved through the house, clad in various costumes. Iban penghulus strutted proudly in their official uniforms. Other chiefs wore the full panoply of warriors of olden times, the tall plumes of their war-caps nodding majestically above the heads of the throng. Humbler men were more simply but no less picturesquely dressed, their long black tresses and naked brown bodies adorned with silver necklaces and coloured loin-cloths representing savagery at its handsomest. Among them the European officers in western tropical kit appeared like odd travellers from far-off lands. A touch of the freakish was added by a pair of albino natives with red hair and pink, freckled skins.

The women's dresses, too, presented fantastic contrasts. Some ladies wore the many-beaded costumes of pagan priestesses which I had seen in Jinggut's house, but most women were more lightly clad, in the style of slave girls in Eastern romances. Among them a small company of especially lovely damsels hastened to and fro, bearing dishes of food which they laid in rows on the mat before me.

The gallery was decorated extravagantly for the occasion, appearing as gaudy with flowers, flags and foliage as the Mall in London on a Coronation morning. Among this riot of decoration the sacred heads of the house were almost hidden, but I spied them slung from a beam close by me—a dozen skulls covered with human flesh so smoked that their skin looked like parchment black with age. Through the passage of years the detailed features of their grim faces had mostly disappeared. They might have belonged to mummies buried countless centuries ago, instead of to men who lived and fought in our own lifetimes. Temonggong Koh explained to me that no Iban victims hung among them. They were all Kayans, trophies from battles fought in earlier years against those hereditary foes.

The grand chief bore marvellously well the almost eighty years which he now boasted. He was a perfect example of mellow and noble old age. His step was firm and dignified, his carriage proud, his gaze serene, sagacious and benevolent. As he moved among his people an aura of sanctity seemed to surround him. Everyone stood aside for him and looked upon him with affection, as if he were the patriarch of whom the rest were children. In the evening of his life he had acquired unrivalled prestige among the pagans of Sarawak. During his vigorous youth he had many enemies, but now he had none. In earlier years he must needs fight with a sword to get his way, but now he had only to speak a word to gain whatever he wished. He was the pre-eminent Iban of his time, the wisest, the best and the most honoured. If the natives wrote their racial histories and invented titles by which to remember particular heroes, he would be known as Koh the Great.

He squatted beside me. He had cast off his penghulu's jacket, and sat naked in his wrinkled skin except for a black sirat, a pair of rattan garters, and a white fur turban. Koh always seemed indifferent to every article in man's wardrobe except the hat. He wore neither ear-rings nor bangles, and was unconcerned about the cut and colour of his sirat, invariably favouring a simple old black loin-cloth when other men exhibited more fastidious tastes. Yet he had a passion for fanciful hats. A reckless extravagance about them was his sole sartorial weakness, his one self-indulgence, his solitary concession to vanity. He possessed as astonishing an assortment of headgear as does Sir Winston Churchill. Sometimes he wore a certain straw creation, like an inverted waste-paper basket cockaded with a flurry of hornbill's feathers. At other times he donned a velvet Mohammedan cap trimmed with Scottish tartan ribbon, a conjunction of Islamic and Presbyterian symbols as fetching as it was unique. Another favourite style was a silk scarf wound round his grey locks at the rakish angle of a pirate's turban, and I have sometimes seen him adorn the turban with leaves, as if he were a laurel-crowned Caesar making a triumphal entry into Rome. That afternoon in his house he produced an even more bizarre conceit. He had acquired a length of white fur, and so fashioned it that it appeared like the headdress of a Russian ballerina in a winter scene in a ballet.

No one will wear with more sublime happiness his halo when he goes to Heaven.

Beside the old man sat a boy eight or nine years old, with straggly, long black hair, mischievous, sparkling dark eyes and a slim body clad only in a snow-white sirat. He was Kanyan, Koh's younger son, born to him in old age and now his pride and joy. The elder son had married and moved to a distant part of Sarawak, and no longer played a part in his father's life.

Gradually the great assembly of Iban penghulus, European officials, minor chiefs, long-house bucks, pagan priestesses, pantun

chanters, simple warriors, common housewives, husky children
and tiny infants settled in a deep semi-circle round me, some
sitting, some kneeling and some standing. The handmaidens of
the spirits brought a final set of plates for the bedara and arranged
them before me. A hush fell upon the crowd as Tedong announced
that all was ready for the show to commence.

Koh reached forward, and fitted a copper bracelet round
my wrist. Then I proceeded with the tedious business of concocting a feast for the goblins. Seizing an empty platter, I began
to heap food on it, one morsel joining another until the banquet
was fit to set before the supernatural beings.

When I had done this we were free to forget them for a while,
and to turn our thoughts to the entertainment of mortal men.
The pagans have ideas on this subject which do not distinguish
them greatly from people claiming to be more civilized. They
believe that the principal sources of man's happiness are three in
number, namely wine, women and song. That, at least, appears
to be the reason why the next part of the ceremony invariably
consists of charming females singing pantuns and dispensing tuak.

The girls who were to perform moved forward to the attack.
They knelt in a row before me, a quartette especially selected for
their feminine attraction. Mindun was their leader. She was
handsome rather than beautiful, and nearer her thirties than her
'teens. Her figure was perhaps somewhat too heavy; but she
had a brilliant flash of personality, and her vivacious nature gave
an infectious gaiety to her smile.

Her three companions were younger maidens, with fresh, delicious, beguiling prettiness. One girl I recognized as Siah and
another as her sister Sani. Their faces had tranquil beauty and
their forms left nothing to be desired. Yet the third girl was
the loveliest of them all. She had a touching, tender quality
in her looks. Instinctively I knew that she was Segura, Koh's
youngest daughter, the delightful child whom I had met in Kapit
three years earlier. Now the bud had burst into flower. She
sat before us transformed, in all the glory of young womanhood.

She was shy. Her eyes stared demurely towards the floor, her
lower lip trembled slightly, and one hand clasped nervously

her elder sister Mindun's hand. The words of a popular song passed through my mind:

I took one look at her
And then my heart stood still.

Segura was now the age of Juliet when Romeo fell in love with her, and she had a similar dark, magical, bewitching beauty. In her long black hair exquisite posies of tropical flowers were set. Her slanting, almond-shaped eyes had dark lustre, her nose was small with delicately arched nostrils, her lips were tilted upwards at each corner with an expression like an enigmatic smile, and her chin was firmly modelled. She had golden-brown, flawless skin.

Although there was a touch of sophistication about her careful coiffure and elegant attire, her beauty was as yet immature. She was still too young for more than a hint of her character to appear in her features. That firm chin certainly indicated a strong will. Perhaps the line of her nose and the arch of her nostrils foretold a passionate nature. Possibly, too, a proud glance which sometimes flashed in her eyes was a warning of quick temper. In any case it suggested that she was what is called "spoiled". Nothing could be more natural than that. Her father doted on her, and she was doubtless accustomed now to the admiration of other men. No youth in his senses could fail to be affected by her adorable looks.

Some of these details I observed only later, as I came to know her better. At that first glimpse after the opening bedara I noticed little more than the loveliness of her face and the enchantment of her body. Like Mindun, Siah and Sani, she was scantily and glamorously clad. I have already mentioned the bouquets of flowers adorning her hair. In her pretty ears hung small golden ear-rings, a single gold necklace depended above her bosom, and many silver and ivory bracelets almost covered her forearms. Below her round, twin breasts a girdle of coiled silver encircled her waist and hips, neatly fitting their graceful curves, and beneath it a short, woven red and yellow skirt fell to her knees.

Segura played only a passive part in the first bedara. Mindun sang most of the pantuns. In a subdued, high-pitched, sing-song voice she expressed her people's welcome to me. The extravagance of her flattery was tempered by sobering shafts of wit. Commenting, for example, on the fact that I was wearing a tartan kilt, she remarked that I had come attired in the most extraordinary pair of trousers ever seen on the Balleh River.

There was nothing bashful about Mindun. One of the most practised pantun singers in Sarawak, she was cocksure, artful and friendly. At the end of her song she handed me a tumblerful of tuak, maintaining her purposeful grip on the glass until I had drained every drop.

Then she turned her attention to Dawson, improvising a ditty for him. At the same time Siah raised her voice and composed an ode to Barcroft, while a male singer squatting in front of Jill Dawson droned a saga to her. The gallery seemed to be, like Elizabethan England, "a nest of singing birds".

When this preliminary bout of carolling and carousing ended, I made a presentation to Temonggong Koh. He was an admirer of those ancient Chinese earthenware jars which came to Borneo as trade goods several centuries ago. Indeed, he was as keen and discriminating a collector as any customer of Captain Spink, Mr. Sparks or the Bluett brothers in London. I had found one of these venerable pots in a curio shop in Singapore, bought it for sixty dollars and transported it with loving care by aeroplane, motor car, launch and prahu across the South China Sea, through Kuching, up the Rejang River and along the Balleh to this savage prince of connoisseurs.

As the jar's shimmering green glaze and encrusted design emerged from its packing, his eyes gleamed with acquisitive pleasure. When it was wholly revealed, standing three feet tall, he stroked it appraisingly, scrutinized critically the detail of its pattern, exchanged scholarly comments with other native authorities squatting on the floor, and then pronounced it worthy of inclusion in his collection. Willie Geikie, who shares Koh's and my weakness for such objects, told me afterwards that it belonged to a category of ware which the Ibans value at about two hundred dollars.

The afternoon was now well advanced. Having celebrated the

introductory rites of our merry meeting, we decided to permit ourselves an hour or two of rest and relaxation prior to the programme of amusement arranged for the evening. So the assembly broke up. In any case our hosts had much to do in preparation for the later proceedings. The girls got busy fetching gourds of water from the river, the women retired to their rooms to cook food for the household's evening meal, the men discussed points of etiquette which had yet to be settled in connection with the supreme ceremony to be celebrated on the morrow, and we all had a wash and brush-up for the night's party.

II

I roamed along the outside platform taking photographs, and then descended to the river for a swim. As I dressed afterwards a messenger came to bid me to a cocktail party—of all extraordinary phenomena in the jungle!—in Koh's room.

I entered the chief's private apartment and found it a hive of activity. Food was cooking on a crackling fire. Women stooped over pots preparing our dinner, girls arranged scores of saucers for bedaras yet to be performed, men squatted in a circle on the floor eating supper from bowls of rice, and children scampered all over the place.

In charge of the culinary operations was a small, elderly woman with a wrinkled face and thinning grey hair. She was exceedingly busy, and saw to it that the rest of her team also worked like beavers. Yet she never spoke a word of command, exerting her authority by the subtle force of her quiet character as well as by her own efficient example. As Koh came forward to greet me, he beckoned to her. She joined us, and he introduced me to her. She was his bini, his wife. She beamed a glad, unaffected smile, made a simple welcoming gesture with her hands, and then trotted dutifully back to her labours.

The large apartment was divided by a wooden partition into two unequal sections. The smaller, inner room was Koh's private parlour, his sanctum sanctorum. The walls of this cosy chamber were draped with an array of coloured Iban rugs, giving it the decorated appearance of a miniature tapestry gallery. Here and

there hung a plumed war-cap, a feathered cloak or a parang in
its carved scabbard. Beneath them stood serried ranks of tall
Sung and Ming pottery jars, the finest specimens in the old man's
collection. They seemed numerous and ample enough to hide
the forty thieves, if those swashbucklers should ever turn up in
Borneo. Compared with the refined porcelains produced for
the Imperial palaces, these wares made for export to the barbarians
of the Spice Islands were rough; yet they had simple shapes and
decorations which were truly beautiful.

The room was like a small museum of Bornean works of art.
At that moment, however, it seemed devoted to the indulgence
of man's body rather than to the elevation of his mind. Around a
table sat a jovial group of friends: Jugah, Grinang, Tedong and
my half-dozen travelling companions. On the table stood a
group of bottles. Their only claim to a place in an art gallery
was the fact that they contained samples of the Iban art of brew-
ing rice-wine.

Koh took his place as host at the head of the table, and I
slipped into a proffered chair. Grinang and Tedong, aided and
abetted by Jugah, were in hilarious charge of the proceedings.
Evidently they had known privily of another stock of bottles, and
had already helped themselves liberally to their contents, for
they were in a mood more rollicking than is customary even in
the most naturally cheerful of men. It is time that the reader
knew more about these chiefs, as lively a trio of head-hunters as
ever trod a jungle path.

After Koh, Penghulu Jugah was the most influential Iban on
the Rejang. His manly face, swift to break into a laugh or
pucker in a frown, was a faithful expression of his vivid personality. Rapid in thought, quick in decision and energetic in action,
he was sometimes likened to "a human dynamo"; but the dynamo
was not always wholly under control. His mental processes
sometimes worked too quickly, and sometimes his emotions took
such command of him that those processes did not have time to
work at all. He was then inclined to be erratic in judgement
and impulsive in conduct. His intellect was sharper than Koh's,
but his intelligence was blunter. He produced brighter ideas
than the old man, but lacked the elder's mature ripeness of

thought. So he was a less sagacious leader than Koh. Nevertheless, his sincere, alert and charming nature made him a lovable man, and he was a power in the land.

Tedong was his younger brother. In many ways, in physique and character, they were alike. Yet Tedong had not been promoted from his present post of tuai rumah to the higher rank of penghulu. He possessed Jugah's impulsiveness, but not his intellectual gifts. His talk was as lively as Jugah's, yet his words did not carry the same weight. He was a lighter, lesser Jugah. A marked streak of the superficial in him inclined him to the pleasures rather than the serious things of life. I could imagine that when Jugah's mind was bent on politics and government, Tedong's would stray towards flirting and dancing. He, too, had charm, with a gallant, braggart air.

Penghulu Grinang was a complete contrast to the other two. They had quick, mercurial minds, but his appeared slothful. Their personalities were immediately attractive, while his seemed at first to be the reverse. And while they were both handsome men, he was distinctly ugly. His countenance had coarse, loutish features, like the comic mask of a clown. His eyes looked bleary, on his nose perched a pair of spectacles with lenses so dirty that it would have been difficult for even the sharpest sight to penetrate their obscurity, and his loose-lipped mouth was grotesquely large.

His history was interesting. As a youth he was a rip-roaring public menace. One day he went on a head-hunting spree, and successfully brought home his quarry. Caught by the Government, he was tried and cast in prison for several years. Behind iron bars he developed a surprising tendency to become a member of the intelligentsia. He learned a smattering of English and showed other signs of being a reformed character. In fact, he seemed promising material for the celebrated experiment of turning a poacher into a game-keeper; so when he left the penitentiary he was made a tuai rumah, and afterwards a penghulu—and the experiment worked. He has been a reasonably well-behaved and respected chief ever since, possessing especially an unrivalled knowledge of native law and custom. Yet he is not really a very solid type of character, being more interested in play than in work. Always on the look-out for fun, he had become

a self-appointed court jester in the long-houses of the upper
Rejang.

When Tedong and Grinang depart from the path of strict
sobriety they quickly infect a party with good fellowship. As
I sat in Koh's parlour that evening I saw that they already showed
a tendency to stray in that direction. With reckless generosity
they poured drinks into glasses and pushed them towards us.
When we all had bumpers in our hands Koh proposed a toast
which included hosts and guests alike. We honoured it with
enthusiasm.

Grinang had now established himself the master of our revels.
His uncouth face was lit by diabolical merriment, and his voice
had a husky wickedness like the speech of a witch. He reached
for my tumbler, to refill it. Holding up a bottle marked "Bols
gin", which in fact contained Chinese arak, he peered at the label
through his spectacles, licked his lips, grinned from ear to ear and
cried, "Champagne."

Barcroft warned me against the brew, remarking that it had a
swift and violent kick. So I refused it. Grinang looked dumbfounded. When I asked for a glass of undiluted soda-water, he
realized that this was a case of mental aberration. Looking at
me in sorrow rather than in anger, he humoured me by granting
my request.

Then he flourished the bottle again and pressed its contents
gleefully on the others, each in turn. Heedful of Barcroft's advice,
they all expressed a preference for something else. Not in the
least perturbed, Grinang emptied the arak, alias gin, alias champagne into glasses for Jugah, Tedong and himself. They tossed
it down without drawing breath.

Mindun walked into the room. Grinang called to her to join
us, so that we might have songs to accompany our wine. Ever
ready to oblige, she came to the table. Lifting a glass of tuak, she
held it suspended before my face and burst into the sing-song
gibberish of a pantun. As the verses finished she put the drink
to my lips. After a few sips I showed signs of resistance, but she
laughed and put her free hand half caressingly, half firmly round
the back of my neck. By its pressure she sought to fasten me
more closely to the tumbler as she tilted the wine at an angle

which made it spill down my throat. · But I disengaged myself.

Seizing the glass I said, "Neerup!", which means "Drink the rest yourself!"

Mindun yielded gracefully. Tedong handed her another glass of tuak. She carried it to Barcroft and repeated her performance. This time it had a different ending. Mindun felt that she could take a stronger line with the Resident, an old friend of the Ibans. When her song was over and she pushed the drink to his mouth, she placed her free hand so purposefully round the back of his neck and exerted such force that resistance by him would have meant a tough trial of strength. Chivalrously he resigned himself, and swallowed all that she offered.

Grinang loudly expressed his approval of these strong-arm methods, and with hearty applause we all concurred. Then Tedong shouted an Iban word which sounded like a command.

Grinang, resorting to that knowledge of English which he had acquired in prison, translated it.

"Keess!" he cried jovially, making the smacking sound of kissing with his lascivious lips.

"Keess!" repeated Tedong to Mindun.

She chuckled and did not hesitate. Replacing the empty tumbler on the table, she seized Barcroft's head between her hands and pressed her mouth to his. He accepted the gift in the generous spirit in which it was offered.

Mindun next took a glass of tuak to Dilks. When he had quaffed it and she laid down the empty tumbler, Grinang called jocularly, "Keess!" The whole company repeated the cry like a refrain. But neither Mindun nor Dilks needed any form of compulsion. They saluted each other with robust goodwill.

It was Gilliat's turn next, and then Geikie's and then Dawson's. All acquitted themselves like men, following the pattern now set for every performance. Even Grinang, with his exacting standards in such matters, had no fault to find with them.

At that point a delicate question of etiquette arose. Jill Dawson must have a pantun sung to her, but it could not be by Mindun. Even if she should sing the ditty and hold the drink, it seemed hardly appropriate for her to perform the further service which was now added to the rites. Obviously this was a man's

privilege. Grinang, Tedong and Jugah competed for it, and to
Jill's relief Jugah got his way. He was most gentlemanly. After
chanting a few verses and offering her a sip of tuak, he leaned
forward and touched her cheek ever so lightly with his lips, with
the courtly decorum of a Spanish grandee kissing a lady's hand.

After that Mindun did the honours as hostess to the two
penghulus and Tedong. Hilarity was high as she exchanged
courtesies first with Jugah, then with his brother and finally with
Grinang. The last named was not content with the allowance
of one kiss which was now the established ration. Adopting
the passionate attitude of a lorn lover in a melodramatic opera,
he demanded a second. When Mindun refused it voluntarily,
he stole it by force.

We relapsed into a period of conversation. Koh told us the
latest news of life on the Balleh. His household's padi harvest
was gathered and had been plentiful. Some other houses were
less fortunate. Their crops were below average, and several
would have no surplus rice for sale. A few had insufficient even
to feed their own people, and must buy supplies elsewhere. Wild
pigs were numerous and had helped themselves to large quantities of the grain.

We asked many questions, and the discussion might have been
protracted if Grinang had not felt it his duty to check this serious
turn of events. Two or three untouched bottles still stood on the
table, to be disposed of before dinner. He drew our attention
to them. Koh, too, was anxious that his hospitality should be
abundant. He sent for Segura to come and help Mindun to
entertain us.

The young girl came into the room quietly, unobtrusively, as
if she hoped that her arrival would be unnoticed. She looked
lovely, though her beauty was not lit by a smile. Her face was
impassive, expressing neither pleasure nor displeasure. She was
still so shy of us that any other feeling in her seemed numb. Her
eyes avoided looking at us, except when she thought that she
could steal a quick, undetected, inquisitive glance.

Koh asked her to pour me a drink, and she did so dutifully.
She gave a forced, embarrassed smile when Grinang bade her
compose a pantun for me, mopping her brow with a handker-

chief. The room was warm, but she was coolly clad and no perspiration stood on her forehead. Her gesture was one of nervousness. But everyone awaited the pantun, and she had no choice but to sing. After a few moments she began in a small, sweet voice to recount what she had heard others speak of my virtues. Her eyes never shifted their gaze from the floor.

The company murmured encouragingly when she ceased singing and handed me the wine. I drank half of it, and returned the rest to her.

"Keess!" called Grinang with a joyous cackle.

"Keess!" cried Tedong and Jugah.

"Keess!" said Mindun.

Segura gave a half-hearted laugh, and looked around as if to see where she could escape.

"Keess! Keess! Keess!" repeated the Don Juans in chorus. Others took up the refrain.

Segura still hesitated, a polite but uneasy smile on her lips. To end her embarrassment I rose and gave her a light, paternal salutation on one cheek.

The company clapped and laughed. Koh passed another tumbler down the table for Segura to offer Barcroft.

She sang a brief pantun and held up a cup of wine to each visitor in turn. Every time when the moment came for her to seal the ceremony with a kiss, she held back, reluctant and shy. She had none of the easy light-heartedness of her sister.

When she finished the round, she came and stood near me. I felt sad that I could not speak with her in her mother tongue. Through Barcroft I asked her whether she recollected our last meeting when we watched Iban dancing and a Malay opera at Kapit. She grinned and answered that she remembered it very well.

Conversation started again. Talk turned on the significance of the ceremonial which we would witness on the morrow. I told Koh that we could stay only one night in his house, for we were committed to engagements in Kuching three days later, and so had to leave the Balleh by the following noon. Koh and the other chiefs tried to persuade us to remain a second night, since the celebration should normally occupy forty-eight hours.

We would gladly have agreed, but could not. This involved speeding up the programme of events proposed for the next morning, and there was much discussion about the best means of doing that.

In the middle of the talk Segura brought a chair and sat beside me. Without saying a word she slipped her hand into mine with childish friendliness and held it fast.

The discussion continued for some time. Periodically Grinang and Tedong tried to circulate the bottles again, but we all prudently kept a few mouthfuls of tuak in our glasses as an excuse for refusing further refills. We knew that a long night of pagan sociability stretched before us. Eventually Koh rose to his feet and made a gracious speech of thanks to us for our visit to his house. I replied, saying that the gratitude was due from us to him, since it was a rare delight to be guests in his jungle home.

After that the company dispersed. The Ibans went to resume their various duties in the house, and we visitors stayed to dine in the Temonggong's parlour. We parted with mutual promises to meet again in an hour's time, when the evening's round of gaiety would commence.

III

The first few hours after dinner passed rather dully. There were thirty-eight private rooms in the house, and each family wished us to conduct a separate bedara with it. If our whole party had performed the sacred rites at every door, these solemnities alone would have kept us fully occupied till morning. Therefore we divided forces, each member of the company conducting the ceremony at an allotted number of rooms. By this device many hands made light work. Unfortunately for me, several householders felt particular about the status of the person who should serve meat and drink to their spirits. None but a Commissioner-General for the United Kingdom in South-East Asia would satisfy their requirements, so I had to take on several extra bedaras in addition to my agreed portion.

Hour after hour I crouched on my haunches, throwing rations

of tuak to the hobgoblins, concocting huge dishes of food for their delight, and murmuring words of blessing as I brandished protesting cockerels over the feasts. In each room the family concerned sat round me; each fitted a new copper bracelet on my arm; and every time when the sprites were duly fed, the wife or daughter of the room knelt before me, sang a pantun and held up a glass of wine for my refreshment. The chant ended, I would swallow a few mouthfuls and return the rest to the girl.

Throughout these labours Koh stayed faithfully beside me, though his eye-lids drooped with sleepiness and every now and then his chin fell on his chest as he dozed for a few moments. At length our charitable effort for the good and evil spirits was completed. The last plate of viands was offered, the last pantun sung, the last drop of wine drunk. I was stiff with squatting and bored with reiterated ceremonial, and rose with relief to walk towards sounds of revelry issuing along the gallery.

A large audience was gathered round a space of floor for dancers. My fellow Europeans and such other personages as still remained awake sat in the front row beside the stage. Grinang was there, with Jugah and Rabong. Mindun, Segura, Siah and Sani were also prominent in the company. I had not seen them for several hours. They looked charming in their evening dresses, having taken as much trouble to adorn themselves for the show as fashionable Western ladies do when patronizing the opera. The principle on which they achieved this on the Balleh River, however, was the opposite of that adopted in Covent Garden. In the West women, having covered their bodies amply throughout the day, incline to discard a deal of clothing in the evening. The girls in Koh's house, on the other hand, having been nearly naked all day, now appeared in costumes which covered them from head to foot. They had donned long-sleeved, broad-busted and narrow-waisted Malay blouses, with sarongs reaching to their ankles. It only went to show how incalculable feminine fashions are.

Segura and Siah received me with fond cries, and shifted their positions to make a space for me between them. As I sat down they slipped their arms through mine. Grinang observed this show of friendship with approval tempered by envy. He called warningly to me that the girls were two of his favourite wives. They hotly repudiated his claim and laughed with merry disdain.

Not even their beguiling company, however, persuaded me that the entertainment that evening was high-class. The music was tuneful, but the dancers were unworthy of it. Perhaps I had become too blasé about pagan dancing. I had by now watched some of the finest Kayan and Kenyah exponents of the art, and my trained eye was no longer satisfied with anything but the best. However, the indifference of the floor show did not matter. A festive mood animated the crowd of head-hunters, and the atmosphere was charged with good fellowship. The evening needed no other stimulant.

As the night advanced, some members of the audience tired and drifted away. Barcroft went to Koh's room to discuss with the old chief the order of events to occur when day should dawn. Jill Dawson withdrew to snatch a few hours of sleep. I noticed Christopher Dawson on the outer edge of the crowd engaged in earnest conversation with an intelligent-looking native. He told me the next morning of the topic which so engrossed him during the small hours. The Iban with whom he talked had spoken of the good and evil spirits.

"We all have our attendant spirits," the pagan said. "Not only us men, but the women too. Each individual has his or her constant, invisible companion. I'm not sure whether children have them; perhaps the spirits are only concerned with grown-ups. If you lose your spirit, if it leaves you, you die. While life lasts, it accompanies you everywhere. If it's bad, nothing will go right. If a warrior going into battle isn't followed by a spirit who is a staunch, brave fighter, he'll not come through alive. These companions are always with us. We can't see them, of course, nor hear them, but they're perpetually around. They're in this room, for example—the spirits of all of us. We can't tell exactly where they are. Perhaps mine is sitting here, on this side of me, or perhaps it's over there on the other side. Though we don't see them, they see us and listen to us. They know everything we say and do, and everything that's going on. They're very important. Their influence settles all that happens to us."

The native spoke much more in this strain, and Dawson listened, fascinated. He asked many questions and received answers, catching a revealing glimpse of the innermost pagan mind.

The spirit who attended upon me that evening was evidently in indulgent mood. It allowed me to have an enchanting time. The revels continued late. Dancer followed dancer, performing many wild capers. Every enterprising male in the audience took his turn. Dilks, with the ease of a good District Officer in a Dayak area, did an Iban war dance several times. I performed once, with less skill.

For the rest, I sat and watched the entertainment with deep pleasure. Those who usually spend their time grappling with the awful, frustrating problems which modern civilized societies have created for themselves can best appreciate the sensible simplicity of life among primitive peoples. I felt happy, lolling on the long-house floor and watching with carefree mind the playful gambols of my "savage" friends. The house was wrapped in peace; its tranquillity could not have been more profound. No serious troubles worried these Ibans. Round me in the dim-lit gallery were none but gay, smiling faces; and at my side sat Segura, as contented as a kitten. She watched the dancing with appreciative eyes, and every now and then turned her face to look at me, to make sure that I enjoyed the fun as much as she did. We could not exchange a word with each other, for I was as ignorant of her language as she was of mine. That did not seem to make any difference to our sense of companionship.

The music and dancing continued until past three o'clock in the morning. Then they ceased and we all yawned, grinned, murmured "Salamat teedor", and went to bed.

IV

Barcroft and I pitched our camp-beds in a temporary hut which our hosts had built for us on the long-house verandah. I slept deeply until six o'clock in the morning, when I was wakened by the squealing of a pig.

The disturbance arose just outside our hut. Peering through the doorway, I saw that the sun had not yet risen. The faint glimmer of earliest dawn was hardly strong enough to illumine the scene, but on the platform outside I detected dimly a solitary human figure bending over an object at his feet. Another squeal escaped from the object. It was a young pig lying helpless on the ground, its four legs pinioned to the shaft of a spear. The man was endeavouring to make the poor little animal as comfortable as circumstances permitted, so that it might rest quietly and not annoy us. He stood erect, and I recognized Temonggong Koh.

No one else was stirring, but the remarkable old man was already at work, preparing for the celebration timed to begin some two hours later. It was as if the Duke of Norfolk, the hereditary Earl Marshal of England, who is responsible for organizing the ceremony when British kings are crowned, were to arrive at Westminster Abbey at crack of dawn on Coronation morning to make personally the final dispositions in the church.

The pig was a sacrificial beast, to be killed at a certain moment in the day's rites. Koh felt solicitous about its comfort during its few remaining hours of life. He started to construct an awning over it, to shade it from the heat of the later sun. My heart warmed to the old penghulu.

Daylight slowly increased, and more natives began to emerge from the house. I rose and dressed. As I shaved near the door the pig eyed me in dumb appeal, and I felt guilty, for I knew that I myself would be its executioner. I dislike killing animals. This little creature had done me no harm, and my sympathies lay entirely with it. Yet I could not, without causing deep hurt to our hosts' feelings, resign my post as the principal dignitary officiating at the traditional and, for them, sacred ritual about to be performed. So I averted my gaze from the pig and continued to lather my chin.

Women from the house trooped in small, single file processions across the verandah and down the staircases to the river, to take their morning baths and fetch water for the household. Men likewise went to bathe, and then engaged in various tasks. We ate our breakfast at odd intervals. All the time Koh and his lieutenants were putting finishing touches to the decorations of the house. The whole place was a scene of busy preparation for a grand event.

When all else was ready, the Ibans dressed in their best attire. At many places along the verandah I could see men unwinding long, black work-a-day sirats from their loins, and carefully donning sirats of blue or scarlet in their place. Indoors young women were discarding their plain sarongs and adorning themselves like brides with flowers, jewellery and coloured finery. Chiefs who were to play important parts in the show clothed themselves in the barbaric splendour of feathered caps, fur cloaks and clanking parangs.

I, too, was to appear in wild garb. Tedong dressed me with the professional care of a valet robing an opera singer for a stage appearance. Round my waist he buckled a leather belt with a sheathed sword, over my shoulders he hung a cloak of goat's hair, and on my head he set a beaded war-cap crowned with Argus-pheasant plumes. Then Koh garlanded me with a large, rough copper-wire collar, the emblem of office of a dignitary about to conduct hallowed pagan rites.

At last everything was ready for the special ceremony called gawai nanga rumah, which is performed on occasions when the gods are believed to visit a house. It is naturally a rare occurrence. That is just as well, for customarily the attendant feasting and fun last with little break through two days and nights.

At an agreed signal I descended the main staircase to the river, followed by Temonggong Koh and Penghulu Grinang. There Mindun handed me a bumper of tuak which I flung into the Balleh as a preliminary gesture of goodwill to the spirits. At that a salute of nineteen guns began to roar from cannon on the platform above, and I and my faithful chieftains started with sedate steps to ascend again to the house. On the topmost step Segura gave me a second goblet of wine, which followed the way of the first. I had not seen her since the dancing of the previous night, and was glad to observe that the belated revels left no trace of tiredness on her features. She looked as lovely as a fresh flower.

On the verandah at my feet lay the little pig, surprisingly quiet. Jugah stood beside it holding a spear. He handed me the weapon. Placing its tip above the animal's throat, I swiftly drove it down through the jugular vein. The beast died without a quiver, and a deep sigh of gratification escaped the crowd of natives at this fulfilment of the sacrifice.

I turned my face from the slaughter and saw Segura smiling kindly at me. She held out to me another glass of wine, which I swallowed at one gulp. Then Koh led us into the house, where food for a bedara was spread in the centre of the gallery. We squatted in our places to play our various parts in the well-known drill.

I performed the bedara. Since the meal was to go not to mere spirits, but to the gods themselves, it included a cup of chicken's blood, a drink particularly pleasing to the holy ones. The feast prepared, I was entertained with ditties and drinks by Mindun and Segura. Then Dawson received his meed of song and tuak, and Barcroft and others were similarly honoured. Siah and Sani did duty with Mindun and Segura, chanting pantuns and dispensing wine. All the girls had completely lost their shyness, and were full of joviality.

Grinang was sober, yet still sparkling. Periodically he interrupted the pantuns to shout outrageous gallantries at the singers. His sallies always brought a laugh. The whole assembly of natives was in cheerful, elated mood.

I was permitted to take off my head-hunting warrior's garb, for furs and feathers were hot under the equatorial sun. Dawson, however, had to don the full regalia of fancy dress, for he was to perform one of the most remarkable parts of the gawai. He was actually to wait upon the gods, to hand them the food which I had prepared for them. In fact he played the head waiter to my chef.

On the roof-top of the long-house, over the centre of the building, the Ibans had constructed a small, one-roomed hut, looking rather like a mountaineer's shelter skied in solitude on an Alpine ridge. A bamboo stairway led steeply from the verandah to the eaves of the dwelling and thence up the roof to this refuge. Both the stairway and the hut were fancifully decorated with foliage and flowers.

The pagans assert that on the occasion of a gawai the gods visit this roof dwelling. It would be their lodging for the duration of the festival. Expediency, as well as reverence, therefore demanded that they should be plentifully provided with meat and drink, so that they found no fault with the attentions paid to them. Dawson was to perform this service. Accoutred in pagan uniform, he scaled the improvised ladder to the holy of holies, like a mediæval hermit climbing into a cave in a cliff face. Unlike a hermit, however, he did not make the journey alone. He was followed into his cell by a troupe of attendants such as would have delighted the heart of one of the least worthy ascetics in Boccaccio's *Decameron*. Segura, Siah and Sani all went to aid him in his religious duties. Up the staircase with them went enough food and drink to nourish an army of gods through a protracted siege.

None of us less privileged mortals was allowed to set foot on even the lowest rung of the ladder leading to their paradise. A strict taboo barred access to it. So no eye-witness saw what occurred to Dawson and his elect company in their retreat, and no reliable report of their conduct ever came down to earth. They tarried aloft for half an hour, during which time Dawson states that he officiated at a particularly conscientious bedara. The look of beatitude on his face when he descended certainly seemed to indicate that he had been vouchsafed some extraordinarily inspiring experience. That is all that I can tell about the climax of the day's proceedings.

While Dawson was hob-nobbing with the gods above, we mere men below were far from idle. We engaged in a complex operation intended to assist him in his good work. A stout pole had been erected in the gallery immediately below the roof hut. Rising from the floor to the ceiling, it disappeared through the rafters, penetrated the shingles and entered the house of the gods itself. A long piece of cloth hung from it. When Dawson and his attendants were established upstairs, Koh and Jugah built a rattan fence round the foot of this pole and covered it with Iban blankets and branches of trees. Inside the fence they placed a plate of food.

At this point Koh summoned my aid. I dressed once more in the garb of a barbarian chieftain and held a naked parang in one hand. Into the other hand Jugah thrust a light wooden object shaped like a tambourine, with innumerable long, thin strips of dry banana leaf like strings on a huge mop. They fluttered and rustled when I shook them. Koh was attired in full war garb, and he, too, held a drawn sword in one hand and a tambourine-mop in the other.

Assuming a stance facing the artificial fence, he invited me to join him there, and asked me to follow him in everything that he did. I promised faithful obedience. Koh then opened his mouth, hollered aloud in such a frightening way that for a moment my blood ran cold, and at the same time slashed the air with his sword and violently shook his mop. I imitated his sounds and gestures as exactly as I could. Then he started to march with lolloping, prancing steps round the fence, periodically beating the atmosphere with his sword, rustling his mop, and giving horrid shrieks. There was a distinct suggestion in his actions that he was driving unseen creatures away from the vicinity.

I followed suit, gambolling on my feet, gesticulating with my arms and sounding off with my mouth like a mad mullah, precisely as he did. Round and round the enclosure we went, causing a frightful hullabaloo. In my imagination I saw a host of ghost-like figures rushing helter-skelter from us in all directions.

A crowd of natives crouched on the gallery floor, watching closely every movement that we made. They were agog with interest, regarding our capers as a matter of serious import. For them the strange proceedings were sacred, and the mumbo-jumbo was charged with mysterious and hopeful significance. They observed it all with the reverent spirit of a congregation in church on a day of high religious festival.

After ten minutes of this pantomime Koh seemed to feel that our exertions had achieved whatever could be expected of them. He and I ceased our action and disrobed. Our discarded caps, cloaks and parangs were immediately donned by Jugah and Barcroft, who proceeded to repeat with their own noises and gestures the astonishing charades which we had just played.

Soon afterwards I was decoyed into celebrating another bedara. The episodes of the gawai then became as difficult to follow as

the simultaneous items in a three-ringed circus. Many different
events occurred at the same time. Dawson was still playing host
to the gods upstairs, Jugah and Barcroft were engaged in their
solemn tomfoolery in the gallery, I was back where I started
conducting a bedara on the floor, and Koh was now mustering a
company of fantastically costumed youths and girls for a procession.

Let me pause amidst this baffling multiplicity of frolics to
describe the significance of the ceremony as a whole. It related
principally to the person of Koh himself. To explain the situation I must refer to an earlier incident in his life, which Jugah
related to me.

Many years earlier, in 1916, when Koh was a comparatively
new penghulu, he had a remarkable dream. In his sleep he saw
visions indicating that if he would sacrifice to the gods and hold
converse with them, they would espouse his cause and ensure
that everything in life went well for him. Next morning he
made preparations for a gawai which would be symbolic of
a tryst between himself and the deities. On the roof-ridge of
his house he built a hut representing their residence in the sky,
and when the date for the solemnities arrived he climbed to it,
conducted bedaras, sacrificed a pig and celebrated other rites.
These actions seemed to create a happy impression on the gods,
for that day marked the beginning of his outstanding good fortunes, and ever afterwards he prospered.

The gawai in which we were now partaking was a sequel to
its predecessor thirty-three years earlier. Koh had grown old, and
his thoughts began to turn to the next world. He wished to
ensure that when he died and sought access to the Iban heaven,
he would receive a sympathetic welcome. He resolved, therefore, to make once more a special sacrifice to the gods who had
befriended him, to commune with them and seek their favour.
He chose the occasion of my visit to arrange a suitable event.

The hut on the roof symbolized the home of the gods in
heaven. The rattan fence in the gallery immediately below represented a long-house on earth—Koh's house. The tall post and
length of cloth between the two indicated the connection between
heaven and earth. They suggested the path which Koh would

take when, in due course, he left this world and joined the blessed dead in the Iban Elysian fields.

The feast which he offered the gods as a mark of his petition was prepared by my hands in the first bedara conducted that morning. It was borne to their symbolic dwelling place by Dawson. While he presented it to them above, the rest of us below abetted the general effort to ensure a happy meeting between Koh and his celestial guests. When the Temonggong and I, and then Jugah and Barcroft, indulged in wild antics and war-whoops round the representation of the chief's long-house, we were warding off possible enemies, shooing away ill-disposed demons, so that Koh would be free from unfriendly obstructions and ultimately make an unimpeded passage to the next world.

Some of the principal contrivances in this picturesque jiggery-pokery, such as the god-house on the roof, were copied from other gawais which had a communal rather than a personal significance. Experts told me that various bits of the ceremony were borrowed from different gawais of one sort or another. But several features, as well as the general plan and sequence, were Koh's own invention. In this way the ceremony was unique*.

In due course Dawson and his party descended from the roof. Tedong, martially apparelled, then assumed command of the procession which Koh had meantime mobilized. He walked at its head with a swaggering strut, and behind him came young bucks beating drums and gongs. Maidens dressed in beads from head to foot followed, and in their wake strolled a rabble of men, women and children. With percussion instruments loudly beating a slow, ramshackle, tuneless tattoo, this oddly assorted pageant meandered first the whole length of the gallery and then the whole length of the verandah, like villagers in old England beating the bounds of their land. After that they dispersed.

Then some new fun commenced. Jugah and Barcroft were still dressed in all the finery that they could accommodate on their

---

* When I asked Jugah whether, following Koh's earlier success with his gawai, any other chief had celebrated it for his own personal advantage, Jugah replied in the affirmative. He said that he himself, Penghulu Grinang and Penghulu Sibat had copied it in their homes, and added that the three had all enjoyed more than usual good fortune since.

persons, with unsheathed swords and tambourine-mops gripped in their hands. They left the vicinity of the symbolic long-house and proceeded to a far end of the gallery. In front of the farthest door they shook their parangs and tambourines threateningly, at the same time shouting defiant cat-calls. They were challenging any evil spirits who might still lurk on the premises to come and be vanquished. None appeared, and the two champions accepted offerings of tuak from a grateful female inmate of the room. They then advanced with jaunty, dancing gait and horrid yells of provocation to the next door, where they repeated the operation. No ghostly foes emerged, and again they received from maidenly hands the reward of a drink. As soon as it was swallowed, they pranced to the third door and once more played their part. So it was before every one of the thirty-eight rooms in the house. At each the valiant warriors brandished their weapons, shook their tambourines and uttered their threats, and at each they sipped cups of nectar brewed from fermented rice.

When they had finished, they handed their costumes and weapons to Grinang and Dilks, who promptly donned them and disappeared to the far end of the gallery. Awful yells and merry laughter issuing from their direction indicated that the new pair of knights-errant were repeating the performance of the old. Deliberately they went from door to door, hopping and yelling, gesticulating and drinking, down the whole length of the house. When they finished the journey, they handed their properties to Tedong and Geikie, who in turn started at one end of the long chamber and with hollerings and caperings imitated exactly the conduct of their predecessors. After that Jinggut and Gilliat did it all over again.

Before the completion of this episode, Koh summoned me to officiate at yet another bedara. This time it took place on the outside platform. The food was spread on an Iban mat under the scorching mid-day sun, and all who joined in the event had to wear large sun-hats to avoid being roasted alive. On this occasion pretty Siah sang the pantun and handed me the wine.

Nearly five hours had now passed since the ceremonies began. The programme had proceeded without a moment's halt or hesitation. All of us had been perpetually engaged. When we were not actually performing a part, we were changing costumes between one act and the next. Now it was noon. Rites and revels would continue through the rest of the day, most of the night and into the morrow. But, alas, we European visitors could not wait for more. We must bid good-bye to our friends and return downriver.

Once more they tried to prevail on us to stay, but reluctantly we insisted that we had no choice but to go. So Koh announced that we should celebrate a final bedara in the gallery, and into the house we all trooped. Every man, woman, child and babe in the dwelling gathered for this farewell act. Nearly three hundred people thronged the space round the mats where the fare for the spirits was spread.

My fellow guests and I sat cross-legged along one edge of the mats, like a row of old-fashioned tailors. Before us were scores of saucers filled with the usual food. Beyond them, facing us, knelt Mindun and Segura, Siah and Sani. At their back Koh sat in state on a wicker chair, like a jungle king enthroned. His son Kanyan lolled in his lap, with an odd mixture of childish innocence and royal arrogance in the glances of his eyes. Beside the old chief and the young princeling crouched a row of penghulus and tuai tuai rumah, while all around squatted the vast assemblage of commoners.

Two bedaras were performed simultaneously, one by Dawson and the other by Barcroft. Siah and Sani acted as their serving maids in this last effort at pacification of the sprites. Mindun and Segura stayed strangely inactive and silent. They looked nervous, as if a more testing ordeal lay before them. Even Mindun seemed less composed than usual, appearing affected by some emotional stress. Segura's eyes were downcast and her face was rigidly impassive. It had become once more that beautiful, expressionless mask which she wore when suffering an attack of stage fright. Her breathing, noticeable in the rise and fall of her bosom, betrayed agitation, and one of her hands was outstretched for a comforting clasp in Mindun's.

In due course Dawson and Barcroft completed their culinary tasks and placed their dishes in bamboo lodgements. A loud, throaty mumble of gratitude rose from the crowd.

Then all eyes turned to Mindun and Segura. So something *was* expected of them, and they were now to act their parts. Visibly they braced themselves for a special effort. Mindun unclasped her sister's hand, and at that Segura seemed to come to life again, like a person waking from a trance. Deftly the two girls poured tuak into several tumblers and set them in a row, ready for our refreshment when the moment came. But first they must sing.

A profound, expectant hush fell upon the assembly. For a few more moments the girls stayed motionless and quiet, then they exchanged glances and inclined their heads slightly to each other as a signal. Gently they broke the silence with a song.

In several ways this chant differed from the pantuns with which I was familiar. First, the two girls sang together, and a duet is a rare occurrence in Iban music. Then the song was not, like a pantun, a monotonous dirge, but a sweetly tuneful melody. In addition, whereas a pantun is usually performed in uninspired accents, as if it were mechanically produced, the tones of this singing expressed spontaneous emotion. I could not understand the words, yet quickly realized from the grace of their sounds and the rapt mood in which the audience listened that they too must be unusual. They were, in fact, not impromptu doggerel, but eternal poetry. Mindun and Segura were chanting some timeless ballad of the Iban race.

As they sang, they threw significant glances towards my travelling companions and me.

Geikie whispered to me a translation of their phrases:

> *The flowers and butterflies go together.*
> *If the butterflies do not tend the flowers,*
> *The flowers will fade.*

The soft, tremulous soprano of the girls hung in the air like jewels of sound. The sisters used no tricks to gain an effect; their performance had a sincere, heart-touching simplicity and beauty.

Somehow a sense of sadness had stolen into the atmosphere, evoked by the feelings of all present. It expressed the thought that precious moments were slipping away, that devoted friends were about to part, and that the sorrow, not the joy, of human affection now lay upon us.

At the close of two verses the song ended. No one sought to disturb the quiet which followed, for all were under a spell of sentiment.

After a few moments Segura turned to Mindun and whispered something to her. Mindun nodded assent and soon they began to chant again.

Smiles spread on the faces of the listening natives. Grinang beamed wickedly, while into Mindun's and Segura's eyes crept playful twinkles.

Again Geikie translated the words for me:

> *Many of us women have husbands,*
> *Yet when you leave we shall feel that we are*
> *torn from dear companions.*

Grinang's discordant voice broke into the harmony. "Don't worry," he called banteringly, "I'll still be here."

A burst of laughter greeted this characteristic intervention.

Mindun and Segura continued singing for a while. When they ceased, the audience applauded. Then again Segura murmured something to Mindun, and as soon as the bravos and handclaps subsided they started to sing once more. This time their theme was serious again. Suddenly I saw tears moisten the eyes of many onlookers, even hardened penghulus looking a trifle tender-hearted.

Geikie whispered to me, "The song says:

> *There are moments that can never be*
> *forgotten in a whole lifetime."*

The sweet voices of the girls quivered, for they were now deeply affected, and only with difficulty continued to sing. Their sadness gave the performance an exquisite, fragile quality.

I glanced at Koh. He sat relaxed in his chair, a look of contentment on his old face. One arm was thrown fondly round the shoulders of his son, and his eyes gazed with happiness upon his two daughters. He seemed the very embodiment of paternal pride.

When the song ended and the performers' voices fell silent, no one stirred or spoke. Segura was the first to make a movement. She stretched out a hand, grasped a glass of tuak and raised it towards me. Her eyes and lips smiled enchantingly.

I swallowed the tumblerful of wine.

Segura put down the empty glass, then shifted nearer to me and took both my hands in hers. She tilted her face to be kissed, and we saluted each other with an affection which left even Grinang dumb with admiration.

Mindun held up a glass for me. I disposed of its contents with similar despatch, for this was an occasion to express unreserved gratitude for superlative friendship. The ritual with Mindun also ended in an embrace.

These sincere examples were followed by Dawson, Barcroft, Geikie, Dilks and Gilliat when fair hands proffered them wine and fair faces looked into their eyes. Iban men may have abandoned the practice of taking heads, but Iban women have not lost the art of taking hearts.

When the exchanges were complete, we visitors decided that it was our turn to contribute a song as a grand conclusion to this memorable meeting. We proposed that the whole company should link arms and sing "Auld Lang Syne".

Temonggong Koh and his chiefs and people were mystified by this suggestion, but entered into it with the zest of children learning a new game. Before long a huge chain of handclasps joined everyone round the gallery. We started the strains of "Should auld acquaintance be forgot", and soon the mixed male and female voices of three hundred Ibans were humming the tune with a sound like a gathering storm. As we quickened the pace and began the faster handshakes which introduce its climax, their chanting gained in volume and gusto, until the house began to tremble to the rhythm of the choir. Never in Scotland's hills and glens did the old lament receive a more vigorous rendering.

At last the moment for departure had come. Countless hands were stretched forward on all sides for final comradely exchanges. We were long delayed, bidding good-bye to eager members of the throng who crowded round us, shaking the fists of men, smiling at women and patting children on their heads.

"Salamat tingal!" we called to them.

"Salamat jalai!" they replied.

When at length we emerged from the gallery on to the verandah, we found the penghulus and principal women drawn up in two formal rows to take leave of us. I looked along the rank of feathered warriors and admired the rough, strong character in their faces; then I glanced upon the female column and was touched again by their exotic charm. I felt a close intimacy with these simple, kindly people, in whose homes I had dwelt with so much enjoyment, as if they and I were members of one family.

Moving along the row of women, I shook hands and said "Tabeh" to each in turn. When I came to Siah, Sani and Mindun I kissed them gently in farewell.

I did the same to Segura. At that a sorrowful little cry broke from her. Suddenly she flung her arms round my neck and kissed me many times on both cheeks. For a while our lingering good-bye halted the progress of departure.

Nobody minded that. Various fond adieus were being said. An uninitiated stranger arriving on the scene might have supposed that we were a troop of fighting men about to embark on a dangerous head-hunting expedition, bidding farewell to wives and sweethearts before leaving the security of our homes.

Afterwards I walked along the line of penghulus, taking leave of each of them. When I came to Grinang, I looked appreciatively upon his uncouth, ruffianly features. Our revels owed much to his boundless capacity for fun.

"Keess!" I shouted in grateful mimicry of him, and gave him a filial embrace.

This delighted him hugely, and set a precedent which he, Jugah and Tedong all followed when they said good-bye to the rest of my astonished party.

Last of all I came to Koh, standing at the head of the high stairway sloping steeply from the platform to the river. The Grand Old Gentleman of Borneo looked tired, but that did not affect his imperturbable dignity. In one hand he held a small basket made of fresh banana leaf, containing a boiled egg, some rice and other trifling viands. He gave it to me and begged that I would keep it wherever I travelled for the next three days, as a ticket of safe-conduct through the world of ill-disposed spirits.

Then he led the way down the tree-trunk stairway. Our party followed, and behind us descended Mindun and Segura and all the chiefs.

As we embarked in our long-boats, the group of Ibans stayed at the water's edge. A hot sun beat down upon us all. Segura opened a blue parasol and held it over her dark head.

Our oarsmen dipped their paddles and took a few strokes, and the craft began to move towards mid-stream. Then the penghulus on the bank started a long, haunting wail which is a pagan farewell. Mindun unfolded a handkerchief to wave to us, but burst into tears and hid her face in it instead. For a moment Segura too looked miserable, and laid a hand over her heart in an impulsive gesture of sorrow. Then she asserted her self-control, smiled gaily and waved her sunshade.

The throng of natives on the verandah echoed the wailing cry, and we uttered it mournfully in reply. To an accompaniment of yells and counter-yells our boats gathered speed and slipped down-river.

With heartfelt emotion I reflected,

> *There are moments that can never be*
> *forgotten in a whole lifetime.*

V

The flood waters were swift and we reached Kapit in less than five hours. There we bathed and rested, dined and slept the night.

On one arm I still wore the collection of copper bangles presented by various families at bedaras, and round my neck hung the metal collar which Koh had placed there at the commencement of the gawai. When I undressed I unfastened these rough articles of pagan vestment and laid them with my clothes. Next morning I did not replace them on my body. I felt for them warm attachment, and would have liked to continue wearing them, but I feared lest friends in Singapore might misinterpret

their significance. If I appeared braceletted and cravatted in bits
of old ironmongery, they might suspect that I had turned heathen
or gone cuckoo up the Balleh River.

So I reluctantly decided that I must abandon these relics of
Iban favour. Yet I disliked the thought of leaving them for other
hands to touch. They were mine and mine alone, and in being
presented to me at Koh's gawai had fulfilled their destiny.
Nothing should violate the virtue which they had there acquired
and imparted. They should now disappear from the earth and be
lost forever to prying human gaze, yet remain as intact as treasures
interred in the tombs of dead kings.

I took them to the lake beside the District Officer's house.
Standing on its high bank, I hurled them one by one into the air.
They performed graceful curves of flight and plunged into the
middle of the pool. Each time that a bangle sank, I watched the
ripples of water travel in ever wider, fainter circles across the
surface from the spot where it dived. For a few moments they
quivered on the lake's face and then vanished, leaving the copper
trinket buried below.

One material relic of our frolics up the Balleh remained with
us longer—the small banana-leaf basket which Koh thrust into
my hands as we left his house. This we guarded as a sacred
trust cherishing its egg, rice and vegetables as fondly as if they
were rose petals preserved between the pages of an album in
sentimental, nostalgic memory of a romantic adventure. When
we boarded our launch to continue the voyage to Kuching, we
hung it on a cross-bar at the vessel's prow. There spirit eyes
would detect it and respect its protecting power; and there it
remained until our journey's end. Only when at last we arrived
opposite the watergate of the astana in Kuching did we remove
it. We had promised Koh to keep it for three days, and now
those days were spent.

I carried it down the side of the launch and into the Governor's barge waiting to row us to the astana. As the Malay crew
dipped their paddles and the boat began to glide across the river,
I lifted the basket overboard. Placing it carefully, so that it floated
on the water, I let it go. The current caught it and started to
carry it down-stream towards the coast, the sea and the unknown.

CHAPTER TEN

INTERLUDE IN THE JUNGLE

I

FIVE MONTHS LATER I left Kuching for another visit to the Balleh. The Government was introducing certain reforms which I wished to discuss with some Iban chiefs. John Barcroft, a wise counsellor on native affairs, came with me.

It was September, the northeast monsoon was blowing, and on our way round the coast we spent a tempestuous night at sea. Sleep was impossible, and I lay for hours unwinking on my bunk. As I stared into the darkness beyond the cabin window, I listened to the heaving and straining of the storm-tossed boat, the wild fury of wind and rain, and the occasional comradely calls of the Malay sailors on deck. It was comforting to hear the calm, confident voices of the crew against the uncontrolled whistling and roaring of the elements. Nothing on earth is more remarkable than the way in which men have made themselves at home amidst the most violent manifestations of Nature.

At dawn we entered the Rejang River and proceeded all day along its broad, tranquil course. After a night at Sibu we continued our journey to Kapit. There we tarried also for a night, and Ian Urquhart, the District Officer, joined us.

In Kapit I called on the Baughmans at the Methodist mission school. Since my last visit they had received some new pupils. One of them was a notable and surprising recruit—Segura.

News had reached me in Singapore a few weeks earlier that she had left her paternal long-house and gone to boarding school. I received the tidings with mixed feelings, for the experiment seemed to me of doubtful wisdom. The impulse to give Segura a modern education was worthy; yet was it sensible? Koh's daughter was no longer a child who could patiently acquire a knowledge of such things as reading, writing and arithmetic.

Already sixteen years old, she had reached a period in most girls' lives when their thoughts are turning from classroom studies to more adult interests. Bornean girls mature early. Segura was now a young lady conscious of her womanhood. Indeed, in accordance with recognized Iban custom, she had probably already experienced two or three love affairs. Was she not, therefore, too grown-up to gain benefits from a school curriculum, and too independent to submit to discipline designed for younger, more amenable human beings?

I felt apprehensive, too, on another score. Segura had matured in the traditions and ways of a long-house. It might have been prudent to start her some years earlier on a course of education which would accustom her to other ideas, so that she could adapt herself by a slow, evolutionary process during impressionable youth to totally different habits of mind. The transition from a "primitive" long-house child into a "civilized" modern maiden would then have been gradual and tactful. But for an older person of formed habits would not the change be too sudden, too disturbing, too revolutionary? Might it not upset her whole mental and social outlook?

That day at Kapit I gained no clear impression of the answers to these questions, for Segura was away from school. Baughman told me that, hearing I was on my way up-river, she had left by prahu two days earlier to rejoin her family and welcome me in their home. I gleaned from the schoolmaster's cool responses to my enquiries that she was not one of his aptest and favourite pupils. He spoke with more enthusiasm of other, younger scholars like Penghulu Sibat's daughters. With a wry smile he remarked that Segura's chief interest seemed to be men. It has been well said by a famous philosopher that the proper study of mankind should be Man, but I gathered from Baughman's tone of voice that Segura's preoccupation with the subject was perhaps not conceived in that spirit of objective intellectual questing which the sage intended.

I looked forward with keen sympathy and a touch of concern to meeting Segura again.

Barcroft, Urquhart and I embarked in our long-boats for the journey up-river. A few miles above Kapit we entered the remote and wild, yet strangely serene Balleh. As my boat turned into its mouth I felt instantly that I had left the awful, wearying troubles of the modern world and reached a haven where complexity was replaced by simplicity, frustration by contentment and strife by peace. The leafy boughs of the forest trees seemed outstretched like hands of friends to welcome us, the voice of the river murmured with pleasure at our arrival, and the equatorial sun beamed down upon us with a warm inviting smile. My thoughts raced forward many miles to our Iban hosts, and in imagination I saw them preparing their home for our reception.

We did not go at once to their house, but made a diversion first to that of Penghulu Jugah. I had promised to stay with him and his family for a night.

To reach his dwelling we turned aside from the Balleh and entered a tributary called the Merirai. Jugah himself and a dozen youths from his house hailed us at the point of land where the two rivers met. They brought small prahus with numerous paddles and punt-poles to take us the rest of the way. They also provided expert knowledge of the channel of the Merirai, which is a turbulent and difficult river. Without them we should have run aground, holed our craft and sunk.

Up the Merirai the jungle scenery became magnificent. The river was little more than a narrow lane of water between two lofty walls of rock overgrown with tropical shrubbery and trees. Its stream was twisting and strewn with boulders. In some places the water flowed placidly, as if this were a calm canal, but in others it was wildly agitated. We passed through a dozen stretches of rapids, some of them fierce in temper. Amidst them the unassisted horse-power of outboard motors was not enough to achieve advance; the power of many men must be added to it. Where the rapids were not too unruly, some of the crews stood erect in our prahus and poled us onwards, while others crouched and plied their paddles; but where the galloping torrent was too strong to be overcome by these means, the Ibans leaped overboard and trudged waist-deep in waves, grasping the boats and lugging them by brute force up-stream.

The dense, tangled vegetation on either hand was primary jungle, untouched by man since the beginning of time. Noble, gigantic trees towered over the river. These primæval arbours were a playground for countless parties of monkeys, who scampered and leaped through the foliage like troupes of tireless little demons. Here and there stood a long-house perched like a fortress forty or fifty feet above the channel. All these houses came under Jugah's suzerainty.

At length we arrived at his own dwelling, skied like the rest on a rocky bluff. Its inmates were keeping a keen look-out for us, and there was a flurry of excitement when our boats came into view. Tedong and other notables ran down zig-zag flights of tree-trunk stairways to a shingly beach where we would land, and girls moved to their stations for the reception ceremony. The rest of the population crowded the outer platform of the house.

The ritual of welcome was faithfully performed at every stage of our ascent to the mansion. Its climax came at the head of the stairs, where Siah and Sani and half a dozen other long-house belles were marshalled to offer us libation cups.

First they handed us drinks for our attendant spirits, which we threw over our shoulders to those incorrigibly thirsty beings, and then tumblers of rice-wine for ourselves. After that Siah and Sani flung their arms round my neck and embraced me with unaffected gladness, as if I were a prodigal son who had misguidedly strayed into civilization and was now returning to the wild.

The two gay sisters introduced me to their husbands, a pair of recent acquisitions whom I had not previously met. They were pleasant young men who appeared to be worthy of their charming brides, and I congratulated them on their good fortune.

Jugah led me into his room and presented me to his gracious wife. For several hours after that we enjoyed a boisterous time. No hospitality in the world is more spontaneous than that of the natives of Sarawak, and the sample of it given by Jugah and his family was a heartening experience. There was much gossip, feasting, dancing and merry-making, and little sleep.

II

Early next morning we took leave of our friends and returned down the Merirai. Jugah and a group of youths accompanied us. The penghulu was to stay with us during our travels through

the next few days, but the young men came only to pilot us down
the turbulent river.

The scenery that morning was wonderfully impressive. Early
sunshine bathed the forest in a delicate, mysterious light such as
filters into the nave of a cathedral at dawn. Here and there pale
sunbeams penetrated the vault of leaves and slanted, translucent,
to the ground. No breeze yet stirred, and every leaf and branch
in the jungle hung motionless. In vivid contrast to this silent
woodland immobility was the irrepressibly noisy liveliness of the
river. It swirled and leaped and tossed with ceaseless excitement,
and our prahus shot all the rapids at top speed.

At the Merirai's mouth Penghulu Sibat joined us. Like Jugah,
he was to accompany us on our travels during the next few days.
Changing from our prahus into temois, we turned up-stream into
the Balleh. Soon we passed Temonggong Koh's house where
such memorable celebrations had occurred a few months earlier.
Only a scattering of elders now occupied the place, for its inmates
were almost all on their farms distributed along the river, engaged
in the vital work of planting padi. Koh himself was residing
with his family in a farmhouse ten miles farther up-stream. We
were to stay with him there.

For several hours we journeyed along the Balleh, until at last
we came in sight of our destination. The river had narrowed
to a fraction of its former width, and on either side hills climbed
abruptly from the water's edge. The front ranks of ridges were
steep but not lofty; at their back rose grander heights, wildly
shaped, forest-clad and inaccessible. Some slopes in the fore-
ground were covered with jungle, but others had been shaved
bare of trees for the spring sowing. They bore the scars of
a violent clearance recently achieved by Iban husbandmen. Whole
hillsides were strewn with the trunks of felled trees and pock-
marked with patches of scorched earth, where the burning of
timber and undergrowth had been most fierce. Here and there
grey columns of smoke rose languidly into the air from dying
embers of huge bonfires and many surviving stumps and trunks
were burnt to the consistency of charcoal.

Amidst this scene of destruction and death were signs of new,
burgeoning life. A thin, transparent veil of green on many hill-

sides revealed young rice plants sprouting. Turning my field-glasses on them, I saw that they grew from countless small holes drilled in the earth, where seed had been dropped. In some places the padi stood nearly a foot high.

Among the clustering hills ahead we spied Koh's farmhouse, perched on a promontory overlooking the river, like a Swiss chalet commanding an Alpine valley. The building was small and intimate for an Iban dwelling, containing only seven private rooms. No rustic retreat could be more charming, nor more majestically placed in beautiful highland scenery.

When we landed, Koh stepped forward to welcome us. With him were two young women. One was Mindun, as gay and attractive as ever. The other I did not know. She appeared to be a Chinese girl. Or was she a Malay? Her dress seemed to indicate the latter, yet her short, artificially waved hair, and the powder and rouge on her face, were more in Chinese style. It was odd to find this foreigner staying in Koh's house. Her features were extremely pretty. Her almond shaped eyes had a half-shy, half-bold expression, her mouth was sweetly yet petulantly curled, and her chin was firm. By a strange coincidence her face was reminiscent of Koh's youngest daughter. . . . Suddenly, with a shock, I realized that this was Segura.

I felt appalled. I had never seen a familiar face more transformed. When I thought of the beautiful woodland maiden, the golden-brown girl whom I had known a few months earlier, and then looked upon this painted, dolled-up young lady, I could have wept. I remembered her long black tresses crowned with flowers, her angelic face and lithe body clad only in a pagan skirt, and her vivid grace as she ran barefoot over the ground. Now all that was changed. Her hair had been clipped and arranged in small, sham curls; instead of wild flowers, two genteel velvet bows perched above her temples; her honey-coloured skin was daubed with white face powder and her mouth was smeared with scarlet lipstick. A Malay blouse clothed the upper half of her body, a flamboyant sarong hung from her waist to her ankles, and her feet were strapped in a pair of high-heeled shoes. She looked like a city flapper, and had the air of self-conscious elegance of a gauche pupil in a third-rate school of feminine deportment.

A strange sensation affected me. I felt that the Segura whom I had known was dead. She had passed away, a lovely, elusive person never to be seen again. And I felt that I too must have died, and been re-born after many decades. By some odd chance I was meeting a descendant of my earlier friend. This new girl also was attractive, with features reminiscent of the old Segura. Perhaps she was a great-granddaughter of the original Iban maid, removed from her by a few generations and inheriting similar looks, though possessing the sophisticated style of later times.

Yet this was the very same Segura, only five months older! It was almost unbelievable that so brief an interval could span an age.

She peered at me inquiringly, trying to detect whether I admired her new looks. I sought to hide that my emotions were of a contrary nature, for I did not wish to hurt her. But I felt sick at heart, and hoped that her character had not altered in the same way as her appearance.

We climbed to the farmhouse, where I found that other changes had affected the household since my last visit. Koh's young son, Kanyan, had also gone to school. His long black locks and slim white loin-cloth were things of the past. His hair was now clipped, neatly parted in the middle and smoothed with hair oil, and he strutted around with a self-confident, cocksure air in a blue shirt and khaki shorts, with hands thrust importantly into trouser pockets.

He bowed to me with easy but regrettable bumptiousness and said in a precise, well-practised phrase, "Good evening, sir."

The new styles thus brought to the Balleh by Segura and Kanyan had to some extent influenced the rest of the family. Bini Koh, the chief's wife, and Mindun still wore hand-woven Iban skirts, but they had acquired the respectability which insisted on blouses to cover their chests. Old Koh, too, had forsworn his pristine simplicity of garb, and now wore a striped European pyjama jacket and a long Malay sarong. Only his eldest daughter, Iba, scorned these novel tastes, appearing in customary native undress. I felt that her instinct made her contemptuous of all change, and that deep within her lurked a racial pride which resented this mimicry of alien peoples like the Malays and Chinese. She was an Iban of the old school, a dyed-in-the-wool conservative who would never capitulate to new-fangled notions.

The more I saw of Iba, the more I respected her. Once upon a time she must have been a comely girl, but, like most women of primitive races, the females in an Iban family work hard and age prematurely. Iba's looks had faded. The oldest of Koh's daughters, she had neither the beauty of Segura nor the vivacity of Mindun; yet perhaps she had more sterling character than the other two put together. Possessed of a ready and caustic wit, she was a realist who called a spade a spade, and would likewise never hesitate to tell an idiot to his face that he was an idiot. But she had also a gentle, feminine side to her nature, which sometimes made her extremely thoughtful and kind. She was physically powerful and morally dependable, traits which conspired to give her handsome face a certain robust strength. I often thought that Boadicea, the Queen of the ancient Britons, must have looked like Iba.

None of the lesser inmates of the house had altered their native mode of dress. Only Koh's immediate relatives had adopted the changes, and among them only Segura went to the extremes of cutting her hair, using lipstick and powder, wearing Malay costume and donning high-heeled shoes. In spite of their blouses, Bini Koh and Mindun still looked like Iban women; but Segura did not. She appeared a foreign visitor in her own home.

I quickly learned that her new habit had caused a sad disruption in a hitherto happily united family. Her parents and sisters resented her transformation, suspecting that she now despised the simplicity of long-house life and looked down upon them all as uncouth. I was told that Koh's comments on her new style when she first returned home had been explosive. In particular he condemned her resort to cosmetics and the shearing of her long hair. He spoke of these transgressions with a bitterness which could hardly have been harsher if she had offered him deep personal insult, brought disgrace upon his family and forfeited all claim to Iban virtue.

The old man did not realize that the blame for it all lay less with Segura than with himself. He had conceived the plan to send her abruptly from the untutored jungle to a school in a smart down-river town. His was the odd notion that a young woman of ripening years could be put in a classroom meant for children, to learn dull occupations like spelling and arithmetic; and his was the blunder of supposing that she would not be more attracted by the lessons to be learned in Kapit's bazaar, in its ladies' tailoring establishment and local beauty parlour.

Yet how could the aged pagan foresee such consequences? His motives were good. He felt the time had come when the Iban people should receive modern education, when their younger generation should advance from the stagnation in old-fashioned ways which marked him and his contemporaries, and equip themselves to play proper parts in a fast changing, twentieth century Sarawak. He wished the members of his family to set an example, and so he sent his daughter Segura and his son Kanyan to school.

In Kanyan's case the decision was probably wise. The boy was young enough to mix with other children in the novel environment of a classroom, to gain scholastic benefits from it, and to acquire gradually a new outlook. But in the case of Segura the decision was fraught with tragic possibilities. Some of its first results quickly became apparent to me.

When we settled on the floor in Koh's room, we celebrated a bedara. I followed faithfully the instructions which would have been laid down in Mrs. Beeton's Cook Book, if that eminent authoress had set out to cater for evil spirits as well as human beings. "First take a leaf of sirih, and then a betel-nut—." So, gathering all the ingredients in a huge heap, I made the meal for the hobgoblins. Then Mindun took a bottle of tuak, poured a drink for me and sang a pantun. But when it was Segura's turn to sing, she refused to do so.

She sat beside me, and had helped me once or twice to select the dishes in the right order, or to balance an egg correctly on the popcorn. Yet her attitude to the proceedings seemed detached, even politely aloof. Now she shook her head in vigorous dissent at the suggestion that she should offer refreshment and sing verses of welcome to her family's guests. She indicated that at school such a performance would not be regarded as ladylike, and that it was, indeed, a piece of savagery of which she felt ashamed.

Koh expressed his feelings in an angry tirade, scolding her mercilessly for evading her duty as a daughter in his house. She remained completely unmoved, and there was an awkward silence. Disapproving side-glances from her relatives showed that Segura was isolated in a company of critics.

I spoke gently to her, with Barcroft as interpreter, expressing the opinion that she was wrong, and urging her not to feel aversion to traditional Iban songs and customs. They were part of the proud heritage of her race, and as an Iban girl she should be glad to sing pantuns and try to excel all her contemporaries in the art. I remarked that she must have misunderstood the attitude of the school authorities at Kapit, for they would not intentionally decry native culture. As a European I delighted in listening to pantuns, which were as pleasing musical performances as the national songs of other peoples.

She seemed impressed by this argument, though she still needed further persuasion to perform. I half chided and half coaxed her, and at length she agreed to sing.

Filling a glassful of tuak, she placed it before me and, after a moment's hesitation, began to chant. At the end of a few phrases she stopped and sniggered. A minute of embarrassed silence followed. Then she started to sing again, but once more broke down. She shrugged her shoulders, laughed uneasily, and made no further attempt.

Koh was now thoroughly annoyed with her, and expressed his displeasure sternly. He became utterly unreasonable. First he ordered her to conduct a conversation with me in English. When she pleaded that she could not do so, he asked what was the use of sending her to school if she did not learn to discuss the affairs of the world with government officers in their mother tongue. When I suggested that the blame should attach to me, since I had been coming to Borneo much longer than Segura had yet been to school, and so should by now converse easily in Iban, he dismissed the idea as frivolous.

For a while the conversation became a general remonstrance at the extreme way in which Segura had altered her Iban appearance. Several of us took part, our protests mostly couched in terms of sympathetic friendship. I for one tried to appeal to her feminine vanity as well as to her racial pride. I deplored the massacre of her lovely hair, since her bounteous tresses had been one of her womanly glories, and voiced doubts also about her use of face powder and lipstick. I said that they marred the natural, unblemished beauty of her face. I discoursed, no doubt pompously, on the mistake which peoples make when they adopt the dress of another race and so lose part of their distinct, precious national character. Fortunately I was wearing my own savage national costume, the kilt, and so could prove that I practised what I preached.

Barcroft and Urquhart supported my pleas, and Jugah and Sibat made no secret of their hearty agreement. Segura listened with apparent indifference, yet with actual keen attention. She made no reply, however, beyond an occasional nervous laugh.

I felt sincerely distressed at the change in her appearance, but by itself that need be only superficial. It was not the root of my apprehension. What worried me was the thought that it might be an outward sign of an inner development of deeper significance. If Segura had been so quick to abandon her Iban clothes, might she not discard equally rapidly all the ideas of personal and social conduct which her Iban training had implanted in her? And if that change was occurring, where would it lead her? So far as I knew, her future lay in a long-house. She must maintain her respect and liking for its way of life; otherwise she would suffer emotional confusion. If she grew to despise her own people's society and to hanker after a different, unattainable order, then she might be doomed to terrible misery of mind and spirit.

These thoughts troubled me as I bathed in the river before dinner. A summons to supper dismissed them from my mind, and I climbed to the farm to enjoy Koh's hospitality.

That evening I introduced an innovation into long-house life. It seemed to me that if Western civilization must invade the interior of Borneo, its best gifts as well as some of its less satisfactory offerings should be bestowed there. So I launched a campaign to establish English nursery games as part of Iban custom, and began with a demonstration of blind-man's-buff. The sport proved immensely popular. Koh and his wife, Jugah, Sibat, Iba, Mindun, Segura, Kanyan and other Iban youths and maidens entered into it with enthusiasm.

The long-gallery was a splendid setting for the game, its nicely sprung bamboo floor lending extra bounce to the antics of hunter and hunted alike. The fish-traps, rice mortars and rolls of matting standing against the wall became additional obstacles to be negotiated by a groping blind-man, for the Ibans showed diabolical resource in placing them across his path. Loud shrieks of laughter from an audience of all the house's inmates gave constant stimulus to our tomfoolery.

Koh fancied himself as a blindfold head-hunter. Frequently, when temporarily a free man, he would loiter in the blind-man's line of advance, hoping to be caught and assume again the handkerchief of the chaser. Afterwards, as he moved forward sightlessly, his children encouraged him with loud cries from this or that corner, and then with swift movements eluded his grabs when he was about to make a capture.

It was hot work, darting this way and that, ricocheting off walls and pillars, and avoiding collisions with neighbours in the crowded gallery. After a while we resorted to less active pastimes, such as lying flat on one's back on the floor, balancing a tuak bottle on the forehead, and endeavouring first to rise into an erect standing posture and then to subside again into a recumbent position without spilling the bottle. The agile Jugah carried off the prize in that contest. To follow it we played hunt-the-slipper, here-we-go-gathering-nuts-in-May and other games. The tension in the house caused by Segura's sartorial bombshell relaxed, and she and her family were reconciled in the enjoyment of hearty fun.

By midnight our exercises had tired us out, and we retired to bed.

III

Early next morning Barcroft, Jugah, Sibat and I left the farm. We would return after three days. In the meantime we were to stay in a camp many miles farther up-river, where my companions would fish and hunt while I lazed in the sunshine, scribbled notes for this book and helped to eat the fruits of their sport. In the evenings we would debate the problems which I had come to discuss.

The camp had been built by some natives from Jugah's house, who in the brief space of twenty-four hours selected a suitable site on the river bank, demolished the jungle occupying it and raised a roomy hut and small cook-house in the clearing. The hut stood on stilts, its floor and walls made of slim tree trunks lashed side by side, and its roof covered with large rain-proof leaves. It occupied a commanding position about forty feet above the river.

Its half-dozen builders greeted us on our arrival, for they were to stay as boatmen, cooks, handymen, hunters and fishermen during our sojourn in the wilderness. Except for loin-cloths they were naked, and looked as fierce a group of savages as any romantic seeker after Primitive Man could wish to find. One or two held rifles, but their principal weapons were parangs, spears and blow-pipes.

Soon after we settled in the hut, Barcroft and I decided that a large tree in front of it should have several branches amputated, to give us a clearer view of the river. Jugah issued an order for this to be done. Immediately an Iban youth gave a mighty leap, caught a long, drooping creeper on the tree, swung himself up it hand over hand like a monkey, gained a foothold on a stout branch and ran along the bough. Then he swarmed quickly up the main trunk and lopped off the condemned branches with a few strokes of his parang.

During the next few days we saw many impressive exhibitions of the Ibans' jungle craft. They made platforms for drying clothes, ladders to aid us clumsy white men in climbing trees, bridges for crossing gullies, and pathways through the "impenetrable" forest, swiftly and easily. If matches were not handy, they rubbed sticks together to strike a spark and make a fire. They were adept at cooking food over the flames. It was pleasant to see them squatting on their haunches round the blaze, jabbering like a group of gossiping women as they fried fish or meat, and then cramming the fare with deft fingers and hearty gusto into their mouths.

We had taken few supplies with us, and lived off the jungle. Although the Balleh was in flood and its waters were muddied, Barcroft and Jugah had fair success with their fishing. Sibat and our retainers went hunting and shot several monkeys. After dark the two penghulus made stealthy visits to a nearby salt-lick, and twice returned with the carcase of a mouse-deer; but they had no luck with bigger game.

In the early mornings the forest was full of the conversations of various birds—the melodious, bubbling notes of bulbuls, a gay whistling of sandpipers, sweet snatches of a magpie robin's song, the raucous cackle of kingfishers, an occasional shriek from a brahminy kite, and many other calls. Frequently we heard the limpid cries of Argus-pheasants, though none of us ever caught sight of those shy, lovely creatures.

One night I was wakened by a different cry, the yell of a human being in pain. At first I was not sure whence it came in the darkness. Then the shout was repeated, startlingly close by me. I realized that Barcroft was having a nightmare. Twice more he called incomprehensible words before relapsing into silence.

I heard the heavy breathing of our native companions in the hut. They seemed to be fast asleep, and soon afterwards I dozed off again. I would have forgotten the disturbance had not one of the Ibans referred to it at breakfast the next morning.

"You saved us a lot of trouble last night, Tuan," he said, addressing Barcroft in the Iban tongue. "There was an evil spirit on the other side of the river. It was very angry at our presence and wanted to come across to harm us. I heard it moving about and muttering, and was dreadfully frightened. Then you heard it too, and shouted to it to stop its wickedness. You ordered it to clear out. At first it obstinately refused, but you shouted again and again, and that scared it and drove it away. I heard no more of it after that."

Our brief jungle holiday passed pleasantly. All day, every day, we stayed out-of-doors, making voyages up- and down-river to test the fishing grounds, and enjoying the fresh air and natural scenery. In the evenings we sat by lamplight in our hut, supping and talking. Our policy was early to bed and early to rise; but after the evening meal Barcroft, Jugah, Sibat and I always conversed for a couple of hours about the affairs of the world in general and the problems of Sarawak in particular.

I got to know the two chiefs well during those discussions. Both were attractive men. The reader is already acquainted with Jugah, whose character impressed me again on that sportive jaunt up the Balleh. Never reserved in speech or action, he talked a great deal. I could not understand much of what he said until Barcroft translated his observations for me, but he was obviously a brilliant conversationalist and racy raconteur. His forceful, intelligent personality was reflected in his eloquence, the flow of his words being swift and easy, and his expressive voice rising and falling artfully as he spoke. Sometimes, to drive a point home, he gesticulated with his hands or grimaced with his face like an actor. His eyes, too, aided his advocacy, now sparkling brightly and now dimming dreamily as he sought to indicate a mood. Frequently his chatter was full of fun. He was a humorist, a satirist, a wit, a teaser—but always kindly so. He could be sharp, commanding, imperious, but never cruel.

I remember a typical jest of his. One morning he went fishing. Our larder was almost empty, and we depended on his catch to replenish it. Shortly before lunch he returned with a wry look on his face and a small fish the size of a sardine in his hands. In silent disgust he held it up for our inspection. Speechless with shame, he accepted our sarcastic comments with a dejected, hang-dog countenance as we prepared for a day's starvation.

Ten minutes later one of his henchmen arrived, staggering under the weight of his true catch, a dozen fish of most gratifying dimensions.

Penghulu Sibat, too, had a nice sense of humour, but it was receptive rather than creative. His was perhaps a more thoughtful and deeper nature than Jugah's. Of all the younger Iban chiefs he came nearest to his kinsman, Temonggong Koh, in abilities, with a quiet strength and wisdom which were more reliable qualities than Jugah's clever exuberance. Jugah was his senior by several years, and by reason of his more obvious merits enjoyed greater prestige among the Ibans; but Sibat's unobtrusive and unfailing good sense, his power of convincing argument and his personal charm made him highly respected. He was the only serious rival to Jugah as Koh's principal lieutenant and potential successor as paramount chief.

Our conversation turned sometimes to interesting facts of natural history in the jungle surrounding us. The neighbourhood was notorious as a haunt of pythons, and that intriguing circumstance led talk one evening to the subject of those awful snakes.

Jugah remarked that the Ibans were afraid of only two physical creatures in the wild. One was the bear and the other was the python. The natives disliked bears because these bad-tempered beasts moved silently along forest tracks, and you might come upon them suddenly without warning. The first intimation of a bear's presence might be its claws scratching at your body.

But the python was even more dangerous. The initial revelation of its presence might be a sudden, unexpected embrace, growing ever more insistent until it crushed the breath from your body. The natives in our circle began to tell tales of pythons with which they had been acquainted. They vied with each other, each seeking to produce the most astonishing story, and their accounts became increasingly hair-raising as the talk proceeded.

One Iban told of a python which, in his presence, suffered a severe attack of indigestion and cured it by regurgitating a whole barking deer.

Another capped this by relating how he once caught a python incapable of resistance, since it felt lethargic following a gargantuan meal. When he cut it open, an entire samba deer—much larger than a barking deer—lay in its stomach.

A third story-teller described an attack by a python on a wild pig. He watched the snake strike its adversary with bared teeth. The blow partially disabled the boar, and the aggressor then proceeded to coil itself round the hapless victim's body. Slowly but surely it increased its pressure until the pig was dead. The serpent then unloosed its grip, unslung its horrid jaw and proceeded to swallow the quarry holus-bolus.

Then another pagan described a classic duel which he witnessed one day between a python and a crocodile. Sitting in a prahu on the Balleh, he noticed a tree over the river swaying violently. On closer examination he saw a gigantic snake stretching down from the tree and a crocodile reaching up from the water, locked together in deadly combat. Each had a firm hold on the other, and a titanic tug-of-war ensued. Sometimes the python pulled the crocodile half out of the water, like an enormous water-rat caught helplessly by its neck; but at other times the crocodile's grip proved the stronger, and it lugged the serpent farther and farther towards the stream. The battle swayed this way and that, the combatants being evenly matched, and in the end neither side could gain a mastery. Neither secured a fatal clinch or dealt a knockout blow. After half an hour's fierce conflict the two champions abandoned the fight, apparently by mutual consent, each withdrawing to its own element.

That saga was followed by another. One day an Iban hunter spied a clutch of strange eggs nestling in a hole on a river bank. Going to investigate, he decided that they must be a python's eggs. Interested by this rare discovery, he helped himself to them. Soon his supposition about the nature of his find was proved indubitably correct, for as his hand felt in the hole for the last egg the mother python seized his arm. Until that moment he was unaware of her presence farther along the tunnel. Now she tried to pull him into her dwelling, but without success, for his frame was too bulky to effect an entrance. He for his part sought to extricate his arm, but equally in vain, for her grip was too firm. No one knows how long this frustrating struggle lasted, but all learned how it ended. Some hours later the egg thief's corpse was found on the river bank beside the nest, with one arm pulled from its socket and the flesh and ribs of that side of his body ripped away.

After hearing those stories, I moved more warily when I stepped into the jungle round our camp. The only disadvantage of this precaution was that I could never add a personal experience of my own to my companions' repertoire of bedtime python stories.

IV

In the evenings our conversation usually turned to contemporary Iban affairs. These were the matters which I had come to Sarawak to discuss with the chiefs. Jugah and Sibat felt deeply concerned about the future of their race. They had grown up in a native society which seemed to be rapidly changing, and they were not sure where some of the changes would lead. They expressed their anxieties freely to Barcroft and me.

"You urge," Jugah said to me, "that we should keep our native style of dress, yet the Government wishes us to progress. You plead with us to maintain many ancient Iban customs, but the Government insists that we adopt new ways of doing things. The Government itself is making big changes in the methods of administering our affairs." He suggested that a conflict existed between these two policies.

I answered that there was no contradiction. In some matters a change, a development from ancient Iban habits was desirable, for the old methods were out-of-date and prevented his people from making adaptations which would enable them to survive in the modern world. But in other matters traditional customs were good and should be preserved as an essential part of Iban racial character. So there should be modifications in some features of native life and no modifications in others.

Jugah and Sibat both said that they understood this, but they felt confused. It was difficult to distinguish where there should be changes and where there should be none. They thought that in some directions the authorities were pressing developments too rapidly.

I asked what parts of official policy they had in mind, and in reply they spoke of certain innovations in local government.

These innovations were part of a comprehensive programme of reform in agriculture, public health, education, social welfare and political controls which the administration had pursued since the country's cession. New local government institutions were being created as the best means of training the natives in the wider management of their own affairs. Previously the authority of a tuai rumah, for example, had been confined strictly to the problems of his house, while the authority of a penghulu was limited to the group of long-houses for which he was responsible. These native leaders felt little or no concern with broader questions. The administration of a District was the business of the British District Officer assisted by junior government officials who were Malays or Chinese, while the administration of a Division was the sole responsibility of the British Resident, with such advice as he thought fit to seek from his District Officers. There were no District or Divisional councils on which pagan chieftains sat and expressed their views. Naturally the British officials kept in personal touch with the penghulus, and sometimes sought their opinions, but these contacts were informal, spasmodic and individual. There was no regular, organized, collective consultation with local chiefs, to stimulate in them a sense of corporate responsibility for the affairs of their people in matters more important than small long-house problems.

It was true that one of the supreme pagan chiefs, Temonggong Koh, sat in the national council of Sarawak, called the Council Negri. But he was only one of two Dayak representatives in an assembly of almost twenty, the other members being British and Malays with a few Chinese. Moreover, in the Rajah's time the Council met only once every three years, and had no legislative duties. The purpose of its meeting was to hear from His Highness a general statement of his government's policy, and then to adjourn for social jollifications. Its usefulness as a body where anyone could become familiar with the country's public affairs and be trained in their management had been nil.

All that was being changed under the new British régime, and the size and functions of the Council Negri were both being enlarged. As a foundation for the process by which the peoples of Sarawak would ultimately become self-governing, Charles Arden-Clarke introduced in 1948 the beginnings of a representative system of local administration. It was modelled on the Native Authorities which flourished in some other parts of the Colonial Empire. In certain areas he set up District Councils, the chairmen of which were the District Officers while the other members were a group of nominated local leaders. Similarly in each Division a Divisional Council was established. Its chairman was the Resident, and his colleagues were a picked group of government officers and area leaders. Usually each District Council selected by vote its representatives to sit on the Divisional Council. All these councils met regularly and enjoyed considerable powers.

The innovation was a modest political development, the embryonic beginning of a system which would grow in due course into national self-rule. Yet in Sarawak nothing like it had ever been contemplated before. It was revolutionary.

This was the reform which Jugah and Sibat questioned. They were both members of their District Council, and Jugah sat also on a Divisional Council. They said that they thought the creation of these bodies a good step, but suggested that they had been established too fast, and that they were being given too much power. When I cross-examined them to discover the exact reason for their criticism, it became evident that they disliked the fact that the councils might to some extent reduce the authority of the penghulus.

Previously no individual or group had come between a penghulu and his superior District Officer. In his own sphere a chief was all-powerful. He settled the affairs in which he had responsibility, except where a District Officer might intervene. Now the formation of District Councils created another authority with certain specific functions. Though at least some of the penghulus were members of each council, they had to share responsibility with other local leaders, and this tended to qualify their individual influence in their own areas.

The plain fact was that Jugah and Sibat were chieftains of an old régime who, in their heart of hearts, desired no change.

I tried to counter their argument by presenting certain considerations which would appeal to them.

"Hitherto in Sarawak," I said, "the Malays have been the governing race, under the Rajah and his British advisers. They alone became Native Officers, Assistant District Officers and high officials in departments in Kuching. They were also a large majority of the people's representatives on the Council Negri. Their voice powerfully influenced government policy in national affairs, as did also the voice of Chinese commercial leaders in

Kuching. But the voice of the Ibans was rarely heard outside their long-houses."

The two chiefs made signs of assent that this arrangement left something to be desired.

"The time has come," I continued, "for the Ibans and other pagan peoples to strive towards political equality with the Malays and the Chinese. They're capable of it. Their natural qualities of energy, intelligence and ability entitle them to that position."

Jugah declared that in his opinion the Ibans were a superior race not only to the Malays and the Chinese, but to all the other peoples in Sarawak.

I answered that I sincerely admired the Ibans, but that if they were to prove themselves as good as he claimed, they must exert themselves to take a wider interest in the affairs of their country. To do that they must extend their vision beyond the problems of a local group of villages, and be increasingly concerned with district, divisional and national questions. Otherwise the Ibans would become inferior; the Malays, Chinese and others would rule them.

Jugah and Sibat accepted this statement with sagacious nods of their heads. They had become deeply interested in the argument.

I introduced another thought, asking them whether they favoured education for Iban children. I knew full well what their answer would be.

They replied enthusiastically that their children should go to school, saying that the Ibans were backward because previously they received no education. Only if they were taught new things would they be able to hold their own with other races in a progressive Sarawak. The reason why the Malays had a monopoly of government offices, and why the Chinese were pre-eminent in trade was that these peoples were trained. Malay and Chinese children had long ago gone to school, and it was high time that pagan children did the same. Jugah and Sibat said that they and their fellow chiefs felt very grateful to the British administration for its policy of establishing schools throughout the up-river areas, where virtually none had existed under the Rajahs.

I commented that their children would learn many things at school in addition to the recognized lessons of a classroom. They would acquire knowledge to enable them to be in some cases more competent agriculturists, fishermen and hunters, and in other cases capable teachers and government officials. The most thoughtful among them would pick up ideas about how modern people should conduct their affairs, and they would wish the Ibans to organize their life according to those notions. They would want them to shoulder responsibilities in more than small long-house problems, to begin to exert influence in broader local, and ultimately national, questions. In fact they would demand the establishment of exactly such bodies as District Councils and Divisional Councils.

"Therefore," I said, "if you favour education for your children, you should be in favour of these other changes, for they will inevitably follow. The one produces the others. It's like planting a seed. The seed doesn't stay small in the ground. It grows, bursts through the earth and produces other things which are much more than a seed—a tree and leaves and flowers and fruit."

The two chiefs acknowledged this and approved the simile, but they urged that the pace of growth should not be too fast. A big tree, they said, took a very long time to grow from a small seed.

I replied that they were right to plead that we should not move too fast, but I argued that we should also not move too slowly. We must advance deliberately, step by step. We should develop new forms of government, like local councils, at a rate which enabled the Ibans and other up-river tribesmen to learn their new responsibilities gradually, and to acquire steadily the experience which would make them wise in their exercise.

Jugah and Sibat conceded that a reasonable pace of progress was necessary, but reiterated their anxiety lest the speed should be too fast. In this connection they raised a more particular issue. They said that rumours were circulating that the Governor proposed that penghulus in future should be popularly elected. This would, in their judgement, be a retrograde step. At present penghulus were chosen by the Government from the wisest men. After informal soundings of local opinion, they were selected because of their capacity for leadership. The inmates of the long-houses accepted their authority and followed their directions. Sometimes it was necessary for penghulus to adopt policies which placed unpleasant burdens on their people, such as taxes and communal labour. This was in the interests of government. As long as the chiefs were men of good sense, they would be able to persuade their followers to support such proposals, but if penghulus were to be chosen by the votes of the long-house inhabitants, such chiefs might not get elected. Irresponsible candidates would put themselves forward, promising that they would abolish taxes and other burdens. The voters, in their ignorance, might elect them, expecting benefits to follow. So the wiser men would lose their influence and the Government would lose its revenue. A deplorable state of affairs would result.

I smiled at this revelation that my simple "backward" friends were already familiar with the stock arguments sometimes used for and against democratic political practices, and assured them that they need not feel too apprehensive. So far as I knew, the Governor had no intention of introducing elections for the office of penghulu. Perhaps one day, in the distant future, when the natives' political education had progressed much further, such a plan would be wise, but I agreed with them that for the time being it would be foolish and might bring unfortunate results.

Nevertheless, I added, I did not fear that, even if elections were held, men like themselves would cease to be penghulus. They both seemed to me to possess all the qualities required for successful candidates in a democratic system. In addition to the fact that they were good-looking, they had conspicuous powers of eloquent speech, could impress humbler people with their character and brains, and would no doubt exploit their long-established authority as leaders to defeat the wiles of less desirable demagogues.

They were delighted with this tribute, and laughed uproariously. Jugah winked at me confidentially, to show that he approved of my powers of perception.

I could write at length about other comments made by the chiefs in our discussions, and describe certain shrewd, constructive suggestions which they made for the better working of the local councils system. Their proposals were afterwards adopted, with excellent results. But this book is not a political treatise on Sarawak's machinery of government, nor a study of the constitutional evolution now taking place there. It is a sketch of Sarawak society and some of the peoples who compose it. In particular it presents a picture of the pagan communities, of the changes through which they are passing, and of the disintegration of their old way of life. Political developments were only one among many contributory elements forcing that partly excellent, partly deplorable and wholly inevitable process.

These developments, which bade fair to produce in due course sweeping changes in the organization of native government, presented men like Jugah and Sibat with a serious problem concerning their children's upbringing. It was the same problem as faced Temonggong Koh regarding Segura and Kanyan.

Jugah, Sibat and their contemporaries were long-established penghulus. Whatever changes might come, that system of chieftainship would probably survive their time. For the rest of their lives they would assert authority in their ancient offices, alongside the new, rising influence of bodies like District and Divisional Councils. But what of their sons? In olden days those youngsters would have been trained in the long-houses to assume, if they proved worthy, their fathers' duties and privileges as leaders. They would probably be selected as chiefs. Useful and honourable careers were open to them.

Now, however, that prospect was dimmed. The responsibilities of popular councils might increase, and those of penghulus decline. All sorts of unforeseen, indeed unforeseeable, changes might shift the balance of power between individuals up the rivers. What should the present generation of chiefs do about their sons? How should they train them—as young long-house bucks with knowledge of the traditional ways of their people, who would later be leaders of the tribesmen in their jungle dwellings, or as modern school-taught youths familiar with the life of sophisticated townships, who would become representatives of the Ibans in local councils, administrative departments and, ultimately, a national assembly?

Jugah and Sibat told us that they and their fellow chiefs argued much among themselves about this question. They speculated curiously and earnestly about the future, trying to see clearly ahead, to prophesy accurately about coming events, and to guide their children wisely into ways which would lead to their profitable advancement.

Jugah himself had two sons, and Sibat one. Sibat's boy was a baby twelve months old, so there was time to wait and study developments before making decisions about his education. In the meantime the chief had sent his two daughters to school at Kapit. Nine and ten years old respectively, they were young enough to acquire without mental or emotional stress a partially new outlook. He intended, however, that the girls should return later to his home. Their future lay in a long-house, and they would only stay at Kapit long enough to learn reading, writing and other elementary lessons which would make them more useful and progressive women in Iban society.*

Jugah's sons were already of primary school age, and his resourceful mind had produced an ingenious answer to the riddle of what should be done about their education. I had met both youngsters in his house a few days earlier, and was astonished at the extraordinary difference between them. The younger, named Alo, was a regular long-house child, a little savage wearing flowing hair and a loin-cloth. The elder, Linggi, looked on the other hand like a product of the Western world. His hair was cropped short, neatly parted and brushed, and he wore a blue sailor suit like a smartly dressed boy in an English nursery.

Jugah explained that he was making provision for all eventualities! He would keep his younger son in the long-house and train him in the ancient traditions of Iban life. That boy would become an up-river leader. If the office of penghulu continued, he would probably succeed Jugah as the foremost chieftain on the Merirai.

The other son he had sent to Baughman's school at Kapit; hence his haircut and sailor suit. There the lad was learning new-fangled, modern ways. Later he would leave the long-house,

---

* Penghulu Sibat's capable elder daughter, Bawang, has since been trained in Sibu hospital as a midwife, and has returned to the Balleh to spread modern medical practice there.

enter government service and, if he were capable, become a Native Officer, District Officer or higher functionary in the official hierarchy.

I was impressed as well as amused by this characteristic Jugah effort to make the best of both worlds. I told him that possibly he would find that each boy qualified for distinguished service in a different sphere in future Iban society. His people would need two types of chiefs. The first would be in their local, up-river affairs, and these should be men who shared with the ordinary tribesmen their everyday lives The others would be Iban leaders in the central administration, men who lived in the populated, cosmopolitan centres, who met the Governor, his principal advisers and Malay, Chinese and other politicians, and who could represent the Ibans in the highest national councils.

I said that one of his sons might become the former type of leader, and the other the latter. The two types should always maintain close contact with one another, so that understanding existed between them. It might, therefore, be an admirable arrangement for two brothers to aim at filling each of these offices respectively. I congratulated Jugah on his far-sighted parental wisdom.

Sometimes in our talks Jugah or Sibat was inclined to belittle the qualities of other races in Sarawak, such as the Malays or the Chinese. They betrayed a typical, robust Iban tendency to feel contempt for those who had not the good fortune to be Ibans. I countered all such ideas, expressing the opinion that every racial community had its own particular sets of virtues and vices, and that all should be equal, fraternal partners. Just as Ibans should not be treated as inferiors to Malays or Chinese, so the other peoples should not be regarded as inferiors to Ibans. I explained that future peace and progress in Sarawak would depend on its various communal groups living together as fellow-citizens, feeling a common love and sharing a common loyalty for their same homeland. I added that one of the great values of the new District and Divisional Councils was that they brought representatives of the different races together round the same table, to solve their local problems in co-operation.

The two chiefs assured me that they fully recognized this

truth; but only a man with a more profound understanding of Iban mentality than I possessed could tell how deep, or shallow, was that recognition in their minds.

V

After three days' sojourn in our jungle camp we returned down-river. The passage to Koh's farm was exhilarating, accomplished amidst wild scenery through even wilder waters. We raced down various rapids and shipped a few waves as we went, but none of more than playful size.

Our friends on the farm made merry at our return. We were to spend one night there. Next day I would continue down the Balleh, heading for Singapore, while Barcroft went up-river again to continue his holiday.

Our plea a few days earlier that the Ibans should not discard their characteristic dress for foreign costumes had produced some effect. Koh no longer sported a pyjama jacket and sarong, but strutted around once more in a feathered cap and loin-cloth, like an aged Adam in an almost unspoilt Garden of Eden. His wife and Mindun had also reverted to their customary somewhat Eve-like style. Segura compromised between old and new fashions by casting off her blouse and wearing only a brassiere above her skirt, thus making the worst of both worlds. She told me, however, that she had decided to grow her hair again.

We enjoyed an evening of relaxation. A swim in the river was followed by supper in Koh's room, and that was succeeded by a vigorous spell of blind-man's-buff. Our hosts and hostesses were now zealous and skilful exponents of the game. Other sports came afterwards, until we were in a sufficient state of exhaustion to retire to bed. We had to rise early the next morning, the Ibans to resume their farm work and we visitors to depart.

At that time the household was in the middle of padi-planting. Several hillsides surrounding the farm were shaved of trees to receive the new seed. On some the sowing had already been completed, and a fresh, thin haze of green rice-shoots began to appear. But on others the work had still to commence.

I rose early to join a party of husbandmen on a high hill behind the farm. Iba led one group, which included a dozen women and several men. The area being sown was near to the hill's summit. All over the ground, on the burnt earth among the charred tree trunks, small holes had been poked in the soil. The men marched ahead drilling them with sharply pointed sticks, and the women followed, throwing seed into every hole. They threw casually by hand, dropping about half a dozen grains into each cavity. Sometimes a woman's aim was bad, and the seed fell outside its target. It was left there. The precious particles in the holes also remained uncovered, for the next fall of rain would wash earth over them.

One might have supposed that this careless method would result in birds eating a large proportion of the grain; but, judging from the abundance with which padi-grass soon sprouted, the loss was not too serious. That does not alter the fact that this primitive style of planting is wasteful.

I took some seeds and cast them into the ground. Then an extraordinary thing happened. A woman picked an object from the earth near my feet and held it out for me to see, uttering exclamations of astonishment. Our companions crowded round us to examine her find. It was a live tortoise.

The Ibans grew excited. A few days earlier the hillside had been burned; its slope was then a mass of flames. The tortoise had survived the conflagration. No such phenomenon had ever appeared on a freshly scorched padi ground in the memory of anyone present, and my friends regarded the event as a miracle. Obviously the tortoise was a spirit; otherwise it would have been roasted. Its presence was an omen of superlative good fortune for the harvest, and the natives observed the little animal with reverence and joy.

The tortoise itself took only a casual interest in the situation. At first it hid its head inside its thick armour-plated shell, but after a while curiosity got the better of it. Out poked its little, old man's face with wrinkled skin and mild, contemplative eyes. It surveyed us calmly, blinking sagaciously now and then.

One other creature on the hillside was unprecedented. It was I. The tortoise and I were at once linked in the Ibans' minds as twin messengers from the gods, joint harbingers of glad tidings, sure pledges of agricultural fertility and prosperity for Temonggong Koh and his people in the coming year. They spoke eagerly of this unique circumstance, and regarded me with touching appreciation.

It was high time, however, that I embarked for Kapit. When I announced that I must go, Koh urged that before I left I should perform a bedara in honour of the tortoise. I consented, and we hurried down the hillside, calling to Mindun and Segura in the farm below that they should quickly prepare dishes for the ceremony.

In Koh's room we squatted on the floor, with the tortoise placed in the central position of honour as chief guest among us. At first it refused to take any interest in the proceedings. Withdrawing its head and legs from view, it pretended to be just an empty, lifeless bit of tortoise-shell. Presently, however, it showed reviving curiosity. Cautiously it poked out its face and limbs, gave us a friendly blink, and then raised itself from the ground and strolled around. The Ibans watched its manoeuvres with glee.

I prepared the feast for the spirits, and placed it where they could eat it at their leisure. Then Mindun poured a glass of tuak and sang a pantun for me. Afterwards Segura followed suit. She had recovered some faith in the propriety of such conduct, though she still seemed slightly uncertain and abashed.

Then the two girls acceded to my request for a duet. Sitting side by side and hand in hand before me, they exchanged whispered suggestions as to the ballad they should sing. Soon they reached a decision, laughed gaily at me and began to chant in gentle, lyrical tones,

> *When the full moon shines at night*
> *We think of you.*

Urquhart interpreted their words for me. I found it hard to tear myself away from such sentimental banter, and lingered on the floor. Mindun and Segura needed no encouragement to continue their concert. They began to improvise a cycle of half a dozen brief poetic pieces, inventing the words in hurried, murmured conferences between each verse. There was a merry glint in their eyes as they chanted:

> *When you have gone*
> *We shall kiss your footprints*
> *In the grass.*

The tortoise found these observations boring, hid its head in its shell and dozed off to sleep.

> *Why don't you stay*
> *And lift heavy sorrow*
> *From our hearts?*

continued Mindun and Segura.

I would have liked to postpone my departure, but stern duty beckoned. In imagination I could hear the clamorous ring of telephone bells in my office in Singapore, and see official committees awaiting my attendance. Reluctantly I rose and made ready to go, and my Iban friends trooped towards the river to wave me good-bye.

As we walked down the path to the boat I asked Koh what he would do with the sacred tortoise. He replied that after my departure they would carry it up the hillside behind the farm, with dishes of food and bottles of tuak to celebrate a bedara on the exact spot where it had been found. Afterwards they would cook it and eat it, to acquire in their own persons part of its divine virtue.

Momentarily I felt shocked. Then my grief at the animal's fate was replaced by relief at my own. I remembered that a short while earlier the Ibans had regarded the tortoise and me as kindred spirits, twin messengers come to impart our special supernatural quality to the occasion. They seemed to have forgotten that I also was endowed with virtue which could presumably give strength to them. But for that lapse of memory, I reflected, I too might have ended the day's adventure in the pot.

VI

With marks of high mutual esteem my hosts and I parted on the river bank. Urquhart, too, had a sorrowful send-off. He was a deservedly popular District Officer, and was now returning to his headquarters in Kapit. We waved good-bye also to Barcroft, Jugah and Sibat, who were to tarry a while longer on the farm, before journeying up-river again.

Segura, however, did not remain behind. She came with Urquhart and me. Her short spell of truancy was over, and she would now return to school at Kapit. Complete with face-powder and lipstick, hair-ribbons, baju, sarong and high-heeled shoes, she stepped into our prahu and reclined with ladylike ease on the cushions beneath its awning.

The journey was pleasant and uneventful, and we reached Kapit early that afternoon. We decided to have tea in Urquhart's house, and then to go shopping before I delivered Segura once more into the charge of the missionaries. If she was to have a wardrobe at all, I thought, it should be of better quality than the one she wore. Her sarong, for example, was a cheap, flashy article. I asked her whether she would like one made of Javanese batik. She was delighted with the idea. So we sipped tea and munched cakes in Urquhart's house beside the lake, then made our way to the bazaar.

Kapit's shopping centre was a modest affair. Its single street contained a score of shop-houses, mostly devoted to supplying the local population with food and drink. Rice, dried fish, vegetables, tinned foods, orange squash, Chinese arak, biscuits and other tasty commodities crowded their counters, shelves and floors. Other stores were filled with household goods like kettles, pots, crockery, glassware, lamps and scrubbing brushes. A few shops, however, raised their customers' thoughts above material considerations and attempted to satisfy the aesthetic aspirations of Man, not to mention Woman. It is true that they were primarily concerned with providing clothes for Kapit's citizens, which are a sheer necessity, but they were rarely content to offer plain articles which performed only the utilitarian function of covering a wearer's limbs. Their shirts, sarongs, blouses and sirats strove after decorative effects. Gay colours and bold designs made gallant claims to beauty, and in prominent glass cases were displayed also those dazzling articles of jewellery which we have already seen adorning Iban females.

These were the establishments which Segura and I visited. Their Chinese proprietors bowed and smiled a cordial welcome to us. At our request they fetched from their shelves their finest sarongs, and unfolded them for Segura's inspection. Naturally the materials did not compare with the rich stuffs to be found in wealthy centres like Djakarta, Penang and Singapore, but they included a few specimens of good hand-stamped batik. After much critical examination and careful thought Segura selected the two which she liked best.

As we loitered in the bazaar a downpour of rain began, and we realized that the long muddy path to the mission would become very slippery. So we went to Fort Sylvia for shelter until the return of sunshine. The storm was short but sharp, with lightning and thunder as well as torrents of water. While we waited for it to stop we engaged in an animated conversation.

Koh had done less than justice to Mr. Baughman's success in teaching English, and to Segura's aptitude as a student, when he complained that she was incapable of holding a coherent conversation with me in my native tongue. Two or three times in the long-house she and I had chatted freely and pleasantly in English. It is true that these talks always touched upon the same topics, and that they were subject to certain narrow limitations; but that was to be expected, since Segura had attended her classes for only a few months. We did what we could with her increasing fund of knowledge.

As we sat in the fort, watching the sky for a sign of a break in its sopping greyness, we repeated our conversation. First I pronounced my solitary more or less intelligible sentence in Iban.

"Aku teeda pandi," I observed, "chukkup Iban." Actually this was a mixture of Iban and Malay meaning, "I cannot speak Iban."

Segura smiled with gracious encouragement and said, "Tuan chukkup Iban badas." ("You speak good Iban, Master.")

I made a gesture of dissent and remarked, "Segura chukkup English badas," which of course meant, "Segura speaks good English."

"Nadai," she replied with a laugh, using the Iban word for an emphatic negative.

I expressed disagreement with this statement, held up one hand, pointed to it and said, "Chukkup English."

Segura understood that I was asking, "What is this in English?"

She thought for a moment and then answered, "Hant."

I nodded approval, pointed to my thumb and looked at her enquiringly.

Again she considered for a while and then replied, "Tom."

"Thumb," I said, correcting her.

"Tom," she repeated, for she could get no nearer to the Anglo-Saxon pronunciation. I let it go at that.

I indicated one of my fingers, and at once she exclaimed with delight, "Fingarr."

I grinned assent and pointed to my arm.

"Arm," she cried without a moment's hesitation.

"Banya badas," I said, which signifies "Very good."

Next I stuck out an elbow.

She hesitated for a while, looking nonplussed. Then gradually the light of knowledge dawned in her eyes and she said, rather doubtfully, "Ilbow."

I thought this good enough and clapped my hands in sincere congratulation. She gave a triumphant chuckle.

I made a gesture of enquiry as to the word for my countenance.

"Face," answered Segura promptly. Then she had a further thought, and added, "Very nice face."

We both laughed. No fair-minded person could deny that this was becoming a highly accomplished and intelligent conversation.

Resuming it, I pointed inquisitively to my nose.

"Noce," she said.

"Nose," I retorted.

"Nose," she agreed with a look of abject apology.

I switched my enquiring finger towards one of my eyes.

"Eye," she declared.

I indicated the arch of hairs above the eye.

"Eyebrow," she said as confidently as a Professor of English giving a lesson.

My admiration was such that I could not express it adequately in common-or-garden English.

"Badas! Badas!! Badas!!!" I exclaimed.

Next I pointed to my mouth.

For a few moments Segura contemplated it and then said, "Ear."

"Nadai," I said in flat denial.

Segura looked astonished, and bit her lip in vexation. She gave vent to an Iban sentence which could have been either a polite expression of regret or a string of wicked oaths. Then suddenly her eyes dilated with enlightenment and she burst into a peal of laughter.

"Mouth," she cried. Pointing at that sweet feature on her own face, she repeated, "Mouth, mouth, mouth."

She patted one of her ears and said, "Ear."

"Badas," I said. "Very nice mouth and ear."

She chortled, and the oral examination continued. I put Segura to the test about my teeth, lips, chin, legs, feet, shoes, shirt and trousers. She quickly recognized them all and described them correctly.

Afterwards we transferred our attention to other objects in the room. Strolling round it, I pointed to a chair, a table, a picture, an inkpot and other interesting articles. Segura usually reeled off their names with swift accuracy, but occasionally did not know the English word for something. I confided it to her. She repeated it several times to herself, committing it to memory. Then we moved to other objects to do our exercises before them. After a while we returned to the new item in Segura's vocabulary, and I would ask her to declare its name once more. Usually she recollected it aright.

When I thought that our talk in English had continued long enough to refresh but not exhaust Segura's interest in foreign speech, I pointed at my nose and said, "Chukkup Iban."

She told me the Iban word for nose.

I repeated it solemnly, and she corrected my pronunciation when it erred.

Then I pointed to my eyes, and she instructed me in the Iban description of them.

So we took note once more of many features of my anatomy,

and I learned in what terms my Iban friends would refer to them, if by chance they ever felt disposed to do so. Afterwards we again extended our survey to various objects in the room.

We were so absorbed in our learned discourse that for a while we did not notice a remarkable improvement in the weather. Or if we did, by a tacit, unexpressed understanding we avoided referring to the fact that the sky outside was once more heavenly blue, and that brilliant sunshine was swiftly mopping up the damage wrought by the rain. We continued to call a spade a spade, a table a table, a finger a fingarr, and a thumb a tom, so that Segura's already long overdue return to school could be further postponed.

At last our consciences drew attention to the sparkling afternoon out-of-doors. I pointed a "fingarr" in the direction of the Methodist mission and indicated in dumb show that, with deep regret, I thought we should slowly turn our steps towards it. Sadly Segura conveyed in looks and gestures her dutiful agreement. We picked up her parcel of new sarongs and a basket of possessions which she had brought from the long-house, left the fort and walked along the path to the school.

Mr. and Mrs. Baughman gave us a cordial welcome. Their pupils, too, received us kindly. The children seemed glad at Segura's return, and at once began to ply her with questions about their acquaintances up-river.

The Baughmans and I discussed wider world affairs for a while. Then I said good-bye to them and their young community, and started along the path back to the township. Segura and her schoolmates waved to me until I disappeared from view.

CHAPTER ELEVEN

SEGURA

I

Since I could not visit the Balleh again for a long time, the Balleh came to visit me.

First those three doughty penghulus, Jugah, Sibat and Jinggut, stayed for a few days in Bukit Serene, my sultanic palace in Johore. Jugah had been to Malaya on a previous occasion, but for the others this was a first venture outside Borneo. We all treated the experience as if it were a glorified schoolboy escapade, and had a hilarious time viewing the sights and enjoying the diversions of Singapore.

A few months later an even more formidable party of friends from the Balleh arrived. Temonggong Koh came, bringing Bini Koh, Kanyan, Segura, a companion for Segura called Mary, and Mindun's husband, Jambong. I had invited Iba and Mindun too. Iba characteristically refused, saying that she was a simple up-river woman who would be out of place in the sophisticated surroundings of a modern city. Mindun, on the other hand, was enthusiastic at the prospect of stepping into the dazzling world beyond Sarawak, and she fully intended to come. Shortly before the party left the Balleh, however, illness laid low some children in their house. Mindun's assistance was needed to nurse them back to health, and with a sense of duty worthy of Florence Nightingale she surrendered her seat in the prahu and stayed at home.

The party of visitors was completed by "Shot" Spurway, the head of the Forestry Department in Kuching and one of the most genial men alive. For thirty years he had been a friend of Koh and his family, and he came to Bukit Serene as chosen companion and interpreter for us all.

Martin Gilliat, my Comptroller, met the travellers at Singapore docks and conducted them to Johore. He told me later that when Temonggong Koh saw my glistening Rolls Royce awaiting them, and learned that it would convey them to my house, his eyes almost dropped out with astonishment. He had never imagined that such a beautiful monster existed, and for a few moments he was speechless with incredulity.

I greeted the party at the front door. Beside me stood Ah Tiu, my head Chinese boy, with a trayful of drinks. I shook hands warmly with the happily grinning Koh, gave him a small tumbler containing ginger-ale, and said, "Buai."

The chief conscientiously threw the drink to the ground. Then I handed him a large whisky-and-soda for his own refreshment, which he imbibed with unfeigned pleasure.

To each of the others I gave first a drink of ginger-ale and then a whisky-and-soda. Thus were the customary rites of greeting performed, and the mixed company of human beings and shadowy sprites who honoured me with a visit made welcome in my home.

We proceeded at once to the next stage of the time-honoured ceremonial. I conducted my guests to a verandah overlooking the garden, where we squatted on Iban mats upon the floor. Spread before us were rows of small dishes piled with all the appropriate delicacies for a bedara. I had secured them that morning in the market in Johore Bahru.

Placing a copper bracelet round Temonggong Koh's wrist, I invited him to prepare the feast. He did it with contented grunts. At the right moment a cock appeared and was waved upside-down over the meal. Every detail was performed according to the Iban book, except that, unknown to my guests, the fowl was not slaughtered after its brief entry on the scene. Two feathers plucked from a dead hen—which was already cooking in a pot for lunch—and dipped in its blood were substituted for our bird's plumes. Thus was honour satisfied.

Afterwards Koh carried the dish to a bamboo pole erected that morning on the lawn before the verandah, and placed it on the summit. Then we squatted once more on the mats to consume drink and exchange gossip.

I apologized to Koh for having no girls in my home to chant

a pantun to him. Instead I recited a short speech in the grand
pagan's praise, expressing my delight at his and his family's
visit to my long-house. Then I persuaded Segura to celebrate
our reunion with a song. She complied shyly. As soon as she
ceased singing, Koh tugged at Spurway's sleeve and asked him to
say that the chief wished to address me. When the words had
been translated, Koh solemnly cleared his throat and began to
speak.

Spurway listened carefully, as did the company around. At
one point in his remarks the Ibans all smiled at me, and Segura
stretched out a hand and laid it on my arm. When the Temonggong fell silent, Spurway interpreted his words.

"Penghulu Temonggong Koh spoke thus:" he said. " 'Master,
you are the mightiest man in these parts, for your power stretches
over many countries and numerous peoples. I am but the paramount chief of the Ibans on the Rejang River in Sarawak. Beside you I am like a mouse-deer beside an elephant. But I am an
old man and you are young. In age I am to you like a father to
a son. If you will allow me, I would like to call you my son.
It is fitting, because I and all my family feel bound to you by
ties of deep affection.' "

Spurway observed to me in an aside that this was a rare mark
of devotion, and that Koh had spoken from his heart. He had
used the word "anak" for son, denoting the closest relationship
between an elder and a younger man.

I felt profoundly touched, and thanked the old chief, calling
him "Api", which was the name by which his children and intimate friends addressed him. I said that I was proud to be a son
of such a great and good chief, and of his gentle wife. I felt
happy, too, at being a brother of Iba, Mindun, Segura and Kanyan. I assured him that, as they all knew, I reciprocated their
affection. A hundred times they had been kind to me, and one
of my joys was to stay with them in their house.

At that we filled a loving cup and everyone drank from it.
We sat long on the mats on the verandah, exchanging our news
since we last met. Then we rose and I showed my guests their
bedrooms. They unpacked their few belongings and settled
into the house with many exclamations of astonishment at various

features of a place so strange to them, yet with the natural ease of visitors in the home of a member of their family.

II

They stayed for three days. No period in my life has been more packed with incident. Temonggong Koh and his party were paying their first visit to Singapore, and none of them had ever seen anything of its kind before. They were used to the quiet, peaceful environment of a remote river and jungle where Nature is supreme and Man is merely one of her lowly creatures, where human communities are small compared with the boundless spaces of forest and hills, and where the call of a bird or the cry of a monkey are the only sounds which occasionally break the prevailing silence.

Singapore was to them a new world, completely strange and fabulous. It was the very reverse of everything to which they were accustomed. Here Nature was subdued and Man appeared to be master. Human beings assembled in multitudes, raising everywhere in unbelievable profusion their houses, shops and business premises, and introducing all manner of odd inventions like motor-cars, bicycles and buses, which rushed around like herds of panic-stricken animals whose fearful baying and roaring banished silence and murdered peace.

Almost everything that we did in those days was a new experience for my friends. In astonishing, unanticipated ways I kept realizing this. For example, before we drove into Singapore one evening, to visit a cinema, I discovered Segura and Kanyan standing transfixed beside my car. They were used now to the vehicle itself, but were amazed by the beams of its headlights stretching forward like brilliant antennae into the darkness. They had never imagined any such phenomenon. And as we drove into the city they were thrilled by the spectres of headlamps of other cars racing swiftly towards us.

So it was with almost everything that we did. During the visit my guests had their first journey in a railway train, their first flight in an aeroplane, their first visit to a moving-picture theatre, their first meal in a restaurant, their first ascent in an elevator, their first expedition to a large shop, and their first fling in an amusement park. All these experiences were strange, new and wondrous to them. The Ibans were like travellers landing on a new planet revealing unimagined sights. They were in a constant state of twittering excitement, leading a life in which every successive event was a breathless adventure.

As we sat in a railway carriage travelling from Johore Bahru to Singapore, Koh gazed dumbfounded at the speed with which the landscape flashed past the windows, while Segura, Mary and Bini Koh emitted constant exclamations of frank disbelief. When we peered from an aeroplane on the crowded buildings and streets of the great city below, they all kept moving from look-out to look-out, lest they should miss any detail of the astonishing spectacle. This was Koh's second flight (for had he not directed the bombing of Song from the cockpit of an aircraft?) and he was inclined to assume a superior, knowing sort of air; but the others were unaffectedly enthralled. And in an elevator in Robinson's shop, when the cage door closed behind us and the confined box in which we stood suddenly shot up through space, the old man was as startled as anyone could be. A deep, long-drawn sigh of awe escaped him. Segura and Mary screamed shrilly with fright, Bini Koh gripped my hand as if she needed sudden protection from an unseen evil spirit, and Kanyan gave a shout of half fear and half triumph at this supreme achievement.

Of all our adventures I think that the visit to Robinson's shop was the best. It most staggered my friends. When we entered the vast ground floor, Koh and his family stood for a while silent with amazement, stock-still, as if rooted to the ground. They stared incredulously, first at the crowd of shoppers and then, in even greater astonishment, at the show-cases, shelves and counters piled with merchandise. Each glanced enquiringly at the others, all wondering whether the eyes of their companions could possibly be seeing the same things. Afterwards they gazed again at the scene in front of them, half expecting that, like a mirage, it would have disappeared. But the throng of people and the enormous assembly of all the goods that man or woman could desire remained.

Deliberately the Ibans' eyes roamed from counter to counter. Here stood innumerable dials of miraculously ticking clocks, there were collected more china tea-sets and dinner-sets than they had thought could exist in the world, and in another place hung sufficient gents' trousers and jackets to clothe all the men in several long-houses in Borneo. So many pairs of shoes were assembled that surely people had insufficient money to buy them, and there were pots and pans enough to last the population of Singapore, it would seem, until eternity. Elsewhere were so many rolls of cotton and silk for dresses that not even the greed or vanity of all the women on earth could possibly exhaust them.

Koh made an exclamation of emphatic, uncompromising unbelief. His wife stared at the spectacle with the look of a small child entering fairyland. Segura and Mary seemed under the spell of some joyous but inexpressible emotion, and Kanyan's eyes sparkled with the ecstatic rapture of a holy man seeing visions.

The shock of their first astonishment had frozen their limbs into immobility. After a while, however, as their eyes became more accustomed to the scene, their bodies gradually woke into life again, and they began to advance through the shop. We strolled from department to department, examining their assortments of goods. Koh and his family fingered this article and touched that, to feel their substance and make sure again that these wares actually existed. They were still not wholly convinced that they were not the victims of some colossal hallucination.

If the Ibans were astounded at the shop, the shop was equally agog at the Ibans. The Temonggong wore that day one of his hats adorned with fluttering feathers, with a necklace of yellow beads, a red-tabbed penghulu's jacket and short khaki trousers on otherwise bare legs. His long, pierced ear-lobes and tattooed throat and hands took the shopping public of Singapore by surprise. Some people raised their eyebrows in slight dismay, others smirked with patronizing tolerance, and yet others smiled with welcoming friendship.

Bini Koh and Segura attracted no less attention than the chief. The old lady's rough Bornean features and her daughter's fresh young Mongolian beauty both produced something of a sensation. Shoppers turned and stared after them wherever they moved.

Girls serving behind the counters ceased to attend their customers, gazing instead in astonishment at these sudden apparitions. Business was momentarily interrupted.

I had told my guests that they could buy, on my account, anything in the shop that they chose, feeling confident that the innate courtesy of primitive man would prevent their abusing this rash, un-Caledonian invitation. So we made a preliminary reconnaissance of all the departments on Robinson's ground floor, and then stepped into an elevator and were conveyed to the upper stories. I have already described the startled emotions which affected my friends when the elevator began, like a magic carpet, to transport us through space. Their enjoyment of the journey was delightful; but their capacity for surprise that day seemed inexhaustible. When we arrived in the toy department, Kanyan at first stopped dead in his tracks at the sight of dolls, teddy-bears, model trains, tin soldiers, spinning-tops and other toys galore, and then with a wild cry ran excitedly towards them. Koh was as pleased as his son at the display of children's treasures, and Bini Koh, Segura and Mary were also for a while intrigued. But their feminine fancy was already seduced by the supplies of silks and satins, velvets and cottons, ribbons and sashes, buttons and bows which they had seen downstairs. So their attention kept wandering from the massed attractions of toyland towards the magic elevator, which could presumably drop them again to the dresses as swiftly as it had raised them to the golliwogs.

We therefore decided to divide forces. The ladies descended to the millinery department, with me as their escort, to make a selection of stuffs to add to their wardrobes. Kanyan stayed, with Martin Gilliat as protector, among the toys. Koh and Jambong, with Spurway as guide, started to roam through the whole shop, upstairs and downstairs, round and about, inspecting first one floor and then another in search of trophies to carry, like heads of old, back to the Balleh as souvenirs of this raid on Singapore.

In the end, after many debates, decisions, retractions, arguments, counter-arguments and ultimate resolves, Bini Koh, Mary and Segura selected several lengths of coloured silks to make sarongs and bajus, Kanyan chose a clockwork train with a figure-of-eight set of railway lines, Jambong got himself a wrist-watch

with a luminous dial, and Temonggong Koh acquired a dinner-
set of fine Worcester porcelain. I acquired a not inconsiderable
overdraft at my bank.

We lunched in the restaurant at Robinson's, doing full justice
to an ample menu. Still our party was a centre of attraction.
Other lunchers stared in our direction, whispering their entranced
astonishment at Koh's hornbill feathers, Jambong's long black
tresses and Segura's exotic grace. Rumour ran through the shop
that a party of head-hunters from Borneo had invaded the restaurant, and many people came to enjoy cups of coffee which a short
while earlier they had no intention of drinking. The place did a
roaring business.

The Ibans were indifferent to this unsolicited fame. They
were in merry mood, and our conversation was carefree and gay.
Up to that point the expedition was an unqualified success, and
we had no hint of the tragedy which would soon mar it.

After lunch I went to my office, to do some work which even
the visit of my distinguished guests would not permit me to
neglect. Spurway took Koh and Jambong on a sight-seeing tour
of the city; Bini Koh and Kanyan, attended by Martin Gilliat,
strolled through Robinson's store to enjoy again its sights and
sounds; and Mary and Segura disappeared into the establishment's beauty parlour.

They said that they would not be long; a quarter-of-an-hour
would suffice for the slight adjustments to their hair which they
intended. After half-an-hour Gilliat, exhausted by the day's duties
and eager to transport his charges back to the restful atmosphere
of Bukit Serene, made a tactful enquiry at the beauty parlour to
learn whether the ladies were ready. He was assured that they
would be out almost at once.

So he, Bini Koh and Kanyan settled on a sofa close by, to
pass casually there the brief moments before their companions
would rejoin them. Their wait became somewhat protracted.
Quarter-of-an-hour succeeded quarter-of-an-hour, dragging ever
more wearily as the afternoon advanced. Several times the beauty
parlour door opened to let customers out, but none of these was
Segura or Mary.

After another hour Gilliat made a more peremptory enquiry

about the truants. He wondered whether, perhaps, they could have been kidnapped. Assured that such things did not happen in Robinson's, he asked that a message from her mother should be delivered to Segura. This indicated that if she did not reappear forthwith, the consequences would be dire.

Hopefully Gilliat awaited the answer, and after a few minutes it came. Segura sent her compliments and begged to state that she and Mary were now helplessly incarcerated under hair-driers, and that they could not be set free for a considerable time to come.

At length, after two hours, the door opened again, and out strolled Segura and Mary. But somehow they did not appear to be the same females as had entered the place earlier. Each was now crowned with a permanent wave of astonishing vivacity, their hair positively rippling and glistening with wild seascapes of wavelets breaking all over their heads. The experts who operated in the beauty parlour had evidently given them "the works". The pair were transformed into living advertisements for every curl and ringlet that the establishment could produce.

I was not there to witness the aftermath, but Gilliat reported it to me later. Bini Koh had grown steadily more impatient and cross as the afternoon advanced. Now she contemplated her daughter with that pregnant calm which precedes a storm. Silently she contained her wrath so long as the party remained in the shop, but as soon as they settled in the car outside the tempest broke.

Bini Koh gave a contemptuous look at Segura's carefully created coiffure. She opened her mouth and out of it poured a torrent of abuse. She fumed and raged, indicating in phrases of terrible condemnation that her daughter's behaviour was utterly shameless, and that her character was such as no mother would wish her child to possess.

For a while Segura withstood the onslaught with the courage and confidence of revolutionary youth who knows that reactionary old age is blind to the necessity for progress in human affairs. She gazed indifferently out of the car, as if her interest in goings-on in the street commanded her exclusive attention and inadvertently prevented her from realizing that her mother was addressing to her a few pithy remarks. Then a sullen, sulky look crept into her features, betraying that she was indeed aware of the old lady's speech. Suddenly her lower lip quivered, a hurt expression entered her eyes, and she hid her face in her hands. A moment later her shoulders shook convulsively, and a howl of weeping escaped her. Between heartrending sobs she uttered dreadful words of defiance of her mother.

It was a painful, humiliating, tragic scene.

When I returned to Bukit Serene the house was ominously silent. Gilliat apprised me of the cause. Temonggong Koh had returned, and a fresh, flaming row had broken out between Segura and her parents when the chief set eyes on her permanent wave. He was now closeted in his room with his wife, pacing the floor like an angry lion, while Segura lay prostrate in her and Mary's bedroom, tired and ill from weeping.

Mary, a wise and friendly woman, had done her best to intervene, to prevent tempers from rising too high, and to initiate moves towards reconciliation in the family. But she had temporarily lost her influence with Koh and his wife by accompanying Segura into the beauty parlour; so her efforts were in vain. Only time could heal the breach—and it seemed that in this case even time had been set an unusually difficult task.

Koh and his wife were not just Ibans of an old generation, intolerant, as elders sometimes are, of novel ideas in youngsters of their own begetting. The gulf between them and Segura was wider than that of a mere generation; it spanned centuries. They were Ibans of an altogether earlier way of life, a disappearing epoch. She was an Iban of a new age, acquiring a completely different outlook, hankering after a modern, revolutionary mode of living. Her dress and manners, appearance and notions were powerfully influenced by sudden impact with the vital, exciting, infectious habits of alien peoples, Malays, Chinese and Europeans. She was drifting away from her native traditions. That was what hurt her aged parents so deeply.

The clash between them was awful. The incident of the permanent wave was not its cause, but only a symptom. The old couple felt that their child was turning away from them, that she despised her family and race, that she now preferred other society—and their resentment was bitter. It was all the more violent because they loved her truly.

Poor Segura, it was not her fault. She was a victim of social circumstances far beyond her comprehension or control. On her were being inflicted the pains of the birth of a new order. She was a scapegoat for a system of society which had remained too long conservative, and which was now suffering an inevitable, yet too swift, too sudden, almost too catastrophic transformation from one stage of evolution to another.

Outwardly friendly relations between her and her parents were gradually re-established during the next two days at Bukit Serene, but beneath the surface the misunderstanding between them remained.

III

Apart from the violent disturbance of her temper produced by the beauty parlour incident, Segura seemed very gay and happy during those days. She entered with zest into all our activities. In the amusement park at the Happy World she sampled every thrill offered for our entertainment, laughing often as she sped on horseback on the merry-go-round, floated upwards on the giant wheel, drove a motor-car round the miniature race-track, shied wooden balls at leering Aunt Sallies, and engaged in all manner of other sports. Again, when we played blind-man's-buff, touch-last, hunt-the-thimble and similar games in the evenings at Bukit Serene, she was as full of fun as anyone.

She looked exceedingly pretty. By now she had abandoned for ever any attempt to retain the appearance and habits of a simple, untutored Iban girl. She dressed, made herself up and brushed her hair much as did famous contemporary Malay film actresses. Her models were photographs of glamorous local stars like Siput Sarawak which found their way in magazines into the bazaar, if not into the school, at Kapit. Naturally she had not the accomplished, professional sartorial art of these successful beauties. She had neither the money nor the experience to dress as finely as they. Her sarongs and bajus were of cheaper materials, and her style was an inferior copy of theirs. But it was a young amateur's brave attempt to emulate their grace, and the natural physical attributes which she brought to the effort were as enchanting as theirs. Her face at the age of seventeen had an unblemished, flowerlike loveliness, and her figure a trim sweetness which attracted notice wherever she went. Always when we strolled through the streets of Singapore, people turned to gaze at her.

She was aware of this, and seemed to accept the compliment as a matter of course. Admiration did not spoil her, nor make her vain and silly. She recognized the fact that she was good-looking, was pleased by it, and did her best with her little brush and comb, powder-puff and lipstick to accentuate her beauty. But her manner and conduct remained natural and modest. She had a charming, unaffected smile.

Yet in reality she was at that time profoundly unhappy. The contradictions in her life baffled and confused her. Moreover, she was involved in an unfortunate affair of the heart. She confided this to me in a talk at Bukit Serene, with Spurway as our interpreter.

The story seemed to be as follows. Before she went to school at Kapit she had already experienced two or three long-house love affairs. As the reader knows, such temporary liaisons were, within limits, an accepted part of the social and moral code of Iban society on the Balleh. They were regarded as a natural and proper means by which a girl could eventually find a congenial husband, and a boy a suitable wife. The system permitted a number of experiments before youngsters made their final choice.

Each of Segura's affairs so far had ended in her rejecting her suitor. According to the custom in which she was brought up, and which she had never heard challenged, it was inevitable and right that in due course she should find herself in love again, and be intimate with the youth of her fancy.

At that moment Koh sent her to the mission school in Kapit. She was not really a bad pupil, but nature had now loosed in her stronger impulses than an inclination to sit at a desk developing her intellectual capacities. She felt the normal, instinctive desire of a young female for attractive masculine company. The school did not cater for that particular requirement. Though its scholars included one or two girls of her own age, its male pupils consisted only of a few boys not yet in their 'teens. After a while she began to miss badly the company of the opposite sex to which she was accustomed, and which it was natural for her to enjoy.

Young men from the township were not allowed to visit the school. Occasionally, however, the students were led on expeditions into Kapit, where they strolled round Fort Sylvia, viewed the lake and inspected the bazaar. Segura was attracted by the bazaar, and made a few purchases there. Encouraged by the missionaries, she had already discarded her native Iban dress and adopted a new style, a baju to hide her naked bosom and a sarong to cover her shapely legs. She liked the pretty designs of the blouses, and the colourful folds of the long skirts were as gay as they were novel. Soon her feminine delight in such things led her to adopt other fashions which were advertised in Kapit's shops. She bought a pair of red shoes for her brown feet, and some blue ribbon for her black hair. Then, one day, she allowed an expert in the art of beauty culture to shear off her long, straight tresses, and to contrive instead artful little curls all over her head.

The magnetism of the bazaar for Segura grew gradually stronger. Here was a new, fascinating, tinselled way of life, more exciting than the old-fashioned manners of long-house society up the Balleh. And the shops at Kapit hinted at another, more fabulous life led by people in the greater world beyond. Tales of it came up-river with traders from centres like Sibu and Kuching.

One afternoon she met a young Chinese trader in the bazaar. She liked his looks, and was glad when she found that he could speak Iban. They conversed together. He had travelled, and he talked to her of the wonders of the wide world. He seemed to be himself a part of that freer, more spacious existence, with his business contacts, his neat European clothes and his pleasant, courteous speech. Soon she fell in love with him, and how could he do other than lose his heart to her?

Her feeling for him was quite serious, and in that situation it was right and proper for an Iban girl to accept all his advances.

She realized, however, that for some inexplicable reason her school teachers would not approve of this. They did not seem to understand. She wished to have her love affair openly, as she would at home, but the mission put barriers in her way. It gave no facilities for her and her friend to meet; so she was forced to see him by stealth. At nights she climbed through her dormitory window, dropped silently to the grass below, and ran with fast-beating heart to their secret trysting place.

That, at least, is my reconstruction of how the episode started. The narrative is right in substance, though it may be incorrect in some details. Segura did not tell us the complete story, but only its general import.

When she came to Bukit Serene her affair with the young Chinese had continued for some time. It had the magic touch of romance for her, yet already showed signs of being only a half-happy arrangement. Many circumstances worked against its success. The fact that she was forced to conduct her friendship clandestinely cast a shadow across it. She wished it to be a publicly acknowledged alliance, a companionship as irreproachable as it was sincere; but secretiveness gave it an air of guilt which troubled her.

The element of conspiracy also gave it a tenseness which had not characterized the previous pleasant but comparatively light liaisons in which she had been involved. They were frankly recognized as experiments entered into genuinely but tentatively, to be abandoned if they proved mistakes. She began this new venture in the same spirit, intending that it should have a provisional character until she learned whether it satisfied her and could blossom into true, abiding love. In the latter case, of course, she would be ready to commit herself wholly to her new-found partner; otherwise she would wish the incident to end by common consent with mutual goodwill. She soon discovered, however, that the concealed nature of the affair made it somehow more committal, more difficult to treat as temporary, an entanglement from which it would be hard to escape.

Moreover, her Chinese lover never regarded it as the tentative trial which Iban custom decreed. An old-fashioned Cantonese brought up in a different social tradition, he assumed that any young woman who gave herself to him was willing to become either his permanent wife or his regular concubine. From the beginning, therefore, he thought the affair more final than she did. How could she have realized that his attitude would differ from hers? She knew only the Iban view of life, and did not comprehend that the Chinese had other ideas.

In this complicated situation she had hoped for friendly help from her parents when she returned home and told them of her latest love affair. Instead she received a fierce blast of their displeasure. It was the occasion which I have already described, when her relationship with them was spoiled by their disapproval of her head shorn of its long hair and her face painted with powder and lipstick. Koh immediately flew into a rage; and he was in no mood later to consider with sympathy the news that she was conducting a "trial marriage" with a Chinese. Had the youth been an Iban, he would have regarded the incident as a matter of course; but that she, the daughter of the paramount chief, should be thus involved with a foreigner filled his cup of disappointment to the brim. He scolded her mercilessly, and his lack of consideration aroused rebellious feelings in her which only increased her emotional difficulties.

Incidentally, Koh had by then conceived the idea that Segura, after leaving school, should quit the long-house and settle permanently in Kapit. At that time another new development occurred in Iban society. The chiefs thought that the Chinese monopoly of trade on the Rejang should be broken, and that Ibans should share in the profits of commerce. They planned to acquire shops in the bazaars at Kapit and elsewhere, reckoning that their natural ability for such work would be at least as great as that of the Chinese, and that in addition the pagans, who composed a vast majority of the customers on the river, would prefer to deal with their fellow natives. So they looked forward to engaging in lucrative business. Progressive penghulus like Jugah and Sibat were discussing the project, and Koh himself was a party to their scheme. Pondering the question of who could manage a shop for him, he hit on the plan that Segura should devote the talents derived from a modern education to this purpose.

An assumption of the proposal was that she would marry an

Iban who would be her helpmate in the venture. No other matrimonial possibility had ever entered his head. Now he was flabbergasted by the suggestion that she might wed a Chinese, and the fact that the young man was already established in business in Kapit seemed to him tantamount to selling the pass of his commercial interests to an enemy. This unpalatable thought increased the fury of the terms in which he expressed disapproval of her romance.

In her trouble poor Segura had no one to turn to. Her parents were hostile. Others whom she might have relied on for sympathy, like her sisters and Jugah and Sibat, shared Temonggong Koh's dismay at her conduct. She dared not tell the authorities at the mission school, for she realized that they would sternly rebuke her. In her distress only her Chinese friend was gentle and kind to her, and this increased her dependence on him.

Yet—she told Spurway and me with tears in her eyes—she was inclined to think that she did not want to marry him. She was fond of him and grateful to him, but her people's prejudice against a Chinese affected her deeply, and made her sceptical about the decisive step of matrimony. At the same time it was difficult for her to break the association so long as she stayed at Kapit—and she had no wish to leave Kapit and return to the long-house. She was in a cruel dilemma.

Spurway and I found it extremely difficult to decide what, if anything, we could do to help solve this affecting personal problem. In theory it seemed best that Segura's breach with long-house life should now be confirmed, that she should be transferred to reside in a "modern" centre where her transition from the old Iban ways to the new could be continued, and where she would in due course marry some young Iban policeman, government official or other youth whose future lay in up-to-date society. She would be an ideal wife for such a man, and he would give her the niche in life for which she was suited. Failing an Iban, there was no good reason why she should not happily wed an eligible Malay, Chinese or other young citizen of Sarawak.

Yet it was hard to see how this theory could be translated into practice. Where could Segura go? Who would look after her? And how would she occupy herself? My first impulse was to arrange for her to stay for a while in Singapore, where I could keep a fraternal eye on her (for was she not now my sister?) and she could continue her education and adapt herself to urban life. But the risks of failure, of misfit and misery for her, were too great for this idea to mature seriously. My wife was at that time away in Canada, and so was not available to give the girl sympathetic feminine help. Moreover, if Segura stayed in Singapore, she would probably never wish to return to Sarawak. That would mean permanent separation from her family, and a loss of her to her people. It seemed wrong, for she was just the type of young woman who might play an important part in the tactful transition of the Ibans from their present primitive state into the more progressive society which was their destiny.

But where in Sarawak might Segura go? There was nowhere in the colony a training school for young Iban ladies desirous of quitting their long-houses. Nor could we think of anyone sufficiently free, interested and understanding to take Segura into their home and give her the care and instruction which would complete the change begun by the school at Kapit. Spurway might have made some arrangement in Kuching which would enable him to act as guardian to her, but he was due to retire a few months later from the Sarawak service, and to live in England.

There seemed no practical alternative to Segura's return to her father's house when the time came for her to leave school. And in any case there was much to be said for that course. She would go back to the circle of her family, where she belonged. Her roots lay in traditional Iban life, and she might slip easily again into its manners. Many of the new ideas which she had acquired in her brief sojourn at Kapit might pass out of her mind as quickly as they had entered it.

Yet things might not turn out that way. Her new notions might prove an enduring part of her make-up. Then she would be an incompatible element in the house, a frustrated, unhappy stranger there. Above all she might no longer feel disposed to take a husband who was just an old-fashioned, near-naked, primitive native, ignorant of modern ways. Her womanly life and contentment would then be destroyed.

We pondered the problem anxiously, and could find no satis-

factory solution to it. There seemed no way in which we for-
eigners could with certainty make a helpful intervention. It
appeared better to let matters take whatever course Koh and his
wife, their Iban friends and Segura herself decided to be best
for her. We tried to discuss the matter with Koh, to induce in
him a warmer understanding and sympathy for his baffled
daughter; but a tactful sounding of the old man revealed that he
was in obstinate mood, not amenable to reason. So Segura's
problem was as confused as ever when she and her parents left
Bukit Serene and I waved good-bye to them aboard the ship which
carried them back to Sarawak.

CHAPTER TWELVE

RETREAT FROM PAGANISM

I

Two MONTHS LATER astonishing news arrived from the Balleh. It came without warning, and seemed as inexplicable as it was surprising. First a rumour announced, and then official report confirmed, that Temonggong Koh and Penghulus Jugah, Sibat and Jinggut, with more than a dozen other leading pagans on the river, had been baptized by Burr Baughman as Christians.

My first intelligence of the event came in a characteristic message from Jugah. A few days before Christmas he sent me a telegram saying, "Merry Christmas! I am a Christian now. Love from Penghulu Jugah."

I was dumbfounded, and when I learned later of the extent of the baptisms I felt a mixture of pleasure and concern. The mass conversion of such an impressive group of Iban leaders on the Balleh was of course a triumph for Baughman and the Methodist mission, but it seemed impossible that, on the part of some at least of the chiefs, it was authentic. Undoubtedly Jugah, Sibat, Jinggut and several other serious-minded penghulus were genuine, and had real comprehension of what Christianity meant; but I doubted both the understanding and the sincerity of others. As for Koh, he was far too old and set in his ideas to adopt, except in a most superficial manner, a profound new faith. Presumably he had been talked into this sudden change by some of the younger men, who perhaps thought it politically opportune and spiritually harmless.

I was told by a mutual friend afterwards that Baughman himself shared these doubts. He had known for some time that Jugah, Sibat and Jinggut were intelligently attracted by Christianity, but it was something of a surprise to him when a much larger group of chiefs asked to be christened. His first instinct was to refuse one or two of them; but then he realized the difficulty which he would cause if he accepted some and rejected the rest. In particular it would be hard to shut the door of the Church against the paramount chief while opening it to his juniors. Moreover, by receiving so many leaders as avowed Christians he could increase his influence with them, and secure better opportunities for educational missionary work among their people.

Feeling, however, that he should not himself take a decision on this somewhat dubious matter, he referred it to his Methodist superiors in Singapore. They approved the baptisms. So, at a historic service at Kapit, Temonggong Koh and an array of distinguished ex-pagans were received into the Church.

As I anticipated, this remarkable event did not produce any change in Koh's outlook on material, intellectual or spiritual matters. Some time earlier he had invited me to attend a great Hornbill Ceremony which he planned to hold. This was one of the rarest of all traditional pagan celebrations, and was to mark the final stage on this earth of his intimate personal association with the Iban gods. It did not strike him that there was any contradiction between such solemn heathen rites and his recent profession of Christianity, for he now renewed in pressing terms his invitation to me to attend the ceremony. No doubt the Almighty, who loves with deep compassion all us miserable sinners, accepted the situation with His infinite benevolence and mercy.

I promised to visit Koh after the harvest in the following year, 1951; so the Hornbill Ceremony was fixed for that time. Then another piece of unexpected news arrived from the Balleh. Bini Koh died. The old chief's house was plunged in mourning. Various funerary taboos had to be observed, and in any case sorrow forbade jollification. The Hornbill Ceremony and my visit to the Balleh were therefore postponed, and before they could take place the next padi-planting started. It delayed for several months my journey to my friends.

I was surprised when, only a few weeks afterwards, a third piece of remarkable intelligence reached me from the Balleh. Koh had married again! The aged chieftain wedded a buxom,

presentable Iban lass in her late twenties. She seemed a girl of
personality, for report said that she had now assumed control in
his long-house with complete acceptability to everyone concerned,
including her step-daughters, Iba and Mindun. They, too, were
women of strong character, and both were older than she.

The same budget of news informed me that immediately
after her mother's death Segura left school and returned to her
father's house. Precise tidings of her were difficult to get, for I
was largely dependent on chance communications from travellers.
Reports about her were conflicting. Some alleged that she had
settled comfortably again in her home, become reconciled to its
way of life, and grown obedient to her parent; while others
declared that she was unhappy, that the situation between her
and her relations was strained, and that her spirit was rebellious.

Information about her romance with the young Chinese was
also contradictory. One visitor from Borneo assured me that it
had ended, and that Segura was once again an unattached, heart-
free Iban damsel; yet from another source I heard that the friendship continued secretly with unabated affection on both sides.

Uncertain of the situation, and fearing difficulties between
old Koh and his impetuous daughter, I sent him a message
urging understanding and sympathy towards her, and another
message to her advising calmness, sweetness and prudence with
him. From both I received replies that they would heed my
advice, and each begged me to come and see them soon.

I needed no persuasion. The various changes in the household made me curious to revisit my Iban family. In particular
I felt it my duty to pay filial respects to Koh's bride, my new
mother. So I planned to travel up the Balleh immediately after
the padi harvest in April, reckoning that the chief would hold
his long postponed and keenly awaited Hornbill Ceremony then.
Suddenly, near the end of January, he sent me word that it was
imperative for the celebration to be held before the crop ripened,
that all his other guests were invited, that the occasion would
be a fiasco without me, and that he hoped I could join them in his
house in the following week. Hastily I readjusted a programme
of engagements in Singapore, and obeyed the summons.

II

I could spare only a few days away from Malaya, and had to hurry. Flying to Kuching, I picked up the Governor, no longer Sir Charles Arden-Clarke but a successor, Sir Anthony Abell. Thence we flew to Sibu, where we alighted on the Rejang and embarked in a motor-launch.

As we went up-river I saw many changes. In Sibu spick-and-span buildings were the first fruits of a grand new town-plan; in Kanowit a street of imposing cement shops rose amidst the decaying remnants of the wood and attap bazaar; at Song the settlement's original, precipitous site had been abandoned, and a modern Song was being created on flat ground on the opposite side of the river; and in Kapit immense developments were taking place. The old bazaar, with its earthen road and ramshackle timber shop-houses, had disappeared, and in its place stood a handsome new shopping centre worthy of any sophisticated town. Its wide roadway was hard-surfaced, flanked with stone pavements and dignified by an occasional lamp-post; its buildings were large concrete structures with spacious rooms and an air of smart prosperity; and the area which they covered was much larger than of yore. Modern government offices, a pleasant new church and a massive warehouse completed the impression of a flourishing young settlement.

The contents of the shops also showed laudable enterprise. In the departments selling ladies' clothing the supply of sarongs and dresses was better in quantity and quality than when Segura and I made our purchases there two years earlier. The variety of other goods was also eloquent of ambitious commercial progress. I noticed some significant details. In the show-cases of jewellery the silver belts which Iban women wore with their native skirts were scarce; in their place Malay bajus, European blouses and Javanese sarongs were plentifully displayed. Moreover, there were fewer silver ear-rings and other ornaments of traditional design, and large stocks of necklaces and brooches bearing the Christian cross lay on the counters instead. Not only sartorial, but also ethical fashions were changing.

I learned that some of the new shops belonged to Iban chiefs;

so their desire to enter trade was being realized. Jugah owned a
fine emporium, and another was almost ready for Temonggong
Koh—the establishment which he once hoped that Segura, suitably husbanded, would manage. None of these places was actually operated by a native. In every case the penghulu let his
property to a Chinese towkay, who paid a rent and pocketed
the rest of the profits. The landlord reserved for himself an
upstairs room where he and his relatives could stay when they
came to town. To the Ibans this arrangement seemed more advan-
tageous than becoming merchants themselves, since it assured
them regular incomes, without either the hard work or the grave
risks of personal participation in business.

I heard that Penghulu Grinang had also owned a shop, rented
it to a Chinese and for a while enjoyed from it a desirable income.
Unfortunately he invested the whole of this money in fluid assets
—in other words, drink. The result was that before long his
business went literally as well as technically into liquidation. He
was forced to sell the property and revert to a less extravagant
scale of self-entertainment. This extraordinarily bibulous period
in Grinang's life left a permanent mark on the map of Kapit,
for it gave a new name to the lake beside the District Officer's
house. Let me recount the tale of this interesting geographical
fact.

Late one night the penghulu, after a bout of drinking, paid
a courtesy call on the District Officer, now a curly-headed, intelligent young man called Richards. Being more or less incapable
of coherent speech, the chief was a tedious visitor, and before
long Richards led him to the door. In the darkness Grinang
recognized the lights of the distant fort, and started to walk
straight to them. Before Richards could stop him he had crossed
the path, descended the slope to the lake and waded into the
water. In reply to Richards' shouts of warning the penghulu
emitted a number of light-hearted yells imitative of jungle animals, and persisted obstinately on his way. He was in that state
of happy emotional elation which makes a man's body somehow
impervious to physical obstacles. The proper path to the fort
wound circuitously round the lake; but Grinang was blissfully
conscious of only two things: first, that the lights ahead were

those of the fort which he wished to reach, and second, that he was taking the shortest cut to them. As he advanced the water rose from his knees to his thighs, from his thighs to his waist and from his waist to his chest, but he continued his bee-line progress, singing with ever wilder jubilation as he sank lower into the lake. Fortunately at its deepest spot it reached no higher than his shoulders, so his neck and head remained above water. Eventually he emerged on the farther shore, shook himself like a dog landing from a swim in the sea, and then continued in a straight line over hillocks, flower beds and hedges to his goal.

After that the lake was christened "Jalan Grinang", which means "Grinang's Way".

As Abell and I strolled through the bazaar, we met a Negro with crinkled hair, tender eyes, smiling lips, pearly teeth and a natty American tropical suit. Richards introduced him to us as Mr. Tom Harris, and explained that he had recently arrived to help Burr Baughman in his work on the Rejang. So Baughman's little troop of Methodist crusaders now consisted of his American self, his Chinese wife, a Negro principal, a Sumatran assistant and an increasing cohort of Iban and Chinese converts. It was an impressive demonstration of the cosmopolitan camaraderie of Christianity.

Harris told us of a programme of expansion which the mission planned on the Rejang. The original school at Kapit now boasted sixty students. Soon a second small academy would be built in the settlement. Meanwhile a classroom had been established near Penghulu Jinggut's house up the Balleh, and the founding of other schools along the river was in the planning stage. Baughman was at that moment up-river settling their sites. The most important among them would be that at Nanja Nujong, the mouth of the river where Sibat and Rabong lived. It was to be partly a farm-training centre, and would be Harris's own headquarters, for he was an agricultural expert engaged to teach the Ibans improved methods of husbandry.

From Richards I sought news of Temonggong Koh and his family, and especially of Segura. He confirmed the report that her unhappy romance with the young Chinese in Kapit was over, though he could not tell me why or how it ended. Her

future seemed uncertain. Rumour whispered that her father,
feeling no confidence now in her capacity to choose a suitable
husband for herself, intended to marry her to a young Iban schoolmaster from a neighbouring district. The lad was reputed to
be a pleasant, well educated "modern" youth—but Segura's private
thoughts on this plan remained, I gathered, her own secret.

That afternoon we embarked in temois for the journey up-
river.

III

When we turned into the Balleh I felt, as always at that point,
like a traveller who, after long wanderings, returns home. The
wild yet peaceful jungle gave us its familiar welcome.

Towards dusk we arrived at a modest long-house of some
twenty doors, where we were to spend the night. Its inmates
gave us a friendly greeting and treated us to a characteristic sample
of Iban hospitality. But we retired early to bed, for prudence demanded that we should snatch ample sleep before the morrow's
celebrations in Koh's house.

At first light next morning we departed. Dawn mists still
hung over the hills, but gradually they dissolved and revealed
beautiful, savage landscapes. Here and there small patches of
hillside cleared of forest sprouted with padi. The crop was
almost ripe, and the harvest looked good. As we advanced up
the Balleh we passed successively the mouths of its various
tributaries, each the domain of a famous Iban chief—first the
Su'ut where Jinggut's writ ran, and then the Nujong where Sibat
and Rabong dwelt, and after that the beautiful Merirai where
Jugah was lord, and finally the Ga'at where Grinang ruled the
roost. Occasionally we saw evidence that in these remote places
the phenomenon called progress had taken several paces forward
since my last visit. In particular we noticed signs of the penghulus' ventures into trade. Our friends were fast becoming
shop-keepers. On the river bank opposite the Merirai we saw the
timber skeleton of a half-built hut, and learned that it would be
a store owned by Tedong. Sibat had employed a different technique. Acquiring a temoi and stocking it with merchandise, he

engaged an agent to skipper it and sent it up- and down-river conducting business on the mobile principle adopted by street vendors of ice-cream.

Again, when at mid-day we reached the point of land where the Ga'at flows into the Balleh, we saw a trim new shed standing on the bank. From its door ran Jugah's wife and his pretty daughter Sani. They gave us a warm welcome when we disembarked, and announced that this was Jugah's shop. They told us that Sani and her husband now lived there, managing the place for the penghulu. This was indeed a small symptom of a great revolution, for it meant that the Iban couple had abandoned communal life in a long-house for family life in their own home, and had exchanged the collective enterprise of Iban husbandry for the individual venture of private trade.

Sani seemed plumper than in earlier years. I hoped that this was testimony that Jugah's business prospered. Her husband was away that day, fetching goods from Kapit. She told me proudly that he managed the shop, and that she was his helpmate. But on further investigation I discovered that their control of affairs was purely nominal. A Chinese clerk who in theory was their assistant, in practice did most of the work.

During lunch Sani gave me an example of her feckless incapacity to run the business. The mid-day sun was scorching out-of-doors, and we ate in the shady room of the shop. To quench my thirst I asked for a bottle of orange-squash, such as scores of Sani's customers must have received regularly from her hands. She brought it with the professional grace of an Iban maiden dispensing glasses of tuak, but when I held out money and enquired the price she laughed and shrugged her shoulders.

"I'm just a stupid native," she exclaimed in her mother tongue. "I don't know the prices of things."

She asked the Chinese assistant, who perhaps added a commission to the actual tariff. The fact was that in most of those trading enterprises on the Balleh at that time the Chinese outsmarted the Ibans. The natives were capable of learning, and with experience would become reasonably competent business men; but in the beginning they had no knowledge of such matters, and depended on their Chinese subordinates.

Sani told me that she lived almost always at the shop. When I asked whether she missed Jugah's great mansion and her pleasant companions there, she replied that she preferred her new existence. She found it novel and amusing.

I was disappointed to learn that she did not intend to come to the Hornbill Ceremony at Temonggong Koh's. She explained that she could not neglect her duty in the shop for many days. When I said that I would stay but a short while at Koh's house, that I would return down-river on the following afternoon, and that I could take her in my boat that day and deliver her back the next, she was delighted with the proposal. She disappeared into her private room to pack her belongings, and five minutes later reappeared with a small suitcase ready for departure.

Jugah's wife accepted a similar invitation, and asked whether she could bring her son Alo, who stood at her side. He was the child whom I had seen wearing long hair and an Iban sirat in Jugah's house two years before, the boy whom his parents intended to rear in traditional style as a man of the jungle. Imagine my surprise when I saw him now, an intelligent, bright-eyed lad with neatly cut hair, a beautifully washed face and an immaculately laundered white shirt and shorts!

On later enquiry I learned that his change of fashion had been forced upon his parents by himself. He flatly refused to remain a wild man of Borneo while his brother, Linggi, became a modern gentleman. So stubborn was he in opposition to his parents' plan that eventually Jugah capitulated and sent the boy to Baughman's school in Kapit. Alo's rebellion was eloquent of the aspirations of the young generation of Ibans on the Balleh.

So when Richards and I re-embarked in our temoi we were joined by Bini Jugah, Sani and Alo. They squatted at ease beside us. As we went up-river, Richards lolled on cushions and read a book, I relaxed and scribbled some notes in my diary, Rabong fell asleep, Alo maintained a keen watch on all the sights of the river, and the ladies made their toilets for Koh's party. With graceful movements they combed, oiled and dressed their long hair, rubbed cream on their skins and adorned themselves with jewellery. Thus in pleasant companionship we travelled to the Temonggong's house.

Two incidents during the journey were worth recording. At one spot in mid-stream the branch of a drifting tree protruded, and on it crouched a baby crocodile. The little creature measured less than two feet long and seemed endowed with the pretty innocence of a kitten—until I saw through field glasses its fierce, glaring eyes and ugly, trap-like jaw!

The other incident was even more unusual. As we went up-river a drizzle of rain began and formed a thin, transparent veil between us and the sunlit scene. Suddenly a brilliant rainbow appeared close by us, descending in a bold curve from the sky and touching the water's surface only ten yards away.

I drew Richards' attention to it, remarking on its marvellous beauty and astonishing proximity.

"Yes, it's lovely," he replied. "But don't point it out to the Ibans. They regard such a rainbow as a very bad omen."

I felt a stab of foreboding in my heart. Somehow I attached significance to the Iban superstition. The rainbow, I thought, was in truth a prophecy of evil, and I wondered what tragedy would happen in the next few days.

IV

Late that afternoon we arrived at Koh's home. Our reception was as vociferous as ever. Ancient brass cannon fired a salute, and as our boats came to land shouts of welcome rose from the throats of the people waiting ashore.

First among them stood Koh himself in all the dignity of pagan dress. His three daughters were at his side. Iba and Mindun wore their customary attire, except that even Iba had now added a Malay baju above her Iban skirt. Only Segura was completely different. Her powdered face was paler than the rest, her hair was set in Western style, and she wore a white blouse and smartly tailored green skirt of European sports-girl cut. At a distance she looked like some beautiful English miss on a visit to strange Bornean friends.

Koh muttered blessings as he shook my hand, and Iba and Mindun chortled as they offered me drinks for my attendant spirit and myself. Segura took no part in this primitive ritual,

but there was a kind welcome in her eyes. I noticed at once that
her expression was more mature, her face indefinably older than
when I last saw her. It was more womanly. Her manner, too,
had subtly changed. Instead of clutching my hand with childish
impulsiveness as she used to do, she slipped an arm through one
of mine with easy, assured, adult friendship.

We ascended the flight of steps to the house and celebrated
forthwith in its gallery the customary bedara. Our host's recent
conversion to Christianity caused no change whatever in the
substance or the spirit of the ceremonial. When the feast was
spread for the demons and deities, Mindun chanted a pantun to
every visitor in turn; and Segura crouched on the mat before me
and sang a few verses in my honour.

Then Koh introduced me to his latest bride, my new mother.
Rumour in this instance had not been a lying jade. The girl
was a buxom wench, said to be now in her twenty-eighth year.
Her face was pleasant, and she made no pretence of being anything but an untutored Iban woman. Except for her colourfully
woven skirt she was naked. Her limbs were strong and smooth,
and her breasts hung as large as melons. She favoured me with
an unaffected smile, and I gained an impression of a modest,
sensible, capable character. Her name was Mantai, but Koh
never referred to her as anything but "bini bahru", which simply
means "new wife".

Among my fellow guests were Jugah, Tedong, Grinang, Sibat
and Sandai. We greeted each other like brothers, and were soon
garrulously exchanging scraps of news. Jugah was delighted
that I had brought his wife and Sani and Alo. I, on the other
hand, was disappointed to learn that Siah and her husband
had not accompanied him. They had stayed on the Merirai to
gather the harvest, a task which had already begun.

For the next few hours the house was filled with a din of
hammering and carpentry. On the outer platform squads of men
were making architectural adaptations for the Hornbill Ceremony next day. Little time was left for the work, and with
feverish haste they chopped at lengths of tree trunk, chiselled
them into smooth tall masts, knocked bits and pieces of joinery
together, carved effigies of birds and beasts, painted these with

lurid features, arranged decorative foliage, hung flags and performed a hundred other acts of noisy construction.

Abell and I held a conference with the chiefs in the Temonggong's private chamber, to discuss government policy on local
problems. The women worked at their multifarious domestic
duties elsewhere in the room. Mantai was in command of them,
and Iba and Mindun too were deeply engaged. Among the busy
females was Segura.

I watched her closely, wondering whether she had fitted
again into the environment of her home. The answer to the
question was hard to discover. It seemed to be neither an unqualified affirmative nor a negative, but a mixture of the two.
In some ways she appeared a normal member of the household.
I was glad to see how hard and willingly she worked. Perpetually active, she carried dishes, rinsed rice-bowls, tended the
fire, set food on plates for bedaras, and undertook a score of
similar labours of a kitchen maid. Her superior education and
polished manners made no difference between the tasks which
she and the others performed.

Yet she seemed to be a separate creature from them. Her
dress distinguished her even from those who adopted the modern
fetish of covering their nakedness with a baju. It was true that
she had changed now from her English blouse and skirt into an
Asian style of costume; but this, too, had a sophistication hitherto
unknown on the Balleh. Her brightly flowered batik sarong
worn in the style made famous to film fans by Miss Dorothy
Lamour was more akin to Hollywood than Borneo. Her made-up
face also marked her from all her companions.

Yet she worked as one of them, seeming perfectly content. It
was difficult to decide what was her exact position. And if the
appearance of things was reassuring, what about the hidden
reality of her thoughts? Had she contradictory secret feelings?
Was there a conflict in her heart? She gave no inkling of her state
of mind. Whenever she passed near the table where we sat, she
threw a glance in our direction and smiled at me. That was all.

Gradually I picked up scraps of the story of her return from
school. When she first arrived in the long-house, several months
earlier, she received a cold, unfriendly reception. Her conduct

with the Chinese youth at Kapit was well-known, and universally condemned as scandalous. Her relations with her father were bad. He treated her with apparent indifference, and the other Ibans modelled their attitude on the chief's. They ostracized and ignored her. She herself was partly to blame for this, for she felt rebellious and made no attempt to hide her feelings. She lent no hand in the housework, but sat always sulking, always alone. Her family addressed a minimum of remarks to her, and as often as not she refused to answer even their scant enquiries. That period, when she was despised and rejected and yet ever present, must have been one of terrible strain for all the principal persons concerned.

Such a tense situation could not long remain static. It must either grow worse and end in dreadful disaster, or gradually improve. Providentially it took the latter course. Koh's affection for his erring child slowly reasserted itself and melted his heart. After a while he began to speak occasional kind words to her. She for her part was helpless to translate her rebellious sentiment into action in the form of escape, for he forbade her ever to leave the house, and posted sentinels to watch her. She soon got bored with complete inactivity, and so made a concession by starting to help in the housework. By gradual processes a reconciliation took place, until she more or less resumed her position as a member of the family. At that time my messages to Koh and Segura arrived, urging each to be understanding and friendly with the other, and I gathered that they were a protective influence in her favour and a helpful element towards achieving their reunion.

Yet Segura never resumed completely her rightful place in the house as the chief's youngest, best-loved daughter. That was partly because the past could not be wholly forgotten, and partly because she herself did not wish to revert to all her earlier Iban ways. She worked hard, but it was almost always in the background, and she rarely appeared as a prominent performer in our ceremonials. Least of all did she return to her proper office as leader of the troupe of belles who officiated at bedaras. She did not even rejoin that choice company as a member. In her different dress she occasionally poured a drink and sang a pantun; but for me and me alone.

In spite of the apparent reconciliation between her and her father, I sensed a restraint in their relationship. Perhaps it was caused by the fact that over them hung the shadow of the future. Did Koh know what he intended to do about a marriage for Segura? And if he did, was she a party to his design? No one in the house seemed to know, but rumour was busy. That evening I heard again that Koh was resolved to marry her to a young Iban school teacher, though nobody could say with confidence whether the decision had been finally taken. Nor could anyone venture an opinion on Segura's attitude. Could it be that she knew of the proposal, and that her calm spirits were a sign at least of resignation, if not of happy consent to her fate? I had no means of telling, but to me the uncertainty seemed ominous. If Barcroft or Spurway or some other sympathetic person accustomed to act as interpreter for Segura and me had been present, I would have learned more; but in their absence I had no chance of enlightenment.

That evening was devoted to informal relaxation. No official part of the Hornbill Ceremony would commence until the morrow. Then it would start early. We would rise before the sun and continue all day and far into the night the solemnities and gambols which were to be the climax of Temonggong Koh's life on earth.

We intended only some mild frolics that evening, and then an early retreat to bed. But those good resolutions got broken. First we performed a grand bedara with merry rounds of singing and drinking; then young bucks of the house and visiting penghulus exhibited their prowess at dancing; and after that we visitors had to do our parlour tricks. Finally we started the nursery games from the Western world which were now a regular part of our ritual on these occasions, playing hunt-the-slipper and other such light-hearted sports until two o'clock in the morning.

Throughout them Koh was astonishingly active. Before the visit I had been warned that I would find a great change in the venerable chief. I was told that he had aged immensely in recent months, some of my informants even suggesting that he was growing senile. I expected, therefore, to find a feeble old man, and was delightfully surprised to discover instead a veteran who showed his three-score years and nineteen in grizzled locks and wrinkled face, but belied them in strong arms and vigorous legs. It was true that he seemed somewhat quieter, a trifle more reserved than of yore, but his energy never flagged and when we engaged in his favourite game, blind-man's-buff, he was second to none in exuberance and stamina.

Abell, Jugah, Sibat, Grinang, Richards and all the other Sarawak chieftains, brown and white alike, were tireless in these manly activities, and young Kanyan, too, played a lively part. The females proved no less zealous. This was Mantai's initiation into these particular rites, and she joined in them with zest. Iba and Mindun were practised players, and showed their mastery of every trick of obstruction and evasion, while Segura entered into the fun with a gloriously carefree spirit.

Once more she had changed her dress, appearing now in a chic short jacket of red velvet over a high-collared, snow-white blouse, with a flamboyant sarong falling to dainty silver slippers. She did not allow this costume to cramp her style. Throwing away her coat and kicking off her shoes, she darted hither and thither in escape from the blind-man until she was utterly breathless, got caught and became herself the pursuer. She seemed to be the happy Segura of old. Laughing with joy, she appeared to have no care in the world. I wondered, hopefully, whether the truth could be that she was fully aware of her father's plan for her marriage, that she approved his choice of a bridegroom, and that her gaiety was the expression of a girl head over heels in love.

Some time in the small hours we began to tire, and my suggestion that it might be prudent to spend a short while in bed was favourably received. We bade each other "Salamat teedor" and dispersed to our sleeping quarters.

My mattress and mosquito-net were spread in a corner of Koh's apartment, with Tony Abell's close by. The Temonggong, his wife, Mantai, and other members of their household were to sleep in the same chamber. Iba and Mindun, with their husbands and children, retired to a cubicle in the loft, while Segura had her bed in the next room. Some of the Ibans did not settle at once to slumber. As I undressed, Koh and a few cronies squatted for gossip round a lamp on the floor. Its acetylene flame filled the place with brightness, but neither the noise of their talk nor the glare of the light kept me awake. As soon as my head touched the pillow I fell asleep.

Some subconscious communication in my mind must have wakened me shortly afterwards. As my eyes opened I heard again the mumble of Iban conversation. The room was still aglow with lamp-light, yet my bed seemed more shaded than before. Looking up, I saw a blanket stretching along a wire to act as a screen for me, and on the screen, thrown there by the light beyond, was the silhouette of a girl. She stood on tiptoe on the farther side of the blanket, pinning its edge to the wire. When she turned sideways, I recognized from her shadowy profile that she was Segura.

I felt touched by her thoughtfulness in thus shielding me from the glare, and coughed to attract her attention. Her shadow hesitated and listened. When I whispered her name, the silhouette moved swiftly across the screen until it disappeared off the edge, and round the curtain slipped Segura in person. Barefooted and half undressed, she must have been preparing for bed when she thought of hanging a blanket to shade me from the light.

I lifted my mosquito-net and sat at the end of my mattress. Segura glanced furtively back into the room, to make sure that its other occupants were not watching; then she came and knelt beside me. She smiled and at once began to speak in low, eager tones. Her words poured forth in a torrent, but I could not understand them. In dumb show I indicated my lack of comprehension. She looked disappointed and bewildered, then started to speak again, this time more slowly. Her manner was extremely earnest; she was trying to explain something. I cursed my folly for not learning her language during the last few years, so that she and I could talk together.

Clearly she wished to confide to me some important information. Once or twice she glanced backwards nervously towards the group beyond the screen and listened intently, to ensure that they had not noticed her whereabouts. Then she turned to me and began whispering once more. From her manner she seemed to be making statements and asking questions, seeking my opinion on some critical matter. But her efforts were in vain. I could not understand a word of what she said.

Suddenly her father's voice was raised among the gossipers round the lamp. She froze into immobility and held her breath. Koh's voice subsided, and someone else took up the talk. Segura relaxed, grinned at me, stretched out a hand and touched mine in friendship, then rose silently, stepped to the hanging blanket and started again to pin it on the wire. After a while she moved to its farther side, and once more I saw her graceful, girlish shadow on the brightly illumined screen.

As I lay back on my pillow I thought to myself how much of life is just shadows thrown upon a screen, unsubstantial forms reflecting and yet obscuring realities beyond our ken, a continuous succession of illusions.

V

At six o'clock that morning we were wakened by the booming of a gong. A native beat it as he walked the length of the gallery. Its beautiful, deep, resonant voice was a magnificent summons from sleep to the events of the day.

When I stepped on the outer platform and went to the river for a swim, the earth was still half hidden in darkness. Mists hung over the jungled hills, and wisps of their grey vapour dipped and swept the water's surface. Already the verandah and its surroundings presented a scene of extraordinary activity. Girls climbed the stairways fetching water for the household, old women scrubbed sacrificial pigs which squealed in protest, young men daubed final coats of paint on grotesque wooden images of hornbills, penghulus raised tall ceremonial masts at intervals along the platform, and matrons lit fires and cooked their families' morning meals.

After breakfast we made our final preparations for the great ceremony. When the time came, I donned my pagan vestments and descended to the river to perform the opening gambit of the show. Sir Anthony Abell, Temonggong Koh and Penghulu Grinang, all suitably clad, accompanied me.

At an agreed signal I started my solemn ascent, followed by

these illustrious retainers. The thought of the pig condemned to death above made me feel like an executioner climbing a scaffold, yet I had no choice but to accept philosophically the bad with the good features of Iban life. On the top step Mindun and Sani greeted me with a dish of food and a glass of wine. As I cast the concoction of eggs, rice and other morsels into the air, a sharp explosion shattered the silence. One of the eggs was so ancient that it could contain itself no longer, and burst its shell. Like echoes of this unrehearsed rudery, a battery of Brunei cannon immediately began to bark a royal salute, and I stepped forward and plunged my spear through the neck of a gigantic porker lying at my feet.

After that we moved to our places for the opening bedara, and thereafter one curious ceremony followed another in quick succession. Sometimes half a dozen different strange actions were being performed by various troupes of actors at the same moment. It was all delightfully diverting but hopelessly confusing, and I shall not make confusion worse confounded by attempting to describe it. In any case the reader has already had more than his fill of pagan celebrations.

Moreover, I could not stay longer than the first six or seven hours, and so did not witness the later, most significant features of this rare revel which distinguished it from all others. At its climax suitable salutations were made, I was told, to fantastic effigies of hornbills which graced the tops of the highest ceremonial masts. I could not perform this duty, since I had by then left for Singapore. In my place Abell undertook the tasks which on such occasions fall to the Representative of the British Sovereign. No official labours are more exacting, and no Excellency whom it has been my pleasure to meet performs them with a more devoted and happy sense of duty than does Abell. Sarawak has been fortunate in its Governors. First Charles Arden-Clarke gave it sagacious and kindly rule; then Duncan Stewart brought to it for a brief, tragic moment (which I shall describe) his brilliant gifts; and afterwards Anthony Abell arrived. He has a genius for friendship. His capacity for fun, coupled with a sincere respect for native beliefs, always enables him to make suitable distinction between the frankly ludicrous and the essentially sacred portions of Koh's and other pagan ceremonies. As a result of this quality, combined with his administrative wisdom, Abell's influence for good among the peoples of Sarawak is very great.

I was kept so busy throughout the morning that I caught only occasional glimpses of Segura. She, too, worked ceaselessly. Most of the time she stayed unobtrusively in the background, washing dishes, preparing food for bedaras, cooking meals and fetching objects needed for our antics. Whenever I celebrated a bedara she came and sat beside me, poured my rice-wine and sang a few verses of a pantun; then she rose and returned to her labours. Our respective tasks were so continuous that even if some friendly interpreter had been present we would not have had a chance to talk. So there was no opportunity for me to learn what she had tried to tell me during the night.

As the hour for my departure approached, she, Mindun and Iba neglected their duties and attached themselves to me in all my final ritual acts. Another of our brief family meetings was ending, and we felt sad.

Once more the last episode before I left was a performance of duets by Mindun and Segura. The whole assembly crowded round them as they sat on the gallery floor and chanted snatches of the poetry of the Iban people. Then we took our fond farewells. As I entered my long-boat, Koh handed me a basket of food to hang at its prow for the appeasement of the evil spirits. The temoi started to speed down-stream, and I waved to my friends until they and their fluttering handkerchiefs were lost to view.

VI

Sani and her mother had decided to stay until the end of the festivities, so I did not have to deliver them back at their shop. Sulaihi was at the helm of my boat, and no pilot is finer on the river. Having delayed until the last moment, we now had to hurry if I was to keep to my time-table. I must reach Kapit later that afternoon, embark immediately on a launch, continue my journey through the night to Sibu, and at crack of dawn next day fly to Singapore. The reason for my haste was that I wished to greet a new High Commissioner of Malaya when he landed in the

city. He was the successor to the murdered Sir Henry Gurney—
a certain General Sir Gerald Templer, whom I did not know. He
would alight at Kallang airfield at ten o'clock the next morning,
and I must be there to welcome him.

Sulaihi rose superbly to the occasion and broke the record for
the passage from Koh's house to Kapit. On the upward journey
we had taken more than twelve hours to cover the distance, and
he said that his average time for the downward trip was about
six. That afternoon he completed it in four hours and ten minutes.

When we reached Kapit I climbed aboard my waiting launch,
the crew weighed anchor and we slipped down-stream. I sat on
deck and watched darkness fall. Later a half-moon rose and
helped to light us on our way. On my arms hung the copper
bracelets of countless bedaras, and round my neck was a collar
of bright-coloured paper flowers made for me by Sani.

Beside me sat a young Iban police officer, John Nicoll, who
sometimes came as my aide-de-camp on these Sarawak expeditions. The son of a family in the Second Division, he was an
example of the modern type of Iban from down-river areas,
where good schools had for some time been available to educate
the rising generation of this naturally intelligent race. Handsome, neatly dressed, well mannered, fluent in English, and competent at his job, he was a model of what many up-river youngsters, like Kanyan, would become when similar opportunities
reached them in Borneo's interior.

John had recently attended a six months' course at the Police
Training College in England. As we sat on deck, he told me
of his English journey. He was enthusiastic about his treatment
and experiences in Britain, where his eyes had been opened to
many remarkable things. Evidently he had made the most of
the liberal education of travel.

Among other episodes, he described a visit which he paid to
London. The great capital amazed and staggered him, and he
was filled with admiration for its multitudinous life.

I asked him what was his first impression when he found himself standing in a London street staring at the vast buildings,
ceaseless traffic and teeming crowds.

He replied at once, "I felt as if I were in the middle of the jungle. Houses everywhere—nothing but houses as numerous as trees. I didn't know which way to turn, and felt lonely and lost."

It was an illuminating commentary by a wild man from Borneo on one of the most admired achievements of modern civilization.

I retired early to my bunk, for I was tired after the exertions in Koh's house. Sometime in the morning we arrived at Kapit, but I remained blissfully unconscious that we had reached our destination.

Then a loud knocking on my cabin door woke me.

"Come in," I called drowsily.

Mr. Waite, the District Officer, entered.

"I'm afraid, sir," he said, "I've got very bad news for you."

"What's up?" I asked.

"His Majesty the King died last night."

I felt stunned. The news was shocking. All the world had believed that King George was making an excellent recovery from his severe illness. A sense of profound loss and sorrow swept through me. Then I remembered the beautiful rainbow which, scarcely twenty-four hours earlier, had appeared on the Balleh— according to Iban superstition, an evil omen.

I dressed hurriedly, went to the Sunderland flying-boat moored in the river, climbed into it and flew to Singapore to greet Queen Elizabeth the Second's new High Commissioner.

VII

The final episode in that period of Segura's life can soon be told. I received a letter recounting it a few weeks later.

It seemed that Koh had indeed resolved to marry her to the Iban schoolmaster, but that she had not consented to the plan. She did not know the young man at all, and strongly objected. Her father was adamant, and so my high-spirited sister expressed her disagreement in the most decisive way that lay in her power. She fled from the long-house and eloped with someone else.

So that was the project which she had wished to confide to me, and on which she hoped to get my advice, in the middle of the night!

Presumably she was already secretly in love with the boy whom she chose as her partner in this escapade for the two laid their plans carefully. Creeping from her father's house one midnight, they stole a prahu and paddled swiftly up-river. At daybreak they went ashore, hid the boat and slept in the jungle until nightfall. Then they continued their journey and by the following morning had reached Koh's farm. They lived together there for more than five consecutive days and nights, the period which by Iban custom on the Balleh constitutes legal union, making a pair husband and wife. Segura believed that by this bold stratagem she had successfully thwarted her parent; and now she set herself to enjoy her romantic honeymoon.

Soon afterwards, however, they were rudely interrupted. Old Koh was not so easily deflected from his purposes. When he heard of Segura's escape he flew into a rage and ordered a crew of his followers to chase her. When the next report brought the news of her marriage he remained calm, for he had determined on his policy.

Jugah led the expedition for the fugitives' apprehension, and they made no resistance when they were both "arrested". As I have said, Segura no doubt counted on her marriage as her protection. It had been performed according to Iban custom, and must therefore presumably be recognized by her family and friends. She forgot that what is legally done can be legally undone. If Koh had been helpless to prevent her marriage, she was now helpless to prevent her divorce.

Like an ignominious captive, she was brought back to Koh's house. Her husband was removed elsewhere, and disappeared from her life. By the adat lama of her people, their union was declared null and void.

A few days later she was married to the Iban schoolmaster. The ceremony took place in his father's house, far away from the Balleh. The groom's family and every member of the household were witnesses of the wedding, which was performed with all the ancient rites of the pagan faith. In spite of its simplicity the occasion cannot have been without touches of drama.

The letter informing me of these events told no more. It did not say whether the bride wore a smile or a frown on her wedding day. I could only reflect that sometimes life among the Ibans is as rough as it is simple, as cruel as it can be good, and that these profoundly sensible people learn to adapt themselves to all kinds of circumstances. Segura was a typical daughter of her race, and possibly even her passionate nature accepted this rapid change of fortunes, not to mention husbands, with philosophic resignation. Moreover, hers was a temperament capable of swiftly altering moods. If her bridegroom pleased her when she got to know him, then she might take to him as strongly as she had rejected him before she acquired that knowledge. Clearly he was in some ways well fitted to give her the station in life for which she had been prepared, and perhaps old Koh, in choosing a "modern" Iban teacher for her mate, had shown perfect parental wisdom.

Anyway, I hoped that, now that she was married, Segura would live happily ever after. If the reader wishes to know whether my hope was realized, he must exercise his patience until later in this book.

PART FOUR

THE KAYANS AND KENYAHS

CHAPTER THIRTEEN

INTRODUCTION TO THE KAYANS

I

My tale of travels in Borneo now moves from the country of the Ibans into the land of their neighbours, the Kayans and Kenyahs.

Most British officials in Sarawak have a definite preference for one or other of the pagan tribes. Some like the Ibans best, while others prefer the Kayans, and yet others favour the Kenyahs or the Melanaus or the Kelabits or the Punans. I have never heard anyone give pride of place to the Land Dayaks. A man's choice is largely a matter of personal taste or prejudice. Often his judgement is determined by which of the various natives happened to be his first love, and that depended on the accident of where he chanced to be initially posted as an out-station officer. Alternatively, a man may grow to like best the tribe among whom he has spent most of his working years. Far from familiarity breeding contempt, it usually produces a deepening regard for these simple, warm-hearted peoples.

I remember the first occasion, in August 1946, when I travelled along the Baram River, the main artery of the Fourth Division in Sarawak and the central highway into the country of the Kayans and their Kenyah kinsmen. I sat on board a launch with a group of congenial characters discussing the comparative merits of the various pagan tribes. In the party were John Gilbert, the Resident of the Fourth Division, Denis White, who in earlier years served long at various posts on the river, Bob Snellus, who likewise had laboured much among the Kayans and Kenyahs, and Toby Carter, an official of the Shell Oil Company who was a member of the expedition which parachuted into Borneo in 1945. At that time he had led a band of Kenyah and Kayan warriors down the Baram on the heels of the retreating

Japanese, just as Bill Sochon had led the Ibans down the Rejang.
My companions all knew the Kayans and Kenyahs well, and their
prejudice was in favour of these sturdy clansmen.

To provoke them, I expressed my admiration for the Ibans. I
had recently caught my first glimpse of the Rejang's natives,
and repeated some of the praise of them which I had heard
from Barcroft and others, adding my own initial enthusiastic
impressions.

My companions responded to the challenge. Being clever
advocates, they began by paying a few mild compliments to the
Ibans. They admitted that the Ibans whom they knew best—
those living on the Baram—were comparatively recent immigrants
to the area who only moved into it because they could not hold
their own among their fellow Ibans on the Batang Lupar and
the Rejang, and that they were therefore inferior examples of
the breed. They also agreed that the Ibans as a whole were more
virile, intelligent and enterprising than the Kayans and Kenyahs.
They confessed as well that some of the Kayans' and Kenyahs'
superstitious practices were stupid and horrifying and that these
sapped grievously the natives' health and well-being.

Then they poured cold water on some of the commendation
of the Ibans which I had heard. The natives of the Rejang, they
said, had not given as much help to Bill Sochon against the Japanese as was sometimes claimed. Their decision to support the
British was neither spontaneous nor taken regardless of consequences. The original daring and far-sighted resolve to aid the
parachutists was made by chiefs of the Kenyah, Kayan and related
peoples living farther in the interior. In particular the great Kenyah leader on the Baram, Penghulu Tama Weng Ajang, and the
Skapan chieftain in the upper reaches of the Rejang, Penghulu
Puso, had given the initial bold lead. These were the men of true
courage, wisdom and vision. The Ibans, said my travelling companions, only declared for the British later, when it was certain
that the Japanese were doomed.

The critics then argued that, with brilliant individual excep-
tions, the Ibans were not brave fighting men. Their method of
head-hunting had always been cowardly. They were more
partial to assault on an enemy from the rear than to attack from

the front, and they showed more courage when chasing a defence-less old woman than when engaging a well-armed young man. Moreover, the Iban lust for heads—so much more exuberant than that of other tribes—had eventually become mere bestial savagery. The Kenyahs and Kayans were more restrained and gentlemanly in pursuing their favourite hobby. They were braver in battle, wiser in council, finer in character and nobler in culture than the Ibans. Especially as craftsmen and artists they were the Ibans' superiors and teachers.

This was a formidable piece of advocacy, and much of it was true. The talk was lively and stimulating, and it was a good introduction for me to the Kayans and Kenyahs. I listened with especial care to everything that my companions told me of Penghulu Tama Weng Ajang and Penghulu Puso, for I knew that they were the grandest chieftains, and that I would meet them both.

II

I met Penghulu Puso some months later, on a day in March 1947 which I have already partly described. Arden-Clarke and I had struggled in long-boats through the Tekok Rapids up the Rejang River on our way to a Kayan centre called Belaga.

Some time before we reached the rapids we had passed a tributary called the Pilah, the boundary between Iban and Kayan territory. On the river bank at that spot stood two pillars fashioned from gigantic tree trunks. Though half overgrown with jungle vegetation, I could see their surfaces covered with bold carvings of grotesque creatures conceived by inventive, barbaric imaginations. On the summit of each lay a large, flat stone. It looked like the high platform sanctuary of one of those mediæval religious fanatics who banished themselves to such lonely pinnacles beneath the open sky in a passion of self-abne-gation. The pillars were not, however, the homes of living Chris-tians, but the tombs of dead pagans. They were examples of Kayan mortuary architecture, built as lofty, airy resting places for the remains of deceased chiefs. The illustrious corpses were exposed on their high platforms to disintegrate at the will of the spirits, amidst thunder and lightning, wind and rain. Lower in the columns large holes were bored to house the bones of children and other lesser dependents of the noble dead.

These massive monuments, decorated somewhat in the style of Red Indian totem poles, made an impressive entry to the land of the Kayans. They were evidence of their artistic genius. We saluted them respectfully and continued on our way.

As we approached the small administrative centre called Belaga, we passed an occasional long-house much vaster in size and finer in build than any dwellings of the Ibans. They were samples of the architectural masterpieces of the Kayans and kindred tribes. In due course we came to Belaga itself, standing in a clearing on a point of land where a tributary joined the Rejang. On its grassy bank was a white wooden fort, with a court-house and police station near by. A row of Chinese shop-houses constituted a small bazaar where local pagans came to trade, and a few shacks raised on stilts in an untidy banana grove completed the buildings of this jungle village.

At the river's edge stood a native chieftain accompanied by a retinue of savage henchmen. He was Penghulu Puso. An aristocrat of the Skapan people—a minor branch of the Kayan group of clans—he was the paramount chief of the region.

At first glance he did not give me an impression of particular character or power. In one way he appeared a considerable figure, for his body was large; but it seemed to carry more fat than muscle, and to be gross rather than strong. Nor did his face convey an idea of outstanding intelligence, personality or force. The flesh seemed too loose, the features too common and the eyes too dull. I felt disappointed, for I had heard great things of Puso.

His reputation was solidly founded. In 1945 he showed sterling quality when Major Sochon and Sergeant Barry, in the early, most dangerous days of their adventure, arrived friendless on the upper Rejang. The British intruders revealed themselves first to Puso, and placed their fate in his hands. This was long before they could move farther down-river, where they made contact with Penghulu Sandai and his Iban braves. In fact, Puso had the first refusal, so to speak, of the reward which the Japanese would undoubtedly give for their capture. He could betray them at the very start, and thereby greatly improve his financial standing. Instead, for many weeks he hid, fed and encouraged the outlaws, while using his influence among the Skapans and Kayans in their favour. Thus he gave them security in their original base and laid the foundation for their victorious progress down the river. All this he did at the risk of his life.

So the chief, I thought to myself, must be as big as his reputation. How strange, then, that he should appear rather weak and flabby. Part of the explanation might be that, unlike Ibans, the Kayans do not always exhibit in outward manner and speech their inward qualities. They are reserved and modest. Behind Puso's ordinary appearance lay, no doubt, extraordinary strength of character. Yet I felt that some additional explanation of the apparent contradiction in his personality was needed. Some dark mystery must lie beneath the enigma of his weak appearance and his grand fame.

It was high afternoon when we landed and received from him a cordial greeting. As we climbed a path to the village, he told us that a vast assembly of his followers would gather that evening. They were coming to Belaga from every long-house for many miles around to express in dancing, singing and feasting their pleasure at our arrival. I was delighted at the news, for I knew that the Kenyahs and Kayans were the finest exponents of head-hunters' dances in Borneo.

We went to the fort, where we would lodge during our stay. When I had unpacked my toothbrush and the other few articles which are essential on these Bornean expeditions, I strolled along the stronghold's upper gallery, leaned upon the parapet overlooking the river and surveyed the scene.

The gathering of the Skapan clan had already begun. From my vantage point I watched the picturesque proceedings. Below me an acre of rough lawn surrounded the fort and sloped steeply to the river. Across the water a high, abrupt hill densely covered with tropical vegetation rose like a solid green precipice towards the sky. On its summit stood an ornate, carved wooden tomb of a dead Skapan leader, and at its foot flowed the Rejang, still broad and ample though we were 200 miles from its mouth. A considerable stretch of the river was in view, and along it now came an armada of boats filled with natives.

Some of the craft were light prahus carrying only two or three people, others were larger vessels bringing half a dozen voyagers, and yet others were long, roomy temois manned by a score or more passengers. Every few minutes a new boat or group of boats glided into view. The oarsmen swung their paddles vehemently, shouting challenges to rival crews as they raced towards the landing stage. Their cries were borne far across the tranquil water. A hot sun bathed the scene in brilliant light, which glistened on the bodies of the natives and sparkled on the small, swirling wavelets rippling from their flashing paddle blades as they sped to shore.

Most of the men were bare-limbed, bare-torsoed and bare-headed, impervious to sunstroke. They wore gay loin-cloths, and a few bead trinkets on their ears and necks. The women wore sarongs in the Kayan manner, tucked under their armpits and over their breasts, whence they hung in a graceful sweep to their ankles. These robes displayed various bright colours, and in addition the ladies sported ear-rings and necklaces and large straw sun-hats.

As each craft came to land, its crew shipped their paddles, leaped overboard, and lent eager hands to guide the vessel to a mooring in the shallows. Soon a veritable fleet of prahus was tethered to the bank, like an expeditionary force of native war-boats gathered for attack. But no bustle of unloading supplies or arming warriors ensued. This was a peaceful invasion. The landing parties were bent on jollity, not battle. They climbed the path to a wide, grassy space near the fort, where dancing would take place.

The very atmosphere that afternoon seemed to breathe a festive air, and the throng was in rollicking, carefree mood. They jostled each other cheerfully, the children clinging to their mothers' skirts, the women chattering excitedly and the men talking and laughing. As the moment for the performance approached, they settled in a large circle, many ranks deep, round the lawn which was to be the stage.

At the appointed hour Arden-Clarke and I joined them. We

were led to chairs draped with coloured sarongs, where we sat like rustic emperors enthroned. Close by lolled the master of ceremonies, Penghulu Puso, amidst a group of native worthies. The responsibilities of his office rested lightly upon him; indeed, he seemed blissfully unaware of them. Beneath the bench on which he sat were propped several bottles of burak (the Kayan equivalent of tuak) and I noticed that a flagon of it was gripped between his feet. Even before the dancing started he transferred it from his feet to his hands, uncorked it, raised it to his mouth, and sampled the brew. Approving it, he smacked his lips enthusiastically, poured drinks into several cups, and distributed them among his cronies. This simple little exercise he repeated periodically throughout the evening.

The day was far spent and the sun inclined towards the horizon. Its fiercest heat had abated, the temperature was comfortable out-of-doors, and shadows lengthened gradually across the ground. A hush of expectation fell upon the crowd.

Then the quiet was broken by a gong and drum summoning dancers. Their monotonous, throbbing music had an elemental, timeless quality, like the tramp of primæval creatures through a jungle. A handsome Kayan youth stepped from the multitude into the centre of the arena, a plumed helmet on his head, a cascade of monkey-fur hanging from his shoulder, and the two ends of his sirat appearing like tails below. His naked limbs had magnificent athletic grace, his step was self-confident and jaunty, and his face wore a proud look. Inclining his head in salutation to the Governor and me, he froze into a trance-like pose as a prelude to his dance.

It is time that I wrote about head-hunters' dances. Dancing is the noblest artistic achievement of the Bornean tribes. It is a pastime indulged in by men more than by women. The reader already knows that Land Dayak girls enjoy a little simple jigging, but theirs is a very elementary form of art. I am concerned now with the truly dramatic and aesthetic performances watched eagerly by discriminating audiences in long-houses far up-river. These are primarily masculine efforts. I have rarely seen an Iban woman dance. Kenyah and Kayan ladies trip a measure in a slow-moving, graceful way which I shall describe, but it is always

a secondary entertainment to that of the men, and arouses little
of the enthusiasm and none of the higher criticism which male
dancing provokes. Often it appears to be included in an evening's
programme as an afterthought, and is regarded perhaps with a
certain amount of amused tolerance as a concession to the weaker
sex.

Male dancing, on the other hand, is a serious occupation. It
is a proper pastime for red-blooded he-men, true warriors. Like all
human beings, the head-hunters have an artistic sense lying deep
within them. They feel an urge towards beauty, but their means
of expressing it are few. In their society no literature or painting and scarcely any music exist, nor is there drama apart from
this dancing. So there are no poets and painters, no composers
and playwrights for the community to honour as men of genius
who personify the highest attainments of their race. The craftsmen who make mats, carve shields, design clothes and fashion
trinkets with notable skill express something of the people's
aesthetic instincts, but their work does not qualify as high art.
Only dancing among long-house activities reaches that supreme
standard. So good dancers are held in esteem, their fame spreads
beyond their own houses, and within local limits they win the
admiration of "fans", just as Hollywood film stars do in wider
and often less discriminating circles.

In earlier days the most revered art among the pagans was
fighting, and the most successful warriors were doubtless hailed
as the greatest artists. In their dances, therefore, both then and
now, the virtues of fighting are extolled. The finest dances are
tributes to battle, representations of valour in war, salutes to
head-hunting.

A dance is usually a solo performance. Sometimes two or
more men do their steps together, but that is not the most popular
form. Almost invariably a man dances by himself. The first
performer is succeeded by a second, and then by a third and a
fourth and many more in turn; but they all dance separately.
They execute the same dance, though with variations in each
man's interpretation of it, like a succession of competitors in
Scottish Games each striving to be judged the best exponent of the
highland fling.

The classic Bornean dance represents a head-hunter's combat. The dancer plays the part of a hunter strolling casually through the forest. Suddenly an enemy appears. This second character is not evident to the audience, being an imaginary figure. The performer engages him in battle, in mortal duel. The two are well matched, for the contest is protracted. But eventually, after many a shift of fortune, the dancer triumphs and cuts off his opponent's head.

All the settled pagans of Sarawak perform this dance with greater or less verve. Even the Land Dayaks have adopted it as part of their entertainment on festive evenings, though in olden days they abhorred head-hunting as a sport in which they invariably came off second best, giving more heads than they took. The Ibans, on the other hand, execute it with the nostalgic fervour of one-time champion murderers. But its noblest exponents are the Kayans and Kenyahs. Their best dancers are astonishingly, breath-takingly fine artists. I have seen all the famous dancing of South-East Asia, and admire beyond measure the dramatic brilliance of the Kandyan dancers in Ceylon, the fabulous charm of the palace dancers in Siam, the exquisite fantasy of the royal *corps de ballet* in Cambodia, the magnificent skill of the court performers in Java, and the fairy-like grace of the temple dancers in the paradise called Bali. All these are actions of unforgettable loveliness; yet in its own way the rude art of the savages in Borneo has as rare and memorable a beauty. Their battle dance is a perfect translation of fierce emotion into graceful action. Although its inspiration is fighting, in it violent passion is expressed with restraint, and brutal gestures are made with polished elegance. The movements combine vigour with poise, ardour with sincerity, and savagery with stateliness.

The dance has another quality which is perhaps the secret of its artistic greatness. As performed by its best exponents, it seems to be as much a spiritual as a physical exercise. Some scholars aver that head-hunting had originally a religious significance for the simple, superstitious people who engaged in it. Possibly a dim tribal memory of that time, transmitted through countless generations in the subconscious mind of the race, reasserts itself in the pagans' finest artists, their dancers, inspiring them with a

sublime impulse at the moment of action. They spring into
energetic physical motion, but their bodies seem to be subordi-
nated to their spirits, to be mere vehicles for the expression of
their souls—or rather, the soul of their race. Watching them,
I have often been aware of that quality. A dancer's mood
is one of solemn reverence, his steps are like the genuflections of
a priest at worship, and into his face comes a look of exaltation
such as might glow on the face of a novice at his initiation into
holy orders. The spectacle has moments of thrilling beauty. It
is a glimpse of Primitive Man suddenly revealing all the potential
civilization lying within him.

The first performer that afternoon at Belaga gave a good
exposition of his theme. After remaining for a few moments
motionless, in a graceful statuesque pose, his limbs woke gradually to life, responding to the insistent beat of the gong and
drum. His arms raised themselves sideways, like the wings of a
bird uplifted for flight. For a brief while he maintained that
posture, then took a slow pace forward, bending his knees and
dipping his waist in a half-curtsey. His eyes gazed upwards
towards the sky with a serene, contemplative look. Drawing
himself again to his full height, he strutted forward with deliberate steps, and of a sudden, with a swift twist of his body, leaped
sideways and landed two yards away on silent feet. His arms
were outstretched, and they swayed like branches of a tree in a
gentle breeze.

Forward again he sauntered, gaily and proudly now, with a
touch of swagger. After a while his eyes lost their far-away look
and seemed to concentrate on some nearer object. He had sighted
an enemy. His poise remained calm, yet by almost imperceptible
transitions his movements lost their carefree air and became
cautious and furtive. His arms fell to his side, where one hand
gripped the scabbard on his hip as the other drew the sword
from its sheath. Flourishing the weapon above his head, he
stepped to a shield lying on the ground, stooped, picked it up and
held it defensively along his free arm.

Hitherto he had moved with stately, measured tread, but now
he truly began to dance. His gestures became more brisk and
complex as he leaped and curtseyed, swooped and pirouetted

across the grass. The sweeps of his arms were as gay as the kicks of his legs, while he swung his shield and brandished the sword with joyous bravado. Evidently his foe drew near, for the flourishes of his blade became more purposeful, lunging occasionally like a fencer's foil towards a target. Soon the battle was joined in earnest. There was a suggestion of thrust and parry, of advance and retreat about the dancer's vigorous movements. Through a series of wild, prancing acrobatics he fought as unerringly as he stepped, and ultimately overcame his adversary. With a flash of his sword he claimed the head.

The audience watched his performance intently, and now they broke into loud applause. The artist bowed to the Governor and me, took off his helmet, doffed his war-cloak, laid down his shield, and unslung his sword. Another young man took his place on the stage. An aged native, who did duty as squire to every champion, handed him a glass of burak. A taste of wine was thought essential before a dance, for it helped to give suppleness to a performer's joints and ardour to his spirit. The youth quaffed the drink at one gulp, the gong and drum began to beat their seductive rhythm, and before long he was strutting and leaping over the ground.

So it was with a succession of dancers. One after another they exhibited their skill through the rest of the afternoon and far into the evening. While they danced, the breeze died, the sun sank beyond the rim of the horizon, and countless stars were lit in the twilight sky. When darkness fell, a crescent moon rose in the heavens.

The audience sat in rapt attention, allotting praise or muttering criticism to each performer. Eventually the last dancer retired and the entertainment ended. The attention of the crowd relaxed, and on all sides a murmur of conversation began.

Puso had sat throughout with his group of cronies, gossiping and drinking. Now he rose, walked towards the Governor and me and squatted at our feet. In his arms he hugged a bottle of burak. Summoning a group of husky youths, he ordered several to sit on the ground beside him while others knelt or stood at his back, like a team of athletes posing for a photograph. When they had gathered, the chief poured rice-wine into a tumbler and raised the glass towards me. But he did not yet deliver it into my hands. This was to be a ceremonial drink preceded by a song, and in anticipation of it the crowd once more fell silent.

Kayans and Kenyahs are splendid singers. Some of their songs are as ancient as their dances, and have as strong a tradition and almost as fine an art. Their music is melodious, their voices are lusty, and they have a natural talent for choral singing reminiscent of the Welsh. They perform several types of songs, but their favourites are drinking songs. These are sometimes sung by men alone, sometimes by women only, and at other times by a mixed company. A soloist sings the verses, and his solitary voice is interrupted periodically by the deep tones of the choir chanting a refrain. The effect is as dramatic as it is harmonious.

Puso now honoured me with one of these songs. He himself was the soloist, and his fruity voice did justice to a rollicking tune. He sang numerous verses, and at short intervals the male choir repeated his notes like the sound of a thunderous musical echo. At the climax of the piece he raised the glass of burak to my mouth, indicating that the drink should be swallowed with no heel-taps. While I fulfilled this injunction the audience hummed in unison a rising scale of notes, which ascended as steadily as the wine descended, until the accompaniment reached a high, triumphant roar when I held the glass upside-down to prove that it was empty.

Afterwards Puso sang a ditty in honour of Arden-Clarke, and then others for each of our travelling companions in turn. Every time the choir supported him with splendid, sonorous chanting. There was a haunting beauty about that Kayan singing in the still night under a crescent moon.

III

Our days at Belaga were full and fascinating. Throughout them Penghulu Puso acted as our host. He was a good guide and friend, introducing us to many of his people, organizing a programme of entertainment, and conducting us on various expeditions.

We made journeys to two long-houses in the district. Both

were vast buildings raised in the grand Kayan style, the first the home of forty-three families and the other the home of sixty. Their rooms were large and high-raftered and, although constructed wholly of jungle timbers, had something of the spacious, lordly aspect of baronial halls in mediæval European castles.

The second house was Puso's. We visited it in mid-afternoon. First we sipped cups of tea with a bevy of decorative ladies of the chief's family in his private room, and afterwards drank a glassful of a rather more potent beverage with the men. Then we repaired to the public gallery to witness another show of dancing.

I expected that the handsomest youths in the place would give another exhibition in the traditional style which we had seen on the previous day; but instead a wizened elder stepped on the floor and performed a very different type of dance. In confidential long-house evenings, when men's conversation turned to the lighter side of life, I had heard tell of it. Rumour whispered of its merry prankishness, indeed, of its calculated immodesty and unbounded licence. Let me prepare the reader for an account of the old man's performance by stating that this type of pagan dancing is conceived in a contrasting spirit to that of the dances which I have hitherto described. Whereas they strike a tragic note, it belongs to the school of comedy. Whereas their steps have become formalized, its action is distinctly natural and free. And whereas they are confined by a classic restraint, it is marked by an exuberant, boisterous lack of restraint which dispenses not only with the conventions sometimes imposed by prudery but also with those normally dictated by decency.

These dances are studies in the behaviour of birds and beasts. The Bornean natives are keen, competent naturalists. They have acquired an intimate knowledge of the habits of their neighbours in the jungle—the crocodiles, monkeys, deer, hornbills, iguanas, pythons and other forest folk—and have invented a series of dances to imitate these creatures' ways of life. Thus the Frog Dance is a hilarious take-off on episodes in the private life of a frog, the Pig Dance is a faithful representation of the character and customs to be observed in wild boars, the Bird Dance is a homely dramatization of a hornbill's joys and sorrows, and other items in the natives' repertoire mimic the foibles of other wood-land friends. All these performances are rendered in a clownish spirit; they leave no detail, however intimate, unrecorded; and occasionally they are about as shameless as could be.

The most famous, or infamous, is the Monkey Dance. After tea and a sip of burak in Puso's house, we were favoured with a rendering of it. Overawed by Arden-Clarke's and my presence, however, the dancer gave only a mild version of the skit, an expurgated edition so to speak, confining his actions to the drawing-room behaviour of a monkey as distinct from its bath-room and bedroom conduct. Even so the dance was in parts a piece of uproarious and hair-raising naughtiness.

The actor was a wiry little veteran. The pinched and wrinkled features of his face were so ape-like that they made his imper-sonation of a monkey all the more convincing. On his head he wore a cap topped with splendid Argus-pheasant plumes, the upper half of his body was clad in a close-fitting coat of real monkey's fur, and his sirat provided a natural tail. The man's skill in imitating simian movements was astonishing. At his first ges-tures the floor seemed to disappear beneath his feet, and in its place spread imaginary branches of thickly foliaged trees. With steady balance he walked along one of these, and then with swinging leaps travelled from bough to bough. Reaching with his arms, clutching with his fingers and gripping with his toes, he per-formed a remarkable series of aerial acrobatics, without actually leaving the ground.

Then with a somersault and one or two handsprings he descended from the tree tops to the earth in theory as well as practice. Striding forward with bent knees and out-turned feet, he dragged his fists along the floor. The expression on his face was one of lugubrious, apish melancholy, and the audience roared with laughter. Suddenly he made a grab at the empty air, plucked an imaginary banana, and crouched on his heels to eat it. With a delicately crooked thumb and forefinger he started to strip the skin from the fruit. The operation was interrupted by a sudden urge to catch a flea crawling over his chest. Dis-turbed, the insect leaped from that position and alighted on his posterior. While the dancer's hand pursued the trespasser there, his gaze wandered over the audience with a look of bored indifference. He blinked his eyes superciliously, screwed his features into various monkey-like grimaces and occasionally uttered a small, scolding cough.

When at length he captured the flea, he first examined it with a critic's eyes, then sampled it with a connoisseur's lips, and finally threw it away in disgust. His attention returned to peeling the banana. Its skin removed, he munched contentedly at it, but with increasingly frequent diversions to track down small guests taking liberties in various parts of his person. Sometimes their situation was surprisingly daring.

When he finished his fruit, he paid more deliberate attention to these pests. First he picked a few intruders neatly from his navel, held them up between a finger and thumb, contemplated them with expert scrutiny, and chewed them up with relish. Of a sudden he realized that he was itching all over, and engaged in a frenzy of scratching. With both hands he raked himself on the stomach, under the armpits, along the thighs, all over his buttocks and across his face. Next he grabbed his sirat, examined its length minutely, and plucked several visitors off the tip of that counterfeit tail. All these actions he achieved with a look of serene nonchalance on his face, as if the operation were a matter of dull routine. Even when a flock of fleas apparently assaulted the most private corner of his anatomy—where he pursued them and made several kills—he gazed straight ahead with an unblinking stare indicating that his thoughts had wandered elsewhere. In the middle of that particular incident he yawned.

At last he was rid of his assailants, at any rate for the time being. He rose, lurched a few paces forward with hands dragging once more over the ground, and then leaped into space, caught hold of a bough which was yet another figment of his imagination, and scampered along it on all fours until he disappeared from view.

Throughout the skit the native audience was convulsed with laughter, some rolling on the floor holding their sides with mirth, others rocking to and fro and wiping tears of merriment from their cheeks. Occasionally cat-calls greeted the dancer, coaxing him to ever more outrageous acts of mimicry. Not all these ejaculations were sounds employed by cats. Many were expressions borrowed from the monkey language, and the one most frequently heard was, someone told me, the love call of an orang-utan in the mating season. Its authors sought to induce the performer to illustrate the amatory tendencies of monkeys, to present in detail the love life of these interesting creatures. But the old man desisted, too much impressed by the Governor's and my restraining presence, a flattering yet regrettable tribute to our good taste and delicacy of feeling.

Thus we were denied a glimpse of the customary climax to this notorious dance. Usually the portrayal of the monkey's zeal as a hunter of small game on its person is followed by representations of other episodes in its sportive career. As the performance proceeds it becomes increasingly unseemly. The coarseness innate in human nature receives uninhibited expression. First come imitations of the homely gestures of the animal when answering the call of nature, and then an exhibition of its antics when it answers the call of love. The dancer's capers are bound by no limitations of propriety, his friskings growing ever more ribald and suggestive. Sometimes at the crisis of his act a second dancer makes a fleeting appearance on the scene, and is chased and captured by the first. The resultant obscenity brings the long-house roof down.

I have since witnessed the whole, unexpurgated, romantic drama in a long-house up the Baram River, but I shall not venture upon a more detailed description of it. I should add, however, that the performance is conceived in a humorous spirit. It is burlesque, even if unbridled burlesque. Its inspiration is pure comedy rather than impure "dirt". The pagans live close to nature; in a long-house the facts of life cannot be concealed behind veils of mystery. They are accepted as a matter of course by youngsters as well as elders, like any other natural actions; and poking fun at them is done openly before all the house, not privily in dens of vice. The jest may be reprehensible, but it is an appeal to the common vulgarity of normal and robust, if rude, human minds, not to the warped senses of depraved individuals.

IV

During those days in Belaga we had many opportunities for serious discussion with Puso and his principal lieutenants. In addition to many private conversations, we twice held public assemblies in the large room of the fort. They were attended by many penghulus, tuai tuai rumah and other men of account in the district. Some came to speak and others to listen. The talk was frank and free, anyone could raise any subject that he liked, and the meetings did not close until everyone who wished to participate had done so.

I was impressed by the forthrightness and intelligence of the native mind revealed in these conferences. In particular Puso showed conspicuous intellectual grasp. An example of his ability appeared in our first discussion.

The date was early 1947, a few months after Sarawak's cession by the Rajah to the King. Puso spoke of his people's attitude towards the change. He said that in most ways they liked it. They felt deep trust in the British Government, which had long protected them. His Majesty's reputation as a wise and benevolent friend of primitive peoples was well known to them, and they welcomed the prospect that cession opened of better, more up-to-date rule. Nevertheless, on one point they were worried.

Seventy years earlier, he said, their forefathers had made a treaty with the second Rajah Brooke, swearing to him an oath of loyalty. That vow was binding on the present generation of Kayans and Skapans, the descendants of the signatories of the agreement. They were now fearful lest support for cession should be inconsistent with it. Could their old duty of fealty to the Rajah be reconciled with their new duty of allegiance to the King? They did not wish to break their word to the Brookes, and so to fall into dishonour. Apart from considerations of morality in principle, they felt apprehensive lest in practice they would be punished, if they erred. The spirits who guide the affairs of men might be offended, and wreak vengeance on them.

Puso asked us earnestly what we thought of the problem.

When Arden-Clarke explained that the King was the lawful successor to the third Rajah; that the Rajah himself, at his own suggestion, of his own free will and with the consent of the Council Negri and Supreme Council, had ceded Sarawak to King George; and that the loyalty owing to the Brookes could therefore be rightfully transferred to His Majesty, the penghulu and his friends were pleased. They listened carefully to a translation of the Governor's explanation, following the argument closely and occasionally nodding assent to it. At the end Puso addressed the audience and told them that the Governor's answer completely satisfied him. The whole assembly murmured approval.

On another topic the Governor and the penghulu did not find themselves in such ready agreement. Talk turned to the economic situation of the natives. It was generally conceded that this was difficult and even precarious. The pagans' manner of growing padi was reviewed. Arden-Clarke gave information about modern methods of cultivation, and promised the chiefs expert advice from trained officers which should improve their strains of rice and increase their yields. Then he mentioned the Kayans' own attitude towards agriculture, and the limiting effect on production of certain customs. With consummate tact he introduced the question of superstitions and taboos. Disclaiming any particular knowledge on the subject himself, since he was a comparative newcomer to the country, he observed that several government officers who had lived long in Sarawak, and who knew the Kayans well and cared deeply about their welfare, advised him that certain local practices were harmful. However strongly these might be hallowed by tradition, there was no doubt that they prejudiced the quality of the crops harvested each year. As an example he referred to the superstition which made the Kayans and kindred peoples seal up their rooms at the appearance of certain omens, and stay for many days religiously indoors. He urged that when this happened, as it often did, at critical periods in the planting, cultivation or reaping of padi, the food supply of the people was endangered. From that he proceeded to suggest that perhaps some ancient pagan beliefs were out-of-date, and that they could be modified in the interests of native well-being. He remarked that in some parts of Sarawak the long-house dwellers had adopted Christianity, and that an improvement in their economic prosperity had followed. Puso and his colleagues listened attentively to a translation of this friendly and cogent homily.

After a few moments of reflection, the chief replied. He thanked the Tuan Governor for his solicitude about the natives' well-being. It was true that their economic situation was depressed, but, with great respect, he felt that His Excellency had been misinformed about the reasons for this state of affairs. Poor crops and indifferent harvests were not produced by the people's taboos; they resulted from natural causes. Conditions of soil, the vagaries of the weather—which frequently managed to produce either too much or too little rain at crucial stages of the padi's growth—and the depredations of wild beasts like pigs and deer were the most important influences determining the quantity and quality of the rice yield each year.

As for Christianity, Puso continued, he and his people were quite ready to turn to that, if they were convinced that it was a superior faith to their own. At present they were not so persuaded. Unless and until they were, they would not abandon their time-honoured beliefs. These had served the Kayans well for centuries. If the pagans abandoned them, the spirits might grow wrathful and punish them. A people with no faith were like lost people, because they had no guide to tell them what was right and what was wrong. They had no sense of direction through life's difficulties. Therefore the Kayan tribes wished to abide by what they believed, until they really came to believe in something better.

Nevertheless, he added, they were willing to hear about Christianity. They would listen conscientiously to its teachings. But, he ventured to comment, this new religion could hardly overcome the alleged difficulty caused by the taboo which decreed that the natives should sometimes stay indoors and neglect their fields. Christianity had a similar taboo. It insisted that every seventh day should be a day of rest. That meant that for fifty-two days every year people were forbidden to labour in their padi-fields. The pagans' taboo did not involve nearly such a serious loss of time as that.

The audience, who had listened with keen attention to their leader's reply to the Governor, broke into smiles and exclamations of approval at this clever debating point. When he sat down, an animated gossiping began among them. They were airing their own notions on the controversy, and their opinion, we were told, was emphatically in sympathy with Puso's cautious but broad-minded exposition of the subject. Indeed, they echoed his words, partly because he had accurately expressed their own sentiments and partly because he was their chief, in whose wisdom they felt firm confidence.

Arden-Clarke did not at that time continue the religious part of the argument. He had dropped in his word of scepticism about the infallibility of paganism, and thought it better to leave the matter there. He merely said that this was a subject upon which the chiefs and their followers should ponder, with a view to considering what was best for them and their wives and children. Then he turned the conversation to practical questions of hygiene and public health. The natives were eager to receive instruction, and we had a long and lively discussion on these improving topics.

Through all our talks and activities in Belaga I observed Penghulu Puso closely, learning much about his character. It was an absorbing study of a man naturally endowed with unusual ability struggling to develop his gifts in the limiting conditions of primitive society. His shrewdness of judgement, breadth of vision and creativeness of mind were powerful qualities, but latent more than actual. Their growth beyond a certain point was hampered by lack of exercise among his simple-minded fellows. He had no peer against whose wits he could sharpen his own wits, beside whose ability he could extend his own ability, and in response to whose ideas he could improve his own ideas. He was like a promising sculptured figure of a giant, half-hewn from granite, and then left unfinished—rugged, strong and yet impotent. The stuff of greatness was there, but its development was arrested by lack of opportunity to fulfil itself.

Watching his face one evening, when it was animated by a vigorous argument in which he was engaged, I was reminded of another countenance that I had seen, years earlier. The features of the two were much alike, and both portrayed similar mental power and strength of character. The other face which I recalled was not that of a living person. It was the life-mask of a man long dead, kept in the library at Chequers, the country home of Britain's Prime Ministers. It represented Oliver Cromwell at the climax of his career. Seeing its similarity to the rough visage of Puso, I reflected how the great Lord Protector of England might have been like this man, if he had been born into a savage tribe in a remote land on the sultry equator.

Yet when Puso's face was in repose it betrayed again that touch of puffiness which seemed to indicate weakness. The trait constantly bothered me. It did not seem natural. I felt worried by the apparent contradiction in the chief's qualities, the conflict between his strength and his feebleness. It was as if a shadow of illness lay across his face, almost like the expression of a man who sometimes smoked opium.

CHAPTER FOURTEEN

LONG LAPUT

I

THE MOST IMPORTANT CENTRE of Kayan and Kenyah population in Sarawak lies up the Baram River, the mightiest waterway in the country after the Rejang. Along the lower Baram and its tributaries live many Ibans, while the Kayans and Kenyahs congregate farther up-river, in Borneo's true interior. They are not numerous in Sarawak, their main populations being settled across the border in what used to be Dutch Borneo and is now Kelemantan. On the Baram only some 4,000 Kenyahs and approximately 5,000 Kayans live; but what they lack in quantity they make up for in quality. Both peoples are endowed with attractive characters and considerable gifts. They have much in common, yet are two distinct communities living in separate societies in diverse territories under different chiefs.

Early one morning I drove from Miri, the capital of Sarawak's Fourth Division, to Kuala Baram, a rustic group of huts beside the sea at the mouth of the great river. My travelling companions were John Gilbert, Toby Carter, Denis White and Bob Snellus. It was the occasion of the talk on the relative merits of Sarawak's pagan tribes which I have already recorded.

We were to embark on a launch at Kuala Baram and journey far up-river, our ultimate destination being a notable Kayan house called Long Laput, 130 miles from the coast. There we would pay our respects to a famous Kayan lady, Lallang, who many years earlier had made history by becoming the first woman tuai rumah of a long-house. I would have liked to continue the trip for another 70 miles, to meet the greatest Kenyah chieftain, Tama Weng Ajang, in his home at Long Akar. There he had held in the previous year the historic conference of native leaders which resolved to support Toby Carter and his party of parachutists. But that journey would have taken more days than I could then spare, and I had to postpone it until a later visit.

We drove in a jeep from Miri to Kuala Baram along the beach, which at low tide provided a sandy highway as smooth as a race-track. The air was cool, for the sun had scarcely yet peered above the horizon. Our drive was extremely pleasant. The shore was a home of sandpipers, plovers and sanderlings, and many of these charming waders were taking the morning air. On swift-running feet they scurried ahead of our vehicle and then, as we seemed on the point of crushing them, took wing and flew with tremulous piping over the ocean waves.

Other residents of the beach were crabs, thousands of them living in tunnels burrowed into the sand. Obliquely they scampered away from our onrushing wheels and popped down holes to their subterranean chambers. They attracted other creatures from the near by forest, for certain monkeys have a fastidious taste in meat and dearly love to eat the soft, delicious flesh of crab.

One such gourmet strolled ahead of us, indifferent to our approach. As we sped close by, the monkey turned its head and glanced at us with hardly a glimmer of curiosity, its expression supercilious, like that of an aristocrat who cannot avoid observing in passing some rude fellow who should really be beneath his notice. Blinking slowly and deliberately, it went to a large crab-hole, inserted an arm down the tunnel, and groped to discover whether the inmate was at home. Finding the place empty, it walked to another opening and tried again. I am told that these monkeys sometimes let their tails down the holes, as an angler sinks his line into water, and that if a crab nips the tail, the monkey hauls it up and eats his catch. But I suspect that the story should be regarded with the tolerant respect tempered by frank scepticism which is the proper attitude towards all fishermen's yarns.

At Kuala Baram we boarded our launch and started the journey inland. For the first few miles both river banks were fringed by mangroves and nipah palms. Soon these lowly forms of vegetation gave way to mightier jungle, and hour after hour we travelled along a smooth corridor of water between high walls of forest. Only occasionally a small area of ground near the river was cleared, and a hut betrayed the presence of some human pioneer, a Malay or Chinese squatter cultivating ground-nuts or gathering jelutong in the crowded solitude of the primæval jungle.

We entered a land of birds and beasts rather than of men. The unwinged creatures kept out of sight. Doubtless they watched us furtively as we passed—crocodiles, leopard cats, gibbons, deer and other citizens of the wild. We never caught sight of them. Birds were more evident. Darters with snake-like heads flapped along the river and rose heavily into the air ahead of us. Sandpipers whistled from floating logs which they used as rafts. Egrets strutted elegantly, bitterns skulked secretively and herons stood statuesquely in muddy, reedy places among the shallows, while kingfishers lent their brilliant colours to shadowy spaces beneath overhanging trees.

We sat on deck beneath shady awnings discussing the peoples of Sarawak. Our talk continued till afternoon, when we arrived at Marudi. There we held the usual inspections and conferences, and stayed the night. Next morning we left early. The passage to Long Laput would take seven hours.

For some time above Marudi no long-houses appeared. Once more the local inhabitants were mostly birds and beasts. The country remained flat much of the day. Then hills and limestone rocks began to appear. In one place a solitary, steep crag half covered with jungle stood beside the river. A pagan legend related that it was once the wooden long-house of a group of natives. They offended the evil spirits, who promptly turned their house to stone. Its rooms became caves, and afterwards only birds inhabited them. On their lofty walls and ceilings the birds build their nests, the famous abodes which make bird's-nest soup, beloved by Chinese gourmets.

From that point onwards the country abandoned itself to the foothills of the mountainous interior. Among them were many limestone stacks and pinnacles, riddled with caves. The region was a paradise for swifts. Tens of thousands of them haunted the caverns, plastering their walls and ceilings with small, thin, cup-like structures made of the birds' glutinous saliva. Their spittle hardened like other builders' cement, forming a firm cradle for young. Most of the nests, however, never held eggs, for they were stolen as soon as they were built. When soaked in water and judiciously cooked, their odd substance made a pleasant, stringy, jelly-like soup. Some inventive Chinese chef discovered this extraordinary fact generations ago, and ever since the caves in the Orient where these swifts breed have been little better than soup factories.

For this reason the caves on the Baram were valuable property for their owners, who were Kayans and Kenyahs.

The caves were not owned communally by the whole population of a long-house, but individually by chiefs and other important personages. Unlike Iban society, which is rather democratic, Kayan and Kenyah society is constructed on a caste system with clear-cut class distinctions. The inmates of every house are divided into three groups: the hereditary aristocrats, the middle class and the "slaves". Originally the last-named consisted of prisoners captured in battle whose labour was more coveted than their heads, and who performed menial tasks for their masters.

Only aristocrats owned bird's-nest caves. In some houses several such landlords lived, making the dwelling affluent, for the nests fetched a lot of money. When gathered, they were sent to a local trading centre called Long Lama, for auction. Chinese merchants travelled up-river to attend the sale. All day keen bidding continued. The number of nests sold each year at Long Lama varied according to the birds' inclinations and the seasonal conditions, but an average number would be between 40,000 and 50,000. Their prices also fluctuated, but a normal yield for, say, 45,000 would be about 33,000 Malayan dollars. The proprietors thus made good money.

The principal owner of caves on the Baram was the high-born Kayan lady whom we were about to visit, Lallang. No one could rival her in the possession of nests and wealth. Because of her rank and riches, European government officers sometimes called her "The Dollar Princess". Other members of her house also owned caves, though on a comparatively minor scale. Nevertheless, the community as a whole derived a handsome annual income from this lucrative source.

On our way up-stream we halted for a while at Long Lama. The settlement consisted of a single row of Chinese shop-houses with a Buddhist temple and school and a Malay Native Officer's

quarters. We drank scented tea, ate jungle fruits, smoked native
cheroots and talked local gossip with the Chinese towkays, keen,
pleasant, friendly men who dressed more humbly and appeared
more penurious than they no doubt were. The place must have
been a little gold-mine for them.

The afternoon was almost spent and night drew near as we
embarked again on our launch. The cool of evening had crept
into the atmosphere. Myriads of mosquitoes and other flying
insects were issuing from their day-time lairs, and began to dance
over the water. Then countless swifts came to hunt them. As we
progressed up-stream the air seemed filled with the birds, performing wide circles of flight, swooping this way and that, climbing and falling, skimming close above the river and then ascending steeply once more into the sky as they chased their prey.
Often a swift dropped with a gliding action to the water's surface,
dipped its beak to snatch a sip of refreshment, and then swerved
upwards again. The birds were in perpetual motion, and their
manoeuvres were full of beauty.

It was pleasant to reflect that these hundreds of graceful,
sportive creatures were Lallang's flocks and herds, from which
she drew her wealth.

II

As dusk fell we arrived at Long Laput. The Kayan house
stretched for an astonishing distance along the river bank. Its
claim to distinction rested on more than its association with far-
famed Lallang, for it was a great place in its own right. Indeed,
it was the largest house, the longest long-house, in the country.
What Knole is to England, Long Laput is to Sarawak. Not
many years ago it boasted ninety-eight apartments, accommodating as many families. At the time of my visit the number had
been slightly reduced, to ninety, and in them lived about six
hundred men, women and children.

The tremendous timber building stretched continuously for
more than a quarter of a mile, curving gradually with the bend
of the river. Several paths made of tree trunks sunk in the muddy
earth ascended from the water's edge to a flat area where the

dwelling stood. Then other tree trunks, notched to make rude stairways, climbed steeply to its platform, raised on stout piles about twenty feet above the ground. The whole edifice was built in the solid, massive style of Kayan architecture.

Our launch anchored in mid-stream, for no jetty stretched across the shallows into deep water. Going from the boat to the house was like taking part in an obstacle race. First some Kayan youths came in prahus to paddle us ashore. Embarking in their tippy little craft, we managed to survive the jaunt without capsizing into the river. Then we faced the next hazard, the walk along a single tree-trunk path up the river bank. Heavy rain having fallen during the afternoon, the wood was sopping wet and the ground on either side a quagmire of mud. Once I slipped off the trunk and sank above my ankles in slime. But at last we reached the house and confronted the final task. It was to keep one's balance while climbing, with no hand-rails and little foothold, the notched tree slanting steeply to the dwelling's main entrance. When we triumphantly achieved that feat we received a hearty welcome from a throng of natives.

We stood now within the open gallery of the building. It was broad and high and spacious, stretching out of sight in either direction. In the middle of the gallery many mats were spread upon the floor. The headman of the community, who was the first to greet us when we arrived, conducted us there. We sat cross-legged with him to exchange introductory courtesies. This central spot was the house's place of honour, and looking up I saw sure evidence of its special sanctity. From a rafter above our heads hung a dozen human skulls.

The tuai rumah was a middle-aged man whose untidily matted hair, dry, wrinkled flesh and squinting eyes were unprepossessing features. In spite of his office he was in fact of secondary importance in the house. Lallang was the dominant power. Until recently she had been headman, but a few months earlier she became seriously ill and, feeling her strength no longer sufficient to bear the responsibilities of chieftainship, resigned the post to him. If I remember rightly, he was her divorced husband, and was conveniently subservient to her will, whenever she chose to assert it.

Having done our duty towards him, we rose and went to call on her. Strolling along the gallery towards her room, and catching glimpses of the river beyond the open parapet, was like taking exercise on the deck of a modern liner of the *Queen Mary* class, so long and wide was the stretch of floor behind and before us.

Three women approached us. One was small and elderly and walked several paces ahead of the others. Though her clothes seemed dirty and her feet were bare, I was struck by her proud carriage.

"Here she comes," Carter whispered to me.

"Who?" I asked.

"Lallang."

The group of natives accompanying us halted respectfully.

As Lallang welcomed us her gestures were gracious, even queenly. A smile of friendship played on her lips, and a kindly twinkle lit her eyes. She was especially cordial in her greeting to Carter, the hero of the liberation of her people in the previous year, and to White, an old acquaintance of pre-war days.

She was an aristocrat of undiluted blue blood. By all accounts she used to be a woman of conspicuous physical fitness, but that afternoon she appeared thin and frail. Denis White, who had not seen her for several years, observed a terrible change in her; and even Carter, who had met her only twelve months earlier, was shocked at how her body had wasted in the interval. Yet illness could not dim the glow of personality in her face. Her features had a charm which sprang from character rather than good looks, and consisted more of expression than of form. In her glance was the composed, self-assured dignity of authority, but her eyes twinkled merrily as she cracked jokes with Carter and White. She seemed inclined to treat everything as a jest. The more I knew her, the more I became conscious of this trait. Her light-heartedness was due partly to native wit, but partly, I thought, to a philosophy which she had acquired in a long and successful, but often troubled life. Sometimes her laugh sounded like the spontaneous, carefree outburst of a schoolgirl, but at other times like a cynical defence against sorrow maintained by a suffering woman. She looked worldly-wise, but also understanding and sympathetic in a deeper way. Nevertheless, I would not have put wickedness past her, and certainly not naughtiness.

She introduced us to her attendants, two girls in their late 'teens. They were good-looking maids, if a trifle plump. Their costumes displayed to perfection the Kayan style of feminine dress. Each wore on her head a coquettish hat like a coronet perched at a gay angle. One was made of leopard-cat's fur with a cockade of jungle grass sprouting above an ear; and the other of beads as finely patterned as *petit-point* needlework, with an upside-down bouquet of a kingfisher's feathers brushing the wearer's cheek. A smart Parisian hatter could not have designed creations more fetching. Each girl also wore a long, coloured sarong hanging from above her bosom to her ankles. No belt or sash clasped its waist. This simple, dignified gown is favoured by Kayan women on gala occasions, but for work-a-day purposes they wear shorter sarongs reaching from the waist to the feet.

The girls' costumes were embellished by two forms of bodily adornment peculiar to Kayan and Kenyah ladies. First, their faces were marred by a remarkable feature which one never saw on Iban belles. The lobes of their ears were pierced and stretched to an appalling length. As a result of years of gradual, artificial elongation they drooped at least six inches lower than the Creator intended that they should, forming long fleshy loops. In each hung several thick brass ear-rings. This seemed to me a frightful mutilation, but in the eyes of Kayan men it is a supremely lovely touch. The longer a woman's ears and the more rings she carries in them, the greater is her reputation for beauty. The ear-lobes of Lallang's companions reached so low that they rested on the forward slopes of their bare shoulders. Incidentally Lallang, too, wore this disfigurement, but her loops were empty of ornaments, for sickness had left her so weak that she could no longer bear their weight.

The girls' second extraordinary bodily adornment was their plentiful tattooing. On their arms a blue-black pattern extended like mittens from the elbows to the fingers, and on their legs a similar design appeared like stockings. The decorations on their legs continued from the base of the toes almost as high, I was told, as their hips.

Such was the striking costume of Lallang's attendants. The elder of the two, named Ubong, wore in addition the radiant looks of a bride. She was Lallang's adopted daughter, and a few months earlier had married a youth called Kallang, the eldest son of the powerful Kenyah chief, Penghulu Tama Weng Ajang. Thereby hangs a tale of pagan politics and diplomacy which I shall tell in due course.

Our introductions over, Lallang invited us to her room. We followed her into a vast apartment with a general air of well-being. In one corner stood an inner chamber like a cubicle, the private quarters of Ubong and Kallang. It was customary for newlyweds in a Kayan house to stay a considerable time with the girl's parents. To accommodate them a small private sanctum was built by erecting partition walls within the family's larger apartment. Sometimes there were two or three such cubicles for different relatives.

We squatted with Lallang on the floor as she ordered a servant to bring burak to regale us. Ubong called to her husband to join us. Kallang came forward modestly, a swarthy, muscular, well-made young man with pleasant features. Like almost all Bornean men, his face was beardless, with the smooth complexion of a schoolboy. The baldness of his countenance was accentuated by a Kenyah haircut. Most of his scalp was shaved, leaving only a neat circle of hair on top of his pate, the central locks of which tumbled far down his back.

He wore certain trinkets affected by Kayan and Kenyah bucks. Through holes cut near the tops of his ears protruded a small pair of ivory tusks, the long eye-teeth of leopard-cats, and in his slightly stretched lobes hung ear-drops made of brightly coloured beads. A necklace of yellow beads, a silver bracelet on each arm, a scarlet loin-cloth and a pair of rattan garters were his sole other attire. His lithe, bronzed, athletic limbs were more splendid than any dress.

The burak circulated and we drank to Lallang's health, wishing her a speedy recovery from her illness. She made cigarettes for us, picking the tobacco from a box of beaten brass, rolling it in dried banana leaf, lighting it between her own lips at a spirit-lamp on the floor, and then handing it to us. As our talk proceeded she herself puffed at one cheroot after another, slowly inhaling the smoke and blowing it out in rings through her pouting mouth.

She spoke of the harsh times that the natives suffered during the Japanese occupation, and of the Kayans' trust in government by the British. They felt no qualms about cession. Since the Rajah in his wisdom had decided that the change was good for them, they were happy to be ruled by the King.

"We're simple and ignorant people," she said. "We're like children. We need your guidance."

Much of the talk was light and merry, but she kept returning to this serious theme.

"Without you we don't know what to do," she reiterated. "Tell us what we should do. Come and see us often."

A group of natives crouching in the background nodded approval of her sentiments.

After a while Lallang sent Ubong to fetch certain prized possessions from a safe hiding-place. When the girl returned, she held a bundle tied in a dirty handkerchief. Lallang took it, laid it on the floor, undid its knots and extracted carefully two strings of beads. They were multi-coloured, marble-sized glass globules bearing marks of antiquity. Lallang said that she did not know their age, but that they were heirlooms inherited through countless generations of her forbears. Such beads were rare possessions among the Kayans, and were regarded with deep veneration. Their owners, she declared, would not part with them for thousands of dollars, for to do so would bring bad luck. According to local tradition, they arrived many centuries ago in Borneo, brought by Chinese traders in exchange for camphor and other desirable jungle produce. Lallang's tale was undoubtedly true. I could see that the oldest beads on her strings belonged to the T'ang or Sung dynasties.

I expressed admiration for the fine quality of Lallang's and Ubong's tattooing, and enquired about the technique of its application. Lallang replied that such decoration was an essential part of Kayan feminine beauty. It would be unthinkable for a lady of style to be without it. Affixing it was a painful process, and the operation was performed gradually by skilled old hands experienced in the art. The design was pricked and the dye soaked into the skin bit by bit, with intervals for healing between each fresh addition of a section of pattern. Three years were needed to complete the whole adornment of arms and legs, and usually a girl began to submit to this beauty treatment at the age of eleven. So she was a specimen of fully tattooed womanhood by her fourteenth year.

I was later to learn that one of the signs of modernity now creeping into Kayan and Kenyah society was the refusal of some young ladies to comply with this custom. In a few cases they even carried their revolutionary ideas further, and objected to the elongation of their ears. Other reforming females who had already had their ears mutilated occasionally visited hospitals to have the long, fleshy loops of the lobes amputated, and the ears restored to their natural size.

But such strange new notions had not yet invaded Long Laput. It was a stronghold of native conservatism.

III

The padi harvest had been poor that year, and Long Laput, with six hundred mouths to feed, was short of food. Knowing this, we arranged to dine aboard our launch, and to return to the house afterwards. After a while, therefore, we took leave of Lallang and descended to the river. Kallang and other youths escorted us, carrying oil-lamps to light us on our way. Night had fallen, and the stars were insufficient illumination to guide our steps along the tree-trunk paths.

After dinner we climbed again to the house. Everything was ready for a party. A vast throng of natives squatted in the gallery, their animated faces dimly lit by a few flickering lamps. We took our places in their centre, beside a space for dancing. Above us the skulls of dead enemies stared vacantly down, and all around the visages of our living friends grinned in the lights and shadows.

After a few moments Lallang entered. Like a ghost suddenly materializing, she appeared from the darkness in the direction of her room, walking with feeble yet stately tread. A procession of eight ladies-in-waiting followed her, first among them Ubong.

The crowd made a passage along which they could parade to join us.

Lallang sat on the mat beside me, and her attendants settled in a group close by. Some of these high-born girls wore chic Kayan hats, while others favoured unadorned hair arrangements. All were dressed in customary Kayan style. Clusters of earrings rested like bunches of strange fruit above their bosoms, several carrying nearly a dozen heavy brass coils in each lobe. I realized then that this fashion is responsible for the sedate walk which characterizes Kayan and Kenyah women, for if they did not move with an erect, smooth carriage, their loads of ear ornaments would jerk painfully at the lobes and break the loops of flesh in which they hang.

When all were settled, the audience fell quiet. Two musicians sat at the edge of the dance floor, each holding a string instrument in his lap. It was a characteristic product of Kayan art called a sapit. Shaped like a mediæval viol, it had sometimes two and sometimes three strings. Their notes were feeble, with a volume of sound about as great as that from a couple of keys on a harpsichord; but the music was sweet and tuneful. It had a pervading air of gentleness, shyness and restraint. Kayans and Kenyahs were fierce and often brutal warriors, and it was significant of more likeable and civilized traits in their natures that, in leisure hours between hunting and fighting, they loved to sit and listen to the soft, sentimental sighing of a sapit.

Now the minstrels began to stroke the strings of their instruments, and the sapits responded with thin, twanging notes. During the dances this soft music was the only sound in the silent long-house, except for an occasional stamp of a dancer's foot or his sudden wild cry as he expressed aloud his emotion.

Each man danced solo. Their talent varied. Among them were some of the best exponents of this dramatic jungle art that I have ever seen. Finest of them all was the bridegroom, Kallang.

For a long time he would not dance. I urged him to do so, but he declined, seeming reluctant. One by one other performers followed each other, but he would not be prevailed upon to take the floor. Then at last he rose.

When he fitted on his war-cloak, helmet and parang, and started the slow, introductory movements of the dance, I understood why he had waited. He had given the others their opportunity first, for none would be so foolish as to appear after him. They would be ashamed to display their awkward posturings after such a brilliant exhibition. He was a supreme master, an incomparable "ace" of perfect dancing, a glorious flash of genius.

When he had sipped his burak and the sapits commenced their faint, whispering tune he stepped into the circle of light. For a few moments he stood relaxed, his arms limp at his sides and one knee slightly bent, as if he were undecided what move to make. His head was bowed and his face wore a contemplative look. The single tall Argus-pheasant plume rising from his cap, the war-cloak of hornbills' feathers falling from his shoulders to his naked buttocks, and the sword sheathed in its scabbard on his hip were touches of splendid savagery. His honey-brown skin glistened where the lamplight caressed it.

Deliberately he raised his head, and his eyes gazed at the ceiling. He seemed lost in a dreamy kind of reverie. Raising both arms slightly from his sides, he let them fall again, like a preliminary, uncertain flutter of the wings of a bird about to fly. Though he made no other visible movement, I was conscious of his whole body waking into life, becoming tensely alert and ready for action.

After a few moments one of his feet began to tap the floor, repeating the beat three or four times to give him the sapits' rhythm. Then he took a forward step. His torso swayed gently as he advanced several paces, slow and stately yet easy and graceful, like the relaxed, nonchalant walk of a wild cat. He raised his arms sideways to the level of his shoulders, with elbows sharply bent and hands upraised. The movements were restrained, like the actions of a dancer in a slow-motion film.

Suddenly he broke from this subdued mood. With swift, twisting leaps he executed three violent, whirling steps. His balance and control were perfect. No sound of falling feet or straining limbs was audible. It was astonishing how such vigour could be so silent. The only noises were the dry clicks of feathered quills on his cloak as they rose and fell with each leap, and the gentle, ever so gentle, sighing of the sapits.

He reverted to a brief series of slow-motion steps as abruptly as he had broken from them. Soon, however, he sprang again into quick, energetic action. Then for a second time he seemed to relapse into inertia. A sleeper who has slumbered deeply for an age might wake by this fitful, gradual process.

The audience watched with fascination, as if held by a spell. Once more Kallang's progress returned to its sharper pace. Making a swift, feline, sideways leap, he landed on noiseless toes, then crossed one leg in front of the other and began a downward, spiralling curtsey. By some miraculous trick his body made two complete revolutions as it descended and two more as it circled upwards again without any apparent change in the position of his feet. At the lowest point of his pirouette he squatted on the floor, with arms stretched sideways while slow, undulating ripples of motion passed along them. As he rose and attained once more his full height, one hand felt for his scabbard and the other clasped the hilt of his sword. He drew the weapon and flourished it deftly in the air, its blade flashing in the gleaming lamplight.

The expression on his face was sometimes serene, sometimes fierce and sometimes lit by a kind of ecstasy. He was representing not so much an individual, personal sentiment as a deep, collective emotion of his race. Fighting was their tradition, and when physical combat was joined to capture a head it had spiritual, religious meaning. A bloody, severed mask was a sacrificial offering to one of the great dead.

Strutting jauntily, Kallang approached a shield lying on the floor, stooped and lifted it in his free hand. With consummate grace and agility he swept first the sword and then the shield through the air, holding them aloft as if they were holy vessels for display. As he did so, he pranced this way and that with proud steps. Round and round the circle of the stage he passed. Gradually his arms fell into battle positions and his gestures became warlike, now defensive and now offensive. Twice he repeated the exquisite pirouette movement, the shield and sword both poised to protect him as they swung downwards and upwards with him. The tempo of his performance increased. The crisis of the dance was approaching. He was now engaged in deadly contest against a grim, though imaginary, foe.

Then came the most brilliant moments of all. Kallang was hard pressed by his enemy. The duel was a desperate hand-to-hand encounter, and the thrust and parry were quick. Leaping, side-stepping, twisting, whirling, he evaded his opponent's lunging strokes, and drove in his own. His movements seemed as swift as lightning. His shield swung this way and that, and his sword was a flashing silver flame searing the air. The space for his performance was confined, for the hushed, crowded audience narrowed it all round; yet he appeared to move with absolute freedom, as if he had acres of ground in which to manoeuvre. His self-confidence was superlative. One slip of a foot would cause disaster; his naked blade would plunge among the faces peering close beside him and instantly inflict a terrible wound on some spectator. Indeed, the fury of its strokes and the sharpness of its cutting edge were sufficient to slice through a neck and claim for the hungry weapon another grizzly prize. But with complete self-control he swirled within a few inches of the audience's crouching figures, slashing his sword through the air a few inches above their heads. The onlookers too felt thoroughly assured. They neither stirred nor murmured.

In a series of breath-taking, whirlwind spins, culminating in a shout of triumph which shattered the silence like a thunderclap, the dance ended.

The great assembly of natives broke into loud shouts of delight, which gradually changed into a joyful, melodious, multitudinous chanting. This chorus of praise lasted several minutes.

Kallang laid down his shield and parang, and took off his war-cap and cloak. At my beckon he came to sit beside me. Perspiration poured from his body, his chest heaved violently as he panted for breath, and his heart pounded as if it would burst. He smiled and accepted a glass of burak. Drinks passed round the group of leading men sitting near us, and Lallang sipped some rice-wine from a teacup. Her ladies lit fresh cigarettes at a spirit-lamp on the floor, and a babble of conversation began. The tension created by Kallang's amazing, unforgettable performance relaxed.

Hitherto all the artists had been men. After a decent interval I asked Lallang whether some of her women would dance. She chortled, and passed the suggestion to them. They made shy, simpering, deprecatory gestures, but she laughed at them, and waxed caustic at their bashfulness. They still resisted, staring at the floor as if they were a company of deaf mutes incapable of either hearing or uttering speech. She continued to address them in chiding tones. Then one of them nudged another, and two or three sitting near the chosen victim gave her little pokes with their fingers. A stirring of half-suppressed mirth passed through the group as they tormented her. They smiled and sniggered and whispered among themselves. For a while the girl pretended not to notice their hints, but at last her resistance broke down, and she rose and walked into the circle of light. The string instruments struck up their inconspicuous little tune, and she began to sway her body to their faint rhythm.

After that the ice of feminine modesty quickly melted, and all the ladies-in-waiting danced in turn.

Their actions were not dramatic like the men's, but restrained and placid. In the dance their feet hardly moved at all. One explanation was no doubt, again, those heavy bunches of ornaments hanging from their ears. Had a woman engaged in any violent movement, her extended ear-lobes would have swung out and the ear-rings, breaking the long, slender strings of flesh, would have flown in all directions like stones slung from catapults.

So each dancer stood erect, her feet close together, her arms raised outwards from her body, and her gaze concentrated ahead. Throughout the performance she scarcely stirred from that pose. With the toes and ball of one foot she tapped on the floor a monotonous beat, and both feet advanced very slowly, each in turn shuffling forward a fraction of an inch at a time. The main effect was gained by a continuous, sinuous, snakey rippling and swaying of the arms.

Most of the girls confined their whole performance to this rather lovely, if unexciting exhibition, but a few executed an additional movement of singular charm. With feet pressed to-

gether they bent their knees, turned their bodies slightly sideways and descended floorwards in a slow, pirouetting curtsey.
Having almost swept the ground with their bodies, they then
rose again in the same deliberate, graceful, spiralling manner.
All the time their arms were held outwards with a bend at the
elbows, while their upraised hands undulated with slow, beautiful waves of motion. These hand gestures sprang at the wrists
and did not cease their rippling until it flowed off the tips of
their fingers. It was the cunning motif renowned in some Indian,
Javanese and other Oriental dancing, though these untutored
jungle women had not the polished artistry of professional palace
and temple performers in more sophisticated lands. Nevertheless,
the theme hinted that the origin, the inspiration of all these
dances in southern Asia was similar. Whence, for example, came
those surprisingly beautiful movements of remote head-hunters in
forest-bound Borneo? No one knows, but probably from some
far-off, half-wild, half-civilized beginning in the Burmese highlands, the Sumatran hills or elsewhere where their ancestors
tarried for generations in an earlier period of their migrations,
living and mixing with the local tribes before travelling onwards
to Borneo.

One girl caused merriment by a hint of abandon in her
performance. She was a pretty minx. Her steps were more
lively than those of the others, and there was a mischievous
twinkle in her eyes. At the beginning of each languid pirouette
she swung her hips with a seductive motion, and occasionally into
the undulations of her hands crept an inviting, beckoning, "come
hither" gesture.

When all Lallang's other handmaidens had performed, Ubong
rose to take the floor. Immediately Kayan wit was let loose at the
bride's expense. Ribald voices shouted that she should be occupied otherwise than in dancing in these days. Some jesters warned
her to be careful about her condition. Every sally was greeted
with guffaws of laughter, but the jokes were good-humoured and
friendly. For a while Ubong withstood the barrage, pretending
not to hear it. She posed statuesquely, raised her arms sideways,
and then commenced the slow, stately, foot-tapping amble of the
dance. Her arms and hands began to flutter like branches and
leaves on a tree in a gentle breeze.

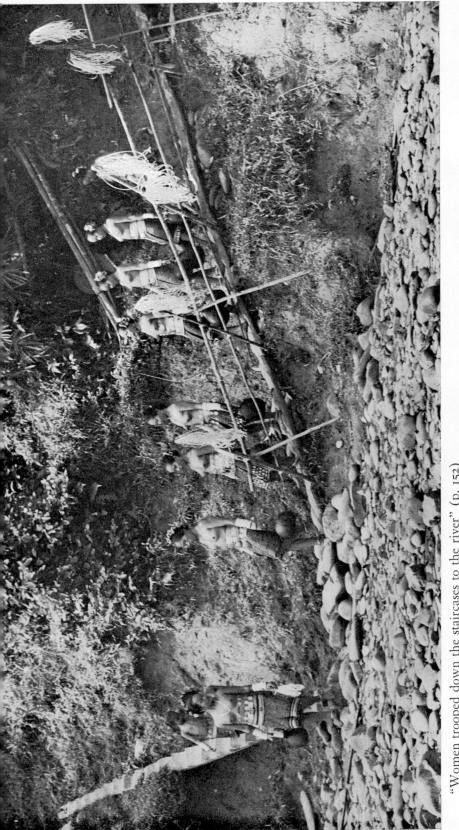

"Women trooped down the staircases to the river" (p. 152)

Temonggong Koh with Mindun and Segura (p. 88)

"...sides were strewn with ...e trunks of felled trees" (p. 171)

Koh's farmhouse (p. 172)

"Enjoying the natural scenery" (p. 180)

"On its summit stood an ornate, carved wooden tomb" (p. 249)

"Boats filled with natives" (p. 250)

"He pirouetted across the grass" (p. 254)

"The foothills of the mountainous interior" (p. 268)

Lallang (p. 272)

"From a rafter above our heads hung human skulls" (p. 271)

"The Kayan style of feminine dress" (p. 273)

"The lobes of their ears were pierced and stretched" (p. 273)

"Arden-Clarke had held an investiture in Miri" (p. 292)

An orchestra of Iban girls at Igan (p. 370)

"Houses stood along either bank" (p. 363)

Ong Tiang Swee (p. 379)

"Anchang, wearing a tiara of flowers on her head" (p. 409)

"Temonggong Koh: an august eighty-one" (p. 410)

"Careful! Careful!" exclaimed some rude fellow.

The girl made a nervous grimace, faltered for a moment, and then started to dance again. No movement could be more discreet, or less calculated to strain even the most delicate human frame.

But the chorus of banter increased. Ubong looked embarrassed. Some anonymous admirer gave a flirtatious wolf whistle. A pink flush rose in her cheeks. Suddenly she halted, hid her face in her hands, burst into laughter and retired from the unequal contest.

The dancing was over. We passed to the next diversion in the programme of entertainment.

Lallang called for a tumbler of burak. Shifting her position until she sat immediately in front of me, she told her ladies to do likewise. The rest of the audience drew close around us.

In one of her aged, delicate hands (the skin and bone of which seemed as fragile as a piece of Venetian glass) Lallang raised the tumbler towards me, held it suspended in mid-air, and started to sing. The princess was to lead a Kayan drinking song in my honour. She carolled the solo parts, and her ladies-in-waiting chanted the refrains. First her thin, high-pitched, old woman's voice quavered a couple of lines on its own, like an antique musical instrument cracked with age; then their sweet young voices took up the tune, giving it sudden melodious volume. As they fell silent her croaking contralto rose again in solitary incantation, to be sustained once more a little later by their clear trebles. After a few verses some of the youths joined the choir. Reinforced by their rich tenors and basses, the harmony had solemn, powerful beauty.

Kayan drinking songs, like Iban pantuns, are veritable sagas in which the qualities of a guest are celebrated in countless verses. The soloist improvises the words as he or she proceeds, while the phrases of the chorus are fixed and oft-repeated. That evening Lallang composed about a score of stanzas. Each time when she launched upon a new line it seemed that the frail vessel of her voice would founder, that it would break and of a sudden disappear in unfathomable silence. But her spirit bore it up undaunted, and she maintained her effort to the end.

At last she finished the long, imaginative recitation of my

virtues, and her voice fell a key in tone into the monotonous humming which is the climax of these songs. The whole audience of hundreds of natives now swelled the chorus of sound. Lallang handed me the glass, and I quaffed its contents, as honour demanded, without drawing breath.

The hour was past midnight, and I could see that the events of the day had tired Lallang. Much of the evening she had sat quiet, only occasionally making jocular comments on the proceedings. The liveliness in her was half-dead. She revived for the song, but that was a special, gallant last flicker of energy. Now in an instant she seemed exhausted.

In earlier years none could excel her in robust vivacity. A European government officer once told me that she was then rather gay. He realized this forcibly one night, twenty years earlier, on his first visit as a young cadet to Long Laput. When he had retired to bed and was about to fall asleep in the dark longhouse, the mosquito-net surrounding his couch was parted by strange hands. On to the mattress beside him slipped a naked woman—Lallang! He was an innocent youngster, and felt astonished, shy and shocked. With scant chivalry and prim inhospitality, he pushed her out of bed and she sprawled on the floor.

Time had wrought great changes in her physique, but her generous, friendly spirit had not altered. As the party broke up that night, and I was wishing her sweet dreams, she said that she would like to make me a gift. She sent Kallang to fetch it, and after a while he returned carrying a bulky parcel. As Lallang handed it to me she apologized for the contents' insignificance; but when I unpacked it I found inside a hundred dollars' worth of her precious, delicious edible bird's nests.

IV

With this mark of her favour I withdrew to my sleeping quarters. I was to spend the night on a dais built for special visitors in a corner of her vast apartment. Many others would sleep in the same room. At one end camp-beds for my English fellow-travellers stood like a row of bunks in a schoolboys' dormitory;

at the other Lallang and a group of friends squatted round a dish
of rice, eating, smoking and gossiping before going to rest; and
in their cubicle Kallang and Ubong were likewise having an
evening meal.

Their door was half open, and I caught glimpses of them as
they moved about the room. I watched a domestic idyll in the
life of pagans. Ubong cooked rice and brewed tea on a small
stove on the floor. When their supper was ready, the young
couple sat cross-legged on a mat to eat it. In whispered tones
they conversed together, and every now and then they softly
chuckled. At one moment they seemed on the point of being
convulsed with merriment, and only with difficulty stifled their
desire to laugh loud and long. They controlled the impulse, no
doubt, for fear of disturbing us strangers beyond the wooden
partition. Possibly they were recalling the events of the evening,
and sharing private jokes about them. I noticed Ubong's happy
glances at her husband. At the point when they had to check
their laughter he appeared to be teasing her, for she blushed and
playfully slapped his arm. Perhaps he was reminding her of
the jests which greeted her when she rose to dance, and of her
failure to complete the performance.

When their meal was finished he rose, took a towel from a
peg on the wall, stepped through the cubicle door and left the
house. He had gone for a bathe in the river. She cleared away
their cups and dishes, then fetched a broom and swept the floor.
The little boudoir cleaned, she peered through the door to see
whether Kallang were returning. He was still away. She went
to the middle of their room, stood poised for a few moments, and
then raised her arms in the attitude of dancing. Into her face came
the serene expression assumed by performers. One foot began to
tap the floor lightly, her arms commenced to ripple, and she
shuffled slowly forwards in the oft-rehearsed movements of the
dance. Soon she passed beyond my line of vision, but I could still
watch her as a shadow on the wall. For a long time she danced,
tapping and swaying, ambling and pirouetting without a faltering
step. Sometimes I saw her in person and at other times only as a
shadow while she moved round her chamber. She was reassuring

herself that she could dance as faultlessly as any girl in the house, and she was still dancing when Kallang returned.

He stepped through the door and closed it behind him.

I retired to my dais, undressed and lay down. A medley of sounds issued from the gallery and neighbouring rooms, but I soon fell asleep. Paradoxical though it may seem, easy lies the head that shares a head-hunter's room.

Next day we left early and returned down-river.

"We're ignorant savages," said Lallang as she bade me farewell. "We need your help. Don't forget us. Come and see us again."

I promised that I would.

CHAPTER FIFTEEN

BARAM WORTHIES

I

I DID NOT FORGET my promise to Lallang, and fifteen months later, in November 1947, returned to see her and her people. This time my wife, Audrey, came with me, filled with curiosity to meet the "Dollar Princess".

When our launch left Kuala Baram and started up-river, a select party of old and new friends embarked with us. Arden-Clarke was there, though he was to accompany us only as far as Marudi. John Gilbert would come with us all the way to Long Laput, and we picked up the new District Officer at Marudi, a young man called Morgan, who had a sympathetic, constructive attitude to native affairs. In addition three notable characters whom I had not previously met came aboard: Father Jansen, the doyen of Christian missionaries in Sarawak, an able young Kenyah chief called Penghulu Gau, and the redoubtable Penghulu Tama Weng Ajang.

I had long looked forward to meeting Tama Weng, and my high expectations of his appearance and character were not disappointed when I set eyes on him. But before I write of the great man, I must acquaint the reader with certain facts about the politics of the Baram which are relevant to his story. Gilbert, Morgan and I discussed them as we lolled on deck travelling from Marudi to Long Laput. I then learned of some developments which had occurred since my visit in the previous year.

As the reader knows, along the banks of the upper Baram lived numerous communities of Kenyahs and Kayans. Though they had much in common, they were two distinct peoples, each organized in its own tribal society under its own chiefs. Among the Kayans Lallang was the outstanding individual, and among the Kenyahs supreme authority lay with Tama Weng.

One or two other Kayan chieftains were abler than Lallang, and had more official status; but in the past the force of her character, supported by remarkable energy and unrivalled wealth, made her pre-eminent; and the magic of her personality still counted for much. Moreover, the numerous inmates of her house composed about fifteen per cent of the entire Kayan population on the river, and she and others in it remained, by pagan standards, fabulously rich. Current reckoning indicated that their collective income from the ownership of bird's-nest caves amounted to between $12,000 and $15,000 a year.

The way in which this wealth was spent is a sorry revelation, which will lead to a discourse on the place and influence of Long Laput in Baram society. The affluent community could spend its money well or ill, could invest it for the benefit or squander it to the detriment of themselves and their neighbours, could set a good or a bad example. I regret to say that they chose the latter course.

It may seem churlish to criticize their marked fondness for festival after I had myself enjoyed so hugely an evening of it; but I must faithfully present the facts. The Kayans of Long Laput had a poor, indeed an outrageous reputation. They were a bad lot. This was not wholly their fault. In other circumstances they would doubtless have been as sober, self-respecting and commendable savages as any in Sarawak; but, alas, too many riches had fallen into their hands. They were ruined by money. This happens to people in the most civilized societies, so who are we to criticize? People in glass houses—whether they be glass long-houses or not—should not throw stones.

During my first visit to Long Laput I was not made aware of the darker side of its inmates' lives for, owing to circumstances beyond their control, they were then on their best behaviour. Their padi harvest had been poor and they were somewhat short of food. A fortunate result of this otherwise unfortunate condition was that they were automatically short of drink also, their wine being made from rice. Nor had they then any appreciable income from bird's nests with which to purchase extra supplies of food and drink, for in 1946 the trade in nests had not recovered from neglect during the Japanese occupation. So they were suffering a period of enforced abstinence.

I did receive one or two whispered hints that on other occasions my hosts were not all that they should be. For example, it was alleged that during the Japanese occupation they had been guilty of an act of cannibalism. Such conduct was regarded even by passionate head-hunters as showing rather bad form. In the days before Sir James Brooke arrived in Sarawak, in the golden age of head-hunting, cannibalism was not a common practice. On the contrary, it was an extremely rare occurrence which was frowned upon by the long-house dwellers. To eat a fellow human being after you had punctured him with a poisoned arrow, executed him with a parang and humiliated him by hanging his head in your house was thought to be carrying things a bit too far. It was adding insult to injury. Yet during the recent war some men from Long Laput had committed this gross offence, feasting off a dead enemy.

Prior to the war the inmates of Long Laput already had an unenviable reputation, being notorious as light workers and heavy drinkers. Not sedulous agriculturists, they failed to grow as much padi as they needed to feed themselves. Moreover, they had a strong inclination to transform much of the rice which they did produce from invigorating food into intoxicating liquor. The catastrophe of Japanese conquest encouraged this tendency. The occupying army confiscated the pagans' shot-guns, with the result that wild pigs raided the padi-fields and ate much of the crop before it ripened; and then, when the depleted harvest was gathered, Japanese soldiers came up-river to collect most of what was left. These circumstances persuaded the Long Laputians that it would be an act of patriotism as well as prudence to disguise their rice in the form of liquid hidden in jars, and so deny it to the enemy.

The habits thus formed aggravated an evil state of affairs. As we went up-river for my second visit to Long Laput, Morgan complained bitterly of the situation. The people of the house, he said, were now rolling—literally rolling—in money. This wealthy community, instead of setting an example of decorous conduct, had broken all records for depravity; instead of being the best house on the river, it was the worst; instead of being a paradise of peace and plenty, it was a hell-hole of riotous living.

This was all very sad. After each thrice-yearly auction of bird's nests at Long Lama between $4,000 and $5,000 came into the mansion as income for Lallang and other cave-owners. Had they devoted even part of these sums to communal improvements, Long Laput might have become a model of pagan domestic life. But the minds of its people pursued a different train of thought. Since the labour of birds building nests, they reflected, provided them with a comfortable income, they need not themselves labour hard in their fields. If they ran short of home-grown padi, did they not possess the wherewithal to buy more rice? Yet they did not, in fact, save their spare cash for that purpose. They had so much money, they argued, that it did not matter if a little were devoted to the pleasures of living—and in the end they squandered almost all of it on carousals.

Their orgies of drinking sometimes reached astonishing proportions. At the same time the community spent next to nothing on repairing their house, buying new furniture, acquiring better agricultural implements, introducing modern household conveniences, and adding other amenities to their home. Still less did they think of purchasing medical supplies for the sick or financing a school for the children.

The situation was made worse because to their own particular defects they added their share of the shortcomings of Kayans in general. The Kayans and Kenyahs had a seamy side to their natures, clinging with morbid devotion to certain ancient superstitions which led them to observe stupid and even diabolical taboos. I have already noted that if bad omens decreed that a long-house population should lock itself indoors for a period of days or weeks, regardless of the fact that it should then be planting, cultivating or harvesting padi, it would sit religiously at home and let the crop deteriorate. Another taboo was extremely damaging to the well-being of the race. The delivery of a new-born babe was somehow regarded as an unclean act which should not occur inside a house, lest it doom the whole community to disaster; so pregnant women about to give birth were driven from their homes, to suffer their confinements in miserable, un-hygienic jungle solitude. The effect of this on maternal and infant mortality was a serious contributory cause to checking the natural increase of the Kayan and Kenyah peoples.

The Kayans of Long Laput followed these customs faithfully, in addition to indulging in their own favourite excess. It was a thousand pities. Sarawak's tribes had reached a crisis in their history. They stood on the threshold of far-reaching changes. Modern notions were creeping into their country from the outside world, and the natives must adapt themselves to inescapable revolutionary conditions. The inhabitants of Long Laput, employing their wealth as an instrument of policy, could have given a lead in the direction of reforms which would reconcile what was best in their traditions with what could be most beneficial in up-to-date ideas; but instead they were hopelessly sunk in some of the worst practices of their old, primitive way of life.

Unfortunately Lallang's influence was not exerted on the side of wisdom. She was a remarkable personality, but not a remarkable leader—a great pagan of the old school, not a great pagan of the new. Her thoughts were cramped and confined within the narrow limits of ancient, conservative beliefs, and she remained unaware of the presence of fresh, expansive, progressive ideas. In any case she was now too aged and ill to make any effort at adjusting herself to fast-moving times. Her force was a spent force.

That was where Tama Weng Ajang came in. He differed strikingly from her. She represented the old order in native society, while he represented the new. She was the past, and he was the future. They were a fascinating study in contrasting personalities.

Born and bred like her in the ancient tradition, Tama Weng rose above it and could see beyond it. His natural gifts of insight and wisdom enabled him to perceive, no doubt dimly and as yet only half comprehendingly, that strange, vast changes were pending in his country, and that the prospect for his people might be either utterly destroyed or wonderfully improved by them. He was groping after the right solutions to many difficult problems, and was prepared to experiment, to consider novel suggestions, to give a bold lead in a forward direction. He was no ordinary, petty pagan chieftain, but a man of character, courage and vision who, in his small world, attained the stature of a grand statesman.

II

The reader will remember that we British had reason for deep gratitude to Tama Weng for his actions during the last phase of the war in Sarawak. Before our parachute party split into separate expeditions down the rivers, before Bill Sochon went to Penghulu Puso on the Rejang and Toby Carter began his advance down the Baram, the whole force was dependent on the goodwill of Tama Weng. He was the paramount chief in the remote interior where they started their adventure. They declared themselves to him, telling him of their purpose, and throwing themselves completely on his mercy. He could either betray them to the Japanese, or hide, succour and aid them in organizing a revolt against the occupying army. Alternatively he could salve his conscience by evading the issue, refusing to have anything to do with the uninvited visitors, and asking them to take themselves elsewhere.

He did not hesitate. Calling the Kenyah and Kayan penghulus and tuai tuai rumah into conference in his house at Long Akar, he gave a determined lead in favour of rebellion. For three days the discussions continued. In the end, after many arguments and counter-arguments, the chieftains resolved unanimously to offer their help to the handful of British invaders. Once they had taken the decision they never wavered, but worked and fought with unremitting zeal for the cause.

On the day that I met him, Tama Weng was returning from a ceremony which was a sequel to those events. Arden-Clarke had held an investiture in Miri, and among the recipients of awards was Tama Weng. He became that morning a Member of the Most Excellent Order of the British Empire, in recognition of his part in the liberation of Sarawak. When he stepped to the Governor to receive his insignia, he wore the full battle dress of a great Kenyah leader, with plumes, war-cloak, shield and parang. Two attendants escorted him to the dais, one a fellow Kenyah

attired also in wild tribal costume, and the other Toby Carter
wearing the neat uniform of a British major. Carter himself
received the D.S.O. that day.

Tama Weng was now making the return journey to Long
Akar. Our launch would carry him as far as Long Laput, where
a prahu would meet him to take him onward to his home.
Before we embarked, Arden-Clarke introduced me to him on the
jetty, and we exchanged affable words as we went aboard. When
I congratulated him on his M.B.E., he spoke modestly of his part
in the war-time exploits, giving the main credit to Carter, Harrisson, Sochon and their men.

I observed the chief with keen interest. It was difficult to tell
his age. The pagans keep no account of dates or years, and look
mystified if you ask them how old they are. The milestones of
time for them are not years, but memorable events in their local
history.

"That happened about the time of the great flood on the
river," they will say, or, "That happened when the chief at Long
This or Long That died."

If those events are recorded in the official annals, you can
tell to which year the speaker alludes. The favourite historical
occurrence remembered by true veterans in the long-houses was
the eruption of Krakatoa off the Sumatra coast in 1883. The volcano's upheaval was so violent that for days afterwards in distant
Borneo the sky remained darkened by a pall of ash and smoke,
and septuagenarians reckoned their ages by that unforgettable
spectacle.

Tama Weng was probably in his early forties. Though he
stood less than five-and-a-half feet high, he appeared massive, for
he was broadly built and carried a deal of flesh. His head was
cropped in Kenyah style, his countenance was round and chubby,
and his ear-lobes were artificially extended. These features,
coupled with a serene, benign expression in his face, gave him a
striking resemblance to the Buddha. His manner was in keeping
with that character. Placid and contemplative, he talked little
but thought much. His tranquillity was the calm of self-
assurance, and his silence the quietude of strength.

When our launch started its journey, his likeness to the Buddha became even more impressive, owing to the posture which he adopted on board. He sat cross-legged on deck, his hands folded in his lap and his eyes gazing benevolently upon the passing scene. He seemed like a life-size image of the deity stolen from a temple. Had he been born in Tibet, he could scarcely have avoided selection as the Dalai Lama.

As he sat there, outwardly so passive, his inward thoughts were no doubt active. Perhaps he was ruminating on the problems of his people. During his visit to Miri (he might be thinking to himself) the leaders of other Sarawak races as well as of his Kenyahs were in town, and the Governor held conference with them all. Weighty matters were discussed. Certain administrative reforms, the creation of new consultative councils, some awkward questions of taxation, and the Government's policies on agriculture, education and public health came under review. The times were changeful and hopeful, but difficult and in some ways baffling. They were especially confusing to his people, the Kenyahs, and to their friends the Kayans, and also to those strange, restless characters the Ibans, for they were all ignorant folk who could not readily understand the goings-on of the modern world. The Malays and Chinese did comprehend, because they had been to school; but the pagans had never been tutored. They needed guidance through this period of transition from an old to a new order. He was doing his best to lead them, and other chiefs also were helping. His principal aide was that wise young man, Penghulu Gau, who had come to Miri with him and now sat on deck beside him. Gau and he were firm friends and allies, with a relationship rather like that of David and Jonathan in the story which old Father Jansen, the Christian missionary, sometimes told.

Such, possibly, were Tama Weng's thoughts as we made our way up-river; and perhaps they continued in this manner. His authority over the Kenyahs on the Baram was supreme. They would follow his advice. But the Kayans were more uncertain, more incalculable. They had no outstanding leader, and were like a prahu with no guiding oar amid turbulent rapids. They spun round and round, and were in grave danger of losing direction, and even of getting sunk. For example, there were those unsatisfactory people in the enormous house at Long Laput. They just ate and drank and were merry, with no thought of the morrow and its problems. Lallang was a fine woman, but she did not comprehend what was happening in Borneo in these days. A few years ago she might have understood, but now she was too old to learn, and so Long Laput was leaderless. Therefore he was trying to introduce his own influence into that important house, so that his authority might gradually extend among the Kayans as well as his own people. For that reason he had married his son Kallang to Ubong, Lallang's adopted daughter. Lallang had no son, no male heir, so her wealth would pass to Ubong, and perhaps her power among the Kayans would pass in due course to the girl's husband.

I need not seek to trace beyond that point the train of thought of the great Kenyah. Let me explain the rest of the story in my own way. As I have remarked earlier, the union of Kallang with Ubong was an act of high politics, a shrewd stroke of statecraft, like one of the dynastic marriages between children of royal houses in mediæval Europe. It united two important governing families in two neighbouring societies. For long Tama Weng had planned it, and in achieving it he gained a diplomatic triumph.

It was not the first link of its kind between the two families. Tama Weng's father, a famous chief called Akam Jau, had arranged just such a marriage for Tama Weng himself. Tama Weng's wife was Lallang's own daughter, the princess's only child. So Tama Weng was already Lallang's son-in-law, and Kallang was her grandson. The wedding between Kallang and Ubong was a further confirmation, a fresh strengthening in a new generation, of ties of matrimony which bound together the foremost Kenyah family and the principal Kayan family on the Baram.

It would be foolish to suggest that Tama Weng's motives were wholly altruistic, that they were concerned solely with the public good. In them was an element of selfishness, a desire for material private gain. Lallang was enormously rich, and since she would presume that Tama Weng could provide for her actual daughter's —his wife's—future welfare, she might leave all her wealth to her adopted child, Ubong. In that case Kallang's marriage to

Ubong would make the boy joint heir to the old lady's possessions. Moreover, his residence as son-in-law in Lallang's apartment at Long Laput could bring additional advantages. He
might eventually succeed as the headman of the house. So he,
and through him his father, might gain control not only of the
financial wealth but also of the political power at Long Laput.

That was the selfish aspect of Tama Weng's scheme. Cynical
observers were inclined to emphasize it. But the chief's policy
was not merely a piece of personal power politics. It was a means
to the achievement of a grander aim. Tama Weng's ambitions
were broad, patriotic and enlightened. He wished to have a say
in the disposal of Long Laput's riches so that they could be
used not for private but for social ends. He despised the drunken-
ness of the large Kayan household, and feared the disastrous
consequences if such evil habits spread. And he realized what
benefits could flow from Lallang's fortune, if only it were wisely
spent.

There was a wider purpose in the marriage which he contrived
for his son. Kallang's partnership with Ubong was a great step
towards closer kinship between all the Kenyahs and all the
Kayans. The two peoples would be stronger united than divided.
Already inter-marriages among them occasionally occurred, but
the wedding between the Kenyah chief's son and the Kayan
princess's daughter might open the way to an actual merging of
the tribes. If in due course Kallang did prove himself worthy,
he might become not only tuai rumah of the greatest Kayan
house, in Lallang's footsteps, but also paramount chief of the
Kenyahs in succession to Tama Weng. So he would combine in
his own person both races on the Baram River. Tama Weng's
dynastic ambitions were no less magnificent than that.

Through them he hoped that his forward-looking ideas would
prevail in Kenyah-Kayan society. On public affairs he held strong,
original opinions. To put it bluntly, he realized that the old
pagan way of life was doomed. The only method by which
the natives could survive amid the stresses of modern developments was, he thought, by adapting themselves to huge changes.
He understood that the traditional life was condemned because

some of its customs were bad. The taboos, for instance, interfered with good agriculture and undermined the people's health. If these practices continued, the Kenyahs would never rise above a sordid level of poverty and disease, and might even gradually die out. The taboos, however, were deeply founded. They were rooted in fundamental concepts of the pagan faith, and could not easily be disturbed. Indeed, they could only be destroyed by striking at that faith itself.

Tama Weng had the extraordinary insight and courage to decide that his people should abandon paganism, the whole body of beliefs which had sustained and guided them for centuries. Something better, something more creative should take its place. In his opinion this should be Christianity, the religion about which his friend Father Jansen often spoke to him. For the past six months he had professed himself a Christian.

Yet he was not a fanatical convert to the new religion. His wisdom was intuitive and broad. He realized that the reforms which he wished to introduce should not be too sudden or sweeping, for his people were simple and conservative, and violent shocks would upset them. They could be led to accept necessary changes only if they were allowed to grow accustomed to them slowly, progressively. The process would be aided if at the same time unnecessary innovations were avoided, so that the general atmosphere of native life was not abruptly altered. He recognized, too, that though some important features in pagan society were evil, others were good. They suited Bornean conditions and fitted the natives' character. While preaching the abolition of certain ancient customs, he therefore urged the preservation of others. He encouraged the wearing of traditional Kenyah dress, and disapproved of men donning shirts and trousers in the long-house. Such sophistication might be appropriate in towns, but it was not sensible in the jungle. The simple bead necklace and cloth sirat were a distinctive native costume, and were, besides, more convenient and healthy. He strove to maintain other manners congenial to life in the tropical forest, such as communal existence in the long-house itself. But he advocated the sweeping away of the entire collection of harmful superstitions and taboos. And with his whole heart he desired that medical clinics, schools and improved agricultural training should be brought to his people.

He believed that the salvation of his race lay in the adoption of Christianity. So great was his influence in his house at Long Akar that its population was prepared to follow him *en masse* in this conversion. Recently he had asked Father Jansen, long known and beloved by the natives of the Baram, to baptize them at one fell swoop.

The good Father's response to this appeal was characteristic of that sage missionary's deep understanding and sympathy, his humanity and true Christianity. By chance he too was on board our launch that day. A seventy-year-old Dutchman, he was the Grand Old Man of the Christian missions in Sarawak, having lived there for half a century. His pate was bald, his face appeared pinched and sallow, his gentle, friendly blue eyes peered through steel-rimmed spectacles perched on a broken nose, and below his sensitive mouth sprouted a small, grey tuft of beard. His figure was short and slight, and his body seemed dried and shrunken after long exposure to the equatorial sun. He wore simply an old khaki jacket and trousers and a pair of sandals.

The priest moved about the launch as quietly as a mouse, much of the time sitting in a wicker chair, reading a well-thumbed copy of the Bible and sipping lemonade, or puffing at an old briar pipe. He welcomed the chance to talk with us, for all too rarely did he meet fellow Europeans. His conversation was keen and interesting, packed with scraps of fascinating information about the pagan peoples, and enlivened by a whimsical wit. When he spoke, his open mouth revealed a collection of deplorably crooked and broken teeth. His outlandish life gave him no opportunity to visit a dentist.

Since early manhood he had been ceaselessly engaged on his Heavenly Father's business among some of His humblest and most ignorant creatures. Through all those years he lived in obscurity, humility and virtual solitude, for much of the time he was alone in the wilderness except for his friendship with the natives and his companionship with God. Living with apostolic simplicity, he travelled up rivers in pagan canoes to perform healing works, delight people with his cheering presence, and practise as well as preach the Christian ethic. In the course of many journeys from the Arctic to the Antipodes I have met innumerable missionaries belonging to various sects, and most of them led unbelievably selfless lives; but none was more saintly than Father Jansen.

He knew Tama Weng well, admired the chief, and approved of his efforts to abolish harmful traditions and taboos. For many years he had striven to bring Kenyah and Kayan leaders to that point of view. Nevertheless, when Tama Weng asked for admission into the Church he declined to receive him immediately. He praised the native's inclination, but protested that it was not yet a conviction. The conversion must have more depth and passion. Tama Weng, he said, wished to become a Christian for negative reasons, not for positive ones—because he desired to deal blows at heathen superstitions, not because he believed in the Christian faith. The motive was good, but it was not good enough. The chief was courageous and wise in rejecting paganism and emptying his mind of its teachings, but now he must go further and fill his mind with an understanding of Christ's message. The people of his house must wait and do likewise.

Father Jansen realized that he would do a grave disservice to the Kenyahs if he encouraged them to abandon old beliefs without ensuring that in their place they truly accepted new beliefs. Much of the natives' code of individual and social conduct was based on sanctions decreed by their traditional faith. If this were shattered and no new religion took its place, their system of morals might also collapse. That had often happened to primitive peoples. They would become mere non-believers, recognizing no compelling reason for good behaviour as distinct from bad, becoming sceptical of all previously held notions, and not yet deriving guidance from new convictions. They would drift into disbelief of anything and everything, and lack the inspiration of the notion of some supreme supernatural being benevolently concerned with the affairs of men.

So Father Jansen said that he would instruct Tama Weng and the inmates of his house in the elements of the Christian religion. It would take time, but the day would come when the chief and his followers would sincerely believe. Then the missionary would baptize them all.

The priest urged this with such clarity and friendliness that Tama Weng was not offended, but comprehended and accepted the situation. He began to think more seriously about the positive implications of Christianity, and spoke of the problem with the principal men in his house. Father Jansen began a regular course of lessons in the Word of God. He was on his way to Long Akar for further discussions on these matters with the chief, when he embarked on our launch that day.

Tama Weng and Father Jansen were both remarkable men, notable creative influences in the development of contemporary Sarawak. Yet perhaps the most potent personality of the three local passengers on our boat was Penghulu Gau. I had already heard much of this young Kenyah chieftain. Gilbert, a dour and common-sense individual who is cautious in his judgements of men, declared that he liked Gau best and regarded him as the ablest of all the natives on the river. Morgan agreed and went even further. He said that Gau was the finest gentleman he had ever met, either in Borneo or outside it.

The penghulu was about ten years junior to Tama Weng. Both men were alike in all the superficial appearances of Kenyahs. Their Mongolian features, half-shaved heads, light-brown skins and native costumes were similar. In figure Gau was a boyish edition of Tama Weng, younger and slimmer. But different personalities showed in the two men's faces. Tama Weng's countenance rarely betrayed emotion, remaining unwrinkled and displaying monumental calm. Gau's face, on the other hand, was engraved with wrinkles which expressed instantly every passing sentiment that affected him, puckering into a frown, smoothing into thoughtfulness or curving into a grin in quickly alternating moods. Whereas Tama Weng was slow to smile, Gau smiled easily and quickly. Tama Weng's smile when it came was benign and Buddha-like, while Gau's was joyful and puckish. Gau's slanting eyes, protruding ears and playful, full-lipped mouth were also puckish. His face was a sensitive mask reflecting a nimble, half-serious, half-gay character.

Politically his association with Tama Weng was close. He

was the paramount chief's faithful pupil, his disciple in promoting progressive policies. On public questions they planned and co-operated together, both sitting as representatives of the Kenyahs on the recently created District Council. They were like an elder statesman and a younger statesman of their people, and, in the absence of outstanding Kayan leaders on the Baram, were becoming acknowledged as spokesmen of the Kayans also.

Yet if Gau was at present Tama Weng's junior partner in affairs, he might not always remain so. His own merits and his popularity with the natives might make him, in due time, an independent leader, at least equal in authority with his powerful mentor. Already he, not Tama Weng, had been chosen by the Kenyah and Kayan members of the District Council to represent them on the superior Divisional Council. That elevation was made with Tama Weng's approval, for the older man lived far up-river and could not readily attend the necessary meetings in distant Miri. Gau was the penghulu of several Kenyah long-houses on the middle Baram, and so was more handily placed for visits to the divisional capital. Tama Weng therefore authorized his colleague, in effect, to represent him. Nevertheless, Gau's selection was significant of the younger man's increasing reputation, of his rising star.

When Tama Weng's days as paramount chief ended, perhaps Gau rather than Kallang would succeed him as the leader of their peoples.

III

Such were the personalities of my new acquaintances on the journey up the Baram. We travelled the first day as far as Marudi, spent a night there, and left early the next morning to complete the further stages of the trip. On our way we stopped at Penghulu Gau's house to deliver the young chief back to his family. We planned to make a more leisurely visit to him on our return journey next day.

At Long Laput, where we arrived in the late afternoon, Lallang and her teeming household thronged the river bank to give us a boisterous welcome. The princess seemed in about the same state of health as in the previous year, neither frailer nor more robust. She was happy that Audrey had come to see her, and made much of this unusual phenomenon—a white woman—in a long-house. For more than a hundred years white men had travelled up the Sarawak rivers, and they were familiar guests in Kayan homes; but in 1947 European ladies rarely felt disposed to make the rough journeys, suffer the discomforts and run the risks of tropical ailments which these jungle ventures entailed. Since then the amenities of travel in the interior have improved, and more white women make the trip; but, at that time, Audrey's arrival was an exceptional occurrence almost like one of those epic events, such as the eruption of Krakatoa, on which the chronology of pagan history is strung.

Unfortunately Tama Weng was unable to accompany us to the house. On the previous night he had suffered a mishap at Marudi. Walking through the bazaar in the dark, he accidentally placed a foot in a storm-drain, fell and broke a rib. His massive frame was now partly encased in plaster, and so sharp was the pain that he could not comfortably climb the river bank and steep tree-trunk stairway to the dwelling. Instead he lay in a prahu moored at the river's edge, and received visits there from the local leaders, like a royal invalid giving audience to ambassadors in a private yacht. He was to leave at first light next morning, to continue his homeward journey, so I bade him farewell in the prahu. He made me promise to visit him at Long Akar when next I came up-river, a proposal which I enthusiastically accepted.

Then the rest of us climbed to the house. Soon we saw signs of the deterioration among its inmates which Morgan had described. Our reception was attended by an inordinate amount of drinking. Etiquette required, of course, that on our arrival we should squat on mats below the human skulls to toast our friendship with the tuai rumah, and that afterwards we should do the same with Lallang in her apartment. But no further liquid refreshment should have been offered at that early hour. However, when we had partaken of Lallang's burak, puffed at her tobacco, examined again her precious strings of beads, listened to her gossip and talked for a while with Kallang and Ubong, we were invited to join in similar courtesies in the private rooms of several other leading characters in the house. We were advised that refusals might cause hurt feelings among our hosts, so we dutifully complied. These receptions completely filled the three hours between our arrival and supper-time.

Audrey quickly acquired the art of accepting readily in theory invitations to imbibe a continuous flow of drink, and then in practice resisting pressure to implement her promise. After a first glassful she took little more. Whenever a brimming tumbler was passed to her she smiled devastatingly, seized it eagerly in both hands, dipped her lips a fraction of a centimetre into its brew, and then handed it back with a gesture of deep gratitude. If challenged to do more, she pleaded that a delicate feminine constitution made over-indulgence inadvisable. Thus she survived unscathed the gay tribulations of Long Laput hospitality.

Being too ashamed to confess that my masculine constitution was no more iron-clad against the disrupting effects of rice-wine, I accepted whatever was offered to me. Normally I consume little but water, for I suffer from an internal stomach weakness which is instantly aggravated by food or drink with acid content. Probably because of this, I had never acquired a liking for the bitter-sweet taste of arak, tuak or burak. I can go further and state that I thought the stuff filthy and revolting. Duty, however, is a stern task-master, and I felt it a matter of some diplomatic importance to accept the pagans' generosity in whatever lavish degree they chose to offer it—within, of course, the bounds of sobriety. They appreciated government officers who shared with them the simple pleasures of primitive life, and I felt that their good opinion of the Governor-General, and therefore of His Majesty the King (of whom he was the visible incarnation) depended partly on his capacity to imbibe with unimpaired dignity but also unfaltering delight unlimited quantities of native wine.

So whenever I travelled up-river in those days I reconciled myself to the obligation of consuming large amounts of this detestable and, to me, damaging fluid. Invariably for several days afterwards I paid the penalty in indisposition. It was a small cross which I gladly bore in the cause of friendly government in Sarawak.

Usually the amount of refreshment thrust upon a visitor in an evening was moderate. In spite of its deleterious effect on me, it did not threaten to do me irreparable harm. Early that afternoon at Long Laput, however, when dusk had not yet fallen and the party had hardly begun, I realized that this time I was to be more severely tested. My endurance was to be tried to the extreme. The supply of burak in every room was more plentiful than I had ever known, and the determination of the natives to dispense it liberally seemed equally unbounded.

When we had finished our round of primitive cocktail parties, Audrey, Gilbert, Morgan and I returned to Lallang's room for dinner. Ample dishes of rice and chicken were set before us, and we paid the Kayan chef the compliment of demolishing them all. Then we sipped some native port, none other than an extra glass of burak, and a liqueur, which to me looked, smelt and tasted exactly like yet another tumblerful of that brew.

Lallang was enchanted by Audrey's charm and intrigued by her beauty. Perhaps she did not fully appreciate her loveliness, for my wife does not happen to have mutilated ear-lobes laden with innumerable brass rings; but the princess was enthralled by her blonde hair, blue-grey eyes and fair skin. On her side, Audrey liked Lallang immensely; but she confided to me in a whisper that she feared lest some of the other rougher-looking natives nursed a secret desire to take our heads. I assured her that our hosts and hostesses were perfect gentlemen and ladies, who could not possibly entertain such a caddish thought.

As we ate and drank, preliminary twangs from sapits and thuds from gongs were borne to us from the public gallery. Attracted by the resultant cacophony, a great crowd of spectators gathered for the evening's entertainment. When the assembly was ready we took our places in its midst, subsiding on the floor in the front row. Lallang sat between Audrey and me, while Ubong and other ladies of the nobility squatted close by. At that moment Father Jansen appeared. The old man had rested and dined by himself on our launch in mid-river, and now rose like some ecclesiastical Neptune from a mist enshrouding the water. With the skill of half-a-century's practice, he strolled nonchalantly up the tree-trunk staircase into the gallery.

He was dressed in the austere, dignified evening robe of a Catholic priest in the tropics, and looked spruce in this long, snow-white gown with a purple sash. His few grey hairs were neatly brushed across his bald pate, and he had trimmed the little goatee beard beneath his lower lip. It was typical of his respectful character that he took as much care about his appearance for a pagan spree on the Baram as if he were about to wait on the College of Cardinals in Rome. With courtly bows and smiles of greeting to Lallang and the rest of us, he walked to a space prepared for him, and squatted on the floor.

The sapits struck up their faint, insect-like music, and two gongs punctuated it with brazen booms. A young buck clad in the full panoply of a head-hunter stepped forward and quaffed a glass of burak. Uttering a challenging yell, he assumed the jaunty pose with which some performers start their capers, and then glided into the first movements of his dance. As usual, one dancer followed another in long, dramatic succession. The men did not monopolize the floor. Lallang's female attendants also entered heartily into the fun. Of their own accord they rose and danced one after the other, and when Ubong's turn came she performed with as much distinction as any in the company.

Once or twice Audrey repeated to me in half amused, half anxious undertones her suspicion that our hosts were unmitigated savages who would greatly like to slice off our heads.

On my previous visit the climax of the evening's entertainment had been Kallang's performance. A vision of it still lingered as a brilliant memory in my mind. I hoped now to witness his triumphant act again; but, alas, this time it was not repeated. Kallang could not dance that night. By mischance he had trodden a few days earlier on a rusty nail, which pierced the ball of his foot and caused a nasty injury. Now he walked with a limp. It was a sad blow to my expectations.

And yet, looking at him, I wondered whether the rusty nail was the sole cause preventing a display of his artistry. He had put on weight since I saw him fifteen months ago, and his face

had grown fat and his body flabby. There was even a suggestion
of coarseness, of dissipation about his appearance. The sparkle in
his eyes had dulled, and he wore a sullen look. I noticed that he
never let a glass of burak pass him without tasting it. Could it
be that the depravity of Long Laput was infecting him and that
he too was on the slippery downward slope?

But who was I to comment critically on his consumption of
liquid? I, too, swallowed every tumblerful of rice-wine which
friendly hands held out to me. There were many such hands.
I did not encourage our hosts to regale me frequently, but did not
refuse any offer spontaneously made. Following my self-imposed
principle of diplomatic conduct—that I should not spurn their
hospitality as long as I was in no danger of inebriation—I abandoned myself to duty and to fate. As the evening wore on, my
head remained willing but my stomach proved weak. A distinctly painful sensation began to make itself felt in my duodenum.

It was midnight before the succession of native dancers completed their acts. As they performed, and as the sense of a happy
occasion grew, the temper of the assembly became ever merrier.
The challenging yells of dancers betrayed a slightly hilarious
note, the watchful silence of the spectators was now and then
broken by an intemperate call, and the grunts and handclaps
which hailed a skilful artist grew steadily less restrained. A few
weak brethren passed beyond the stage of sober comment on the
proceedings and expressed their feelings in wild, incoherent
ejaculations. They were suppressed by their fellows, and borne
away to the muffled obscurity of their rooms. It became evident
that, though a goodly measure of light-heartedness was expected,
Kayan authority had sent word round the house that undue
exuberance should not occur that night. An excess of spirits
would be not only improper, because disrespectful to us visitors,
but also inexpedient, because it would invite our wrath. Lallang
and her lieutenants knew that we strongly disapproved of intoxication.

So the party was kept, roughly speaking, within decent bounds.
Sometimes on such occasions, when local native talent has exhausted itself, the guests are invited to add whatever parlour
tricks they know to the programme of entertainment. I realized

that the moment for this had come when I saw a slight commotion in the region where Father Jansen sat. Two or three men close by him were asking him to perform. With beautifully mannered gestures he resisted their suggestion, protesting that his dancing was but a feeble, inartistic effort unworthy of public exhibition. But the clamour from his neighbours begging him to grant their request increased. He continued with charming modesty to oppose it. A wider audience then grew interested, and from farther away coaxing calls were made to him. But he still refused. Eventually two pretty young ladies-in-waiting, knowing his pacific temper, rose, walked towards him and added their forceful persuasion to the rising demand. Laughing gaily, each girl seized one of his arms, and they pulled him to his feet. Being a perfect gentleman, he could not refuse such a summons.

Like children choosing a victim in the game here-we-go-gathering-nuts-in-May, the damsels led him to the centre of the floor. The vast assembly of head-hunters roared with delight. The priest responded with a shy grin and a resigned shrug of his shoulders, as a heroic saint might when about to suffer martyrdom. The girls fitted a war-cap crowned with pheasant plumes on his head, and then returned to their seats in the crowd.

For a few moments Father Jansen stood motionless in the middle of the stage, like an effigy of some fabulous half heathen, half Christian character. His head resembled the god Wodin, with its war-cap shaped like a Viking helmet, and his broken nose and his small tuft of beard reminiscent of some battle-scarred Scandinavian pirate; yet his spare body dressed in its long priestly robe appeared like a Biblical figure stepped from a stained-glass window.

Cocking his head wistfully on one side, he listened for a right accent in the sapits' tune. Of a sudden he woke into momentary action. Raising his arms outwards, with the wide sleeves hanging down like angels' wings, he fluttered his hands a few times in playful mockery of a Kayan woman's dancing gestures. Then he discreetly jiggled a hip and essayed two or three high-kicks—no mean feat in his Mother Hubbard skirt. His eyes twinkled and his mouth grinned like a mischievous child's. It was a delicious little piece of clerical comedy, of staid yet sincere tomfoolery. Afterwards he halted abruptly, bowed respectfully to the laughing and cheering crowd, doffed his feathered cap and left the stage.

He came to where I sat.

"If you'll excuse me, Your Excellency," he said with a cherubic smile, "I'll retire now. This party's getting a bit too hot for me."

He shook hands with Lallang and wished her and her entourage peaceful slumbers.

Turning to the whole company he said in the native tongue, "Goodnight and God bless you," and withdrew from the scene.

He left early the next morning with Tama Weng Ajang, and I never saw him again. But I shall not soon forget the tolerance, kindly humour and superb dignity of Father Jansen that night.

The frolics continued. When my turn came to perform, I endeavoured to demonstrate for the head-hunters a national dance of another race of fierce, fighting tribesmen. Laying a parang and its scabbard across each other on the floor, I attempted the steps of a Scottish sword-dance. It was not easy to succeed without bagpipes. The whispered tones and slow tempo of the sapits accorded ill with the swift pace and skirling exuberance of the highland leaping. Indeed, the moods of the music and of my steps were hardly compatible, and my feet kept straying into the restrained movements of a Kayan dance. The effort was a sort of shot-gun marriage between the artistic impulses of the Scottish clans and the Bornean tribes. The Kayans perceived that it revealed some dim, remote spiritual kinship between their ancestors and mine, and they hailed it with loud grunts of pleasure.

Not till the small hours did the revels cease.

IV

On the dais built as a couch for the principal guests in Lallang's apartment a vast mattress was spread for Audrey and me. Covered by its white canopy of mosquito-netting, it looked in the dim room like a ghost of the Great Bed of Ware. We crept within it to rest.

Exhausted by the party, Audrey soon fell asleep; but I could not follow suit. For the last hour I had been feeling extraordinarily ill. Pains of distressing sharpness now afflicted my interior, and they began to increase in viciousness at a galloping pace. I tried to lie still and silent, so as not to disturb Audrey; but that proved impossible. In my agony I wanted to writhe and cry aloud. It felt as if clumsy surgeons with blunt knives and no anaesthetic were cutting me to pieces. I even wondered whether my last hour had come, for my torment seemed too terrible to be produced merely by pints of acidulated burak.

At last I could bear my anguish in silence no longer. I must go to some place where I could wriggle and moan, beat my breast and swear. As stealthily as possible I crawled through the mosquito-net.

Audrey heard me stir, woke and asked me what I was doing. I replied that I was going to talk to a man about a dog, and that I would soon return.

Running on tip-toe through the room, I fled down the back stairs into a rough orchard of banana and coconut trees. At a fair distance from the building, where I hoped that I would not be heard, I flung myself on the ground, writhing and groaning horribly.

The duodenal attack lasted some time, but ultimately passed its zenith. The aches grew less acute. After half an hour I felt able to pick myself up and return to the house.

As I reached the foot of the steps I was startled by a spectre. Dimly I saw a white-robed figure descend the stairs. In the pitch dark the apparition astonished me; but my first shock was at myself, not it. My mind reeled in horror at the thought of what this illusion might portend. Was I imagining things? Was I a prey to hallucinations? Was my illness mental as well as physical?

Then the ghost whispered to me in Audrey's voice.

"Are you all right?" she asked.

When I answered, she responded with a cry of delight, as if she had not expected to find me alive. Her relief was indeed of that order.

Increasingly concerned at my long absence from the house, she had jumped to an awful conclusion. She said to herself that she was right to suspect those wild natives round us. Their passion for head-hunting lay close beneath the surface of their feigned friendliness, and all that vicious sword-play during their dancing had whetted their appetites for murder. Now, she feared, one of them had followed me as I left the house, caught me unawares in a defenceless position, and gleefully severed my head from my body. In the morning our hosts would hang it among the other gruesome trophies in their barbaric gallery.

She thought she might have to shed a widow's tears upon my decapitated corpse.

V

Next day we returned down-river. Our minds were filled with grateful memories of Lallang's and her people's hospitality, yet also with gloomy forebodings about their future. It was plain that they lived solely for today with no thought of the morrow, and only for pleasure with no thought of its cost. They had chosen the road which they would follow in life's journey, and it appeared to have some of the familiar landmarks of "the primrose path to the everlasting bonfire".

Even during the fifteen months since I last visited them they had deteriorated. The change did not appear in Lallang herself, for her character was too set and strong to be influenced now; but it was obvious in other members of her circle. It affected, for example, young Kallang. In the previous year he had been a bright youth conspicuous for freshness and vigour, but now he wore an air of lethargy and dilapidation. He was evidently falling into bad habits.

Forces of decay were at work in this large, important community. These Kayans clung to the old ideas, the ancient adat, the pristine way of life, which now spelled destruction for their race. They did not care to know new ideas which might enable them to adapt themselves to the changing, modern world. Unless external influences came to their rescue, they were doomed.

On our way down-river we called on Penghulu Gau, the Kenyah chief whom we had delivered the day before at his house. Called Long Ikang, it stood amidst a grove of fruit and nut trees on the river bank. He waited beside the water with one arm upraised in salutation to us. The members of his family and his principal henchmen were at his side, all dressed in their best beads and sirats, sun-hats and sarongs, a colourful group.

We climbed the steps to his house. It was much smaller than the mansion at Long Laput, but even more conspicuous than the difference in their sizes was the contrast between its spotless neatness and the dirty untidiness of the other dwelling's rooms. The women here were house-proud and took infinite pains to make their home a model of cleanliness.

We sipped tea and munched cake in Gau's private room. He, his wife, a brother and a sister-in-law, with a brood of children, sat with us. The women appeared shy, though they were self-possessed and joined quietly in the conversation.

Gau's brother was his lieutenant in managing local Kenyah affairs, and they both talked eagerly of their plans. They told us of an experimental agricultural plot which they had just ploughed, where they would grow species of vegetables hitherto unknown on the Baram. They spoke gratefully of the Government's new scheme to send mobile dispensaries up-river, and discussed local health problems, the game laws and the evils of deforestation. They confided to us their ambition to build a school for Long Ikang's youngsters. There was much jesting and laughter, but also keenness, intelligence and sagacity in their talk, which sometimes made it difficult to believe that we were still in the heart of Borneo's jungle.

Against a wall in the room stood two blackboards. Chalked on one were some elementary problems of arithmetic, and on the other was a spelling lesson. On enquiry I learned that these were the properties of a night school conducted in the house. Each evening, after the day's work, some forty pupils of various ages, from youngsters in their early teens to septuagenarians, attended it. Gau's brother was the schoolmaster.

Here was a glimpse of the fresh outlook, the new life, the resurgent hope which Tama Weng Ajang and Penghulu Gau, with others like them, were introducing into pagan society. In a different setting and circumstances these men were as true pioneers as the Pilgrim Fathers.

CHAPTER SIXTEEN

TAMA WENG'S HOME

I

MORE THAN TWO YEARS passed before I travelled again along the Baram. In the meantime many changes had occurred on the great river. Only a few weeks after my previous visit Father Jansen died. The good old priest never spared his energy or strength, and suddenly his aged body could take the strain no longer. Gently he obeyed the summons of the intruder, Death.

Shortly afterwards Lallang also gave up the ghost, and went to join her ancestors in whatever Elysian long-house they occupy in the next world. So when I journeyed up the Baram again, towards the end of 1951, the river was like a landscape from which some familiar features had been removed.

Other landmarks, however, remained unchanged. John Gilbert was still the Resident at Miri, and once again he accompanied me. With us came also a long-legged, bespectacled, smiling American journalist, Howard Sochurek, who brought with him three cameras, two hundred rolls of film, a satchel full of lenses and filters, and various other photographic gadgets; for he was to take pictures of domestic life among the head-hunters for the edification of the readers of that well-known magazine, *Life*.

On our way up-river we took aboard my friend Francis Drake, now the District Officer at Marudi. We also stopped at Long Ikang to embark Penghulu Gau. The young chief's house was the same neat dwelling that I remembered, and beside it now stood a more modern building with trim steps leading to its front door, spick-and-span whitewashed walls, and large European-style windows admitting light and air. It was the realization of one of Gau's dreams—a school raised by himself and his people, and daily filled with youngsters eager to learn reading, writing and arithmetic. Thus far had the local Kenyahs progressed since two years earlier, when only a couple of black-boards symbolized their passion for intellectual advancement.

The master of Long Ikang stood at the water's edge, awaiting our arrival. He climbed aboard our launch, his family waved good-bye to us, and we headed up-stream.

Gau's face was as expressive as ever, lined with wrinkles of thought and care and laughter. His charm of manner was positively courtly, and the assured dignity of his bearing was somehow enhanced by his semi-savage dress. Gilbert told me that the penghulu grew ever more impressive. His zeal for introducing the benefits of modern knowledge among his people was increasingly infectious. Though frequently disappointed at the slow pace of progress, he patiently understood that the Government's limited financial resources and the Kenyahs' conservative habits necessarily put a brake on the speed at which up-to-date public health measures, improved methods of agriculture and enlightened educational provisions could be effectively established among the long-house dwellers. He was learning what Sidney and Beatrice Webb used to call "the inevitability of gradualness".

His reforming influence was spreading steadily along the Baram and beyond. In addition to being a member of the District Council at Marudi and of the Divisional Council at Miri, he was now a member of the Council Negri at Kuching. In this he had again outstripped his one-time mentor, the great chief Tama Weng Ajang, who occupied no seat on that supreme body. The situation had arisen with the older man's consent. Tama Weng lived so much farther up-river that the long journeys to Kuching would have involved him in a tedious loss of time. Moreover, at certain seasons, when bad weather made the upper Baram unnavigable for days on end, he would sometimes have found it impossible to make the trip at all. So Penghulu Gau became the representative of the Kenyah people in the national council.

He was to come with us all the way to Tama Weng's house at Long Akar, the ultimate Mecca of our present expedition. At last I could spare time to make the long journey to the great man's home, and I looked forward to meeting him in his seat of power. Our plan was to travel up-stream all day every day for three days, resting the first two nights at long-houses on the way and reaching Long Akar before dusk on the third. We would stay with Tama Weng for the better part of twenty-four hours, and take another three days for the return voyage.

During the first day's journey above Marudi we went ashore at Long Lama, to sip tea with the Chinese towkays while our baggage was transferred from our launch to the temois in which we would travel the rest of the way. Embarking in them, we soon passed the great mansion at Long Laput. Being pressed for time, we did not stop, knowing that if we tarried in that hospitable place we should not escape in a reasonable time. Besides, Lallang was dead. Without her the house would seem like a shell from which life had departed.

We knew, too, that its surviving inmates whom we wished to see, Kallang and Ubong, would greet us at Long Akar, where they were visiting Tama Weng. So we hastened forward. But I looked nostalgically upon Long Laput as we glided past. Its immense length was as impressive and almost unbelievable as ever. From its shadowy gallery a few residents stared at us, silent and listless, like mournful ghosts haunting a scene of former good fellowship. They seemed to be spectres from a dead past—and they did indeed represent an old order which was swiftly disappearing.

II

As we advanced up-stream we saw signs of many changes creeping into Borneo's interior. The crews in the prahus which frequently passed us, for example, no longer appeared as splendid savages with bare, bronzed bodies glistening in the sunlight, but as brown men aping white men in coloured shirts, khaki trousers and felt hats.

We saw evidence of change, too, in the house at Murik where we stayed the first night. A large and well-populated Kenyah dwelling, it bore many marks of a society in a state of transition in both material and spiritual affairs. The stairway climbing to its entrance was no longer a notched tree trunk, but a broad, professionally carpentered flight of steps. Inside the building the central wall dividing the public gallery from the private apartments was smartly panelled in pseudo-Jacobean style, and its dozens of doors were furnished with modern handles and keyholes. In the rooms the window spaces were much larger than they used to be. In fact, much of the structure was the work, not of the Kenyahs themselves, but of a Chinese contractor hired to provide the dwelling with up-to-date fittings.

Its inmates also showed signs of a significant change. Most of them had abandoned native dress. The men wore European cricket shirts and football trousers, while the women favoured Malay bajus and sarongs. Only from the neck upwards were the ladies still Kenyahs, with saucy Baram hats, long black tresses and heavy brass ornaments hanging from mutilated ears.

Another innovation was remarkable. Above the doors of many family rooms hung carved wooden crosses, and several natives carried similar emblems on their own persons. A group of small girls, for instance, wore clusters of brass rings in their ears in traditional pagan style, while round their necks hung fine gold chains with golden crucifixes bearing the figure of Christ. Many of these Kenyahs were recent converts to Christianity.

We spent a quiet evening at Murik, with neither feasting nor dancing, as became a community preoccupied with the solemn business of changing its religion. Next morning we left early and made good progress up-river. All day our boats sped forward, and shortly before night we reached a house called Long Kiseh, where we would sleep.

It was a formidable edifice containing nearly fifty rooms. Unlike the house at Murik, it was a Kayan dwelling. Constructed by the inmates themselves, it had every customary detail of primitive, massive architecture; and just as there was no sign of a Chinese contractor's work in the building, so also there was no glimmer of a foreign religion among its inmates. They were still pagans from the tops of their heads to the tips of their toes, unredeemed and unrepentant in body and soul. The almost-naked men wore their hair shaven in front and long behind, while the women retained completely their Kayan form of dress. This community evidently felt no discontent with manners and beliefs which had satisfied their ancestors for centuries.

The contrast between one house and another on the Baram at that moment of social and cultural transition was interesting. Some dwellings showed no trace of modifications in ancient customs; while others bore evidence of startling changes wherever you looked. Generally speaking the Kayan homes were strongholds of conservative tradition and the Kenyah houses were pioneers of new ideas. It was eloquent testimony to the influence of Tama Weng and Gau.

After supper at Long Kiseh a space in the gallery was cleared for dancing, and an audience of several hundred crouched round the stage. The dancers performed in a delightfully free spirit. No inhibitions appeared to check indulgence in time-honoured hilarity. The people's high spirits were spontaneous, for there was little drinking; but the place seemed to be full of clowns and humorists. Among the skits in their programme was a witty burlesque of a lugubrious Punan jig, and another was an unexpurgated edition of the notorious Monkey Dance. Then half a dozen old crones stepped the hallowed quadrille which in olden days was performed when new heads came into a house. As young belles forty years ago they had perhaps executed it holding in their hands the fresh, bloody heads of their enemies, but now they twirled for our amusement antique skulls wrapped in banana leaves. The aged harpies' limbs lacked the lithe, maidenish grace of their girlhood, but still they were light of foot and dignified in carriage; and their gentle, elegant movements made the dance a spectacle of strange, melancholy, haunting beauty.

III

At first light next morning we left Long Kiseh, for we must lose no time in pressing forward. The Baram wound ceaselessly ahead of us. Along its course were many treacherous passages which our boats negotiated with a mixture of caution and boldness born of long experience of the fitful whims of Borneo waters. We were travelling beyond the foothills into the true highlands. The river-bed cut deep into the ground, and a lofty landscape loomed everywhere around us. In some places the channel was so confined and the walls of hills so precipitous that we passed through literal gorges; but in others the slopes receded more gradually from the water's edge, and a wider variety of mountain scenery met our gaze.

When we started, patches of early morning mist hung over the earth. Here wisps of vapour trailed along narrow valleys, with hills protruding above them like huge boulders suspended in mid-air; and there white, fleecy clouds avoided the low ground and wreathed themselves instead round the mountain peaks. So sometimes the airy shapes of fog sprawled underneath dark masses of earth superimposed above them, and at other times that order was reversed. The density of different cloud-forms varied as much as their altitudes. In some spots the mist was so opaque that all terrestrial matter behind was hidden, but in others it was so transparent that the hills beyond were partially revealed. According to the degree of its translucence, the outlines of slopes were silhouetted darkly or faintly, like objects seen through veils of varying thicknesses. So the landscape appeared like the half-actual, half-ghostly, beautiful and mysterious world portrayed in classical Chinese paintings.

Later the mist dissolved, but always the heavens were overcast with a threat of rain. Sometimes a rift appeared in the clouds, and for a while the sun broke through. Then steep hillsides intruding close upon the river stood brilliantly exposed, their tropical vegetation luxurious, with every twig and leaf etched precisely by the sunlight.

At last, towards evening, we rounded a bend and spied on a distant promontory the white fort at Long Akar. We had arrived, and sped over that last stretch of water with the relief of a marathon runner who, after a gruelling race, exerts his final effort to dash home.

IV

When we came to land, Tama Weng Ajang stood there to greet us. He was now Temonggong Tama Weng Ajang, having been elevated to the rank of temonggong a year earlier, thus sharing with the illustrious Iban, Koh, the distinction of the highest native title in the Government's gift.

He appeared as chubby and benevolent as ever, and was clad in a strange mixture of Oriental and Occidental, pagan and Christian styles which perhaps reflected accurately the rather confused state of his mind. On his head perched a Kenyah hat topped with hornbills' feathers, his hair was trimmed and combed in native fashion, and from his ears hung leopard-cat's teeth and brass ear-rings. A European blue pinstripe jacket, an American white singlet and a pair of khaki shorts covered the massive middle sections of his body, while below them his legs and feet were bare except for a pair of Kenyah garters. So at his two extremities—from the neck upwards and from the knees downwards—he looked like an unregenerate Bornean, but the intervening portions of his body might have been outfitted by an assortment of haberdashers from the Western world.

His house was situated about three miles above Long Akar at a spot called Long San; so as soon as possible we re-embarked in our boats for that last lap of our journey. In the brief twilight which precedes the tropical night we arrived at Tama Weng's house. When our outboard motors fell silent a sound of rushing water filled the air, as if lively falls splashed near by. In the half-dark I perceived the source of this sweet snatch of nature's music, the leaping white forms of breaking waves and flying spray among innumerable shadowy boulders. The whole width of the Baram above our landing stage was a seething mass of rapids, and all night and all day long their lisping, bubbling murmur reminded the inmates of Long San of their proximity to the wild.

Along a pathway leading to their house stood rows of Kenyah notables marshalled to give us friendly greeting. I was astonished at the neat Western clothing of the men and the beautiful modern dresses of the women. I had expected to see a degree of sophistication in Tama Weng's household, but not to meet a company of people clad almost as smartly as a well-groomed party in Singapore.

In the gloaming out-of-doors I gained a fleeting impression of their sartorial elegance; and when I saw it afterwards in the glare of lamplight indoors my astonishment at its splendour was heightened. Perhaps there was nothing very remarkable about the style of the men's attire, which consisted uniformly of Kenyah hair cuts, necklaces of yellow beads, variously coloured vests or shirts, blue shorts and native garters. What was surprising was their spotless cleanliness. They betrayed none of the casual dirt which invariably, and even unavoidably, gathered as a stain here or a splash there on the garb of other long-house dwellers. Not only were the faces of these Kenyahs perfectly washed and their hair immaculately brushed, but their shirts and trousers looked as if they had just returned from a high-class laundry.

The same quality marked the appearance of the women, but their gowns were distinguished also by unusual style. It was a sign of their shrewd taste that they did not discard their traditional hats, chic little bits of nonsense contrived of wisps of grass, strips of animal fur, patches of coloured beads and gay bird's feathers which would cause a sensation if they appeared on the race-course at Ascot, in a mannequin parade in Paris or at a theatrical garden party in New York.

Their hair also the ladies wore in native styles. They must have been aware of the contemporary popularity of permanent waves, Grecian curls, Eton crops and other beauty-parlour conceits; but they scorned this modern urge to turn women's hair from a lovely natural product into a highly manufactured article. In this too their judgement was sound, for the most glorious adornment of Bornean females is their magnificent tresses, so long that, when loose, they fall to below the waist, and are as glossily black as a raven's wings.

The females' elongated ear-lobes with clusters of heavy earrings were in more doubtful taste; but they were a dramatic, savage touch, and without them the most distinguishing feature of Kenyah and Kayan women would have been absent. Some of the younger girls, however, lacked this trait, their ears retaining natural shapes and sizes. These maids had grown up since new ideas crept up the Baram, and their parents decided not to subject them to the painful distortion. Yet most of the damsels concerned regretted the fact, feeling odd freaks with features different from their friends'. Almost they thought that their natural ears, not the disfigured ones of the others, were the deformed objects!

From the neck downwards the ladies at Long San had abandoned customary tribal costume. Bare shoulders and long Kenyah robes had disappeared, gone the way of blow-pipes and poisoned arrows, banished to the limbo of discarded antiquities. In their place a new fashion was popular based on the Malaysian baju and sarong. But whereas among many Malay women such articles are somewhat shapelessly made, fitting the body loosely, these Kenyah beauties were particular about their cut. The blouses fitted their figures with sleek precision, following obediently every graceful curve; and the skirts, of brilliant colours, fell in elegant folds from their waists to their feet. The natural taste of these allegedly wild jungle women showed artistic genius.

Observing them, I remembered the report on my previous visit to the Baram that, though Tama Weng favoured many reforms in Kenyah society, he insisted on his people retaining their traditional garb. I wondered what had happened to modify his earlier resolution, and he confided to me later that he strongly disapproved of the women's partial abandonment of Kenyah dress. He had done his best to prevent it, telling them that they should abjure foreign styles and maintain unspoiled the beautiful costume which their mothers, grandmothers and female ancestors through countless generations had favoured. The ladies flatly refused to listen to him. They had a notion—which many other women in various countries seem to share—that the robe of yesterday is a discreditable garment, a deplorable throw-back to some dark, uncultured age, as outmoded as a fig-leaf. Even the pleas of their husbands added to the orders of their chief could not uproot this little piece of femininity from their minds. No doubt Tama Weng's own sartorial foibles enabled them to destroy his argument with a fatal retort, for they could point out that his blue pinstripe jacket, white vest and khaki trousers would scarcely have found favour with his father, grandfathers and male ancestors through countless generations.

He told me, however, that he would insist on the ladies preserving their small Kenyah hats and their large Kenyah ears.

After greeting his wife on the river bank, and shaking hands with all the leading personalities there, we walked to the dwelling. Climbing a flight of well-carpentered steps, we entered a sumptuous apartment. This was not the chief's permanent home. He was in process of erecting a new house, and the place which we now visited was only a temporary lodging to serve until the other was finished. The future edifice stood close by, and before complete darkness fell we went to inspect it.

Its massive posts, beams and struts stood already in position, not yet covered with walls and floors and roof. They formed the colossal inner framework of a long-house, like the gaunt, intricate skeleton of an oversized prehistoric monster in a geological museum. On the ground around lay a scattering of scores of poles, hundreds of planks and thousands of shingles, all the bits and pieces required to finish the structure. Their craftsmanship showed excellent quality, and had a modern style. Clearly many of them had been supplied from a professional builder's yard.

The erection of the house was at that time the principal occupation of its inmates-to-be. In the meantime they lived in a smaller, temporary structure made of slim poles, narrow planks and light attap. Yet their pride in creation had inspired its making too. Its main communal chamber, into which Tama Weng now led us, was large and high, made artistic by carved pillars and comfortable by benches, stools and small tables. My attention was at once attracted to its principal feature, a Christian altar in the centre of one wall. On it stood a massive wooden crucifix, and behind it was the most astonishing reredos that I have ever seen. In the place of sacred honour among its assortment of pictures hung a sad-eyed portrait of Christ, cut from the Christmas number of some Catholic magazine. On either side were coloured photographs of His Majesty King George VI and Her Majesty the Queen, Their Royal Highnesses Princess Elizabeth (as she then was) and the Duke of Edinburgh, and Generalissimo Chiang Kai-shek. The regal British couples were posed in the peaceful gilded apartments of Buckingham Palace, but the Chinese leader was represented directing an assault by his troops on a field of battle. Companies of infantry charged an enemy, while batteries of guns fired shells and squadrons of aircraft dropped bombs all around him.

This impressive evidence of Christian piety did not mean that Tama Weng had been baptized. He still wished to be, but I was told that he had not yet attained a sufficient state of grace. The religious instruction which Father Jansen started was being continued by the old man's successor, Father Bruggermann, who joined us later that evening. He said that the chief was making good progress in his studies, and that probably his baptism, with that of most of his followers, would not be long delayed. Some members of the house had already been christened.

A Catholic mission was now established at Long Akar, and Father Bruggermann resided permanently there. He managed a school and encouraged among his parishioners clean habits, the wise care of health, a progressive outlook in agriculture and other reforming tendencies, as well as the deeper Christian way of life. The priest was popular, and exerted considerable influence over his flock.

I sensed a remarkable spirit animating Tama Weng's household. The community possessed an *esprit de corps* which I had not previously met in any long-house. They seemed conscious that they were a significant people, a progressive society, a band of pioneers achieving some historic purpose. Every man, woman and even child appeared to be imbued with this idea. Their feeling of self-importance was expressed not only in cleanly dress, but also in confident bearing, unaffected good manners, a natural approach to us government officials, and obvious pride in themselves and their home. The impression that they were a people of destiny was deliberately fostered by their chieftain, who moved among them with quiet, dignified, massive authority.

How different was all this from the careless, aimless, soulless atmosphere of the other great house at Long Laput!

V

We squatted on stools in the living-room for preliminary converse with our friends. In a Kenyah or Kayan home there is no introductory ceremony like a bedara, even where the people are still pagans. Visitors are merely regaled with welcoming glasses of burak. At Tama Weng's, however, we received a different refreshment. We were served with cups of tea and plates of sweet biscuits, as we might have been in an English drawing-room. It was a revealing touch of gentility, a kindly effort to cater for our particular native tastes.

Members of Tama Weng's family gathered round us. His wife was a gracious hostess, but she stayed in the background organizing the many details of household management which arise on such occasions. We saw more of the chief's two sons, Kallang and Nawang, and of Kallang's wife, Ubong. It was good to meet this pair again, and to be introduced to their child, a chubby-faced girl two years old.

I learned that most of the time they lived at Long Laput, where, as expected, Ubong and Kallang had fallen heirs to Lallang's wealth. Both were important personages in the great house, and Kallang might one day become its tuai rumah. But they visited Long Akar frequently, for Tama Weng wished to maintain his influence over his son. The young man looked well. The signs of deterioration evident when I last saw him had completely disappeared. Now there was an intelligent sparkle again in his eyes and a ready smile on his lips. His complexion was fresh and his body trim. Tama Weng had taken him in hand, asserting his paternal authority to prevent him from succumbing to Long Laput's fatal habits. And already, I heard, through the chief's influence the whole community in the Kayan house showed promise of reformation.

Kallang acted with friendly efficiency his part as the eldest son in a great chief's house, and Ubong, too, was genial. Maternity had left its mark on her in the shape of comfortable plumpness, but it had not banished the youthful bloom on her face nor the girlish gaiety of her spirits. Time passed pleasantly as we renewed acquaintance with them. Afterwards we went for a dip in the river, changed our clothes and returned indoors for the evening's entertainment. We had been promised a celebration worthy of the occasion.

But first we sat long on the floor, engaged in political discussion. Tama Weng squatted in our centre, his solid mass of flesh planted cross-legged on a mat in the attitude of the Buddha. His strong, imperturbable personality dominated the room. Even the most important men sat respectfully at his back, while numerous lesser characters settled at a distance in a circle round him. At Long San the aristocratic system of Kenyah society was fully preserved; the chief's reforming zeal did not extend to introducing any element of democracy.

My travelling companions and I reclined beside him, and Penghulu Gau sat with us. Gau's lively speech often broke into the conversation as we discussed Kenyah affairs. Tama Weng answered all our questions on problems in Long Akar and its neighbourhood, speaking in slow, emphatic, authoritative tones; but when subjects of wider import arose he usually left his younger colleague to provide the information. He seemed aloof from public affairs outside his own locality, while Gau was vitally concerned in them and discussed them with statesmanlike acumen.

As we lolled and talked with a sense of homely ease, Howard Sochurek scurried about the room, as busy as a bee gathering honey in the form of photographs. He set tripods and arc-lamps in various corners, and kept squinting at us from every conceivable angle through his view-finder. Many times he felt dissatisfied and shifted his position, but now and then his artistic taste approved our grouping, he pressed a button of his camera, and for a fraction of a second a flashlamp lit the scene with the brilliance of lightning. He took about twenty snapshots of that gathering, and a few months later one was accorded the honour of publication on a page of *Life*.

Afterwards a feast of boiled rice and roast pork was spread before us. We partook of it heartily, until our appetites were satisfied and the dishes borne away. Then the evening's more light-hearted business began.

For the last two hours we had seen little of the women. They had disappeared into inner rooms to prepare our meal. Now they reappeared, and their entry was like the raising of the curtain in a glamorous drama. They came into the room in a long file, like a procession of Eastern princesses. Walking silently on bare feet, with casual feline tread, they bore themselves with stately carriage. Though wonderfully decorative, their appearance seemed effortless, yet it was of course the result of artful care. An occasional swift, sidelong glance from modest, downcast eyes, or a hint of self-consciousness in the lithe movement of a limb beneath silken drapery, betrayed the ladies' intense awareness of their potent feminine charm.

Particularly striking were a dozen girls who led the procession. Their costumes had superlative elegance, being contrived with that mixture of simplicity and brilliance which is the perfection of taste. But their chief adornments were their own good looks, and their beauty was all the more bewitching because of a certain quality of mystery. At a first glimpse their characters seemed elusive: their features might be the faces of faultless angels or the masks of vicious devils. Observing that their grace appeared as decorous as it was decorative, I gave them the benefit of the doubt, and endowed them with many sweet, innocent virtues. As my narrative progresses the reader will be able to judge whether that verdict was correct.

Gilbert, Drake, Sochurek and I sat relaxed among our hosts on the floor. As the troupe of damsels approached us they broke their ranks, and two came to sit at the feet of each of us. An enchanting couple settled before me. They were mature young females with composed manners and ripe curves. I learned that their names were Bungan and Lohong.

Bungan's face had the slanting eyes, high cheek-bones and ivory-smooth complexion of a Mongolian goddess. She wore a cap of leopard-cat's fur cockaded with a jaunty egret's feather, and many brass rings jingled in her ears. As she reclined at my side she favoured me with a frank stare of curiosity, clearly asking herself, "What sort of person is this odd-looking stranger?"

I reciprocated her mental enquiry. Of one thing there could be no doubt. A commanding look in her eyes and the firm modelling of her mouth indicated a young lady possessing strength of will.

Lohong seemed a gentler creature, perhaps finer or perhaps just weaker. Her head was unadorned except for a mass of magnificent hair. Brushed back sleekly from her forehead, it was caught in a hair-net at the nape of her neck and hung in thick, limp coils down her back like a bagful of serpents. She was a modern Kenyah damsel with ears left as God made them. Her other features, too, were more refined than Bungan's, the arched eyebrows, lustrous eyes, small nose and sweet mouth being exquisite. Here certainly, I thought, was a maiden of genteel modesty.

Ubong sat in the next group, attending Gilbert. She and her companion also appeared models of demure young womanhood. All the handmaidens reclined in prim silence while Kallang and other youths brought bottles of burak to refresh us.

With businesslike despatch Bungan uncorked a bottle, filled a tumbler, held it towards me and started to sing a ditty. Her tuneful voice conveyed that same hint of a forceful character. When at length she raised the drink to my lips, I took a few sips and then resisted her further invitation. She looked at me courteously, but with an unmistakable suggestion that she thought I must be mentally defective. Nor did she seem impressed when Father Bruggermann, who sat next us, explained that my doctor forbade me to indulge in rice-wine because of my delicate stomach. She treated the comment with respect rather than credulity, retorted swiftly that no doctor had yet made disparaging remarks about the good Father's inside, and pressed the liquor to his mouth until he drank it all.

Most conscientiously all the young women devoted themselves to their duty of dispensing refreshment. Maidenly reserve began to dissolve. When a guest showed signs of reluctance to finish a glassful, the girl concerned would brace herself to make a supreme effort in the cause of hospitality. With smiling mouth and sparkling eyes she would coax, persuade, argue, threaten and finally, if necessary, force her client to obey. The insistence of these hostesses on acceptance of their gifts was in any case hard to resist, for it is surprising how easily strong-arm methods succeed when the strong arms are attached to divine faces.

Nevertheless, neither Bungan nor Lohong achieved success with me. My unhappy experience on my last visit to Long Laput had taught me a severe lesson. I was now compelled to admit that several years of dutifully imbibing tuak, arak and burak— all poison to my system—on these official Bornean visits had resulted in such damage to my interior that I could no longer, even in the cause of diplomacy, risk further serious discomfort.

With engaging solicitude the girls kept trying to induce me
to enjoy the drink, but beyond taking an occasional sip, I refused.
They received a poor impression of my manliness.

When these preliminary libations were finished, Tama Weng
called for dancers. Two youths with sapits composed the orchestra.
An audience gathered round while an elderly man stepped on
the dancing mat. As usual, actor succeeded actor. The quality
of their artistry was good. This ancient pastime had evidently not
been discarded with other items of hallowed custom by the
zealous reformers at Long San. Their iconoclasm did not con-
demn this mimicry of savage fighting as a shameful relic of an
age better forgotten, but honoured it as high art, a precious
heritage of their race to be transmitted unspoilt from generation
to generation.

When the other male dancers had performed, Kallang took
the floor. At first he stepped and gestured with restraint, moving
quietly and smoothly across the stage, placing his feet, executing a
leap and flourishing his sword with a disciplined skill wondrous
to behold. Imperceptibly he passed into the more complicated
movements of the dance as if they were as easy as the rest—
swirling and curtseying, jigging and pirouetting, thrusting and
recoiling with faultless grace and yet joyous, violent abandon.

His performance was brief, not sustained like his act on the
memorable night at Long Laput. Abruptly it ended, like an
incomplete poem broken off at some inscrutable whim of the
author. In the middle of a vigorous passage of arms he suddenly
ceased to fight, his hands fell to his sides, his legs stopped their
capers and he restored his parang to its scabbard. Perhaps he
was tired, or perhaps inspiration at that moment left him—or
possibly the thought struck him that he was no longer the premier
dancer in the house, that another performer was his equal if not
his master, and that his steps appeared inferior to the other youth's
exhibition.

That other individual was Nawang, his younger brother.
Many people whispered that Tama Weng's second son was more
promising than the first, and that in due course Nawang might
excel Kallang in power and influence.

At Long San that evening he looked an exact, if slighter, phy-

sical copy of Kallang. Better educated than his elder brother, he
had attended the Teacher Training College in Kuching. Three
years earlier I had happened to visit the place soon after his
arrival, and I first set eyes on Nawang that day as a raw, shy
native lad fresh from the jungle, wearing only a feathered cap
and loin-cloth and feeling a misfit in the civilized environment
of a classroom—like a wild animal caught in a cage. Afterwards
he adapted himself to his new circumstances, did well at his
lessons, and showed the natural aptitude for learning which one
would expect from his father's son. Nor did education spoil him.
Though he soon spurned the sirat and donned instead short
trousers, he retained his pride in being a Kenyah and continued
to wear uncut hair, a yellow bead necklace and black rattan
garters. The longer he stayed at college the more his abilities
flowered, till from a rough, coltish boy he became a disciplined,
well-mannered and conspicuously capable youth showing bright
promise as a potential leader of his fellows. Recently he had
returned to Long San with a knowledge of various matters
unknown to his people. In particular he had received a training
in modern methods of husbandry, which we hoped that he
would devote to the economic betterment of the Kenyahs and
Kayans.

He had already danced that evening at Long San, and it was
true that he showed brilliant skill. His sauntering steps were as
stately, his wild leaps as cunningly silent, and his ecstatic swirls
as breathtaking as those of Kallang. But not more so. The two
brothers were equals in dexterity and artistry, both dancers of
surpassing, unforgettable beauty.

Yet, strange to say, when the girls danced immediately afterwards there was no sense of anti-climax. Indeed, the feeling that
we were privileged to watch a rare aesthetic performance remained
with us. This was not due to any strict comparison between
the young women's technical attainment and that of the young
men, for Kallang's and Nawang's art was superlative, and by
contrast the girls' movements were elementary. They did little
more than occasionally shuffle a foot or tap a toe, raise an arm
or gently wave a hand. Their effects were gained by other
means: by the beguiling feminine necromancy of their good

looks, the theatrical splendour of the costume which they donned
for this play-acting, and their cleverness in executing certain
simple yet extraordinarily dramatic gestures.

Bungan performed first. She stepped on the stage with the
self-assurance of a brazen hussy well aware that she possesses
what it takes to subdue men and silence other women. I began
to realize of what tough stuff she was made. Unabashed by
hundreds of staring eyes, she dressed herself publicly for the
dance. First she took off her chic hat and laid it aside. Then
she loosed her hair, unfastening here a golden comb and there a
glittering pin, until of a sudden all of her tresses tumbled in a
black cascade over her shoulders and down her body almost to
her knees. They were so thick that they hung round her like a
flowing cloak ample enough, had she worn no other garments,
to hide her nakedness. With deft flicks of her fingers she now
gathered the hair up again, arranged it in a tight heap on her head
and, before it could scatter once more, jammed a man's dancing
cap on top of it. She looked magnificent, with this tall-plumed,
bright-beaded warrior's helmet crowning her handsome girl's
face above clusters of savage ear-rings dangling from elongated
ears. Deliberately she next unfastened the sarong round her
waist, held it casually in one hand whilst the other smoothed
the baju over her bosom, and then fixed it again more tightly,
so that it would not slip during her performance. Finally she
stooped and picked from a chair a pair of fantastic bouquets made
of hornbills' feathers. The striped black-and-white quills were
loosely strung together. Bungan held one of these feathery posies
in each fist, grasping them by an artful method which enabled
her to control exactly their movements. With the plumed helmet
on her head and the bunches of feathers in each hand she looked
like a Winged Victory.

She posed briefly in the middle of the stage; then, as the
sapits began to whisper a tune, started the slow, sedate motions
of a dance. Her footwork was as simple as could be, consisting
only of a succession of short, shuffling forward steps. Her carriage was erect and proud, though occasionally she dipped her
body in a gentle curtsey or swung it in an elegant half-twist
above the waist. Her head, too, scarcely moved from a fixed

position, with her face up-tilted and eyes gazing dreamily towards
the ceiling. Meanwhile her arms and hands were in almost
perpetual motion, though their gestures were slight. At regular, short intervals she lifted her arms a little from her sides,
then let them fall again. As she did so a toss of her fingers
made each bunch of feathers unfold like a spreading fan, and
immediately afterwards a counter-toss made them close again.
So she progressed, alternately opening and closing the fluttering
bunches of feathers as her arms rose and fell and her hands
deftly flicked and unflicked—as a bird might constantly stretch
and fold, stretch and fold its wings over and over again. It
was a pretty action, heightened in effect by the supple movements
of the gracious creature who made it.

Afterwards two or three more girls presented versions of the
same pleasing little drama. Then other maidens did other
dances. Lohong, for example, joined three companions in a
lively quadrille. Adding to the soft sighing of the sapits the
music of their own sweet voices, they sang a lightsome air as they
jigged to and fro, swung this way and that, and then clasped
hands in a revolving circle.

After that all the girls advanced in array towards us masculine spectators. Each chose a victim and invited him to be her
partner in a round dance. Bungan dutifully selected me, and I
needed no prompting to answer her invitation. Some of my
companions were more reluctant, but quickly learned that resistance was not permitted. Like regimental sergeant-majors in
a brigade of Amazons, the women descended upon them, seized
them by both arms and pulled them to their feet. These Baram
ladies made it almost brutally clear that they regarded men as
the weaker sex, whose duty it was to hear and obey.

We formed a large, single-file circle composed of perhaps two
dozen people, alternately male and female, and began to progress
with jaunty gait round the room. The natives chanted a lilting
tune with the rhythm of a marching song. The words belonged,
I was told, to an ancient ballad celebrating certain tribal heroes
whose exploits were as daring in love as they were in war. The
tale was a mixture of the martial and the romantic, and unfolded
slowly in an apparently endless series of short verses followed by

resounding choruses. I soon learned the oft-reiterated accents of the refrain, and augmented its noisy rendering.

As we paraded round and round the apartment, spectators began to rise from the floor to join us, inserting themselves here or there in the ring, which broke for a moment to admit the newcomers and then closed again before and behind them. So the company grew ever larger, the circle stretched ever wider, and the volume of singing swelled ever louder. The movements of the procession became more rollicking, the performers bowing first to one side and then to the other at each step. Still more members of the audience kept joining us, and the ring expanded until the room could scarcely contain it, and we were crushed in a friendly mêlée with our neighbours. Bungan followed behind me, and close in my ear her voice carolled the incomprehensible gibberish of our song.

As the merriment increased, several girls took off their smart hats and set them instead on the heads of their male partners, while the men put their feathered helmets on the crowns of their favourite females. The scene assumed a carnival air. None of this was lost on Sochurek and his camera. He moved ceaselessly about the room, studying with professional care the party's appearance from various angles, and taking a dozen pictures of the chanting and prancing crowd. I kept seeing his face peering from the most unlikely places, from a rafter overhead, or the floor underfoot, or the darkness of the night beyond a window or, suddenly, from within a foot of my nose. Always he was smiling genially, his eyes twinkling behind their spectacles and his round countenance looking like the Man in the Moon in benign mood. Periodically his flashlamp exploded with a fierce white light which for an instant blinded us.

The communal mob dance continued for the better part of an hour, and the song accompanying it was similarly protracted. Verse followed upon verse, and a score of verses followed another score of verses, like the interminable incantations of a Tibetan prayer. At length some people wearied, and pairs began to drop from our circle. So the ring contracted again. Smaller and smaller it grew, until ultimately only a dozen of us remained. The others squatted on the floor around, recovering their breath,

or so utterly exhausted that they collapsed and snatched forty
winks where they lay.

Soon afterwards the dance ceased altogether, having accomplished its apparent purpose as a test of endurance. The time
was already past midnight, and many elders crept away to sleep
in their private rooms. For the brighter, younger spirits, however, the party was only in its early stages. They alleged that it
would last all night.

Various capers followed. Among others, we visitors were invited to entertain our hosts. Gilbert and Drake gave personal
interpretations of a Kenyah war dance, Sochurek favoured us
with a frolic reminiscent of the tomahawk dances performed by
Red Indians among the wigwams of his native Middle West,
and I walked across the room on my hands.

Later came the sternest and most convivial test of all. It was
a drinking competition. Against a pillar stood a vast jar with
an ample belly filled with burak, and into it dipped a long, hollow
piece of rattan to act as a drinking-straw. Beside the straw, on the
wine's surface, floated a contrivance which registered when one
inch or two inches, or any other desired measure, of the liquid
had been sucked through the cane into a consumer's mouth. Our
hostesses decreed that each of us should imbibe a couple of inches
of the jar's contents.

It was one of those challenges which sounds easy, until you
try to honour it, and then you realize that it is almost impossible
to achieve. Unfortunately in this instance the word "impossible"
had no place in the Kenyahs' vocabulary. The girls would not
acquiesce in any failure by a man to imbibe his allotted portion
of wine.

They were utterly unscrupulous in the methods which they
employed to accomplish their purpose. First a pair of the prettiest
young women would take one of us visitors gently by the hands,
and draw him with every mark of kind solicitude towards the
formidable jar. Other fair maids would nod coaxingly at him,
laying fingers affectionately on his shoulders or insinuating arms
round his waist as they helped to guide him forward. Flattered
by their deliciously friendly attentions, he would allow himself

to be led to the pot, as an innocent lamb might be led with music, garlands and laughter to the slaughter. With a self-confident smile he would put his lips to the rattan and start sucking at the liquor. After a while his powers of imbibing began to flag, and he would try to disengage himself. Sweet female voices would then tell him that his task was not yet finished, and that he should persevere a little longer. If he sought to lift his head from the straw, the pressure of their hands on the back of his neck would increase. Indeed they forced him to stay where he was.

After a few more mouthfuls he would feel again that his capacity was becoming exhausted. Moreover, he felt sure that the float would now record that he had accomplished what was expected of him. So once more he sought to disengage himself, but immediately disapproving feminine chatter arose. Some of the damsels adopted persuasive tactics to keep his face bowed over the wine, fondling his hair and stroking his cheeks in an attempt to convince him that his situation was enviable, and that he should not hastily retreat from it; while others applied force by strengthening their grips on the back of his head. Realizing now the Machiavellian nature of their conduct, and painfully aware that he had drunk more than enough burak for comfort, he would grow impatient and heave his shoulders or stretch his arms in an effort to break loose. The response to this was a kick on his shins or a smack on his behind from some seductive little cutie like Bungan or Lohong, accompanied by wicked titters of mirth from all the misses, and a vise-like tightening of the discipline of fair hands holding him in position.

Yet this compulsion was accompanied still by a great show of friendly sympathy. The ladies laughed and jested with their prisoner, and a pinch on one of his cheeks was invariably followed by a caress on the other. When next he asked whether he might raise his head for a few moments to examine the float and see how near he was to the attainment of his aim, they readily agreed, provided that he would restore his lips to the drinking-straw and resume his task immediately afterwards. Having no alternative, he promised to comply. At once they relaxed their hold sufficiently for him to unbend somewhat and study the situation

revealed by the yardstick. Mistrustfully, however, they still clung
to his wrists and kept their arms locked across his shoulders, lest
he should try to escape from their clutches.

He fully expected that the measure would show that he had
all but reduced the level of burak by the ordained two inches.
Imagine his horror when he discovered that little more than
half his duty was done! The circumference of the jar was
wider than he had reckoned. Feeling already over-full of fluid,
he begged his jailers to excuse him; but they were deaf to his
appeal. He pleaded with them; but they remained adamant.
With nudges and pinches, pushes and slaps, merry jests and
imperious commands the stern women compelled him to bend
his face again to the rattan conduit-pipe. The fanatical harpies
of the French Revolution, who sat knitting beside the guillotine
counting the heads of aristocrats as they fell from the knife, could
hardly have shown more indifference to the fate of a fellow being.

The victim was virtually helpless. His tormentors were all
females; not a solitary male stood among them. Chivalry prevented him from kicking, punching or biting to liberate himself.
Had any of the ladies been old and ugly he might, in desperation,
have brought himself to lash out at her, to frighten the rest; but
every one of them was young and beautiful, such as no man of
taste would wish to injure. That was perhaps the meanest advantage of all which they took. Incidentally, they were as strong as
they were attractive, being girls accustomed to planting and
harvesting padi, paddling canoes, carrying heavy gourds of water
and performing other lusty manual labour.

I need not describe the rest of the unequal struggle. Suffice
it to say that the captors did not release their captive until he had
done his full penance. Then with cordial goodwill they unhanded
him—and at once sought the next victim.

With cowardly common sense I avoided participation in this
ritual. Once more quoting the instructions of my squeamish
medical adviser, I explained to the high priestesses of Bacchus
that, alas, the delirious delights of drinking were not for me.
So they exempted me from their conscription, and busied themselves with its enforcement on stronger men made of sterner stuff.
Drake, Sochurek, Gilbert, Gau and other personalities who had

dropped into the house for the evening were all given the burak treatment.

These strenuous exercises tired some of the less buoyant inmates of the house. More and more of them disappeared to snatch a little sleep in their family quarters, yet at three o'clock in the morning our company of revellers was still considerable. Wine was followed by song. We sat on the floor, serenading the ghosts and goblins of the night with a series of Kenyah drinking songs. The incorrigible girls still endeavoured to make the men match the words of these chants with appropriate deeds; but more resistance had developed and a successful masculine revolt against matriarchal tyranny was staged.

By four o'clock some of the weaker, or perhaps merely saner, members of the party were ready for bed, and they slipped away quietly. Others felt rested by the sedentary period of community singing, and were eager again for more energetic action. So I introduced for the first time on the Baram the game of blindman's-buff, and it quickly became as popular in Tama Weng's home as it was in Koh's. Feminine shrieks, manly tally-hos and children's laughter filled the dwelling as a sightless hunter darted this way and that, grabbing in search of a capture. Many sleepers were wakened by the noise and, seeing with amazement our novel antics, rose to watch the fun; but others slumbered undisturbed through this tempestuous scene—a tribute to the state of exhaustion to which they had been reduced.

Every wakeful individual wished to have a turn as blind man, so the game continued for a long time. Before it ended, dawn began to break. Darkness slowly dissolved out-of-doors, and gradually the shadowy forms of hills and trees took shape against the eastern sky. As light increased, details of nearer objects appeared, and the murmur of the rapids came to visible as well as audible life in the leaping forms of a myriad wavelets. I looked at my watch and saw that it was six o'clock; so we really had kept up the sport till morning. I felt as virtuous as I used to feel after an all-night sitting in the House of Commons.

Early risers in the house began to stir. Men started to stroll towards the river for their morning baths, and women emerged from private rooms with gourds in their hands for fetching water.

It was time that we night-hawks went to bed. I lay on my mattress, and within a few seconds was asleep.

VI

An hour later I awoke, partly reluctantly because I still felt drugged with sleepiness, and partly willingly because it seemed shameful to waste time lying unconscious in a house so full of vitality. I rose and hastened to the river's edge to bathe, shave and dress.

When I re-entered the house an old acquaintance sat with my companions, drinking coffee and eating eggs at our breakfast table. At first I did not recognize him. His young, refined English face seemed familiar, yet his long dark hair growing almost to his shoulders appeared strange. He wore a dirty shirt and shorts and looked generally untidy, as if he were an explorer just returned from many weeks on some particularly rough expedition.

Suddenly I remembered him. Several months earlier he had lunched with me at my house in Johore—a well-groomed young Oxford graduate in anthropology travelling to Borneo to work as a field ethnologist. He told me that he would do research among the pagan peoples, and that he planned to live with them as one of themselves in their own environment. So, probing into their ways of life and beliefs, he would learn at the original source about one of the world's few remaining types of primitive man.

As we breakfasted that morning at Long San, this remarkable young man, Rodney Needham by name, described how he had lived ever since our last meeting with nomadic Penans on the upper Baram. He still resided in the deep jungle with a group of them, having ingratiated himself so successfully among them that they accepted him as a member of their tribe. He travelled, hunted, ate, gossiped and lodged with them. Hearing that I was to be at Tama Weng's that day, he had journeyed by forest paths and river to see me.

With him he brought two members of his Penan family, a boy and a girl in their late 'teens. They sat as quiet as mice on a bench in a secluded corner of the room. Their furtive, inquisitive eyes watched us closely. Occasionally they whispered and laughed over small secrets together, no doubt at the expense of us strange, uncouth creatures.

Needham had grown fond of his Penan friends. Their unsophisticated natures had commendable streaks, and for him they were also charged with anthropological fascination. As I watched his pale, thin, ill-nourished face framed in its flowing hair, and listened to his account of existence on native food in Penan society in jungle solitudes, I realized that the devotion of such men to science is as heroic as the devotion of selfless missionaries to religion.

He turned our conversation to the subject of the missionaries.

"I came to see you," he started, "to tell you that when we talked at Bukit Serene we were quite wrong about the Evangelicals."

I remembered our conversation many months earlier. I had expressed doubts about the work of some Christian missions in Borneo. I spoke approvingly of men like Father Jansen on the Baram, but was sceptical about the efforts of certain Evangelicals whose headquarters were on the neighbouring Lawas River. During an earlier trip to Sarawak I had visited the place briefly, and gained a superficial knowledge of their activities. I met their principal, an elderly Australian named Southwell whose lanky, angular figure and gaunt, bearded face made him look like an Old Testament prophet. His faith burned in his deep-set eyes and earnest conversation, and it was shared eagerly by his wife and a small band of helpers.

They worked then mostly among the Muruts of the Lawas and Limbang districts, and had achieved gratifying results in curing those wild tribesmen of dipsomaniac tendencies. Whole communities of drink-loving natives had become reformed characters, whose absolute teetotalism would have done credit to the strictest temperance society. Consequently the Muruts' health, as well as their conduct, had distinctly improved. Their maternal and infant mortality started to decline, and their society in general began to stand, like countless individual Muruts themselves, more steadily on its feet.

No one could fail to be impressed at this miracle performed
by Southwell's dynamic religious zeal. But it was not the whole
story. I was told that in some directions his enthusiasm carried
him too far, making him insist on outlawing from native society
much more than jars of rice-wine. At his order, I was informed,
traditional dress suited to the tropical climate was abolished, and
old pagan songs, games and dances which had their origin in
savagery were swept away in a floodtide of reform. When I
heard this from his critics, I felt sad, for I admired the indigenous
arts and crafts of the Borneans, and felt that they were a harmless
as well as vital expression of the people's racial character. Why
should their preservation be any more incompatible with Christianity—if the Muruts must become Christians—than our maintenance of the folklore connected with Santa Claus and his rein-
deer? I jumped to the conclusion that the worthy members of
the Evangelical mission were zealots whose goodness ran to
fanaticism, and whose labours might perhaps be more destructive
than creative.

This impression seemed to be confirmed when I learned some
time later that the Southwells had extended their activities from
the Lawas to the Baram, and that they were making multitudes
of hasty converts among the Kenyahs and Kayans. Tales reached
me of their preaching the Gospel to entranced crowds in long-
houses, and of wholesale baptisms of entire communities within
a few days. The Evangelicals seemed to be embarked on a mili-
tant crusade against heathenism which exploited an emotional
mood among the natives to register them as Christians, without
giving them careful grounding in Christianity. I did not feel
much sympathy with that type of proselytism, especially as I
suspected that with it went a forbidding intolerance of many
innocent native customs.

When Needham lunched with me in Johore I had recently
heard of this development on the Baram, and I remarked upon
it to him, adding that I was not sure of the report's accuracy, but
that it seemed to be supported by evidence. If it were true, then
I thought the activities of the missionaries unfortunate. In my
opinion our policy should be to persuade the pagans to abandon
only such of their ancient habits and beliefs as were harmful, and

to introduce them only to those modern ideas which would help them. We must encourage them to preserve all that was good in their indigenous culture.

Needham agreed with this view, and expressed concern at the rumours of the Evangelicals' excess of zeal. Now, several months later, he had made a considerable journey from the deep jungle especially to tell me that the rumours had been false.

"Southwell and his mission are doing wonderful work," he said enthusiastically.

I asked him to tell me more about it.

"You know that I hold no particular brief for missionaries," he answered. "Sometimes they do great harm among native peoples, because they don't really understand them and their needs. But Southwell doesn't belong to that type of preacher. He feels true sympathy with the pagans, and deals wisely with them. He's doing remarkably constructive work."

"That's very different," I observed, "from what I've heard. Tell me what constructive things he's doing."

"He and his wife and their Evangelical colleagues are turning the natives from dirty savages into people with a sense of cleanliness, from heavy drinkers into abstemious beings, and from an unhealthy race into a race with a good prospect of life. It's on the health side that they've achieved so far their greatest successes. Everywhere they go they teach people the simple facts about proper medical treatment for ailments, the importance of proper sanitation and hygiene in a house, and the prudent care of children. They make them take pride in the spotless neatness of their homes. It's all very elementary; but done in a systematic way it's something new in these communities, and it's producing good results. The people see those results and are very grateful."

"That's admirable," I agreed. "But doesn't Southwell mix his sips of healing physical medicine with too strong, indigestible doses of spiritual refreshment? I was under the impression that in his hurry to smash the natives' pagan beliefs and convert them to Christianity he destroys more quickly than he creates, and so tends to leave the natives without any deeply felt faith at all."

"That's not true," Needham answered emphatically. "Southwell doesn't force Christianity on the natives. He doesn't preach it in a house unless the leaders there invite him. In any case he couldn't compel changes in the people's faith unless they wished them, for the pagans are strong-minded, self-respecting characters who don't abandon old beliefs against their will. Change has its origin in their attitude of mind, not in Southwell's. If they want a change, the Evangelicals offer them an alternative to their old religion, and the measure of the missionaries' success is generally a measure of the people's spontaneous desire for change."

"But isn't Southwell too intolerant of harmless old pagan customs which make some of the brightness in the pattern of native society—of their hallowed songs and dances, for instance. Doesn't he, in his puritanical fervour, forbid them to enjoy these pleasant pastimes? Doesn't he, in fact, sweep away a lot of the good with the bad in local life?"

Needham shook his head and answered, "The stories about that are exaggerated. He doesn't stop the natives singing their old tunes. What he does is write new Christian words to the old tunes, and the natives sing these latest hymns with their accustomed pagan enthusiasm."

That was certainly a tribute to the missionary's subtle, sympathetic understanding of his problem. Not even the most cunning ideological propagandist could improve upon the technique of adopting a simple people's ancient, popular song tunes and devising new words for them—new slogans expressing a new faith!

"As an anthropologist," continued Needham, "I don't think religious conversion is essential to the people's progress. Logically, scientifically, a Bornean system of ethics is equivalent to that of Christianity. If I encourage one rather than the other, that's purely personal and I have no anthropological support. My approval of the Evangelical mission is chiefly for their medical, material and educational care of the people. Their first-aid for wounds, ointments for sores and medicines for ailments show healing powers which win the natives' gratitude; and many of the missionaries' lessons in better household management, food storage, child care and the like bring practical benefits to these

simple folk which they badly need and deeply appreciate. Moreover, the friendly, inspiring power of the Evangelicals' personalities works its own magic. They're good, admirable men and
women. Southwell's astonishing influence over the natives springs
from the strength of his own character, from his spiritual force.
He's a fine man, an inspiring man."

There was a ring of deep sincerity in Needham's voice. I
felt that only a man of God of rare quality could capture so
completely his enthusiasm.

VII

That morning Tama Weng was to take us to inspect two local
works, typical samples of his ambitious plans for his people's
progress. The first was an area of land down the river where
he conducted an experiment in the cultivation of wet-padi, and
the other was a local school where Catholic missionaries were
helping to make his dream of education for the young generation
come true.

Soon after breakfast he led Gilbert, Sochurek and me on an
excursion to see his effort at growing wet-padi. We travelled in
prahus a mile down-stream, and disembarked at a spot where a
muddy path led upwards among thickly growing trees. As we
sped down-river we heard overhead the drone of an aeroplane.
It seemed a strange, discordant intrusion into Borneo's silent interior, far from the airfields and hangars of the sophisticated
coast. Presently a Dakota appeared, flying straight towards Long
San. It travelled surprisingly low, as if it were either in distress
and seeking a landing-place, or deliberately trying to attract the
attention of people below.

As it passed over Tama Weng's house it dipped a wing and
made a sharp turn above the roof. Veering away, it circled and
returned again over the dwelling. Three times it repeated this
manoeuvre, and then flew the short distance to the fort at Long
Akar and did the same there. As the aircraft passed above our
boat I saw a man standing at its open door, ready to cast
some object from the 'plane.

Probably the aircraft was looking for me. If it were, what

message could it have brought? My admiration for the speed
and efficiency with which such emissaries from modern civilization could locate insignificant travellers in the remote heart of
a dense jungle was tempered by annoyance that even in such
distant, peaceful fastnesses one could not escape the clutch of
the official world.

Slightly huffed, I leaped ashore and beckoned to my companions to follow me along the muddy path, where closely inter-
lacing forest foliage would soon hide us from view. No doubt the
aeroplane would drop its message at the fort, and in due course a
native runner would bring it to me. It could wait. I did not
wish it to disturb my enjoyment of Tama Weng's company as he
showed me his remarkable attempt at producing wet-padi amidst
Sarawak's highlands.

After a short walk we emerged from the jungle and stepped
into an area of flat, cleared ground. Only burnt tree stumps
betrayed that not long before it too had been woodland. Then my
eyes observed something which I had never previously seen in the
interior of Borneo. Long, narrow ramparts of earth, elevated
above the rest of the ground, ran criss-cross over the whole area,
and between them large spaces were filled with water, like a
group of shallow fishponds. The raised earthworks were the
balks carrying footpaths, while the pool-like spaces between
were the cultivated fields of a wet-padi farm. This was the site
of Tama Weng's great experiment, his laboratory for testing the
practicability of such husbandry, his revolutionary effort at an
entirely new form of agriculture for the jungle people. Hitherto
only dry-padi had been grown on rough hillsides, with no controlled irrigation, no scientific treatment of the soil, and every
unfortunate consequence of shifting cultivation. I looked upon
the chief's work with as much interest as if it were the pilot
scheme of a great project of agrarian reform in some modern,
progressive state.

The spot had none of the trim, well cultivated appearance of
the boundless acres of rural padi-land seen on the Burmese,
Siamese and Indochinese plains. It was unkempt. In addition
to numerous charred tree stumps jutting from the ground, patches
of wild grass, bushes and other persistent relics of forest marred

the smoothness of the prospect, and in places the mirrors of water were cracked with twisted branches of trees from the recent clearance. Already, however, the surface of the miniature lakes in the patchwork of fields was fractured also by countless shoots of sprouting verdure, covering the shining water with thin, filmy, golden-green veils. They were the young rice shoots which Tama Weng had planted two weeks earlier.

His calm face broke into a proud smile as, slowly and deliberately, he swept an arm in a wide circle round the view, to indicate the extent of his endeavour. His property contained about ten acres, of which several were already ploughed and planted. This was its first year as farmland. Its soil had lately been claimed from the wild, and was now producing its first cultured fruits. In the baking, breathless, tropical sunshine you could almost see them grow. Much depended on the volume of that year's crop. If it were poor, the Kenyah tribesmen would pay scant heed to their chief's bold initiative; but if it were good, their enthusiasm would be kindled, and in the next season they would follow his lead and clear a larger acreage of flat land beside the river.

He led us along a path between adjacent padi ponds. Here and there the balk was partially broken to permit a hollow, slanting stem of bamboo to act as a water-pipe. It was primitive but effective; the rudiments of scientific irrigation were there. Tama Weng brought us eventually to a rickety wooden bridge spanning a stream. Below it was a wall of close-fitting planks to dam up the water, with a trap-door to control the flow. On one side of this the water level was high, and on the other it was low. In a rough and ready sort of way the contraption worked.

Tama Weng demonstrated for us the ease with which the dam could be operated. He personally had directed its building earlier that year. It was the key which unlocked the door to a new manner of farming, a prospect of richer crops and a higher standard of living for his people. The experiment showed every promise of success.

From the bridge he guided us along balks threading their way across numerous fields. In many pools an emerald green haze of rice-shoots appeared above the reflective water. Not far away solid ranks of jungle trees stood motionless, exactly as they and their kind had done for centuries. Overhead was the infinite blue canopy of heaven, just as it too had appeared in this place day after day, year after year and age after age since the beginning of time. Nothing in the prospect stirred; not even a puff of wind whispered its message of life. All things seemed unchanging, and unchangeable—yet imperceptible movement was proceeding all around us. Those new, young shoots of grain were growing, representing much more than the burgeoning of another spring in the eternal cycle of Nature's birth and death. They were the budding of a new era in the history of a section of the human race.

As the chief stood on the path, shading his eyes with one hand and surveying the extent of his experiment, I gazed with admiration on his portly figure. This man had now taken his place in the grand succession of adventurous spirits, of significant innovators who, each in turn, have led mankind a few paces along the road of progress. His name would not be remembered in history; like many another remarkable benefactor of humanity, he would remain forever anonymous; but his work would fructify continuously, and bring every year fresh benefits to his posterity.

VIII

As I contemplated the scene, reflecting on the slow yet restless pulse of life, and on mankind's gradual, painful advance from savagery to civilization, a stranger appeared from the woodland along the river and ran towards us. He was a young Kenyah carrying an envelope in his hand. This he delivered to me, explaining that it had dropped on a small parachute from the aeroplane, landed in the grass beside the fort and been retrieved by Francis Drake, who directed him to bring it to me.

I slit the envelope and extracted a letter. Unfolding it, I saw from the royal crown at its head that it came from the astana in Kuching, and from the signature at its foot that it was sent by the Governor, Tony Abell.

As I scanned the first sentences my heart turned sick. They said:

My dear Malcolm,

This brings bad news for us all. Henry Gurney was killed in an ambush today at about one p.m. on his way to Fraser's Hill. . . .

Henry Gurney killed! The thought was dreadful. The sting of tears started in my eyes. Gurney was much more than the High Commissioner in Malaya and the head of the government fighting the Communist terrorists. He was a statesman of rare wisdom and ability, and a friend of unsurpassed chivalry and charm. So the murderers had slain the noblest of their enemies— caught him in a trap and done him to death. These were appalling, almost unbearable tidings.

I looked at the date on the letter, and saw that it was written on the previous afternoon. I read the rest of it, which said that Gurney's funeral would take place in Kuala Lumpur on the following day, and that an aeroplane would be sent at once to Borneo to fetch me back to Singapore.

Glancing at my watch, I saw that the time was half-past eight. I told my companions of the letter's contents, and they were terribly shocked, for Gurney's name was much respected in Borneo. Gilbert agreed with me that we must return immediately to Long San, pack our bags and order the crews to prepare our prahus for departure within an hour on the down-river journey.

I looked again on the sprouting padi, and congratulated Tama Weng on his remarkable enterprise. I told him that I would report what I had seen to the Government in London, that I felt sure his experiment would be a fine success, and that he was a memorable leader of his people. He smiled modestly, and thanked me for coming so far to visit him. Then we retraced our steps along the path to the river.

While our prahus were being loaded at Long San, I kept my promise to inspect the Catholic mission school. Situated a short way up-river, it consisted of two small wooden buildings; the first the school itself, containing a single spacious classroom, and the second a dormitory for boys who came from distant houses.

Father Bruggermann and an assistant priest greeted me and led me into the class. At rough desks sat an assortment of about sixty boys and girls. As we entered they rose and stood at attention, like a squad of young military recruits. They ranged from seven to twenty years old, and I noticed among them several who had remained awake and lively throughout our revels of the previous night. They looked surprisingly bright-eyed for children who had spent only a brief while in bed after many hours of games and dancing.

I asked them to sit while Father Bruggermann told me of their work. He said that fifty-six boys and eight girls were pupils in the school. Sixteen boys and all the girls came from Tama Weng's house, while the other youths were boarders from more distant dwellings. Many girls from other houses also wished to attend, but the mission had no provision for their accommodation and care. That was a problem which they must solve in future by bringing nuns to Long Akar. Zeal for education was spreading rapidly among the natives, and the school must increase its quarters and staff.

To show me how adept were his scholars, the priest asked them questions, firing a query now at this child and now at that. Always they answered promptly and without any show of shyness. Whether or not their replies were correct I was unable to judge, for the inquisition proceeded on an intellectual plane far above my head, being conducted in the Kenyah tongue. But the intelligence in the pupils' expressions as they spoke was as marked as any that I have seen in classrooms in any part of the world.

Unfortunately I could not stay long. When I told Father Bruggermann that I must leave, he said that the children wished to send me away with a song. Turning to them, he raised his hand as a choir master lifts his baton for the opening notes of an oratorio, and when he gave the signal they began to chant an old Malay ballad. It was so pleasant that I lingered, and when their singing ceased I cried, "Lagi, lagi", which is the Malay expression for "Encore".

Thereupon they sang a Kenyah folk-tune with sweet childish feeling. When it was finished they glanced enquiringly at their teacher, who nodded encouragingly to them. I saw them brace themselves for what was evidently to be a final effort. At his

sign they broke once more into melody, with words which astonished me. I could scarcely believe my ears as they sang,

> *Bonnie Charlie's noo awa'*
> *Safely o'er the friendly main.*
> *Mony a heart will break in twa*
> *Should he ne'er come back again.*

Their diction was excellent, their Scots accents dubious and
their voices as tuneful as a carillon of little bells. Through two
whole verses of the famed lament they remained word-perfect,
and they smiled at me as they sang. When they chanted,

> *Will ye no' come back again?*
> *Will ye no' come back again?*
> *Better lo'ed ye canna be.*
> *Will ye no' come back again?*

my heart seemed to turn over. I thought of the kindness of these
missionaries and children making their gentle plea, and I resolved
to obey their request and return one day to Long San.

And I thought with infinite sadness of my good, gallant
friend Henry Gurney, who would never on this earth "come
back again".

IX

We returned to Tama Weng's house to say farewell to its
inmates. The chief and his wife were full of expressions of
regret at our sudden departure, for we had planned to stay there
several more hours, taking lunch with them and embarking in the
afternoon on the first stage of a leisurely journey down-river.

All the natives seemed disappointed at the abrupt ending of
our companionship. The principal men and women crowded
round Drake, Gilbert, Sochurek and me, shaking us cordially
by the hands and thanking us for our visit.

Last of all in the throng speeding their parting guests were
Bungan, Lohong, Ubong and a bevy of other young women of
the house. They had posted themselves in a row near the exit
from the dwelling, where they would be the last to bid us good-

bye. Dressed in their most dazzling finery, they made no secret of their pride in their good looks. Unlike the rest of us they had been careful not to lose their beauty sleep. While we rose prematurely from bed and dressed, ate breakfast, visited Tama Weng's padi-fields and inspected the school, they still lay dreaming peacefully in their rooms, with long-lashed eye-lids closed over sparkling eyes, gracious countenances passive in repose, and shapely limbs lazily relaxed. Now, well rested, they had come to life again, as radiant as a sunrise. Their dark eyes shone like the glisten of morning dew, and their skins had the clear bloom of freshly opened flowers.

They smiled at us kindly, with no trace of that rough, mischievous trait which had shown in their characters the previous night. Apparently they were in angelic mood—on their best behaviour, no doubt, to bewitch us once more and leave in our memories an impression of perfect gentility matched with unblemished beauty.

When we had shaken hands with all of them, Bungan and Lohong slipped their arms through mine and escorted me across the greensward towards our boat. On the river bank we said our final adieus. Every Kenyah in the place, male and female, old and young, shouted a mighty "Salamat Jalan" as we went aboard our prahus. In the front rank stood Tama Weng and his wife, with Kallang and Nawang, Bungan, Lohong and Ubong. The girls waved their handkerchiefs and beamed enchantingly at us.

As I lolled on the cushions in my boat, waiting for the crew to complete the last minute preparations for departure, I stretched my hands over the vessel's side, dipped my fingers in the water and playfully flicked a few splashes in their direction. I was sitting fifteen yards away from them, above fairly deep river, and they were not only on dry land but also in smart dresses and fine jewellery; so I felt sure that my trick would not invite serious retort.

That was, of course, an incredibly foolish mistake. I should have known better. With shouts of joyful belligerency Bungan, Lohong and Ubong leaped into the river, waded quickly forward until they stood immersed above their waists, and started to hurl great showers of water into the boat. For a while I could scarcely

see them through flying spray. I returned their fire as effectively
as I could, but they did not seem to mind being nearly drowned
in cataracts of river. Sochurek, sitting near me, joined in our
defence, and a tremendous nautical engagement developed.
Soaked to the skins, with their long hair clinging to their lovely
faces and floating round their trim figures, the girls appeared like
outraged mermaids protecting their fishy virtue. Laughing with
reckless gaiety, they presented an unforgettable picture of beautiful fury. It was strange how their mood seemed to alternate uncertainly between the primitive, bellicose instincts of wild women
of head-hunting clans and the drawing-room habits of reformed
ladies in the new Kenyah society which Tama Weng was striving
to create.

In the middle of the fight our engine-driver started the boat's
motor, and the prahu shot suddenly forward, clear of our assailants, into mid-stream. The crowd on the bank cheered and the
girls in the river raised their arms in most friendly salutation. As
I watched their graceful gestures I realized how Ulysses felt when
he sailed impotently out of reach of the Sirens.

Sochurek and I were sopping wet, and our cushioned seats
were pools of water. He was chiefly concerned now with the
safety of his cameras, for they had lain on the boat's floor, and at
one time seemed in danger of being mortal casualties. Gathering
them together with the fond solicitude of a mother-hen collecting
her chicks, he shook and wiped them clean. Meanwhile I started
to dry myself; but before the process was complete Sochurek stole
a snapshot of me which afterwards appeared as a full-page portrait
in *Life*.

Little did the readers of that periodical know that it was a
record of the most vicious naval battle in Sarawak's history since
James Brooke sailed up the Sekrang River and reduced to cinders
its pirate strongholds.

X

Our original plan had been to spend three days travelling
down-river. Now we abandoned that leisurely programme and
resolved to journey non-stop to the river's mouth. We expected

to arrive there by first light the next morning. I would then motor to Seria, where the oil company had a landing strip for aircraft, and hoped that the promised aeroplane would fetch me from there to Singapore. If all went well, I should land in the city soon after lunch. That would be too late for me to attend Henry Gurney's funeral, but it would give me time to fly to Kuala Lumpur for consultations with the Acting High Commissioner, if he needed my help.

It was interesting to reflect that the journey would be accomplished in four stages, in which we should use in turn four different vehicles of transport, progressing from almost the most primitive to the most modern in the world. The first stage would be the hundred miles down-river from Long San to Long Lama, which we would cover in a native prahu; the second would be another hundred miles of water from Long Lama to Kuala Baram, which we would make in a motor-launch; the third was the twenty miles by road to Seria, for which I would resort to an automobile; and finally there would be the thousand miles of sky to Singapore by aeroplane.

All went well with us so long as we relied on the more primitive forms of transport. Our troubles began as soon as we became dependent on man's very latest and most boasted means of travel. Our prahus made the journey from Long Akar to Long Lama in about ten hours, and from there our motor-launch reached Kuala Baram some eight hours later, before five o'clock in the morning. We had beaten all records for the down-river voyage, and if the aeroplane had been as reliable as these more simple craft, I could actually have reached Singapore and flown to Kuala Lumpur in time for Gurney's funeral. A message, however, awaited us at Kuala Baram to say that the 'plane had developed engine trouble in Labuan, that there were no spare parts on the spot to mend the defect, and that the machine would remain grounded for the next two days. A second aircraft would therefore leave Singapore that morning to fetch me back, but it could not land until a few hours later.

As this would involve undue delay, I contacted the oil company at Seria and accepted a friendly offer which they had telegraphed to me to lend me their private aeroplane. I suggested that I should fly in it to Kuching, have the Dakota from Singapore diverted there, transfer at Kuching into the larger machine, and proceed in it to Singapore. The company readily agreed to the proposal, and I motored to Seria. The plan should have saved two or three hours, but owing to further aeronautical difficulties my departure was further postponed. Eventually I landed in Singapore about twelve hours after I had arrived in Kuala Baram, a journey which should have taken less than half that time.

All of which goes to show that human fallibility is still as evident in the most civilized societies as it is among the wild men of Borneo.

PART FIVE

THE MELANAUS, MALAYS AND CHINESE

CHAPTER SEVENTEEN

A MELANAU SCENE

I

I MUST NOW leave the Kenyahs and Kayans, and cast a few glances in the direction of other significant peoples in Sarawak. I wish that I had space to write of additional pagan tribes in the interior, of the nomadic Penans and Punans, the Muruts jigging their jovial communal dances, and the Kelabits tending cattle on a remote plateau. I wish, too, that there were occasion for me to lead the reader down-river to visit other native groups who represent more advanced stages in these people's development—the Ibans, for example, in certain regions of the Second Division, where opportunities to go to school, meet different races and learn about modern agriculture and trade have been more frequent than in the interior, and where the natives' inborn intelligence and restless ambition induce them to adopt many up-to-date ways. There the long-house dwellers have acquired not only Western styles of dress, but such modern amenities as electric light; they produce wet-padi in individual holdings and sell it through co-operative marketing organizations; and some of their ablest young men aspire to enter government service. I have already mentioned a typical representative of these Ibans, my excellent A.D.C., Lieutenant John Nicoll of the Sarawak Constabulary. There are now many such individuals, and the sophisticated down-river native society from which they spring is significant of a social evolution through which the tribesmen of the deep forest will eventually pass.

But I have already written enough to convey an impression of the Bornean clansmen's engaging characters, to indicate the far-reaching changes now affecting their lives, and to express my confidence that they will adapt themselves successfully to whatever circumstances assail them.

I must now mention other groups in Sarawak's population; peoples more advanced, more "civilized", with whom the wild men of the jungle share their homeland, and who add their characteristic touches to the rich, variegated pattern of Sarawak society. Three other principal races live there—the Melanaus, the Chinese and the Malays.

The Melanaus are a small community forming a link between the primitive men up-river and the more modern populations along the coast. I visited them in 1949. The journey from Kuching to Mukah, the principal township of their territory, takes nearly twenty-four hours. In roadless Sarawak the route lies wholly by water, some of it along fresh-water rivers and the rest over salt sea. A traveller sails down the Sarawak River to its mouth, and can then either launch boldly on the ocean and make straight for the Mukah River some 130 miles away, or else hug the coast until he reaches the Rejang, turn up that broad highway as far as Sibu, and thence voyage down another channel called the Igan, from which a short sea trip brings him to the Mukah's bar.

The sea is liable to grow extremely angry during the landas or southwest monsoon, and in those circumstances an official visitor who takes the ocean route is apt to arrive at his destination in no fit state to accept with proper enthusiasm, let alone dignity, the friendly welcome offered by the Melanaus waiting on the quay. When Arden-Clarke and I set forth on this journey, the landas had just begun to blow. Preliminary storms castigating the sea and belabouring the coast showed that they had lost none of their perennial cunning. Reports from fishermen declared that wind and rain, lightning and thunder had arrived off Borneo with all their pristine vigour.

So we decided that duty bade us visit our friends in Sibu on the way to Mukah. This would enable us to enjoy the shelter of river banks during most of the voyage. At first when we reached the Sarawak's estuary, we thought that perhaps our sense of duty had been too sharply developed. The sea was calm, the sun shone with sweet benevolence from a speckless sky, and it seemed that the journey all the way to the Melanau coast would be delightful. I sat on deck reading Gilbert White's *Natural History of Selborne,* marvelling at the strange whim of Fate which sent me to read about rural England along equatorial shores.

Then a dark cloud, no larger than a man's hand, appeared on the horizon. Arden-Clarke and I began to change our minds. We knew that portent. Swiftly the apparition grew, flying angrily across the sky towards us. Soon the sun was blotted out, the sea turned sulky, and a fearful wind began to blow. Thunder crackled in the distance and a pile of black clouds to starboard was fiercely illumined by the bright fireworks of lightning. These ill-omened signs also sped rapidly towards us. Suddenly rain pelted in our faces. The Borneo coast, whose tropical fringe of trees had but a few moments earlier been sunnily displayed, now disappeared behind a deluge.

As the waters from heaven descended in torrents upon us, the waters of earth rose to give us an equally soaking embrace. They heaved and tossed frantically, the white caps of their breakers appearing on all sides. Our little launch, *Karina*, fought them manfully, rising and falling, lunging and rolling in patient, obedient response to their ill-temper. The elements, however, seemed determined to capsize the boat and drown its occupants. The wind sought to rip our awnings to tatters; the rain fell so thick and fast that our decks were swirling pools; and every now and then a flying mass of sea leaped over the side and washed the ship from end to end. Thunder loosed its artillery upon us at close quarters, sounding as if it would at any moment despatch a boarding party of meteors to assault us. But the boat, displacing only forty tons, stuck doggedly to its course. From its mast-top to its keel and from its bow to its stern it was sopping wet, like a playful walrus alternately exposing and submerging itself among tumultuous waves. Yet it remained afloat, and nosed its way steadily towards the refuge of the Rejang River. Arden-Clarke and I felt that our anxiety to look upon the faces and shake the hands of our colleagues in Sibu had not, after all, been misplaced.

Our tossing lasted a couple of hours. I felt high respect for ship-builders who could fashion small craft to face with assurance such dangerous seas. And my esteem for Abdullah, our Malay skipper, also increased considerably. The Malays are splendid, skilful mariners.

I peered over *Karina*'s rail at the mountainous seas, my eyes trying to penetrate the opaque, cascading atmosphere of rain-storm all around. But I could see nothing but water above, water before and water below me. I thought that perhaps we had been blown from our course into the landless wastes of the South China Sea, and my mind started to dwell with Oriental fatalism on the prospect of ship-wreck and marooning on a broken mast. Even as it did so, three curlews dashed through the curtain of rain, flew low above the waves, passed within a few yards of our prow, and disappeared in the gloom beyond. My romantic visions dissolved, for these beautiful birds must be the heralds of a landfall. Sure enough, a few moments later the shadowy sil-houettes of trees took shape in the mist ahead. They were extra-ordinarily close, seeming to loom right over the ship; and as I saw them, we entered the Rejang.

In the sanctuary of the river the water became more tranquil. Then the rain ceased, the wind dropped, night descended, and we voyaged uneventfully to Sibu. Our sense of peace was height-ened by the knowledge that at sea a dreadful tempest raged.

At Sibu, which we reached shortly before midnight, our friends greeted us warmly. They expressed keen appreciation of our kindness in travelling so far out of our way to see them. Such unselfish and gracious conduct, they said, contributed pro-foundly to the sense of good-fellowship among His Majesty's servants doing duty in the lonely outposts of Empire.

II

That night I slept soundly in my bunk all the way down the Igan River. When I woke and stepped on deck, an early morn-ing sun smiled upon a shining mirror of sea, and our launch lay anchored outside the sand-bar of the Mukah River. A mile away an idyllic stretch of South Sea shore appeared, where a white beach, a grove of palm trees and a group of native huts formed a pleasant suburb to the little town of Mukah.

A trim vessel sailing to greet us carried a pilot and the District

Officer. Beyond it a fleet of Melanau fishing-boats floated in a lagoon formed by a semi-circle of waves lapping the sand-shoals of the bar. The craft were dressed for the occasion with colourful pennants and banners, and at their oars sat dusky Melanau crews, the most skilful, intrepid seafarers in all Borneo. I studied them through field-glasses. Their high-cheeked Mongolian faces, sombre dark eyes and mischievous moustachios sprouting above full-lipped mouths made them look like dread Illanun pirates, the only mariners who ever outmatched them at sailing and grabbing loot from those seas. Small, conical straw hats shielding their heads from the hot sun, and slim, naked bronzed bodies added further touches of wildness to their appearance.

As we entered the bar, their shouts of welcome were borne to us across the calm water. We observed then the different styles of their boats. Some were small cockle-shell craft manned by only two or three natives, with a single mast supporting a loose triangular sail. Others were larger vessels accommodating crews of half a dozen men. These were the famous dories, long, workmanlike boats with flat bottoms and shallow drafts which enabled them to cross the treacherous sand-bars of the coast. A few of them supported two masts while others carried three. Nets lay heaped inside the boats. The Melanaus' method of fishing is based on a shrewd study of the habits of their prey. They have noticed that fish like to linger in shady places in the deep; so at a suitable spot in the ocean they heave overboard large bunches of palm fronds. When fish congregate in their shadow, a baglike net supported on wooden booms is lowered over one side of the dory, and the boat is tilted at an angle so that this trap dips beneath the water. A member of the crew then leaps into the sea and literally "shoos" the fish into the net. Afterwards the boat is restored to an upright position, and the catch hauled in.

This type of vessel has been used by Melanau fishermen for centuries. Rare skill is required to keep it from capsizing in rough water; but not rarer skill than the Melanaus possess. They know all that there is to know about sailing small primitive craft. Even in the stormiest periods of the monsoon they take their boats to sea, rowing like galley slaves until they cross the bar, and then quickly unfurling their canvas and letting the craft run before the breeze. Nothing daunts them. On the ocean they are as brave as they are cunning. We felt proud that these courageous men should greet us on our arrival. Their cavalcade of boats escorted us up the river to Mukah's public jetty, as piratical a squadron as ever paid this honour to official representatives of civil government.

Mukah town lies a mile inside the estuary, sheltered from the ocean storms. It is a pleasant tropical settlement with buildings scattered over a wide area. Except for a handful of Europeans, a sprinkling of Malays and the usual community of Chinese traders, its 3,000 inhabitants are all Melanaus.

These people are related in type and culture to the Kayans. Originally as pagan as any other tribe in Borneo, residence in the coastal regions later brought them in contact with new influences. First the example of the Malays inspired them to forswear loincloths and don sarongs with bajus; then it induced them gradually to abandon long-houses and live in individual cottages on family holdings; and finally it made many Melanaus change their age-old ideas. The teachings of the Prophet spread among them, until a large part of the Melanau population was converted to Islam. A lesser section came under the influence of Roman Catholic missionaries and were baptized as Christians, while others retained their animistic faith in the good and evil spirits of earth and sky. An easy, affable tolerance exists among these three religious groups, though each no doubt holds its private opinion about the others' strange faith, and none is above enjoying a few caustic jokes at their misguided fellows' expense.

Another feature distinguishes many Melanaus from the upriver pagans on the one hand and the coastal Malays on the other. They are sago eaters rather than rice eaters. Actually they prefer rice when they can get it, but in some parts of their territory agricultural conditions make sago their staple food. It is almost unbelievable that they should remain content with a fare so indescribably dull. To some extent it is relieved by fish, and their desperate need for this dietary diversion may explain the remarkable heroism of Melanau sailors at sea. But in certain inland districts their menu consists perpetually of undiluted sago. It is not only sago yesterday and sago tomorrow, but also sago today.

This food does not appear to do the Melanaus any harm. No doubt medical authorities could demonstrate that its nutritive value is limited, and that it weakens their physique; but if such a defect exists, its consequences are not visible to uninstructed eyes. On the contrary, the Melanaus present a pleasing bodily appearance. Like all the natives of Borneo, they attain only medium height; but the men are well made and the women have long been famous for their good looks. As I have already written, their reputation for beauty was unenviable in the old days when slave-trading pirates roamed the Borneo coasts, for it caused Melanau girls to be especially prized as booty. In later generations some judges of feminine charm ventured to disagree with the pirates' view on this subject. One writer, for example, said that Melanau women had "pudding faces". The second Rajah took up his pen in their defence, describing them as possessing "agreeable countenances, with the dark, rolling, open eye of Italians". In this controversy I agree with the pirates and the Rajah.

Indeed, Melanau girls are so attractive that it might be worth some beauty parlour expert's while to conduct research into the cause of their sweet looks. He might discover that a diet composed wholly of sago is the right recipe for aspiring Venuses. There may be big money in the proposition. Considering the extraordinary lengths to which women in Western as well as Eastern countries will go to develop every little pleasing feature that they possess, they would doubtless be willing, in this supreme cause, to abandon the joys of other fare and resort to meals of pure sago. In frantic multitudes they would desert the dining-rooms of the Ritz, Maxim's and the Waldorf Astoria and flock to sago restaurants in Piccadilly, the Champs Elysées and Fifth Avenue.

The Melanaus' character is also a commendation of whatever helps to produce it. They have not strong or forceful natures, but that is no bad thing in a world which suffers overmuch from men of tireless energy, boundless ambition and ceaseless aggressiveness. When Melanaus are not doing battle with a raging sea, they are industrious cultivators of rubber, padi and, of course, sago. The men are also competent iron-workers, carpenters and boat-builders, while the women are skilful plaiters of baskets, mats and sun-hats. They take life easily. Their mentality is distinguished by its contented lethargy. They are quiet, shy and unmagnetic at first acquaintance, but a better knowledge of them quickly reveals their unfeigned friendliness and simple, captivating charm. They win the hearts of all who know them.

III

During my stay in Mukah I inspected the process of preparing sago. The finished product is partly consumed by the Melanaus as food, and partly exported from Sarawak for use in the manufacture of starch. Its preparation is Mukah's chief industry, and the work can be studied in a crowded residential quarter built along a small tributary of the main river called the Tillian. The presence of shallow running water is necessary for preparing sago, and the Tillian provides that.

Sago grows in a species of palm-tree called the sago-palm. It does not sprout as an external fruit, like dates or coconuts, but forms internally in the tree trunk. The palms are massive growths of thick girth, covered with an outer bark as rough as the hide of an alligator, and their huge, curving fronds spring luxuriously in fountains of foliage. Orchards of them, called sago gardens, cover wide areas of the Melanau country. They are planted and worked by a great number of smallholders, though rich Melenau owners are now buying up smallholdings and amalgamating them into large estates.

Sago lies packed inside the palm trunks, somewhat like marrow inside a bone. When the trees mature, they are felled, stripped of their rough coating, sawn into sections and shipped down-river to kampongs where the food is extracted. This last part of the work is performed in thousands of individual homes. It is a domestic industry, each family securing from time to time as many sections of palm-trunk as may be necessary to provide sago to sustain the household. Supplies for export are produced mainly in large mills, now owned almost wholly by Chinese business men.

To make my expedition up the Tillian I boarded a prahu. A native at its outboard motor started the engine, and we sped up the Mukah River between long rows of the town's buildings. Soon we entered the Tillian, a small tributary, broad at first, but narrowing quickly to an inconsiderable stream. Houses stood along either bank, ramshackle wooden dwellings erected on piles sunk into the mud. At low tide they stood high and dry on exposed earth, but at full tide waded knee-deep in the river. On each side a continuous succession of them jutted over the water, like rows of cottages in a village street. The Tillian was indeed the village roadway, and the only means of travelling along it was by boat—unless you chose to swim. The place might have been a tumble-down, timber-built copy of a slum in Venice.

Wooden ladders descended from each house to the water, where canoes were moored. A constant traffic of small craft passed up- and down-stream. The boats skimmed noiselessly along, often swerving sharply to avoid children sporting in the river. Bathing parties were frequent. Men, women and children alike would descend the steps from their homes to have a cooling dip, for the Tillian was not only their street, but also their bathroom. Why bother to build a wash-house and erect plumbing for taps of water inside your dwelling, when a plentiful supply of the element flowed constantly past your front door? The villagers performed their ablutions publicly, submerging themselves to the neck at the river's edge, and discreetly soaping their bodies out of sight below. Children used the stream, too, as a playground, diving, somersaulting, fighting and swimming all over its channel to their hearts' content, and to the peril of unskilled boatmen.

The crowd of bathing humanity shared the water with flocks of ducks. These birds thrived in sago-making kampongs. The sago dross which fell into the river was a favourite food of waterfowl, which grew plump on it. In many places the breeding of capons was therefore a by-product of sago manufacture, providing the people with a profitable extra crop. Up the Tillian lived many thousands of ducks. The laughter of children splashing in the river was mixed always with the quacking of frightened mother birds guiding broods of fluffy ducklings to safety amidst the busy traffic.

A final picturesque touch was added to the scene by groves of palm trees growing among the houses. They were not squat, gross sago-palms, but tall, elegant coconut trees such as lend romantic charm to coral island shores. Their slender trunks rose with splendid assurance above the attap roofs of the huts and inclined their lovely shocks of leaves languidly over the water. Above them the infinite blue heaven was a perfect background to an enchanting landscape.

That was the scene which I entered when my prahu turned up the Tillian. I have seldom made a more fascinating journey. A succession of kampongs stood along the rivulet, such a continuous assemblage of huts on either bank that the casual eye of a visitor could not detect where one village ended and the next began. As we progressed, the channel narrowed, its edges drew closer together, and the two crowded lines of houses almost met across the water. The population of human beings and ducks grew ever more dense. Not even the thronged streets of Hong Kong give a more vivid impression of multitudinous humanity.

A first hint of the method of processing sago was contained in an architectural feature common to every house. In front of each protruded a platform made of split bamboo. It stood on wooden stilts above the water, with a roof and latticed screens surrounding it. The screens could be rolled up or let down for light or shade, according to the sun's strength. This flimsy-walled verandah looked like a small sun parlour, but it was in fact the workroom of the house, where sections of tree-trunk were brought for the extraction of crude sago.

Up the Tillian that afternoon the sun shone with truly equatorial heat, and most people had pulled down the screens of their workrooms to maintain a defensive shade. Since these apartments jutted farthest over the water, they provided householders with the best view of what was happening on the river. Word of my journey having preceded me, the people had come to stare. The children plunged into the stream to catch a close glimpse as I passed, the men stood watching from their doorways and the women collected on these verandahs where, by peering through slits in the blinds, they could command an excellent sight of me without themselves being clearly seen. Until you know them and they know you, Melanau women are modest, diffident females. I observed them but dimly that day in almost every house, peeping at me through apertures in the screens, like ladies of a harem gazing inquisitively on the outer world.

An incidental circumstance somewhat marred the enjoyment of the trip. Among its other qualities, good and bad, sago has a powerful smell—and not a pleasant one at that. The river bed was lined with a sediment of sago extract. The water was high that afternoon, which meant that the substance and its evil accompaniment were less exposed than usual. Moreover, I have not a sharp sense of smell, and this was further dulled that day by a bad cold in my nose. Several circumstances therefore conspired to deaden my capacity to detect the odour, and yet the stench was so strong that it almost nauseated me. It reminded me of the stink of a pigsty.

How the Melanaus lived with that obnoxious aroma constantly filling the atmosphere was almost beyond imagining. They shared to a conspicuous degree one of the most remarkable abilities of Asian peoples. The masses inhabiting that continent seem endowed with an infinite capacity to tolerate a multitude of stenches which would make many Westerners vomit. They would, however, return this compliment to us Occidentals, for they declare that we live amidst stinks which would turn their Oriental stomachs. The fact is that likes and dislikes in smell are largely a matter of what you are used to. Easterners are born and bred among their particular brands of odours, and endure them as a matter of course. On the other hand, the scent of a white man is to many of them a disconcerting, unpleasant and even offensive experience. This prejudice is shared by some of their animals, such as the water-buffalo. Whereas those usually amiable beasts relish the fragrance of their Asiatic masters, their sensitive nostrils are so incensed at the whiff emitted by white people that they frequently express their abhorrence by assaulting passing European tourists.

On the Tillian I visited two houses to watch the processes through which raw sago passes before it is ready for human consumption. First I entered a dwelling where a family was engaged in the preparatory work of its extraction from a palm-tree. The master of the household, his wife and a child were occupied on different stages of the job. The man would select a sago log, swing a hatchet and split it lengthwise down the middle. The interior of the trunk was thus exposed, and sago appeared as countless small particles in the fibrous wood. The man rubbed its surface with a metal scraper like a cheese grater, and as he passed the implement to and fro, shavings of "sawdust" fell to the floor, accumulating in a heap.

When a sufficient pile of this substance had collected, the child bore it off to the verandah where the floor was the split-bamboo platform raised over the river which I have described. On this floor lay a loose-woven straw mat with a fine mesh which made it, in effect, a sieve. The youngster unloaded the sawdust on the mat; then the woman stepped on the stuff and with bare feet spread it thinly over the ground. She began shuffling all over the mat, sometimes dragging her feet, sometimes stamping them and sometimes kicking them—treading the sawdust as bare-legged maidens in wine-growing countries used to tread grapes. And just as the juice squirted from the fruit, so now the grains of sago were squeezed from their fibre.

Monotonously and tirelessly the woman continued her little jig, stirring, churning, compressing many times every inch of the dust. Bit by bit the sago was released from its chaff, its grains so small that they passed through the sieve and fell through slits in the bamboo floor below. Most particles of chaff were too gross for this escape, and stayed caught on the mat.

Three or four feet below flowed the Tillian; but before the sago grains reached it they must pass another test. Between the floor and the stream hung, hammock fashion, a sheet of veil-like material, usually a mosquito-net. Its mesh was finer than that of the mat above, and so it acted as an extra sieve to divide the grain from the dross. Only pure sago could penetrate this final obstacle and reach a receptacle waiting below to receive it, a wooden trough moored in the river.

In hundreds of houses along the Tillian these processes were being monotonously repeated. It was a rough and ready method of manufacture. A certain amount of the final product escaped the troughs, falling clear of them or getting capsized into the river. So the bed of the Tillian became coated with sago, and that was how the ducks came to reap their harvest. They were constantly performing somersaults in the water to dive and catch the waste food.

When the sago settled in a trough, only the first half of its treatment was completed. To undergo the second it was paddled along the stream to another type of hut. This was the bake-house, where it was cooked into the dull form which makes it, nevertheless, attractive to Melanau palates. I visited a bake-house to watch the process.

In a roomy apartment two females worked. One was a little old lady with grey hair and a wrinkled, dignified countenance. The other was a girl in the fresh bloom of young womanhood. Her sleek hair glistened as black as night and her nut-brown skin glowed with the warm sunburn of the tropics. Her face had the sensuous features of many full-blown Mongolian beauties. Heavy eye-lids drooped over dreamy eyes, in which passion smouldered like the embers of a fire needing only a puff of wind to blow it into flame. The voluptuous curves to her body made her a sample of the tempting fruit which, in olden days, Illanun pirates came to pluck as it ripened.

The old crone and the young minx demonstrated for me the final stages in concocting edible sago. First the girl poured a basketful of sago flour on a mat. The stuff dropped in large chunks, damp from the river. With nimble fingers she broke the lumps, reducing them to the grain's natural tiny particles. Then she slightly lifted one end of the mat, while her companion raised the other, the middle of the mat resting on the floor. Each in turn, the women made small tossing movements with their hands, causing ripples to pass across the matting which shook the sago in such a way that its grains began to coagulate into numerous small balls. The workers' flips were so skilfully regulated that the transformation occurred as if effortlessly. Soon the mat was full of sago marbles.

The women then laid the matting down, and the girl picked up a rattan sieve. Throwing a heap of marbles on it, she shook them. Most stayed in the tray, but a few puny ones fell through. These were too small for eating, so she cast them aside. The rest she handed to her colleague. Afterwards she threw more handfuls of marbles into the sieve and repeated her action.

Meanwhile the old woman had stoked fires in a brick oven. She spread the sago marbles there and deftly roasted them. When they were done to a nicety, she whipped them off and set another lot in their place. They were now hard-baked little spheres suitable for crunching, if you like crunching that sort of thing. In the trade they are called "sago pearls", but to me they looked more like the small brown pellets which rabbits leave behind them wherever they go.

In this manner is the staple food of many Melanaus made.

IV

From Mukah we toured much of the surrounding country, and then motored twenty miles along the smooth, hard beach to a coastal out-station called Oya. As we advanced, crabs, sandpipers, plovers and curlews fled before us. Oya is a charming village built on a shore where a river flows into the sea. The place has a detached, idyllic air, and has always been a post coveted by District Officers. The bungalow which the reigning incumbent occupies is a cosy dwelling separated from the beach by only a garden laid out with lawns, flower-beds and shady trees. A friend of mine who once lived there told me that his years in Oya were among the most pleasantly idle in all his existence. His Melanau neighbours were companionable, lackadaisical people, and beyond gossiping with them he had little work to do.

We boarded a launch and steamed many miles up the Oya River. Much of the land on either bank was cultivated with sago-palms, forming dense, untidy orchards almost as rough and impenetrable as the jungle itself. Egrets waded in the shallows, monkeys leaped among the trees, occasionally a kite wheeled overhead, and once an eagle soared high in the blue. We seemed to be entering again a kingdom of the beasts.

Yet the country along the riverside was well settled with

people. Every two or three miles we passed a Melanau kampong. In one respect its dwellings were unlike those on the Tillian. Along the Tillian the living quarters of a family and its verandah for treading sago were included under the same roof, but in these hamlets they were separated. The people's residences stood on high ground away from the river, whereas the sago platforms must be at the water's edge. So each household had built a small, square, split-bamboo floor raised on stilts above the stream, with slim poles at its corners supporting a roof from which hung blinds for shelter from sun and rain. It looked like a flimsy wayside stall, and the long row of them stretching along the river in each village was like a series of booths in a country fair.

In almost every one a man or woman was at work treading sago. This occupation seemed ceaseless among the Melanaus. The need to produce food for their family's mouths kept them thus employed much of the day, day after day, week in and week out through all the seasons of the year.

As I watched them, I marvelled again at their infinite capacity for dull, monotonous labour producing dull, monotonous food. Each worker trudged on bare feet round and round the confined space of his platform, as a donkey ambles round the small circle of a primitive mill. Usually he trod with measured, uniform, leaden steps, but every now and then one would give a hearty kick to the sago on the floor, or occasionally break into a lively trot, to give the stuff an extra stir and perhaps to relieve the tedium of his toil. Apparently he was prepared to continue this for hours, the motion being briefly interrupted only once in a while, when it was time to throw a new load of sawdust on the mat.

Usually only one worker at a time appeared in each booth, but sometimes two laboured together. They were probably a man and his wife. Slavishly they followed each other round their miniature track, repeating exactly one another's actions, like a pair of mummers playing a singularly uninspired game of follow-my-leader. The long succession of platforms occupied by a long succession of sago-treaders presented a strange spectacle. During a journey lasting two hours we saw several hundred people going through the same exercise. I thought of the many thousands of Melanaus in all the kampongs on all the rivers in the whole sago-producing country who at that moment were likewise employed. It was a sobering thought.

Next day we travelled through a cutting leading from the Oya to the Igan River. After a jovial evening of feasting, music, dancing and gossip with the Melanau residents and some Iban visitors in the fishing colony of Igan, we voyaged along the coast to the mouth of the Matu River. Sailing up its channel, we came to Matu town, famous for its lovely prospect and for the beautiful sun-hats made by its women.

During the journey the country changed its nature. We had left predominantly sago-growing areas, and had come to regions where padi and rubber were more customary products. Sago gardens still appeared in small, thick clusters here and there, but most of the way up the river rubber plantations and rice fields bordered our aquatic path. Though Matu has a considerable Chinese community, the great majority of its citizens and almost all the rural population are Melanaus, and they are rice eaters. In an elementary fashion they cultivate wet-padi. Building no balks around their plots, they do not employ even the simple system of irrigation which typifies the vast landscapes of rice-fields in most southern Asian countries. Their padi is planted on patches of flat ground in the lower reaches of the river, where the crop is left to be watered, and sometimes drowned, by rain and floods. Government officers are striving to overcome the conservatism which enables these out-of-date methods to persist, and to introduce to casual Melanau minds more scientific agricultural ideas.

In the higher regions of the river sago-making kampongs were more plentiful. One afternoon we took to prahus and went to visit them. As we progressed, the waterway dwindled, shrinking first from a river to a rivulet, and then from a rivulet to a mere stream. The narrow channel wound tortuously mile after mile through flat, fen-like country, our only views being reedy banks close on either hand and a limitless expanse of sky overhead.

Eventually the stream broadened again, a group of huts appeared, and we came to a village. It was a picturesque place. A few score dwellings crowded beside the banks and intruded into the channel. They were kajang cottages, none built on terra firma, but all raised on wooden stilts over the water. The river formed not only the highway but all the byways of the settlement, water flowing below, between and around every shack. Standing above its own reflection in the placid river, the cluster of marooned huts appeared to be suspended in liquid space, an illusion which made it seem all the more flimsy and airy.

We landed on a platform before the headman's house, and then toured the place. Prahus paddled by natives darted along the main channel, giving it the appearance of a roadway busy with traffic. Here and there the stream was spanned by slender bridges made of tree trunks, laid at a height sufficient to permit the passage of boats below. They were footways for the safe crossing of pedestrians; yet their safety seemed dubious to me. None of them had hand-rails to support one's balance, and a man must be a practised pole-walker to stroll at ease along them. The villagers were experts at this, their children in particular scampering over the tree trunks as agilely as squirrels; but untrained venturers on them were liable to grow giddy in mid-stream and plunge headlong in the river. The local youngsters laughed at my slow, hesitant steps, and even the ducks beneath me seemed to quack with a suggestion of amusement as they eyed my unsteady progress. Their exclamations were really, no doubt, expressions of fright, for the birds could hardly fail to recognize that I was an ungainly amateur who might at any moment collapse on top of them.

Wherever we looked in the village we saw the customary small platforms built for treading sago, and on each a man, woman or child tramped monotonously round and round.

V

We stayed two days in a deserted bungalow a few miles outside Matu, once a District Officer's house. It had suffered neglect during the Japanese occupation, and was still empty of furniture. However, its roof and walls provided protection from scorching sun, raging wind and torrential rain, and no one needs much more than that on the equator. We had brought camp-beds and mosquito-nets, and settled agreeably in our simple lodging.

We spent our time inspecting government buildings and schools, visiting the bazaar and residential quarters, eating curry tiffin with Malay officials, manipulating ivory chopsticks with Chinese towkays, discussing local politics with Melanau men and watching Melanau women making hats.

These women produce attractive objects, good in shape, bold in design and vivid in colours. They create a particular style of sun-hat which is one of Sarawak's most attractive artistic products. A small conical affair, it is fashioned of fine straw strips, silver and gold threads, coloured glass beads and bits of sparkling tinsel, all woven into charming, tartan-like designs. No two patterns are the same, each has its own original details, and all bear the human artist's personal touch.

Our visits up the Mukah, Oya, Igan and Matu Rivers had given us a representative glimpse of life among the Melanaus. The organization of their society on an individualist instead of a collectivist basis; their preoccupation with conservative, even primitive, methods of agriculture and fishing; the dependence of many on sago for their maintenance, while rice was the chief crop of others and newer products like rubber played only a small part in their economy; the prevalence in urban as well as rural districts of domestic industries based on family labour; and the division of the population between the pagan, Mohammedan and Christian faiths—all these features were apparent everywhere.

Yet only ten minutes' walk from our bungalow stood a relic of earlier days, a hoary survival from an antique form of Melanau society—one of the few remaining Melanau long-houses. Originally these people were all long-house dwellers, but hardly any now occupy communal habitations. We visited this rare mansion at Matu. It was like turning back the pages of history to a vanished epoch, paying a call on a company of ghosts.

The inmates of the house gave us a friendly welcome. They were impecunious, near-naked husbandmen and river fishermen in curious contrast to the well-dressed, sophisticated Melanaus of Matu little more than a stone's throw away. Their archaic home stood in a grove of coconut trees. In some respects it appeared like a Kayan long-house, and in others like one built by Ibans. Its most curious feature, however, belonged to neither

Kayan nor Iban architecture. The common-room running its length had family apartments leading off on both sides, not on only one side. I never saw this arrangement in any other long-house, and suppose that it belonged to a peculiarly Melanau tradition.

The place had twenty-six rooms, and I learned that 113 people lived in it. The number, however, was steadily dwindling. Disintegration had begun in this solitary, stubborn relic of the past. Already several families had left the house to settle in individual huts close by. The example of other peoples in the district had first tempted a few to make the move. The change would afford them personal privacy, opportunities for development along self-determined lines, and a novel sense of exclusive property in cottage and land. So the influence of inherited tradition was challenged in the minds of progressive thinkers in the old house. For a while their mental struggle, their emotional anguish even, must have been sharp; but eventually the bold, revolutionary decision was taken and the conservatism of centuries broken down. First one family and then another drifted away from the long-house to set up small establishments of their own.

I saw half a dozen such dwellings in the surrounding fields. Their residents continued to visit the long-house, to maintain neighbourly association with its inmates, and to regard themselves as belonging for all collective purposes to the same group; but they never returned to live under the communal roof. Having once experienced the greater freedom of an individual home, their resolution was confirmed.

Sadly the die-hard tuai rumah shook his head and told me that he thought more families would soon depart. I had arrived at a moment of transition in the life of this Melanau community. I caught a glimpse of a great social change in progress, the historic transformation of a primitive people from a collectivist to an individualist society. Already the movement had been completed among nearly all the Melanaus in Sarawak; only two or three inhabited long-houses still remained. The house near Matu was one of them, and in a few years it too would disappear.

I looked on this rare exhibit with curious respect, as if I were meeting the Last of the Mohicans. When my visit ended and

I descended the tree-trunk stairway to leave, I turned to wave good-bye to the chief and his followers with a feeling that I was bidding farewell to a whole human epoch.

What has happened to the Melanaus will happen in due course to the Ibans, the Kayans, the Kenyahs and other up-river peoples in Borneo. Long-house society will gradually dissolve. Modern notions will sweep away ancient customs, one after another. The pagan way of life, which has existed for millennia, will disappear as completely as if it had been swallowed by an earthquake.

CHAPTER EIGHTEEN

CHINESE FAMILY

I

CHINESE TRADERS HAVE VOYAGED to Borneo from time immemorial. The earliest known references in Chinese histories to Borneo, or P'o-li as it was then called by scribes in the Celestial Empire, occur in documents written in the sixth century A.D., before the illustrious first T'ang Emperor ascended the Dragon Throne. These records note the arrival at the Chinese court of embassies from P'o-li. Further allusions occur in later works, all indicating that merchants from China sailed regularly to P'o-li for commerce with its people, and that occasionally official missions from P'o-li repaid the compliment with interest by bringing tribute from their jungle sultan to the Son of Heaven. P'o-li's capital town was graced by a royal establishment of considerable, if savage, splendour, and inhabited by a populous mixed society, partly civilized and partly wild.

Scholars are satisfied that this country was situated on the northwest coast of the great island now called Borneo, and that it was none other than early Brunei.

No one can tell when Chinese traders developed this overseas connection by turning occasional visits into permanent residence in Borneo. By the time that James Brooke arrived in Sarawak several hundred Chinese owned profitable pepper farms in the neighbourhood of Kuching or made comfortable livelihoods mining precious metals elsewhere. At first these industrious settlers were disconcerted by the arrival of the White Rajah. They had flourished in the days of misrule by Pengiran Makota because his inefficient government interfered little with their activities, and such interference as occurred could always be diverted by a little judicious bribery. When Brooke ascended the throne things were different. An incorruptible administration

sought not only to levy taxes in theory but to collect them in practice. Resenting this, the gold-miners at Bau decided to rid themselves of the Rajah and all his works.

Among the old national customs which they had brought
with them from their motherland was that of forming secret
societies. These clandestine organizations were prepared to
pursue shady political objectives by unlawful means. In 1857 the
leaders of one of them staged an unhappy incident notorious in
Sarawak's history as "The Chinese Rebellion". Mobilizing a
fleet of boats and a mob of followers, they paddled down-river
from Bau to Kuching. Landing at midnight, they divided their
forces into two gangs. The first attacked the stockade which
constituted the capital's only military defence, and the other
headed for the astana to kill the Rajah.

As they entered His Highness's garden the latter party met a
young English cadet. Wakened by their noisy approach—for
they were yelling defiantly—he had suspected treachery, and ran
from his near by house to warn his chief. He reached the astana
at the same time as the intruders, who caught and slew him. In
the darkness they took some time to complete this crime.

He saved the Rajah's life, for their delay over his murder
enabled the intended victim to escape. At the first sound of
alarm Brooke dressed and left his bedroom, carrying a sword in
one hand and a pistol in the other. In the corridor he saw a
shadowy figure creeping stealthily towards him, and was about
to despatch the apparition when he recognized the man as a faithful friend, the palace steward. The servant was coming to advise
his master of the danger.

Together they stole into the unlit drawing-room, to recon-
noitre the enemy. The Chinese were now entering the dwelling
and setting its contents on fire. Clearly their numbers made effective defence impossible, so the Rajah and his companion retreated
through a bathroom window, ran across the lawn, dived into a
creek beside the garden, and swam across. On the farther bank
they walked to the house of an official, where English and Malay
friends joined them.

That night the Chinese rebels murdered several European
citizens, slaughtered the Malay guards in the stockade and burned

the astana and other buildings to the ground. Knowing, however, that they had missed their principal quarry, they paraded the town with the head of the young cadet borne on a pike, shouting that it was the Rajah's head. By this stratagem they hoped to make the townspeople submit in panic to their will; but the terrified folk merely withdrew behind firmly-bolted doors.

At daybreak the rebels attempted to win the public's sympathy by a conciliatory policy. Momentarily masters of the capital, they nevertheless knew that the Rajah would try to rally supporters and drive them out. In fact their cause was doomed, for they were hopelessly outnumbered by the local Malays, who remained loyal to their ruler. Moreover, as soon as the Ibans on a neighbouring river heard rumours of their Rajah's murder, they embarked in war boats to avenge his death. When intelligence of their approach reached Kuching, the Chinese decided that it would be sound tactics to withdraw. Filling their prahus with all the loot that they could carry, they started the return journey to Bau.

The Ibans were not to be denied satisfaction. As the retreating enemy paddled desperately along muddy streams, fierce head-hunting warriors caught up with them. Frightful slaughter followed. Many Chinese, preferring to die by their own hands rather than by the cut of Dayak swords, ran their craft ashore and committed suicide by hanging themselves on jungle trees. Some escaped as far as the frontier of Dutch Borneo, but received rough treatment there. Few ever returned alive to their homes.

Among the heads which the Ibans brought in triumph to Kuching were those of most of the rebel leaders. The miserable fiasco was over, and the Rajah never had any more trouble from his Chinese subjects.

II

The Chinese were, of course, short-sighted in regarding the Rajah as an obstacle to progress and prosperity. He was the very opposite. By spreading law and good government throughout Sarawak he created the conditions essential for safe trade, and by extending the boundaries of his state he expanded the area where profitable business could be done. The taxes which he levied on merchants to finance his efforts paid them handsome dividends in better opportunities and larger returns for their enterprises.

As he and his successors increased the territory where order prevailed, the Chinese colony prospered and multiplied. Partly by natural increase and partly by fresh immigration it grew to its present figure of some 125,000, nearly a quarter of Sarawak's population. The community is a typical example of the remarkable Chinese settlement which characterizes many countries in South-East Asia. In Singapore, for example, Chinese compose more than eighty per cent of the citizens; in the Federation of Malaya they account for more than forty per cent, and in Siam, Indo-China, the Philippines and Indonesia they form large minorities. They exercise extraordinary economic power, while their political influence is of varying importance.

Most of these Chinese, or their ancestors, came from the southern provinces of China. Even so, transportation to the coasts and islands of the Malay Archipelago required a notable capacity for adjustment to new conditions and climates. Some races could not survive such transplantation, but the hardy, adaptable, enduring Chinese apparently suffer no harm. On the contrary, they flourish in the countries of their adoption. They seem able to fit themselves into any circumstances in any place. I feel no doubt that if a balloon crowded with Cantonese families strayed in a misguided moment to the moon, its passengers would disembark and at once plant vegetable gardens, found laundries and begin a game of Mahjongg. In a short while they would have established restaurants, pagodas, gambling dens, secret societies, lion-dance kongsis, and all the other familiar features of a Chinatown. Thereafter the Man in the Moon would find life vastly more entertaining than he can have done before.

In Sarawak, as elsewhere, the Chinese have engaged in a multitude of occupations. Wherever I travelled in the country I saw evidence of their penetration. At every trading post a group of Chinese notables stood with other civic worthies to greet me, ranks of Chinese school-children were marshalled to give a friendly salute, Chinese crackers exploded like toy artillery ahead of me as I inspected the bazaar, and bird's-nest soup, shark's fin and other delicacies appeared on the menus of dinner parties offered by the local Chinese Chamber of Commerce. In fact this Chinese element is an essential part of the substance of Sarawak life.

It creates certain problems. The Chinese are easily adaptable, but not easily assimilable. Some of them intermarry with natives or Malays, and the process of unifying Sarawak's peoples into a homogeneous population is to that extent assisted; but on the whole they keep to themselves and preserve with little change the character, customs and ideas which they or their forefathers brought with them from China.

They came to Sarawak for one purpose and one purpose only —to make money. As long as they can pursue a profitable live-lihood they are happy. They all hope to grow rich one day, and in the meantime are content to labour as long and as hard as may be necessary to earn a few extra dollars. Hitherto with few excep-tions they have displayed no political ambitions. Mostly they are traders pure and simple, actual or potential—and traders of genius. Whether the new Communist régime in China will greatly alter this state of affairs remains to be seen.

III

A few years ago there lived in Kuching a truly grand old man who typified in his person the Chinese achievement throughout South-East Asia.

His name was Ong Tiang Swee. His grandfather came from Fukien Province to Singapore in the first half of the last century, and later his father migrated from Singapore to Kuching. Tiang Swee himself was born in the little capital in the middle 1860's, when the first Rajah was still on the throne; and he stayed there until his death in 1951. He bought land, started a business, in-vested his profits in further undertakings, multiplied his interests in various directions, and in due course controlled planting, farm-ing, commercial, shipping and banking enterprises—and a respec-table fortune. The Rajahs often sought his advice in matters of state, and he proved himself as prudent in public as he was in private affairs. He died at the age of eighty-six, remaining to the end in hearty possession of all his faculties.

I knew and loved the old man well during his last few years. Almost bald and completely toothless, with loose, wrinkled skin turned the colour of parchment, his countenance resembled that of a venerable mandarin in a classical Chinese painting. Usually his face wore the placid expression of contented old age; but his interests were lively, his sense of fun was quick, and often his eyes sparkled with humour and his mouth opened to emit dry chuckles of laughter. His mind was as clear as that of a man in his prime; he followed commercial and political affairs closely; and he stated his opinions always with conviction and force. His numerous business concerns still received the benefit of his general guidance, though their detailed management had passed largely to younger colleagues in his family. Before he died the beginnings of deafness, slowly failing sight and rather feeble powers of walking confined him mostly to his own house and garden; but his constitution remained sound, and no one indulged with keener relish in a meal of a dozen choice dishes washed down with champagne.

During my first visit to Sarawak I called on him, and from that day our friendship blossomed. Always when my wife and I were in Kuching he invited us to lunch with him, and his company and his table were temptations which we never resisted. A visitor to his house perceived at once that its furnishings were of a period with himself. In the principal chamber stiff blackwood chairs inlaid with mother-of-pearl stood in rows along the walls, and tables to match added their contribution to the atmosphere of staid formality. Large pictures of Tiang Swee's prim-faced mother and cherub-faced father, autographed portraits of the last Rajah and Ranee in regal dress, and half a dozen photographs of multitudinous gatherings of his family—of whom I shall write later—hung in the room. Here and there stood various ornaments worthy of a late-Victorian landlady's parlour, while the place of honour was filled by a red and gold lacquer altar furnished with brass images, paper flowers, porcelain incense-burners and the other paraphernalia of ancestor worship.

At one end of the room a concession to comfort had been introduced in the form of some genteel wicker chairs; but they too had acquired by long disuse a solemn air. The whole room appeared unlived in. However, the open doorway and glassless windows looked upon a pleasant, overgrown garden, and Borneo's sunshine beyond conveyed its brightness and freshness to the place.

The chamber was primarily a sanctum for the reception of visitors. When we arrived, Tiang Swee would usher us to the wicker chairs, where we sat, sipped sherry and gossiped about the price of rubber, the fertility of pigs, the Government's land policy, the Russian threat to Berlin, the fortunes or misfortunes of Generalissimo Chiang Kai-Shek, or whatever other topics at the moment exercised his mind. Two or three of his sons sat with us, while other relatives were mostly invisible in more intimate apartments farther indoors. Later we would visit them. The women of the household and several of the patriarch's grand-children and great-grandchildren could usually be found in a roofless central courtyard, where lotus plants flowered in great porcelain bowls and grotesque goldfish floated in aquaria. Through the glass walls of their homes the fish would gape and ogle at us, wriggling their bodies and flaunting fabulous long fins, like googoo-eyed, pouting-lipped maidens performing veil dances.

One of the principal impulses of Tiang Swee's life was hospitality. He loved to welcome chosen friends to choice feasts. As I have mentioned, he always invited Audrey and me to lunch with him. The chief bait which he offered was Roast Suckling Pig. Casually he would mention that there would also be bird's-nest soup, shark's fin, fish with sweet-sour sauce and other tasty morsels, with as many glasses of sherry, champagne and liqueur as we wished. But the delicacy round which the banquet centred was Roast Suckling Pig.

Hearing Ong Tiang Swee speak of this dish made its consumption seem not only the sole reason for eating, but also the noblest experience in life, and perhaps the supreme purpose of man's existence on earth. I do not know whether he had read Charles Lamb's famous *Dissertation on Roast Pig*, but whether he had or not, he was undoubtedly a contemporary reincarnation of Bo-bo, the immortal discoverer of the Chinese people's favourite concoction.

At any time a Chinese meal is a formidable affair. To eat it is to enjoy one of the most delicious of worldly pleasures. Were I a skilled man of letters, I would write a volume about it, and at every line of every page the reader's mouth would water. I would describe in detail the odd recipes and astonishing ingredients, the singular meats and unprecedented sauces, the mysterious appearances and seductive flavours of each dish. But the words at my command are too trite to attempt more than a brief comment.

One of the charming qualities of the Chinese—brilliantly represented by Tiang Swee—is their delight in entertaining friends to interminable repasts. I have been a guest at scores of their feasts in private homes, public restaurants and even sacred temples. Usually the courses number between half a dozen and a dozen; but sometimes they greatly exceed that total. The most lavish dinner that I ever attended had twenty-four courses and continued for several hours. It was given by a small Chinese Chamber of Commerce in a remote corner of Sarawak, and was a trifling affair compared with the classic, gargantuan banquets offered in fashionable places in China.

The Chinese are supreme artists, and they display their creative genius as truly in cooking food as in carving jade, casting bronzes, designing porcelain, writing calligraphy and painting pictures. Each item in a menu is a triumph of the chef's skill, taste and imagination. He conjures from the most unpromising materials dainty tidbits of unbelievable exquisiteness. Who would have thought that such lowly stuffs as sea-slugs, birds' saliva, bamboo-shoots and hundred-years-old eggs could be presented in a manner to make discriminating gourmets well-nigh swoon with ecstasy? The transformation is miraculous, and each successive item in a cook's repertoire seems to be more bold and magical than the last.

In my childhood I sometimes took umbrage at a nursery rhyme which ran,

What are little boys made of?
Slugs and snails and puppy-dogs' tails;
That's what little boys are made of.
What are little girls made of?
Sugar and spice and all that's nice;
That's what little girls are made of.

Since dining and wining with Ong Tiang Swee and other Chinese friends in Borneo and Malaya I have lost my sense of grievance against the author of that jingle. I understand now that I should not have taken offence at its innuendo, for its apparent slur on the constitution of small boys was in fact a high tribute. Of slugs and snails the Chinese contrive dishes fit for emperors to eat, and I have no doubt that of puppy dogs' tails they can concoct a feast worthy of the gods.

The cunning necromancy performed by Chinese cooks from the oddest substances is only part of their achievement. Having transformed unlikely raw materials into divine delicacies, these artists then dress them with oils and sauces, juices and spices which add even more to their succulence. Few Chinese, however, lack a sense of humour, and it is perhaps this quality which makes them play a trick on their customers by sometimes serving the finished product in a repulsive manner. The fare often swims in grease or gravy, giving it the appearance of unpalatable slops, or else is hidden in outer coatings of dubious matter which occasionally looks unseemly to the point of obscenity. This habit contributes to the sense of perpetual adventure in encountering Chinese food. It heightens uncertainty and maintains a constant element of surprise. At first sight a timid Occidental diner might turn away in disgust from many items placed before him; but never would mortal man be more mistaken. Courage at a Chinese table brings abundant rewards.

Another admirable feature of the meal is the fact that it lasts a long time and is ever-changing. As I have indicated, there is nothing stingy about Chinese hospitality. Chinese hosts would feel forever disgraced if they served their guests with only three or four courses. A modest dinner includes nearly a dozen successive dishes, a rather special one provides anything up to a score, and a real banquet does not end until at least twice that number have been presented. Each item has its own particular epicurean character, contrasting sometimes subtly and at other times blatantly with its predecessors. One by one, hour after hour, you sample them all. At high feasts the board is rarely without several varied viands at once. If a newly arrived plate contains a specialty which, after trial, you decide is less worthy of attention than some other, you may abandon it and return to your favourite. Later perhaps you will resolve to give it another test. Your taste and judgement are allowed free play. Chinese servants are never in a hurry to remove a dish which appears popular, and you can sample it periodically between excursions in other beguiling directions.

This freedom to experiment among a large assortment of meats is made possible because only a morsel of each need be taken. Hosts in the Western world are apt to limit their offerings to formidable piles of only two or three substances, with the result that—if perchance you do not like them—you are compelled either to hide your grimaces of displeasure as you demolish them, or else to expose yourself to a charge of boorish lack of appreciation of the fare. The Chinese work on the opposite principle. They serve many types of food in countless small quantities, and a guest has no obligation to take more than a tiny mouthful of any individual specimen. Indeed, he may refuse completely many items on a menu. Such conduct does not expose him to accusations of impoliteness. On the contrary, the Chinese would consider it a fault in themselves if they forced any particular style of nourishment on a friend. Therefore they provide enough variety to suit all palates, and in forms which enable each diner to satisfy exactly his preference. For that matter, they provide it so generously that, if he chooses, he may indulge his manifold cravings until he bursts at the table. Such a climax to a meal would be regarded as a singularly sincere expression of enjoyment of it.

That was the form of entertainment to which Ong Tiang Swee frequently invited us—and which we never refused. The summons was for luncheon, not dinner, since the old man was an early bedder; but that made no difference to the meal's magnificence. Possibly it was shorter by a few courses at midday than it would have been at night, but in quality it was as choice as the wise hedonist's impeccable taste could make it—with its promised climax of Roast Suckling Pig.

At noon the privileged guests would assemble on the wicker chairs in his reception room. Tiang Swee's conversation on those days was particularly bright. He felt gay in anticipation of the feast. A servant handed glasses of sherry round the company, and as we sipped our host spoke of the impending pleasures of eating with an expert appreciation which infected everyone with his enthusiasm. The luncheon table was temptingly dressed, its snow-white cloth spread with bright porcelain bowls, polished ivory chopsticks and sparkling crystal goblets. The ceramics were painted with decorative storks, dragons, bats, phoenixes and other emblems of good luck, fertility, longevity and kindred objects of one's heart's desire.

In due course Tiang Swee led us to our seats. His benign old face was now wreathed in smiles, and with many chortles he prepared us for the little pig which would later make its appearance. But the great dish did not arrive for some time. Part of the enjoyment of any pleasure lies in anticipation; and Tiang Swee let us savour that happiness to the full. Ritual decreed that Roast Suckling Pig should be approached gradually; so first a few minor delicacies, mere palate-ticklers like winter-melon broth, shark's fin in chicken gravy, and braised abalone in oyster sauce were introduced.

Then a servant brought in the delicacy of delicacies. Carefully disposed across a large oval platter were the mortal remains of an infant porker. At one end lay its head, its innocent face without a blemish, its eyes closed in eternal sleep, its ears cocked as if to listen for the last trumpet, its snout in repose after an all too short career of grunting, and its mouth half open in—could it be?—a seraphic grin. At the opposite end of the plate appeared the animal's small, curly, whip-like tail still attached to a severed fragment of its rump. In between these two extremities were innumerable tiny slices of meat so arranged as to represent the shape of its body. Its skin was toasted to a delicate golden-brown tint, gleaming like the glaze on a piece of T'ang pottery.

The sight of the dismembered piglet was poignant, for the little creature was but a few weeks old when it fell a victim to the executioner's knife. Its life had been blameless and its character pure. I confess that I could not morally condone its condemnation to death; and yet I stayed deaf to the protesting voice of conscience. I suppose that I should have risen from Tiang Swee's table, expressed horror at the atrocity which had been committed, and stalked from the room. But such conduct would have achieved nothing beyond the ruin of a cherished friendship with a fine old Chinese gentleman, who possessed in a representative degree the charming weaknesses as well as the engaging virtues of his race. It could not have saved the life of the little animal lying quartered on our table, nor of untold thousands of its fellows afterwards. To achieve that, one would need to alter the national habits and character of 600,000,000 Chinese. Many conquerors through the ages, from prehistoric Mongol chiefs to Genghis Khan and the modern Japanese have tried to mould the Chinese nation—and failed. It is a vain, an impossible task. The Chinese are the most numerous, the most changeless, the most enduring and, everything considered, the most admirable people on earth. They do not alter their ideas or customs, still less their natures, for any man. Least of all would they do it for one whom they would regard as that dullest of all bores, a food crank. They love the lofty things of the mind and spirit, but are also favourably inclined towards the physical pleasures of life. They delight in the world's prolific riches, in the fruits of the soil, the scented bloom of flowers, the majestic shapes of mountains, the blue of the sky after rain and the intoxication of wine. And high among the earth's gifts that they value is Roast Suckling Pig. Should anyone dispute the morality of that judgement, they would indicate with infinite politeness that he was a pitiable barbarian unworthy to join the society of civilized men.

So, when the baby pig appeared, I stayed unprotesting at Tiang Swee's table. With my feeble conscience hushed by these weighty considerations, I entered gladly upon its consumption. Let me confess without more ado that, like our good host himself, I belong to the school of taste which regards Roast Suckling Pig as the most delectable food eaten by man. With friendship, therefore, not hostility, I turned up my nose at an odour of peculiar delicacy wafting from the dish. My eye was entranced by the golden-brown tan of the piglet's hide, and soon my tongue too was pleasantly committed. Each particle of pigskin was toasted to a consistency like that of the thinnest and crispest toffees, brittle to one's teeth and yet seeming to melt like butter in the mouth. The white flesh adhering to its under-surface tasted unbelievably sweet, with a tenderness fit for angels. Immediately, irresistibly one became a confirmed addict to the vice discovered by illustrious Bo-bo.

Only when the entire pig was consumed did anyone cry halt to our enjoyment. Even then the festive lunch was far from over. For a while we sat and discussed contentedly the fine points of the particular sample of Roast Suckling Pig which we had savoured; then our deft chopsticks began to toy with other choice courses which led us gently away from the meal's grand climax.

Always on our oft-changing bowls appeared fluttering phoenixes and sportive dragons, those amiable creatures which for centuries have flown and romped their way through Chinese banquets. On them, too, were other emblems of fecundity, longevity and happiness—the gracious ideals which the Chinese people, with the aid of Roast Suckling Pig, have attained more than any other race on earth.

IV

Whether it was as a result of his indulgence in his favourite refreshment, or owing to other causes, Ong Tiang Swee enjoyed in abundance the three virtues of fecundity, longevity and happiness. Not the least of them was fecundity. Additional convincing evidence besides his constitutional stamina proved his physical vigour. It was the multitude of his descendants.

He had married three wives and begotten a score of children. His half-dozen surviving sons inherited his intelligence, and they too were accomplished in the art of living. One, for example, Ong Hap Leong, was a gold miner and business man, a member

of the Council Negri and the Supreme Council, an expert culti-
vator of many species of orchids, the owner of a successful string
of race-horses, devoted husband to a charming wife and the
indulgent father of eight lovely daughters and lively sons.

Incidentally, during the war he risked torture at the hands
of the Japanese by smuggling into the European internees' camp
in Kuching spare parts for an improvised wireless set, so that the
prisoners could receive news from the outside world. Nor did
he limit his gifts to these mechanical contrivances. Occasionally
he slipped through the barbed wire other presents to sustain
the captives' bodies and cheer their spirits. Ong Tiang Swee took
a hand also in these contraband dealings. The generous heart
of the old hedonist wept for the prisoners deprived of liberty to
enjoy the lush beauty of Borneo's landscapes, the bounteous fruits
of the tropical earth, and the civilized pleasures of good living.
Alas, it lay beyond his power to convey to them in their barren
confinement the freedom of green hills and flowering gardens;
but he could occasionally—by pure accident, of course!—despatch
to them through the barbed wire a companionable little pig or a
consoling bottle of wine. With Hap Leong and other discreet
members of his family he maintained this conspiracy through the
early months of the occupation, when the camp for male internees
happened to be in the neighbourhood of his house. Later it was
moved to a more inaccessible place; but the Englishmen never
forgot these courageous gestures of friendship at a time when
the world for them was full of boredom. After their release they
presented their aged benefactor with a handsome silver mug suitably inscribed; and ever afterwards it stood on a central table
in his living-room, his proudest possession.

All Tiang Swee's offspring played their part in propagating
the Ong clan. The number of his children's children and his
children's children's children constantly increased, until at the
time of his death more than 150 of his descendants lived in
Sarawak. The latest additions were some great-great-grandchil-
dren. Tiang Swee's house always seemed full of youngsters,
looking like a troupe of animated dolls. Their sleek black
hair cut in trim fringes, dark, slanting eyes, small noses and
cherry-red mouths were pretty attributes. Some of them were

shy and solemn in the presence of strangers, but others were smiling and playful. Their curiosity about us Occidentals knew no bounds. As we sat in the stiff reception chamber conversing with their grandfather, or great-grandfather, they would gather at the edge of the room and peer fixedly at us. If reproved for ill manners by some unseen mother, aunt or amah in the inner courtyard, they would disappear—and reappear a few minutes later outside the house, poking their faces above the sills of the windows to resume their stares.

Like a patriarch of old, Tiang Swee lived surrounded by this immense family. Nearly all of them resided in Kuching, and periodically the whole company of his progeny, spanning four generations, called to pay their respects to the revered head of their clan. In the centre of the assembly sat the glorious octogenarian, surveying contentedly these most blessed fruits of his life's labours. Among them his word was law. In his small world he was as formidable a figure as the Empress Dowager— "Old Buddha", as she was nicknamed—in the twilight years of the Chinese Empire.

The multitudinous heirs sprung from his loins were a splendid, representative example of the prolific virility which has enabled the Chinese people to spread over so much of the earth. They are increasing rapidly in Sarawak. Their numbers and qualities make them the only possible rivals to the Ibans for ultimate predominance in the country. One day a struggle may develop between the two communities; they must either contend until one is master, or co-operate in a mixed society in which the Malays and other racial groups also take their rightful places.

The latter is the sensible way. Will the Ibans and Chinese both follow it? I think so, but I shall not live to see. The story's unfolding will take longer than the short span of my remaining life.

CHAPTER NINETEEN

MALAY POLITICS

I

THE READER ALREADY KNOWS that at some unrecorded date in the distant past Malays began to migrate to Borneo, and that in due course they founded several sultanates round its coast. The Sultan of Brunei became the most powerful of these Moslem potentates, and until the arrival of James Brooke, Sarawak was a small, misgoverned province in his realm.

For centuries the Malays were the politically dominant race in Sarawak. During the suzerainty of the sultans Malay nobles from Brunei held pro-consular office in Kuching, while local Malays were junior chiefs below them. Together these petty lords wielded exclusive official authority, enjoying a monopoly of such wealth and glory as the country offered, and regarding the Chinese as tax-payers to be fleeced and the pagans as savages to be bullied, exploited and despoiled.

When James Brooke became Rajah he dismissed the Brunei overlords, but confirmed the other Malay chiefs in their appointments. Of necessity he relied on them for the administration of his country, for the pagan peoples were too primitive and the Chinese too occupied in making money to aspire to government posts. Though subjecting his Malay assistants to discipline, and ending their licence to do evil, he renewed their functions as officials with considerable power. When he introduced a novel, unselfish notion of public service they adapted themselves to it. They had learned bad habits only from a bad example, and were equally ready to follow a good one. The innate courtesy and decency of Malay character reasserted themselves.

As the Rajah's territory expanded and its organization of government grew, several new, important administrative offices were created, such as those of Chief Secretary, Treasurer and the

Residents of Divisions. These were filled by men recruited from Britain, but side by side with them the Rajah maintained a team of Malay Officers of State. First among them were the Datu Patinggi, the pre-eminent titular chief; the Datu Shabandar or Bandar, second only to the Datu Patinggi in honourable status; the Datu Temonggong, who was the equivalent of a Malay Prime Minister; the Datu Imam, the principal adviser on Islamic religious affairs; and the Datu Hakim, the supreme authority on Moslem law. To their offices were attached considerable pay and comfortable pensions. They flourished throughout the century of Brooke rule, and some have survived into the present period of British colonial government.

No similar posts carrying national responsibilities existed among the pagan tribes. In the last years of the Rajahs the highest chieftainship was that held by the Iban, Temonggong Koh, but his title gave him no effective status beyond the longhouses of the upper Rejang. It was not an Office of State, nor did it carry a salary or pension. As for the Chinese, throughout the Brooke régime they were regarded as foreign immigrants entitled to none of the fruits of public office. In every locality one of their number was chosen as "Kapitan China", with the duty of representing his community in discussions with the district administration, but his post was honorary and informal.

Supreme power in all matters lay with the Rajah. He was an absolute ruler, but was assisted by a group of officers collectively formed into the Supreme Council. This Council met weekly to review state policy, and in 1941 had nine British, one Chinese and five Malay members. The assembly called the Council Negri was supposedly representative of the population as a whole, and on it sat seven British members, five Malays, four Chinese, and two Dayaks. But this august body was convened only once in every three years. High office in government was therefore in effect an exclusive preserve of the British and the Malays—in spite of the fact that less than twenty per cent of the population were Malays, while twenty-five per cent were Chinese and more than fifty per cent were pagans. A similar state of affairs marked the other ranks of government service. In the central departments in Kuching the senior officials were all either British or Malays; in

the Divisions the British Residents were assisted at their headquarters by predominantly Malay staffs; and in the Districts the
British District Officers were aided by Assistant District Officers
and Native Officers who were almost invariably Malays, though
a few Melanaus, Eurasians and, in exceptional cases, pagans were
appointed.

The privileged position of the Malays was significantly reflected in the education system. The Chinese community was
everywhere well provided with schools, but these were supplied
by the Chinese themselves. The only government-sponsored and
financed schools were establishments for the instruction of Malays,
with a few Melanaus. The authorities provided training also for
Malay teachers. This was necessary precisely because the administration depended so largely on Malays who could read, write, add
and subtract. The Government provided no schools for the up-
river peoples. Only a few classes run by Christian missions catered
here or there for a handful of Dayak youngsters.

Thus the Offices of State and the responsible executive posts
in government, outside those held by British officials, belonged
to the fraction of the population who were Malays. The Malays
were an educated bureaucracy, a privileged governing class. I do
not say that the historical reason for this was unjustified; and
certainly they gave invaluable service to their country. But the
discrimination between them and the others was a glaring fact
which was bound, some day, to cause trouble.

II

When the third Rajah proposed in 1945 to cede Sarawak to
the King, a large majority of the population accepted his decision. Almost unanimously the pagan tribesmen supported the
change, the Chinese overwhelmingly favoured it, and most of the
Melanaus did likewise. Malay opinion, on the other hand, was
divided. While most Malays remained indifferent to the issue,
one group of their leaders warmly approved cession and another
hotly opposed it.

The Malay critics of cession were moved by loyalty to the
Brooke régime, a feeling that Sarawak possessed an indepen-

dence under the Rajah which it would lose as a British colony, and innate conservatism which made them dislike any change at all. Some were apprehensive lest the privileged position which their community had so long enjoyed would disappear under the impartial, reforming British authority. This last reason perhaps explains why opposition to cession was largely confined to a section of Malays.

The views of the pro-cession Malays were voiced in the Council Negri by Datu Bandar, the young leader whom the reader has already met as my companion on a visit to the Land Dayaks on Singgi Mountain. They regretted deeply the passing of Brooke rule, but accepted the Rajah's argument that he could no longer command the financial resources or the trained staffs to give Sarawak modern progressive government. They wished their country to advance with the times, and had confidence in His Majesty's ability to rule with a benevolence equal and an experience superior to that of His Highness. They also showed a wise understanding of the racial problem in Sarawak. They disliked the opposition to cession of their fellow Malays which sprang from a desire to maintain Malay political privileges, for they realized that discrimination would sooner or later produce inter-communal friction. They foresaw that when the pagans awakened to the situation, they would resent it—and they knew that Dayak displeasure would not be an agreeable thing to encounter. Nor did they feel that the Chinese would remain forever content with a subordinate position in their country's administration. So they welcomed a change which would result in equal treatment for the various races, and in the gradual advancement of the capable Chinese and the intelligent pagans to positions of political partnership with the Malays.

The division of opinion between the two sections of the Malay population was unfortunate, but at first it did not seem to forebode evil. The debate on cession in the Council Negri engendered some heat, but afterwards controversy cooled. On the day of the transfer of sovereignty, leading representatives of every community assembled in the courthouse at Kuching to bid a regretful "Farewell" to the old order and a hopeful "Hail" to the new. It was a friendly inter-racial gathering. Those Malays who fervently disliked the change sensibly stayed away. They remained in their homes, peaceable citizens who formally expressed their discontent in a letter sent to me by their aged leader, the Datu Patinggi. No hostile demonstration was held in the crowded streets, and when I drove afterwards through the Malay kampongs many people waved in goodwill. It seemed as if the differences of opinion would be amicably composed.

But then the more zealous local anti-cession leaders organized a keen agitation, and later Mr. Anthony Brooke, the Rajah's nephew, sought to visit Sarawak to assess local opinion. I have expressed in an earlier chapter heartfelt understanding of his feelings, and I do not write in a critical spirit. He is a man of charm, sincerity and honour. During the difficulties which ensued he and I established friendly relations and a practice of discussing our dispute together like reasonable men, which helped to keep tempers within bounds and to lay the foundations of later agreement.

In the autumn of 1946 he left England by aeroplane for Sarawak. The anti-cessionists in Kuching jumped to wild conclusions and began to spread rumours. They said that it had been agreed by influential persons in London that cession should be rescinded and the Brookes restored. On this basis of fable, they invented various other fictions, asserting that Mr. Brooke would dismiss from their posts those who favoured cession, and reward with high office those who declared against it. In spite of government denials, these threats and promises had an effect among the more credulous Malays. Those who were timid wished to insure against loss if the threats proved justified, and there was some accretion of strength to the anti-cession movement. Another section of Malays attempted the delicate political acrobatic feat of "sitting on the fence". Nevertheless, Datu Bandar and his friends did not waver in their support for cession, and the Chinese, Melanau and pagan populations also maintained their opinions. Some long-house dwellers up-river, however, were confused by reports of Mr. Brooke's return, and their leaders urged action by the Government to establish beyond doubt that there would be no reversal of policy.

For this reason Mr. Brooke was forbidden to proceed to Sarawak, and his journey came to an abrupt end in Singapore. I need not write at length about the controversy which followed, nor retail the arguments and counter-arguments which continued between Mr. Brooke and the Government for the next few years. Had he been allowed to land in Kuching, there would have been danger of grave misunderstanding and disturbance of the peace. Some anti-cession leaders showed an unscrupulous capacity for spreading false rumours and exerting secret intimidation. They would have exploited his arrival to start a desperate Malay agitation, and up the rivers blood might have been spilled. I have already mentioned the occasion when Temonggong Koh, with the eager support of all his Iban penghulus, asked Arden-Clarke and me for permission to take the heads of Malay anti-cession propagandists who ventured up the Rejang. Among simple natives passion springs quickly, action is impulsive, and disaster may be unheralded and sudden.

So, to make clear that there would be no reversal of policy, the Government banned Mr. Brooke from Sarawak. The disappointed anti-cession faction in Kuching started a zealous campaign to get the ban lifted, and Mr. Brooke in Singapore naturally encouraged them. They wrote petitions to the Government and manifestos to the press, displayed posters in their kampongs and marched in procession through the streets. The rest of Kuching's population looked on tolerantly. The demonstrators whipped up the tempers of their supporters, but could arouse no wide popular response. The Government deliberately discouraged the pro-cession Malays from holding counter-demonstrations, to reduce the risk of physical clashes.

Believing that they could force the authorities to give way, the anti-cessionists intensified their agitation. They sent agents to centres like Sibu and Miri, and then farther afield, spreading reports that Mr. Brooke would shortly land in Sarawak, that cession would be rescinded and that the Rajah would be restored. These misrepresentations had some effect among Malays, and also in certain Moslem Melanau kampongs. In addition the fanatical anti-cession leaders recruited one or two detribalized Ibans living in Kuching, and quoted them as true spokesmen of the pagan peoples—a stratagem which made the representative up-river Iban chiefs metaphorically sharpen their parangs with rage. But the principal result of the campaign was a deplorable widening of the breach between the two sections of Malays.

It was sad to see the vicious rift which developed between them, and the growing threat of pagan and Chinese hostility to the Malays. By now the earlier apprehension of some natives that British colonial administration might interfere with their well-being had disappeared. The promises made to them were being kept. Their ancient customs and familiar ways of life were respected. The English Governor was like a new Rajah to them, travelling up the rivers, staying in their long-houses, and discussing their local problems with them over glasses of rice-wine and puffs of native tobacco. Peace reigned. Conditions had improved steadily since their liberation from the Japanese, and in some ways the up-river people were already better off than they had been even under the Rajahs. For the first time government schools were being built for their children, for the first time pagans were being regularly appointed as Native Officers, and for the first time pagan chieftains were being thoroughly consulted about state policy. After their initial experience of British rule, the mood of the people of the jungle had changed from passive acquiescence at cession to enthusiastic confidence in it. They believed heartily in the King's rule.

Outside the main centres of population the Malays, too, had at first been happy under the new régime. In every place that I visited during the first six months after cession, they joined freely with the pagans and Chinese in cordial celebrations. Then the anti-cession agitation developed, and the scene changed. I saw the first sign of it in a Malay kampong on the outskirts of Kuching. Knowing that I was to visit the place that afternoon, the propagandists against cession went there in the morning and stuck posters bearing hostile slogans in some gardens. "No Cession", "Sarawak Natives Want the Rajah Muda", "We Want Brooke, not Bureaucracy", they proclaimed.

For several months afterwards such posters were liable to appear when the Governor or I visited Malay and some Melanau villages. Sometimes the local Malays stoutly refused to put them up. This needed courage, for if other methods failed, the agitators were apt to employ intimidation. So they often got their way. Their placards stood beside the kampong paths, bearing always the same three or four slogans. Occasionally the posters did not represent the sentiments of any of the villagers. In one hamlet which I visited a large display of them, scrawled as usual in English, plastered the kampong walls. Knowing that no one in the place could read or write a word of English, the District Officer enquired whence they came. The headman replied that youths from a near by town had kindly brought them that morning. When the District Officer asked whether he knew what was written on them, he answered in the affirmative with a happy smile. On being asked to translate one, he answered in Malay, "Welcome to His Excellency the Governor-General". The ingenious propagandists had secured the ready consent of the villagers to covering their huts with slogans on the understanding that they all conveyed heartfelt greetings to their visitor.

In other places Malays explained to us that they did not wish the placards to be displayed, but that they could not refuse. Some anti-cession enthusiasts in their kampong insisted on this demonstration on their private plots of ground. These people, we were told, said that Anthony Brooke would soon arrive in Sarawak, and that he would punish anyone who did not espouse his cause. Local residents who interfered with the posters would be marked down as enemies, to be dealt with when the day of reckoning came.

For some time the Government did not prohibit these exhibitions. They seemed to do no harm, since everyone in the kampongs understood how far they represented the true feelings of the people. But at the same time the authorities discouraged their Malay and Melanau supporters from putting up counter-posters, to avoid any risk of free fights between members of the factions. Later, however, the patience of the pro-cessionists became exhausted. They refused to tolerate any longer their opponents' monopoly of this form of political self-expression. When the Governor and I went on tour after that we encountered two sets of contradictory placards facing each other in the villages, like appeals by rival candidates in a parliamentary election. One set reiterated the old formulas, "No Cession",

"We Want Brooke, not Bureaucracy" and the like, while the other proclaimed such sentiments as "We Love Cession", "Down with Brooke" and "God Save the King". Sometimes these conflicting declarations stood side by side in neighbouring gardens or even on the same piece of ground, for in places the schism had elements of tragedy. Families became bitterly divided, fathers opposed sons, brothers quarrelled with brothers, and good friends suddenly refused to speak to one another. Feeling on both sides ran high.

After that the Government forbade the display of posters by either party. The decision came none too soon. Shortly before its enforcement I visited Kanowit. The little settlement was *en fête* for the occasion, and crowds of Chinese towkays from the bazaar, Ibans from the surrounding country, Malays from the kampong and children from the schools gathered on the river bank to greet me. Other Malays remained sullenly in their houses, and in front of their dwellings stood the customary protesting notices. The Ibans saw them, and asked curiously what was written on them. When they learned that the billboards bore anti-cession slogans, they grew angry, invaded the kampong in force, tore the offending objects from the ground and hurled them into the river.

After a while the anti-cession campaign ceased to make fresh converts, and then it gradually lost some of its supporters. The local leaders' promises came home to roost. They had asserted confidently that Mr. Brooke would soon arrive in Sarawak, that the Privy Council in London would undo cession, that the Rajah's reign would be resumed, and that anti-cession stalwarts would then receive the reward of high office. In an excess of zeal they made the mistake of announcing a date on which Mr. Brooke would land in Kuching. When the day arrived but he did not, they let it be known that owing to circumstances over which they had no control the event had been postponed, and promptly declared another date for it two or three weeks later. When that occasion also passed without any sign of the visitor, they swore positively that he would appear on a certain morning a fortnight afterwards. When for a third time they proved mistaken, once more, completely unabashed, they promised their

supporters that they would produce Mr. Brooke on another day
to be announced in due course. Their adherents began to feel
disillusioned.

I do not for a moment deny or belittle their sincerity. They
were men in deadly earnest exerting their right to espouse a cause
in which they passionately believed. They sought to advance it by
peaceful, constitutional means; so they were naturally left free by
the authorities to pursue their eager campaign. But they had the
misfortune to be a minority seeking an aim which was impossible of achievement, since the rest of the population opposed it.
They suffered the frustration which all such single-minded groups
must experience in a democratic state, where the will of the
majority prevails.

III

Some supporters of the movement did not believe in constitutional methods for achieving their ends. They were fanatics with
a burning faith, and a few were ready to go to the stake for the
cause. When the anti-cessionists' prospects began to fade, their
sense of defeat must have been painful in the extreme. In the
bosoms of some, disappointed personal ambition fed the fires
of fury.

Led by one such individual, a small group in Sibu was driven
to a mad course. Their chief was a forceful, unscrupulous character called Awang Rambli bin Amit, with a Napoleon complex
and a capacity for spell-binding. He was thirty-seven years old.
All his associates were Malays, and most of them were young men
in their twenties, political adolescents in the first flush of half-
baked, heroic enthusiasms. Numbering a baker's dozen, they
gave themselves the luckless title "The Society of Thirteen".
Meeting secretly in an obscure place, they bound themselves together by a solemn vow, and plotted murder. It was to be no
ordinary murder.

The period of gestation of their conspiracy was more than
a year. During that time various events occurred in Sarawak,
including a change of Governor. By his firm, constructive and
humane administration of the infant colony Charles Arden-

Clarke had earned high opinions everywhere, and in 1949 was promoted to the difficult post of Governor of the Gold Coast, where he has been distinguishing himself ever since.

In his place in Kuching came Mr. Duncan Stewart, one of the ablest of the younger men of high promise in the Colonial Service. New to the East, he came with refreshing, almost school-boy zest to be the chief servant of the peoples of Sarawak. His wife and three children were to join him later.

After a fortnight in Kuching, to meet leading personalities in the capital, he started on tour. First he went to Sibu, the peace-ful administrative headquarters of the Third Division. The citizens turned out in the customary crowd to welcome him. When he landed from his launch the sun shone brightly, sparkling on the gold facings of his tropical uniform as a light breeze played with the cocks' feathers on his gubernatorial helmet. He inspected a guard of honour of policemen, exchanged a few words with the principal government officials, shook hands with a row of Malay, Chinese, European and Iban dignitaries, and admired the exotic costumes of the women from the long-houses. Then it was the school children's turn to be reviewed. They raised their tiny hands in salute and their small voices in song as he walked along their ranks.

When he came to the end of their line a young schoolmaster stumbled forward, as if to throw himself humbly at the Gover-nor's feet. John Barcroft, who walked behind His Excellency, remarked afterwards that he thought the youth had fainted. As he fell, however, he plunged a dagger into Mr. Stewart's side. Another lad ran forward and would have struck the Governor a second knife-blow, had not an onlooker grabbed and held him.

The attack was over in an instant. As policemen took charge of the assailants, Mr. Stewart walked towards a platform erected for speech-making, indicating that he wished the ceremony to proceed without fuss. He held one hand to his side, as if in pain. Then the spectators saw his white glove turn red with blood, and his robust figure stumble and collapse.

It was December 3rd, 1949. Hurriedly the Governor was taken to Sibu hospital, where the local doctor examined him, discovered grievous wounds, performed a successful emergency operation, and sent an SOS to Singapore for the highest medical aid. Next morning Professor Meikie, a skilled surgeon, flew to Sibu. After studying the patient's condition he decided to fly him to Singapore, where he could receive more thorough care than was possible with the limited resources of Sibu's hospital staff. The party made the journey that afternoon.

I met their seaplane when it alighted at the Royal Air Force station at Seletar. Meikie said that I could speak a few words with Stewart on his stretcher, before orderlies took him to a waiting ambulance. Knowing from the facts of the case how desperately ill he was, I was astonished by the calm cheerfulness on his face as I greeted him. I spoke some sentences of encouragement, and he responded with a grin. He thanked me, and then in a matter-of-fact way referred to the attack at Sibu. I saw his smile broaden as he added, "You know, in some ways it was awfully funny. I must tell you about it when we next meet."

We never did meet again. That afternoon Meikie said that the Governor had a chance of recovery, but that the odds were heavily against him. On the next day the surgeon performed a further operation, and Stewart's sturdy response to the ordeal permitted cautious optimism. Meikie told me that if he survived the next two or three days, that would be all to the good, but that the period of gravest danger would be immediately afterwards, when he might suffer a relapse.

It turned out exactly as Meikie prophesied. For a few days, by sheer strength of spirit, Duncan Stewart kept himself alive. His wife arrived by aeroplane from England in time to spend brief periods with him before the end. Then the relapse came with fatal vehemence, and on December 10th, exactly a week after he was stabbed, the Governor died.

IV

Every detail of this senseless assassination was wicked, and most cruel of all was the choice of Duncan Stewart as its victim. Many government officials had been concerned with the policy in Sarawak to which the malcontents objected, but he was not one of them. Indeed, he was the only person in Sarawak who had nothing whatever to do with it. He was new to the country, new to the Far East, new to Asia. Until a month before he had never been within many thousand miles of Sibu, and he was completely free from the slightest responsibility for anything that had ever happened there. Yet on him the political maniacs wreaked their vengeance.

Another feature of transcendent horror in the crime was that none of the principal leaders of the Society of Thirteen themselves committed the murder. Instead Awang Rambli induced two young schoolteachers, Rosli bin Dhobie, aged nineteen, and Morshidi bin Sedik, aged twenty-five, to perpetrate it for them. Rosli, who inflicted the fatal stab, was not even a member of the Society. Evidence given at their trial showed the heartless way in which Rambli persuaded these impressionable, irresponsible youths to do the deed, using a mixture of flattery that through criminal violence they would become national heroes, and of threats that if their courage failed, they might themselves be killed. It is one of the sorriest tales even in the annals of murder.

I need not dwell further on these aspects of the subject. They appear fully in the records of the trials of Rosli and Morshidi for murder, and of Rambli and his colleagues of the Society of Thirteen for conspiracy to murder. After hearings before a District Judge, with a mixed group of Malay, Chinese and Iban assessors, the two youths were found guilty of murder and the members of the Society were convicted of abetment.

Rosli, Morshidi, Rambli and another particularly vicious member of the Society were hanged, and the rest were condemned to long terms of imprisonment.

V

The knife that slew the Governor killed the anti-cession movement. The responsible leaders of that movement had, of course, nothing to do with the conspiracy. That was proved beyond a shadow of doubt in the trials. The anti-cession chiefs were passionately devoted to their cause, but they adopted only lawful means to forward it. Some zealous spirits among them might have been tempted to resort now and then to minor forms of physical disturbance of the peace, to draw dramatic attention to their little crusade, but Mr. Brooke sent insistent messages from Singapore that his followers must employ only methods compatible with democratic British political practices. His personal influence was probably decisive in keeping the anti-cession agitation within proper constitutional bounds.

Nevertheless, Rambli and his associates had posed in Sibu as local representatives of the anti-cession cause, and their criminal irresponsibility dealt a blow to the movement from which it never recovered. The Malay public was profoundly shocked by the tragedy. Many anti-cessionists, realizing suddenly the danger which excessive emotion in politics could bring, lost interest in the barren campaign. The leaders retained their loyalty to their principles, but they lost their following.

In March 1951, when the international situation looked dark and Britain was faced with a possibility of war, Anthony Brooke visited me with proposals for an amicable settlement of the cession controversy. He asked whether the Government would declare that its policy in Sarawak was steady progress towards self-rule, and that the people of the country would eventually be free to choose their own form of government within the Commonwealth, including, if they so desired, a restoration of a Rajah Brooke. He said he believed that his friends in Sarawak would in return agree to end their anti-cession campaign, express loyalty to the King, and co-operate in all things with the administration. He asked also that, if accord on this basis were possible, the authorities in Kuching would welcome the help of their previous opponents.

Neither the Governor in Kuching, nor I in Singapore, nor Ministers in London felt any difficulty about accepting these common-sense suggestions, most of which were already our declared policy. On his side Mr. Brooke proved as good as his word, and a few weeks later the anti-cession movement came to a formal end. The different factions in the Malay community were once more gladly reconciled, and they were soon united again with their fellow citizens of other races in forwarding the interests of their common homeland. That was a most timely event, for the Malays are a vital element in Sarawak's mixed population, and their ripe experience, gentlemanly qualities, and fervent patriotism have a great part to play in the country's future.

The incidents here related were perhaps less manifestations of a temper produced by a local situation in Sarawak than reflections of the dark side of a mood which in recent years has animated all Asia. We live in a generation when one of the gigantic events of history is occurring—the emergence of many new Asian nations, freeing themselves not only from foreign colonial rule but also from "feudal" social systems. It is a period of vast readjustment, of nothing less than revolution on a continental scale. In several countries the change has taken place peacefully, but in others there have been strife and bloodshed, and in all there are impatient political groups who wish the changes to go either farther or faster, and who advocate forceful methods to achieve their ends. These sinister elements are a source of immense danger, for if they were to prevail, reawakened Asia would be cast backwards into a period of savage reaction, not forwards into an era of civilized progress.

It was a grim commentary on the infectious nature of the violent creeds which they and their like preach that a sudden, harsh echo of their strident yells was heard even in remote and peaceful Sarawak. That small land, where most people are still so simple and content that little has yet been spoken of the grand aspirations for political freedom and economic uplift which impel the rest of Asia, nevertheless had a sudden, momentary, bitter taste of political terrorism. It is a reminder that in the modern world no country is insulated against the good or evil influences abroad, and that in Sarawak as elsewhere the Government's policy must be wise and good if the great changes which are inevitable in our time are to be tranquilly achieved.

PART SIX

ENVOI

CHAPTER TWENTY

FAREWELL TO FRIENDS

I

A FEW YEARS HAVE PASSED since my last visit to Temonggong Koh recorded in an earlier chapter, and since my expedition to stay with Temonggong Tama Weng at Long San. On more recent occasions I have several times seen my Iban, Kayan and Kenyah friends.

In February, 1953, I travelled again up the Rejang. Denis White was the Resident, and he and I made the journey from Sibu to Song in a brand-new speedboat which he had just acquired. It raced over the distance in three hours instead of the customary six, so the pagans are not the only people in Sarawak who are beguiled by the craze called Progress. British officials, too, are providing themselves with some of the smart toys of mechanized civilization.

From Song we proceeded to Kapit in more leisurely style, taking an old-fashioned launch. The change was pleasant. Sitting on its quiet deck after crouching in the spluttering speedboat was like enjoying the company of an elderly, well-bred gentleman after consorting with a vulgar young upstart.

The afternoon was windless, the river flowed as smooth as polished marble, and tens of thousands of newly-hatched mayflies skimmed its surface. These frolicsome creatures acted as magnets to the fish below, which rose in large numbers to snap at them, and the fish in their turn attracted human sportsmen. Many natives lurked in prahus to catch them as they fed. So Nature's eternal cycle of life and death was enacted before our eyes—thousands of mayflies feeding on tinier insects in the air above the water, hundreds of fish rising to swallow the flies for their own sustenance, and scores of men killing the fish for their cooking pots. Only the Iban hunters were not a prey immediately to larger monsters, their deaths being postponed until some Greater Will decreed their hour.

The fishermen showed brilliant skill. Several prahus loitered in every stretch of the river. In each were two men, one squatting in the bow to dip a paddle when required, and the other standing in the stern with a spear held ready for attack. The poise of the latter figure had dramatic quality. For long periods he stood taut and tense, like a statue of an athlete holding a javelin above one shoulder, while his eyes searched the water for a glimpse of his victim below. Suddenly his body woke into violent, momentary action, his hand shifting to take swift aim and his arm lunging forward to hurl the weapon at its target. He did not stab the spear like a dagger into the fish, but cast it through the air like a harpoon. Tipped with three small prongs, it flew several feet through space, then plunged into the river and stayed quivering, its shaft protruding and swaying slightly in response to the death agony of the creature it impaled.

The men's perpetually faultless aim was uncanny. Several times I watched a weapon thrown, and every time it found its mark. The water was muddy, and the sportsman could not have seen his prey until it had almost reached the surface to catch a fly. Only a fraction of a second then remained before it would turn tail and disappear again, but in that infinitesimal fragment of time he measured its distance, took his aim, hurled his spear and made his kill. No modern precision instrument is more accurate than the practised eye of primitive man.

We reached Kapit at dusk, and went ashore to view its latest sights. The little settlement's central shopping square was now surrounded on three sides by imposing, brightly-lit emporia. A throng of Ibans, Chinese and Malays wandered along the pavements, inspecting the stocks of articles for sale, exchanging the day's gossip and enjoying the cool evening air. Kapit was becoming a hectic little metropolis. I learned that to its new shops, school and church would soon be added a plush-seated cinema.

Next morning we left in long-boats for the Balleh, to visit first Jugah's house on the Merirai. When we arrived we received a tumultuous welcome from the chief and his people. Our old friends were in good health and gay spirits, and some congenial new acquaintances had arrived on the scene. Siah, for example, introduced me to her son John, a youngster seven months old. She was a proud and happy mother, as well she might be, for he was a lively, laughing infant who could already crawl astonishing distances over the long-house floor. Unlike Siah, Sani had not succeeded in producing an offspring of her own, but she had adopted a tiny daughter who also added babyish gurgles to the usual medley of noises in the crowded house.

So Siah and Sani were now occupied with maternal as well as wifely duties. They were as sweet-looking as ever, but family responsibilities added a touch of seriousness to the character in their faces. No longer the unattached, carefree belles of the household, they had graduated to a somewhat higher station in the feminine hierarchy. Their younger sister, Anchang, succeeded them as the most eligible and beautiful of the unmarried girls. Wearing a tiara of flowers on her head and the traditional Iban maiden's gala costume, she filled the position with lovely distinction.

Jugah's sons Linggi and Alo were at home for the holidays. In contrast to Siah's, Sani's and Anchang's native Bornean dress, they wore modern Western clothes. It was strange to reflect that the five were sisters and brothers, for their attire seemed to separate them by generations as well as continents. Linggi and Alo were now conspicuously attractive teen-age boys, pleasant-looking, neatly dressed and well behaved—eloquent tributes to the excellence of Baughman's teaching of his pupils at Kapit.

Jugah himself was flourishing, and told me of his expanding commercial concerns. He was now engaged in the wholesale business of selling rubber for native smallholders, as well as in the retail trade in consumer goods in his shops at Kapit and the Ga'at. The District Council was the licensing authority for dealings in rubber, and its Iban members were trying to eliminate the Chinese from this branch of activity on the rivers above Kapit. The move was an example of the clash of economic interests between the established Chinese and the awakening Ibans which will be a feature of Sarawak life in the coming generation. No doubt the conflict will be settled by some mutually satisfactory compromise.

In the meantime the native chiefs were not doing badly. Jugah confided to me that from his various enterprises he made profits of $12,000 in 1950 and $8,000 in 1951. The final figure for 1952 was not yet computed, but the three years' surplus had enabled him to repay already the whole loan on his shop-house in Kapit. He owned that establishment jointly with Sibat and Grinang, but was the majority shareholder. The reader knows how Grinang's earlier business went into liquidation; that merry penghulu had not since attempted another one-man venture. Temonggong Koh, Sibat, Rabong and Tedong, however, all owned stores in Kapit or elsewhere. Some were under direct Iban management, others were rented to Chinese, and all contributed to the economic advancement of the chiefs and their households. The ambitious Ibans were on the march.

Since then further modern developments have affected their lives. One of the most remarkable is the Government's installation of wireless sets in the long-houses, whose inmates now listen delightedly to broadcast programmes of news and entertainment in various local tongues. Temonggong Koh, Penghulu Grinang and other authorities on native affairs have gone to Kuching to talk to their people over the microphone; and Siah, now recognized as the best pantun singer in the land, has also made a jaunt to Radio Sarawak to record her songs for transmission through the jungle air. No popular stars in the world are more natural artists, or less spoiled by sudden fame.

II

From Jugah's house we returned down the Merirai and continued up the Balleh to Koh's home. The Temonggong and his family waited at the water's edge to receive us.

"Tabeh anak!" the old man called to me across the water as my temoi approached, just as an American father might cry, "Hi, son!"

At the august age of eighty-one he was easily the senior native on the Rejang in years as well as in rank and honours. That afternoon he looked remarkably hale, and throughout our two days' stay he remained in hearty form. His spry appearance owed

something to large brass ear-rings polished to jewel-like brightness
in his ears, a result of the recent arrival of the first tin of Brasso
on the Balleh. Inordinately proud of them, he frequently un-
hooked them, gave them an extra shine, and then replaced them
in his lobes. He wore an assortment of sartorial fashions, a Malay
turban, a European singlet, a Kayan necklace, and an Iban sirat.

His fitness was a mark of the extraordinarily strong physical
constitution of this survival from the age of head-hunting. Still
in possession of all his faculties, his firm step was so stately that
I exclaimed, "He walks like a king!" His hearing was excellent,
as he frequently demonstrated by ready participation in any
conversation; and his sight was good. When he looked around
him, his unspectacled eyes focussed immediately on whatever
object he wished to see, without the initial vague peerings which
often characterize the gaze of old men. As for his appetite, he
could eat and drink with as much enjoyment as anyone.

He admitted that he occasionally had "off" days, when he
felt "very weak". Especially he complained that he was sometimes tired after several hours' hunting wild pig in difficult jungle.
I wondered how many men even twenty years younger would
so much as dream of engaging in such a gruelling occupation.

The fact was that Koh was almost incredibly tough. One
afternoon during our visit a group of us sat talking in the gallery.
He lolled in a wicker chair, puffing a cigarette and reminiscing
about ancient days in Sarawak. Suddenly his seat tipped back
too far, and he crashed to the floor. His head hit the ground with
a sickening thud which made Segura scream and all of us rise
in alarm. But a grinning Koh picked himself up, rolled a new
cigarette, lit it and resumed the conversation where it had been
interrupted. He was as youthful an octogenarian as ever lived.

Iba and Mindun were their old selves, the former reserved and
wise, the latter vivacious and witty. Kanyan, on the other hand,
was a changed person. Now in his fifteenth year, his boyish
bumptiousness had disappeared. He no longer behaved as the
spoiled, privileged son of a great temonggong, but conducted
himself in a modest, friendly way towards everyone in the house,
seeming inspired with the thought that the first duty of a chief's
son is to be the servant of others in his home. He kept offering

us drinks and tobacco, fetching things for us, and generally attending upon our needs. This he did with an unassuming grace which was engaging, and particularly impressive when one remembered the conceited, selfish child he used to be. Clearly his transformation was not due to any change in his upbringing, for he was still the adored darling of his father and family. It could only be a result of his training at school, further testimony to the admirable education which Baughman gave to the young Ibans who came under his charge.

That the influence of this teaching spread far beyond the limits imposed by the numbers of Baughman's own pupils was well illustrated in Koh's house. Two months earlier a local government school had been opened in a small building raised beside the dwelling. Segura's husband, Seggei, was its master, and the scholars were a score of boys and half a dozen girls from the house. Though most of the other children in the community were still traditional three-quarters naked Ibans, these were all clad in sophisticated attire. The boys modelled themselves on Kanyan, with short-cropped hair, white cricket shirts and neat trousers. Nor was his example confined to sartorial fashions. His quiet, friendly manners were also being emulated by his young admirers.

Seggei was naturally an exponent of the modern style in dress and behaviour. I looked with particular interest on Segura's husband, and was able to talk easily with him, for his command of English was quite good. An unassuming, studious young man with an attractive, somewhat refined face, he was a product of down-river Iban society. Physically less robust but intellectually more advanced than the jungle natives with whom he now lived, he seemed to that extent rather out of place among them. Often when they squatted in the gallery to engage in vulgar rustic gossip, he sat apart reading a magazine or scribbling notes for his classes. He was earnest in his desire to improve himself, and to fulfil his mission to uplift his pupils. Perhaps he was over-earnest. His sense of humour was not conspicuous, and that fact, too, created a slight barrier between him and his companions, for one of their outstanding qualities was a boundless capacity for fun.

Nevertheless, they respected him highly for his educational attainments, and regarded his measure of aloofness as natural, since he had acquired a degree of culture to which they could not themselves aspire, but which they hoped that he would impart to their children. Above all he was an essentially decent and sincere character, anxious to be helpful to everyone. The only person in the house who could write, he sometimes spent hours going from room to room, squatting on the floor with a scribbling-pad propped on his knees, composing letters which parents, wives or sweethearts dictated for absent members of their families fighting the terrorists in Malaya.

His qualities were wholly at Segura's service. He was a devoted, thoughtful husband, possibly a little mystified by her impetuous, emotional temperament, so different from his own, but adapting himself prudently to many of her whims so that their partnership might be tranquil and happy.

Nor did she seem dissatisfied. When she greeted me on my arrival her smile expressed not only the welcome of a warm friend but the calm of a contented woman. At some remark a moment later she burst into laughter, perhaps less carefree and exuberant than of old, but none the less spontaneous and gay. I gained an impression that, after all the romantic thrills and uncertainties of earlier episodes in her life, she had accepted with relief a state of matrimonial security—like a small boat which, after tossing on an exhilarating but dangerous sea, enters at last the quiet waters of a safe harbour.

Her beauty was still evident, but had suffered a change which shocked me. She was thin, a mere shadow of her earlier self. I learned then for the first time that she had been very ill when her baby was born—a daughter now six months old. The child's delivery was extremely difficult, and afterwards poor Segura ailed for a long time, seeming to find it impossible to recover her strength. Now she was much better, but her figure was wasted, her face pinched and her liveliness tempered by a certain listlessness which sprang from weakness of body, not of spirit.

Between her and Seggei a comfortable comradeship existed, and their infant, Daisy, was a strong bond between them. Seggei was a proud father, always ready to take a hand in fastening nappies, filling milk bottles and performing other parental duties. Segura was usually indulgent to her child, flying to Daisy's cradle when she whimpered in her sleep, playing with her happily during her waking hours, and taking great trouble about her feeding, clothing and welfare. Occasionally, however, a little difference of opinion arose between the mother and daughter. Daisy had inherited more of Segura's strong, impulsive nature than of Seggei's calm, amenable disposition, and sometimes she sought obstinately to gain her way in opposition to some notion of her mother's. Then Segura's wilfulness also was provoked, and she would shake or smack her offspring. The more she asserted her authority, the more Daisy's spirit revolted, and the two were soon involved in a vicious little quarrel. It was charmingly reminiscent of the earlier situation between Segura and her father, when old Koh sought to counter her rebelliousness by an exercise of paternal tyranny.

Segura was thus much occupied with maternal duties. In the long-house she also fulfilled all her obligations as a daughter of the chief, the wife of an important person, and a sister with the other women. She had settled back completely into life in an up-river Iban home, bearing her share of all the feminine activities, toiling hard at innumerable domestic tasks, and taking part in any fun that was afoot. The fact that she was no longer alone in wearing modern dress made a great difference to her ease. She had ceased to be an individual apart, a freak, almost an alien in the household. Once more she assumed her rightful place among her own people.

Some months later she, Seggei and Daisy came to stay with me for two weeks in Singapore, Segura to see a doctor about her illness, Seggei to visit the bookstores and buy some primers for his school, and Daisy because neither of them would leave their precious child behind. The clinical report on Segura was satisfactory. If she took a certain medicine, she would put on weight again, recover her health, and be her old self. At the end of her visit she returned to the Balleh armed with bottles of physic and fortified by the hope which they gave her. She also took the latest model of a Singer sewing machine, to help in the making of Daisy's dresses.

So Segura's story was not to end in tragedy after all. The comedy, the pleasantness and the happiness of life had returned to her, combined with the deeper seriousness which attaches to all young human beings as they mature and assume the responsibilities of manhood or womanhood. It did not seem only six years since I first set eyes on her as a small girl in savage nakedness performing the pagan rites of a primitive people.*

III

The second day of my stay in Koh's home was a Sunday. In this great Christian household it was not, however, celebrated by a church service. Instead the Temonggong organized a heathen ceremony. He staged a begawai. With its series of propitiations of the spirits, precautions against interference by hobgoblins, endless bedaras, oft-reiterated pantuns and jumble of superstitious ballyhoo, it seemed to me identical with all the similar performances which I had witnessed before Koh, his family and followers were solemnly baptized.

The only good Christian in the house appeared to be Segura's infant daughter. When she caught sight of the rows of small bedara dishes set precisely on the floor, Daisy crawled to them, trampled playfully on several, picked up others and threw them away, and scattered the feast for the evil spirits. The incident would have seemed to some observers an example of God speaking through the actions of a little child, but old Koh was not struck by that thought. In a huff he ordered Daisy to be kept under severe restraint, and a fresh lot of bedara dishes to be laid upon the floor.

He had not the slightest idea what Christianity meant, nor what beliefs it entailed in its adherents. Some of his younger colleagues were more enlightened. They understood that the old order was crumbling, and for them the ancient ceremonies now had, partially at least, a new meaning. Chief among them was Penghulu Jugah. His consciousness of the need for change, his prudent adaptability, and his sincere respect for the teachings

* Segura has since had a second child, and she, Seggei and their youngsters are all flourishing.

of his friend Baughman had made him by now a devout Methodist.

Realizing that I might be astonished to see the traditional pagan rites performed unaltered, he remarked to me, "We can only introduce Christianity slowly among the Iban people."

He explained that their animist beliefs were deeply rooted and could not easily be disturbed. Conversion to novel ideas must be a gradual process accomplished step by step.

"First we're trying to persuade our followers to smoke less and drink less," he observed. "Then we'll try to curb the amount of adultery among them."

I presumed that he referred to the hallowed system of trial marriages between Iban youths and girls.

"The changes in ideas and beliefs," he continued, "will take longer than the changes in habits. For most of these people a bedara is still an act of appeasement of the evil spirits, and for long it'll remain so. But I and a few others now regard it as an offering to our Christian God."

As usual, the ceremonial lasted all day, and far into the night. Indeed, for a special reason on this occasion, the final act of celebration was maintained ceaselessly till the next morning. The revered Temonggong Koh was growing very old. Everyone realized that he might not remain with us long on this earth. His migration to another world was a matter of almost momentary expectation. The household was conscious of his impending departure, and spoke with sad resignation of its inevitability. Koh himself awaited the event with calm philosophy, his thoughts now dwelling as much on his future in the next world as on his present in this.

He believed that this begawai was probably his last; so it was designed as an act of supplication to the pagan gods to ensure that his reception by them would be cordial. Its climax was an all-night wake by chanting medicine men pleading with the spirits that his passage from earth to heaven should be peaceful. They reckoned that if their performance continued without cease from dusk to dawn, such earnestness would make a favourable impression on the holy ones.

As the twilight shadows deepened through the house, pagan worthies gathered for their astonishing feat of piety. Forty men assembled in a group in the gallery, then divided into a dozen different parties. The leader of each was an elder practised in the arts of heathen voodoo, and the other members were youths who had volunteered for these especially sacred rites. They were dressed, or undressed, in traditional work-a-day native fashion, with an occasional bizarre headgear to lend a touch of magnificence to their otherwise austere garb. Many carried long wooden staves like wands of office in their hands, some of them crowned with clusters of small bells.

The parties distributed themselves along the gallery, extending its whole length. An interested crowd of natives watched their mustering, and women brought drinks to fortify the performers for their ordeal. Darkness had now fallen, and only a few hurricane lamps spaced along the rafters illumined the chamber's gloom.

Of a sudden the leading medicine man struck his stave with a thud upon the floor and raised his voice in wailing. His moan turned gradually into a chant. For a few moments he sang alone, his stave beating the ground with thumping blows which gave rhythm to his tune. Then all the leaders lifted their voices in unison, repeating exactly his words and harmony, and striking the floor with their wands. The bells on the staves tinkled at every blow.

At that all the troupes of pagan priests and acolytes began to move. With slow, mournful tread they marched along the gallery, their steps keeping time with the beats of the staves. Their footfall was silent, for their feet were bare, but the thuds of wooden sticks hitting the floor with monotonous regularity made their progress sound like the tramp of a booted army, and the singing added an accompaniment of dirge-like music reminiscent of a funeral march.

As each band reached the end of the gallery it wheeled and retraced its steps all the way to the opposite end of the house, then turned once more and repeated the journey. This they did over and over again, covering the length of the house first a dozen times, then a score of times, and finally hundreds of times as the night wore on. They were like a constant procession of successive units in a parade, passing and repassing each other repeatedly. The beat of their staves set the time for their stepping, sometimes echoing loud and sometimes softly as the leaders varied the force of their blows on the ground, so that the thudding rose and fell as the tolling of a bell might grow alternately strong and faint in a fitful breeze wafting its strokes this way and that.

The volume of sound was also varied by periodic modulations in the men's singing. Their chant followed a set, oft-repeated pattern. First one voice in each group trilled a few phrases, then that voice fell silent while another carolled a response, and then all the men joined in a resounding chorus. It was a mournful tune, though melodious. Sometimes it had a note of earnest persuasion, sometimes of confident request and sometimes of desperate imprecation as the parading priests invited, prayed and implored the all-powerful gods to grant their leader Koh a safe translation from his mortal life to celestial companionship with them.

All night the marching and counter-marching, the solo incantations and choral responses, the stave-thumping and bell-tinkling continued, perpetually, monotonously, religiously. How the men could endure the test I do not know. Their feet never stopped trudging, their staves never ceased thudding and their voices never faltered in chanting for eleven hours. Yet they grew neither tired nor hoarse. Their limbs seemed as lively and their singing as lusty when dawn broke as they had been when dusk fell the night before.

They were aided by the women, for naturally they required occasional sustenance during this exacting vigil. A bite of food and a sip of drink now and then as they tramped and sang would enable them to maintain the effort without flagging; so their wives, sisters and daughters stayed up all night to serve them. Thus a large part of the population of the house did not go to bed at all, but remained awake in the gallery, chattering, playing games, drinking and singing pantuns to pass the time. Prominent in the company was the author, the *raison d'être* of these goings-on,

Koh himself. He never closed an eye or went to rest, but sat upright in his chair all night, puffing cigarettes and observing with a detached air the ceremony held in honour of his impending death.

My endurance was not so good. I tired early in the evening, and at midnight went to bed. I must have been extraordinarily weary for, in spite of the terrific din, I soon fell asleep. For some hours I remained oblivious to my surroundings, but at four o'clock in the morning woke. At once the noise in the gallery broke like a thunderstorm upon my ears. The trudging of marching men, the singing of pagan priests, the droning of women's pantuns, the mumble of many conversations, and the occasional roars of unrestrained laughter gradually disentangled themselves, one from the other, in my reviving consciousness, and reminded me where I was.

For a while I lay listening, fascinated, almost hypnotized by the medley of sounds. Then, drawn irresistibly to it, I rose and went into the gallery. A yell of welcome greeted me from a party opposite my door, where Iba, Mindun, their husbands and a dozen other revellers squatted in a circle, playing an Iban game like hunt-the-slipper. I joined them for an hour of the sport.

Then I withdrew to bed again. But sleep was now difficult. As often as I dozed off, the mixture of stamping and chanting, chattering and shouting, humming and laughing roused me again. I began to count the number of thumps which the priests' staves made on the floor, hoping that this exercise, like counting sheep, would induce slumber. But it had no success. I was too conscious that the staves did not belong to sheep but to men, that the men were my friends, and that they recited their incantations to ensure a happy departure from this earth—from the beautiful, wild Balleh—of my adopted father, Koh. And I began to grieve that after my departure that day I might never see the old man again. Then I marvelled at the loyalty, the love which all his people concentrated on him, making them, in mixed grief at his approaching death and joy at his impending glory, perform all night these extraordinary antics. And when I reflected on their conduct I found myself wondering how many miles the medicine men had strolled since the previous night. They had begun their journey at dusk, before seven o'clock in the evening, and now it was past five the next day; so they had already walked without halt for ten hours. Their pace was slow; they could not be covering more than a mile and a half every hour. That meant that each man had walked something like twelve and a half miles. There were forty men, which meant that between them they had done about five hundred miles. Had I got that right? Drowsily I began to do the multiplication again, and then for some illogical reason changed the calculation to an attempt to reckon how many verses of their interminable saga they had sung to the long-house rafters. This arithmetical problem so numbed, fuddled and stupefied my mental powers that I yawned, turned over and fell asleep.

I was roused from a deep coma by the explosion of a gun. The first cannon-shot was followed by a second, and then by a third and a fourth. They came from the verandah. Half dreaming, I wondered whether we were being attacked by enemy head-hunters; but light-hearted hoots of laughter outside my door reassured me.

For a few moments the persistent tramping of pagan pandits continued undiminished, then suddenly ceased. Deep silence followed. Not a whisper or footfall disturbed it, as if the whole household had suddenly fallen asleep—or dead.

I opened my eyes and saw the pale light of morning glimmering through a small window in the roof. Then I understood that the cannon-shots were a salute to dawn, a signal that another day had come, and that the people's wake was over. The Ibans' devotions were complete, the classic rites had been fulfilled, the gods should be satisfied. Koh's soul would rest in peace when at last the time came for him to take leave of human kind and join a nobler company.

The long pagan night was over. I lay still, listening expectantly for what would follow. After a while the hush was broken by the first tentative bubbling notes of a bulbul's phrase, and then the sweet song of a magpie-robin greeted the new day.

IV

Six weeks later, at the beginning of June, Her Majesty Queen Elizabeth the Second was crowned in England. Like all the other lands in her wide dominions, Sarawak sent representatives to attend the ceremony in Westminster Abbey. Four notables went, chosen from the principal races in the country. Their leader was Gordon Aikman, now the Chief Secretary, and the other three were a Malay, Datu Abang Openg from Kuching, a Chinese, Chew Geok Lim from Sibu, and an Iban, Penghulu Jugah from the Balleh.

This quartette of worthy envoys stayed with me in Singapore on their way to London. The three Asians were making their first visit to Britain, and were a-twitter with excitement at the prospect. It was delightful to see their enthusiasm for their journey.

I was disappointed to learn that Jugah would not stride into the Abbey on Coronation morning clad in the native finery of a Bornean chief. It seemed to me that a cap of tall hornbills' plumes, and a bronzed, naked body adorned with silver bangles, crimson sirat, black rattan garters and a trusty parang to slice off, if necessary, the heads of the Queen's enemies would have mixed well with the golden coronets and ermine robes of the peers of the realm, the yellow umbrellas and coloured garments of African chieftains, the jewelled turbans and silken tunics of Indian Maharajahs, and the various other fabulous, splendid, glittering costumes of Her Majesty's subjects from all the corners of the earth. I had urged upon the Sarawak authorities that the bare, tattooed figure of the handsome penghulu would represent better than any clothes the peculiar national character of our fellow-citizens in the tropical jungle, and that his skimpy decorations would impress the rest of the Commonwealth and Empire with the artistic nature of the Iban people. But these weighty arguments were brushed aside. Tony Abell and his advisers felt responsible for Jugah's life, and they pointed out that the temperature in Westminster Abbey would be many degrees lower than that in a long-house on the Rejang River. They feared that he might catch pneumonia, and so decreed that he should wear a white shirt, purple tie, blue pin-stripe suit and black socks and shoes. Only his loose, long-flowing hair would designate him as the ambassador of the proud Iban race.

During my last few meetings with Jugah I had noticed a change, a development in him. His charm, courtesy and gaiety were as conspicuous as ever, but he was less impulsive and erratic than he used to be. His judgement had ripened and his character matured. He was more prudent, more thoughtful, and wiser. His ascendancy among the younger Iban chiefs was growing, and he bade fair to be an excellent successor to Temonggong Koh whenever the grand old man went to join his fathers. It was fitting that he should represent the sturdy people of Her Majesty's jungle at her Coronation.*

At the previous Coronation, when King George the Sixth was crowned in 1937, I had sat in a choir-stall in Westminster Abbey. There I saw the regal pageantry, the glorious fragment of living history, the moving religious ceremony with which the monarchs of the British Commonwealth are dedicated for their rule. I had taken a hand in devising the form of service, for it was the first crowning since the overseas Dominions attained a status of sovereign equality with the United Kingdom, and as Secretary of State for Dominion Affairs I had rewritten the passages in the ancient text which refer to those lands. So I knew well the occasion as it appears at the heart of the Commonwealth in London, and the popular magnificence which attends it there.

This time I wished to watch the event from, so to speak, the other end of the telescope. I wanted to go to one of the remotest corners of the Empire, to see how it appeared there. So I went to Miri, the small capital of the Fourth Division in Sarawak, and spent the solemn, joyful day with some of the Queen's most distant subjects.

A dozen different racial communities who live together in Sarawak gathered at Miri to celebrate. Chinese, Malays, British, Indians, Australians, Cingalese, Eurasians, Arabs, Ibans, Kayans, Kenyahs and Kelabits came from the town and neighbouring

---

* Though Koh is still alive, aged 84, Jugah has now been made a Temonggong and is the active leader of the Rejang Ibans.

oil-field, the coast and far-flowing rivers, the padis and the deep jungle. They were of many colours and many tongues. They prayed for the Queen's Majesty in Moslem mosques, Christian churches, Hindu temples, Buddhist pagodas and pagan tabernacles. They celebrated her crowning with Chinese dragon dances, Kayan war jigs, Malay rongging, Scottish reels and the national capers of half a dozen other peoples. They were a microcosm of the populations of the Commonwealth—civilized and savage; black, brown, ivory and white; almost as various as all the fragmentary sections of the human race, and yet united in equality and friendship by loyalty to the same gracious young Queen.

Among those who travelled long distances to join the ceremonies was Temonggong Tama Weng Ajang. He was as serene, sagacious and Buddha-like as ever. He told me that his new long-house was now completed, and all his people comfortably settled in it. He reported that his wife was well, but that she had stayed at Long San to supervise the vast household's own Coronation festivities. Kallang and Ubong were now the happy parents of a second infant, and the little family were flourishing.* Bungan, too, had been blessed with child, successfully producing a daughter who promised to be as handsome, if not as boisterous, as her mother. Lohong on the other hand was still a spinster, not through lack of suitors but lack of desire to lose her independence.

The chief was now a baptized Roman Catholic, so his reformation of Bornean religion was making headway. He told me that his wet-padi experiment had made such encouraging progress that three other leading natives on the river had started similar farming. So his agrarian revolution, too, had taken root. From others at Miri I learned that the great Kenyah had lately achieved a further stroke in his far-sighted policy of promoting unity among the various tribes on the Baram. Just as a few years earlier he had married his first son, Kallang, to Lallang's adopted

* Two years later Kallang suddenly died of an incurable disease, a tragic loss to his father and family, and to all the Kenyah people. In accordance with native custom, the death of his eldest son has involved a change in Tama Weng Ajang's name, which is now Oyang Lawai Jau.

daughter, and thus helped to unite the Kenyah and Kayan peoples, so now he had arranged a dynastic marriage for his second boy, Nawang, to the daughter of a principal chief in another wide district. Quietly and surely his influence was spreading, promoting harmony throughout the land.

Tama Weng was in the ascendant. He had decided to seek membership in the Council Negri in Kuching, and was duly appointed. His first speech in the national assembly was characteristic. Speaking briefly but pungently about the needs of the people in the deep jungle, his peroration was a bald statement of three demands for new amenities at Long San.

"I want running water," he said. "I want a telephone. I want an airstrip." There was no limit to his aspirations.

On Coronation evening John Gilbert and his wife were the host and hostess at a party in their Residency. Two hundred people from every racial community attended. When the moment came for the Queen's health to be drunk, Gilbert invited me to propose the Loyal Toast.

I declined, saying that the honour should belong to Her Majesty's noblest subject in this widely representative gathering. That individual was not myself. He was Tama Weng Ajang.

The Temonggong accepted the task with unaffected pleasure. Mounting a chair, he made in the Kenyah tongue an impromptu speech which for sincerity, eloquence and loyal fervour was not, I'll wager, surpassed anywhere in the Commonwealth that day. He spoke of the deep contentment of the up-river tribesmen under the Queen's rule, declaring, "We have lost our Rajah, whom we loved, but now we have a greater Raj. We feel a greater strength supporting and helping us."

Then, with a sweep of his arm round his audience, he described the many different races there as members of a world-wide family of which Queen Elizabeth was the beloved mother. He said that he spoke for them all when he wished her a great and glorious reign.

The thunderous shouts of approval from the assembly when he raised his glass of burak and cried in Kenyah, "Long Live the Queen," testified that all present shared his sentiments.

A NOTE ON THE AUTHOR

At the conclusion of the Second World War, part of which he spent as British High Commissioner to Canada, the Right Honourable Malcolm MacDonald was appointed Governor-General of Malaya and British Borneo. This marked one more stage of a brilliant career in public service.

Malcolm MacDonald, the second son of the late British Prime Minister J. Ramsay MacDonald, was born in Lossiemouth, Scotland, in 1901. He was elected to the British House of Commons in 1929. Two years later he became Parliamentary Under-Secretary of State for Dominion Affairs and Secretary of State for the Colonies. In 1940 he joined Winston Churchill's Cabinet as Minister of Health, a ministry he directed until he was sent to Canada in 1941.

His sojourn there produced two books, *Down North,* the journal of an expedition through the Canadian Northwest, and *The Birds of Brewery Creek,* a charming record of a year's bird-watching. He is married and has one daughter. He is now in New Delhi as British High Commissioner to India.

A NOTE ON THE TYPE

This book is set in Granjon, a type named in compliment to Robert Granjon, type-cutter and printer—Antwerp, Lyon, Rome, Paris—active from 1523 to 1590. The boldest and most original designer of his time, he was one of the first to practice the trade of type-founder apart from that of printer.

This type face was designed by George W. Jones, who based his drawings upon a type used by Claude Garamond (1510-61) in his beautiful French books, and more closely resembles Garamond's own than do any of the various modern types that bear his name.

Lithography by The Murray Printing Company, Forge Village, Mass., on paper supplied by Curtis Paper Company, Newark, Del.

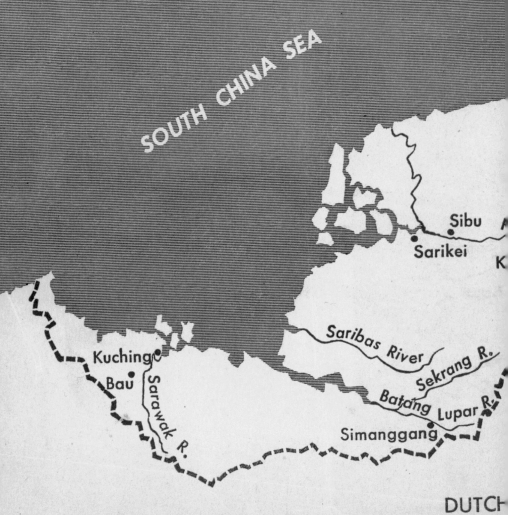

SARAWAK

SOUTH CHINA SEA

Sibu

Sarikei

Saribas River

Sekrang R.

Batang Lupar R.

Kuching

Bau

Sarawak R.

Simanggang

DUTCH